Drawing from Life

Drawing from Life

Memory and Subjectivity in Comic Art

Edited by Jane Tolmie

University Press of Mississippi / Jackson

www.upress.state.ms.us

The University Press of Mississippi is a member
of the Association of American University Presses.

First printing 2013
∞
Library of Congress Cataloging-in-Publication Data

Drawing from life : memory and subjectivity in comic art / edited by Jane Tolmie.
     pages cm
  Includes bibliographical references and index.
  ISBN 978-1-61703-905-8 (cloth : alk. paper) — ISBN 978-1-61703-906-5 (ebook)
1. Comic books, strips, etc.—Authorship. 2. Comic books, strips, etc.—Technique.
3. Autobiography—Authorship. 4. Biography as a literary form. 5. Cartooning—Technique. 6. Memory in literature. I. Tolmie, Jane, editor of compilation.
  PN6714.D73 2013
  741.5'1—dc23   2013018142

British Library Cataloging-in-Publication Data available

Contents

Introduction

If a Body Meet a Body

—Jane Tolmie

What is at stake in comic memoir and semi-autobiography is embodiment. Remembering a scene with the intent of rendering it in sequential art requires nonlinear thinking and engagement with physicality. Who was in the room and where? What was worn? Who spoke first? What images dominated the encounter? Did anybody smile? Unhinged from the summary paragraph, the artist must confront the fact of—to quote Bruce Willis in *The Fifth Element*—the meat popsicle. Accordingly, work on autobiography is increasingly turning to the question, in Judith Butler's words, of the "bodily condition of one's narrative account of oneself" (Butler 2005: 39). Graphic memoirs, or what Gillian Whitlock has categorized as "autographics," offer valuable insights into the various layered processes of memory and self-representation through "the specific conjunctions of visual and verbal text in . . . autobiography" (Whitlock 2006: 966).

Virginia Woolf was premature in speculating that the "impulse towards autobiography may be spent" (Woolf 1975: 79). Autobiography has seen enormous expansions and challenges over the past twenty to thirty years (Rak 2005: 2). One of these expansions has been in the area of comics, and it certainly is an expansion that calls into question any postmodern notion of the death of the author. Accordingly, this collection focuses on relationships between artist/writer and artistic product, or rather, on artistic self-representation in comics. Negotiations between artist/writer/body and drawn/written/text raise the question of whether and how "stories . . . capture the body to which they refer" (Butler 2005: 38). Hillary Chute and Marianne DeKoven argue that graphic narrative's "fundamental syntactical operation is the representation of time as space on the page," but it is also key to analyze the body on the page (Chute and DeKoven 2006: 769).

In the course of a discussion of the need for "more advanced visual and cultural literacies to interpret the intersections of various modes and media and the complex embodiments of avatar, autobiographer," Whitlock and Anna Poletti describe the "confronting bodies that recur under the sign of autographics"; this collection attempts to offer valuable contributions in the area of visual and cultural literacies (Whitlock and Poletti 2008: vi). *Drawing from Life: Memory and Subjectivity in Comic Art* examines autobiography, semi-autobiography, fictionalized autobiography, memory, and self-narration in sequential art. Contributors come from a range of academic backgrounds including English, American Studies, Comparative Literature, Gender Studies, Art History, and Cultural Studies. The book engages with well-known figures such as Art Spiegelman, Marjane Satrapi, Alison Bechdel, Neil Gaiman, Brian Fies, Lynda Barry, Chris Ware, Phoebe Gloeckner, Julie Doucet, Gene Luen Yang and Kim Deitch; with cult-status figures such as Martin Vaughn-James; and with lesser-known works by people such as Frédéric Boilet.

Academic publishing on comics is a rapidly growing field, and this collection aims to make a contribution in the broad area of autobiography studies in sequential art. The international focus of the collection is one of its strengths, thus making it a complement to such publications as Michael Chaney's edited collection *Graphic Subjects* (Wisconsin, 2010), Hillary Chute's *Graphic Women* (Columbia UP, 2010), Bart Beaty's *Unpopular Culture: Transforming the European Comic Book in the 1990s* (U of Toronto P, 2007), Charles Hatfield's *Alternative Comics* (UP of Mississippi, 2005), as well as influential volumes such as Joseph Witek's *Comic Books as History* (UP of Mississippi, 1989). A particular strength of this volume is its thematic focus on memory and subjectivity without a strict definition of autobiographical form, so that the collection includes many allusive—and elusive—types of relationships between artists/writers/subjects. A unifying focus on memory/the construction of the subject encourages readers to work through some of the complicated effects of mixing text and embodiment while remaining sensitive to the need to avoid simple models for truthfulness.

My own recent work on sexual trauma in comics centers on issues of memory and self-representation, so the work of other authors in this collection has been invaluable. Both Debbie Drechsler's intensely creepy

Daddy's Girl and Lynda Barry's *One! Hundred! Demons!* are routinely described as semi-autobiographical and have attracted excellent critical attention. Barry's own by-now-famous term for the status of her truth-telling is "autobiofictionalography"—and she drives her point home by asking, right at the start of her text, "Is it autobiography if parts of it are not true? Is it fiction if parts of it are?" (2002: 7). Similarly, Drechsler has said, "I realized that if I wrote straight autobiography the stories would suffer, so I began to take things that had happened and expand upon them, and mold them into stories that worked better than the 'honest truth' could" (Verstappen: online). While in the original 1992 publication of "Visitors in the Night" in *Drawn and Quarterly*, the abused girl's name is Debbie, in the 1996 *Fantagraphics* publication it has become Lily, which Drechsler relates in her interview in the *Comics Journal* (82).

The truth is not what I am interested in, and of course scholars invested in critical autobiography studies routinely point to the impossibility of direct transmission of lived experience. What I am interested in via Drechsler and Barry are the ways in which their texts and images negotiate private trauma in public, popular-culture formats, using an aesthetic process of reworking childhood events and emphasizing, in each case, a shared community formed from private pain and taboo knowledge. At the heart of each book is an episode or series of episodes of child sexual abuse. Neither artist intended an attractive coming-of-age story, but each makes radically different decisions about degrees of exposure and explicitness, developing two distinct approaches to the artistic representation of sexual trauma and memory. Both approaches, however, ultimately embody productive, empathic, and inclusive solutions to problems of isolation, invisibility, and shame. An image of abuse reaches out and makes—often coerces—emotional connections, forcing a public acknowledgement of private trauma, remaking a closed world of shame into an open book. There is an aesthetics of affect, not an inevitable or natural emotional side effect but a deliberate result of artistic decisions: the image of a forced encounter or an encounter grounded in power inequities is in turn thrust onto the audience.

My own approach to comics study is an intersectional, feminist one, invested in the many and various ways in which a large body of women's comics art makes a point of expressing interconnections between gender, race, class, nation, and sexuality. Both Drechsler and Barry have spoken about the ways in which their respective texts are sourced in painful lived experience, and have expressed the desire to use art both to raise social

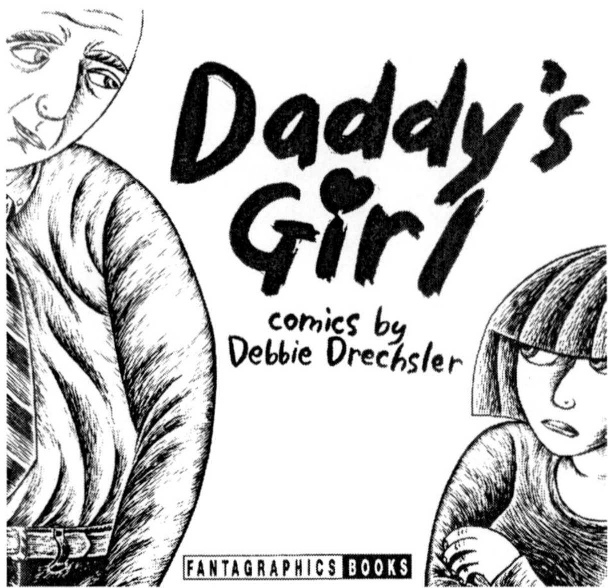

I.1. Note the hunched shoulders and resentful upwards glare, the body language of the daughter cringing away from the father's seemingly benevolent gaze. Debbie Drechsler, *Daddy's Girl*, Cover Art.

awareness and to forge connections with other survivors. Both Drechsler and Barry also make a point of connecting sexual abuse with other forms of abuse such as physical, verbal, and emotional abuse; abuse of animals; racism; poverty; and gender stereotyping. They thereby offer insights that connect dots between different kinds of lived experience rather than insisting on one isolated and isolating theme of female sexual victimization; Chute has similarly observed that the works of Aline Kominsky-Crumb and Phoebe Gloeckner resist simple models for female sexuality, insisting that it is "composed of both pleasure *and* degradation" (61).

The representation of sexual violence, especially violence directed at children or young girls, routinely raises questions of censorship in at least two ways. In the first sense, public anxiety about the display and dissemination of scenes of child rape or sex abuse often expresses itself in the terms of anxiety about pornography and voyeurism. See Chute on Kominsky-Crumb and Gloeckner, both of whom are frequently accused of producing pornography (56, 68–90). Public reaction against Gloeckner's work, in part about lived experiences of child abuse (as well as substance abuse, adolescent desire, and much more), has led to cancellation of speaking events to which she was initially invited. Her work has also been seized by British customs officials and banned from France.

In the second sense of censorship, there are those techniques of silencing and shaming that so key to rape culture and incest culture, the techniques of teaching the victim and people in the know to hide the knowledge and make it *unacknowledgeable*. This sense often aligns nicely with the discomfort experienced by a cultural elite that has the power to censor difficult materials and determine what is in good taste. This alignment, of course, leads disastrously to a an environment in which what Gloeckner labels the "laws of pornography" refuse visual space to victims of abuse with the same logics used to deny narratives of pleasure (quoted in Chute, 68). Such dovetailing of interests are painfully familiar to feminists, highlighting ways in which even opposed groups can cooperate in patriarchal projects of erasure. Comics do a particularly good job of addressing invisibility and silence, however, along with other cultural taboos. Even in non-explicit panels, the artistic decisions made in these comics—the representations of hunched bodies, sideways glances, turned backs, and averted eyes—force the viewer to "see" an often-invisible culture of shaming and silencing. Again, deliberate visual decisions force audience engagement with the dominating and destructive forces of the unspoken and unspeakable. Traumatic memory of something as intangible as being unable to speak can be made visible in the comics medium. The resulting conflation of terms and categories of speech/visibility/affect/bodily experience conveys a strong sense of the complexities of traumatic experience.

For the academic, one problem: how much revelation is *too much* revelation? The ethics of—possibly even forcing—someone to see something profoundly disturbing must be considered, as well as the political implications of making a "wrong" decision, a decision that leads someone or some formal body to identify a voyeuristic mentality or any mentality that is about consumption or even enjoyment of sexual abuse. How is the issue of consent negotiated between academic and audience? How is the issue of consent negotiated between comic artist and audience? They are not the same question because it is not my lived experience at stake—but are related questions. This set of issues is constantly in the minds of the creators of this sort of disturbing work. Barry says in interviews with Chute that she warns parents in particular when purchasing *One! Hundred! Demons!* that the book contains disturbing material about incest, suicide, and drugs (Chute, *Graphic Women* 54, 240 notes). And in an interview

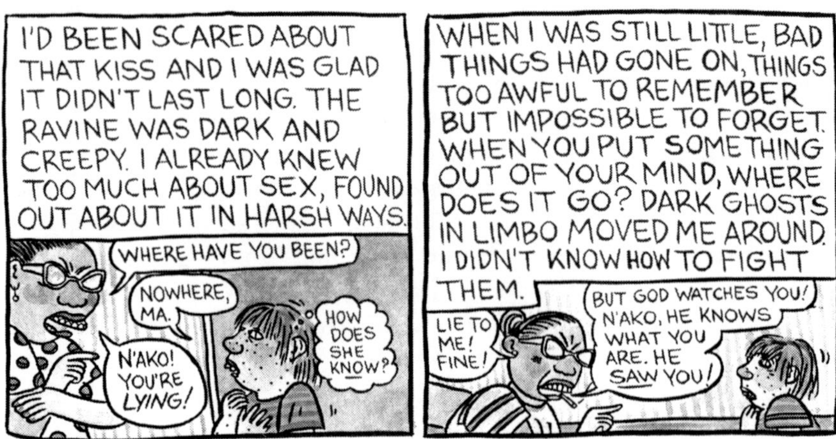

I.2. In classic Barry style, what is remembered is simultaneously forgotten. Lynda Barry, *One! Hundred! Demons!* p. 65.

with *comicsbulletin.com*, Drechsler expresses retrospective worry about maybe having "gone too far" with some of the images in *Daddy's Girl* and acknowledges that even she herself finds them difficult to reread, adding that she found comics to be the ideal way to approach "hard topics" because they are "so much the bastard children of the arts that no one cares what lines get crossed" (http://cotlzine.blogspot.ca/2008/07/deb bie-dreschler-interview.html. That is not quite true, of course, though certainly marginal and alternative publications routinely do difficult cultural work in terms of raising awareness and pushing against boundaries, e.g., as in Jennifer Camper's two edited volumes of *Juicy Mother*.

Comics about abuse offer a visual networking strategy for bringing together survivors in particular and those interested in raising awareness in general; they also extend the borders of autobiography about trauma to make us think about the implications of the image in debates about how prose autobiography forces the reader either to identify or dis-identify. Chute observes that the "disgust and pleasure that the visual carries is related to a bodily rhythm of reading, further underscored, and prompted, by the rhythm of the visual-verbal page, a rupturing alternation between affects" (Chute, *Graphic Women,* 71). In other words, the visual image of abuse is aesthetically and emotionally confrontational, even potentially coercive. Barry steps back from this coercion by leaving the main burdens of imagination to the reader: Only God gets to see what actually happened. Drechsler's approach is totally different.

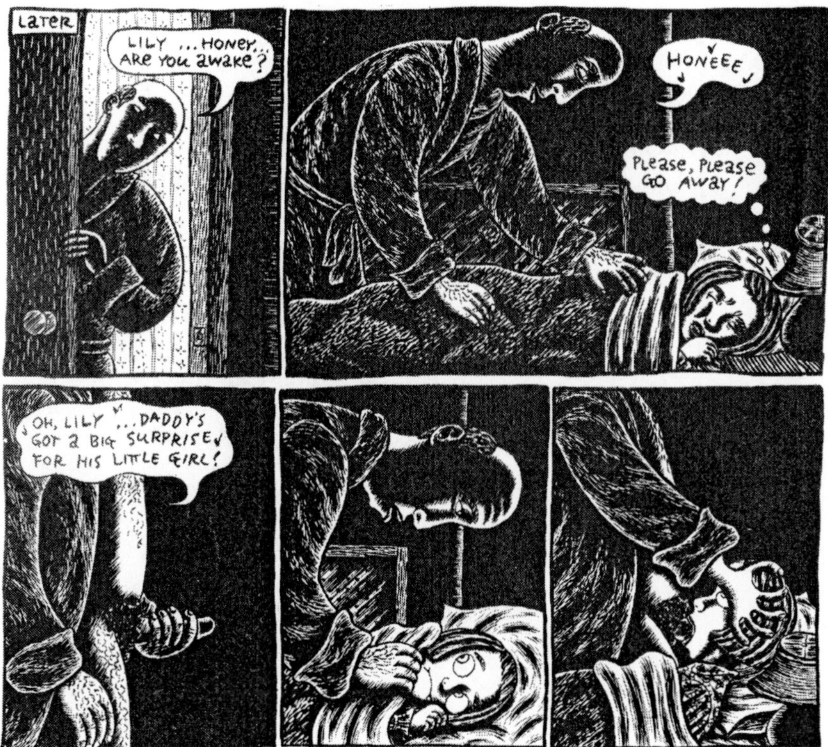

I.3. When the father figure in *Daddy's Girl* enters the bedroom, holding his erect penis, he chirps with a happy smile and some musical notes showing in the air, "Daddy's got a big surprise for his little girl" in a grotesque abuse of the language of a caring parent bringing a present. And then you see his penis in her mouth and you realize that that phrase with its little musical notes is as obscene as anything else in the frames. Debbie Drechsler, *Daddy's Girl*. p. 2.

I have included this explicit set of Drechsler's images of an erect male organ and direct sexual contact with a child for multiple reasons, all to do with confronting different kinds of censorship—and there are, of course, more than two kinds—despite my concerns about the very real dangers of traumatization through such visuals, always keeping in mind that the image can force a reaction in ways that perhaps the word cannot. If we are concerned about the line between what is scene/seen and what is obscene, we must also ask: Who gets to say when reality exceeds the representable? Why is it that so often those primarily concerned with censorship of self-narration are not the ones who have lived the negative realities at stake or

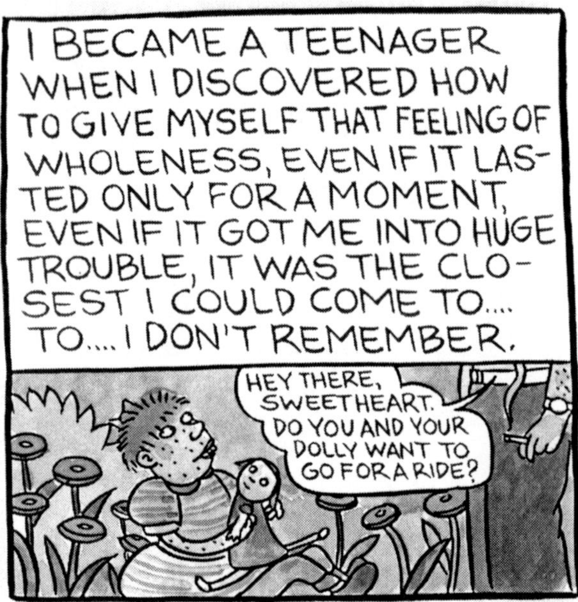

I.4. Lynda Barry. *One! Hundred! Demons!* p. 72.

in question? To what extent does censorship of these images participate in a culture of shaming and blaming? To what extent does said censorship work to obscure connections between individual and community in terms of both affect and shared experience? Perhaps we must think here of Freud and his desperate desire to deny the quotidian nature of father-daughter sex incest, as Judith Herman Lewis observes, "because of what it implied about the behaviour of respectable family men" (9, *Father-Daughter Incest*).

There is usually more buffering in the realm of words than in the world of images. An extensive vocabulary exists to describe incidents of sexual abuse/incest in distant and distancing terms—and no need even to use the word "penis," given the range of available euphemisms: consider Jean Auel, who managed to write an entire series of soft porn using words like "organ" and "member." The phrase "sex abuse" itself is non-specific and leaves the mind free to refuse to imagine in ways that the image does not.

In One! Hundred! Demons! Barry takes that indirect approach in any case, using an aesthetic approach of suggestion and inference—a *less is more* approach sharply in contrast to Drechsler's vivid and explicit renderings. Note the speech bubble positioned directly over the genital

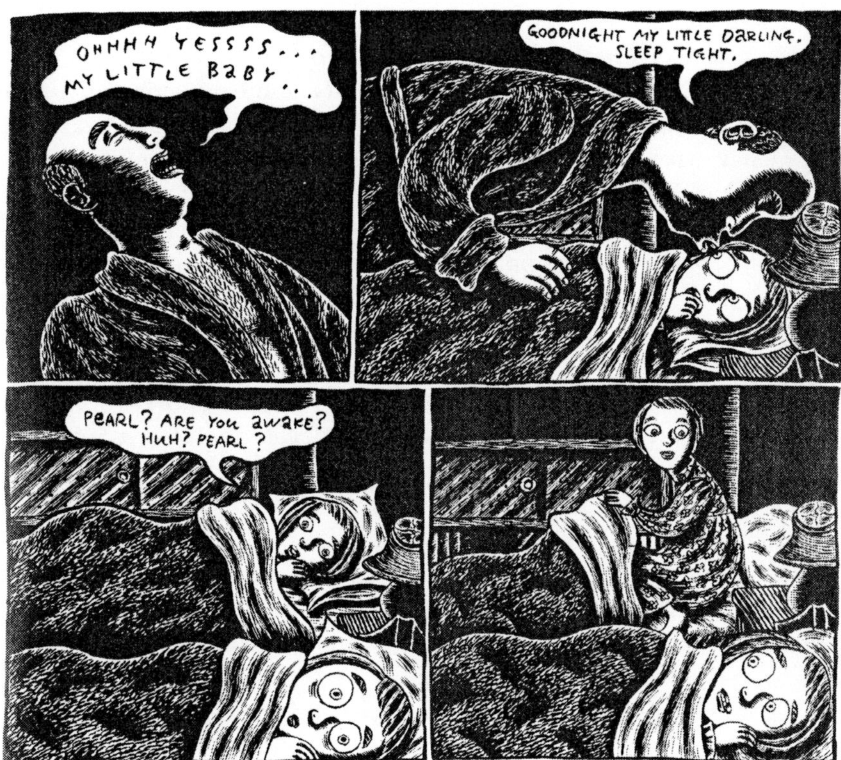

I.5. Debbie Drechsler. *Daddy's Girl*. p. 3.

area. Barry leaves the burden of imagination to the reader; Drechsler, like Kominsky-Crumb and Gloeckner, forces the reader to see what the abuse victim sees. Once again, what is remembered is also forgotten, in a frequent Barry trope that emphasizes memory as a series of choices as much as something that takes shape on its own (72). Memory, like subjectivity, is partial, constructed, and reconstructed. At one point Drechsler's Lily comments, "I never did remember the thing I forgot," even though the reader/viewer has just seen what it was, in all its atrocity (56). Here we see only the head of the father, having an orgasm, and then the sister turning away in denial of what she has witnessed. The sister does and says nothing—here we "see" the refusal of emotional connection, the refusal of acknowledgement, the refusal to confront the situation—the refusal to participate in the reconstruction of memory and subjectivity (3).

Confrontational is an apt word here, recalling Whitlock and Poletti on confronting bodies. It is important to avoid the impression, when talking about affective outreach, that Drechsler's and Barry's visuals offer merely a sort of visual networking system for female victims. Far more profoundly, they offer cultural confrontation and the potential for change or healing through strategies of outreach and uncomfortable transparency. They make clear the value of what might be called feminist art activism, art that deliberately self-defines as a form of creative emancipation. Creative emancipatory work, in the context of the representation of child sex abuse, offers a venue both for the artistic self and for the receiving viewer/reader to do a range of affective and political things: to heal, to make transparent, to undo, and to redo. All of those artistic endeavors are highly politicized. Speaking of Gloeckner, Chute talks of the "urgency of representing trauma" (2010: 74); these comics are precisely about matters of essential cultural urgency at the everyday level. Unique events such as the collapse of the Twin Towers demand and produce acknowledgment of the effects of the extraordinary. These texts do precisely the opposite. They emphasize repeated and quotidian traumas, trauma of gender inequity, traumas set in the home and enacted and re-enacted every day. In a sense, these texts are about what is perfectly ordinary and one thing that is perfectly ordinary is that it is impossible to separate mind and body, word and image, emotion and politics.

The stakes here, unlike those in papers in this collection about the events surrounding 9/11, are precisely about *not* being in a state of exception; the ordinary world itself is dangerous, sexually violent, emotionally difficult, racist, unequal in terms of wealth and class, as the body of Drechsler's and Barry's work makes clearly and undeniably visible. Comics such as these are trouble at its best, destructive of some social norms and creative of new ones. I will not write here about the various ways in which the comics format itself troubles norms of art and of high and low culture, for reasons of space and also because so many comics critics have done such a good job of that already, e.g., troubling norms and comfort levels of art is also something Alisia Chase emphasizes in her essay for this collection, *"You Must Look at the Personal Clutter: Diaristic Indulgence, Female Adolescence, and Feminist Autobiography."* Chase offers a feminist art historian's perspective on women comic artists' deployment of the mess and pain of everyday lived experience to make profound connections that are at once, to use a phrase we all know well but often use tokenistically, personal and political. Barry and Drechsler use sequential art as critique (exposing rape-culture's strategies of shame, blame, and silencing); sequential art as vehicle for self-emancipation, at once political

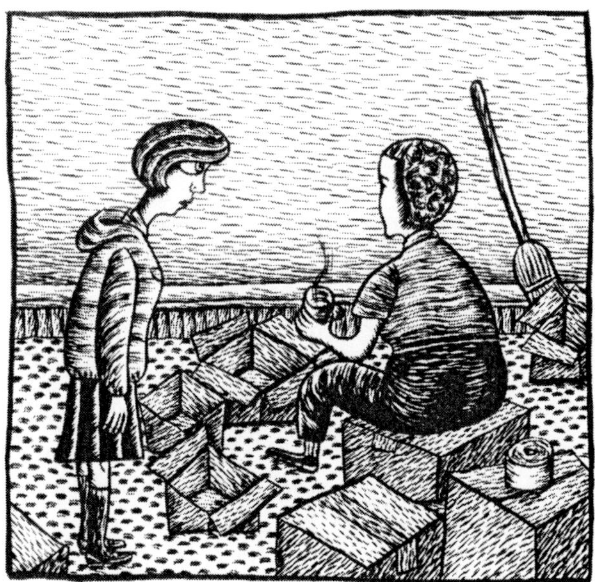

I.6. The mother's turned back and averted gaze echo those of the sister in earlier frames. The viewer is invited into the scene, eyes following the gaze of the child to rest on the mother. Debbie Drechsler, *Daddy's Girl*. p. 25.

and personal, and sequential art as *invitation* to participate in cultural production. By deploying these effectively activist techniques, Barry and Drechsler emphasize ways in which comics art can forge bonds between individual and community.

Drechsler's visual rendering of trauma illustrates rape culture's and incest culture's politics of shame in ways that the word alone cannot, as recognition cannot be refused. The unspoken word does not mean the viewer/reader has not seen and understood. Forbidden things may continue to be unnamed, unspoken, but they are irrefutably there: image forces recognition, empathy, acknowledgement of shame and damage. The shunned or damaged body draws the gaze, and also makes the viewer uncomfortable and afraid of being voyeuristic and thus participating in a culture of dominance and harm.

Both authors have expressed the feeling in interviews that artistic production about the traumatic past is necessary for them, a form of essential performance and public acknowledgment of things the world so often wishes to keep private. Barry's title for the episode specifically about child

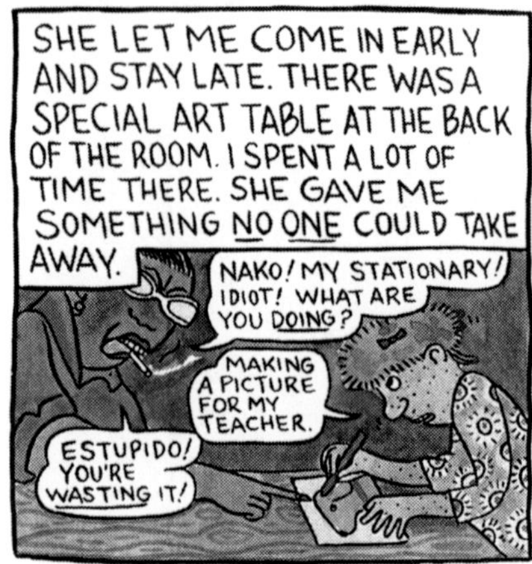

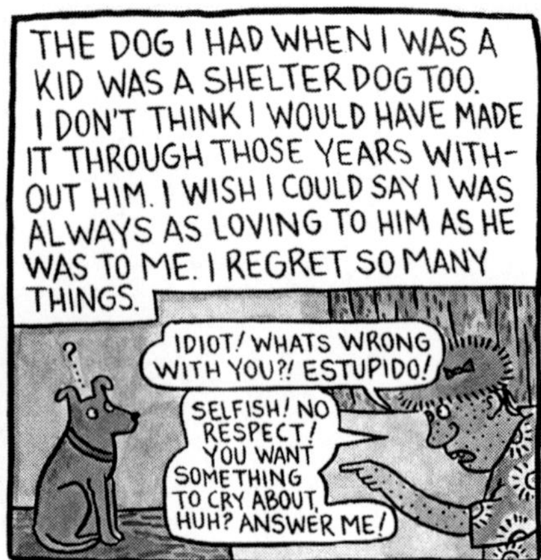

I.7. Note the emphasis on something that no one can take away. Lynda Barry, *One! Hundred! Demons!* p. 177.

abuse is "Resilience." It is acts of artistic reimagining that express this resilience for both Drechsler and Barry. There are scenes in each text in which a supportive art teacher makes a huge difference in enabling access to this form of self-expression. These scenes are tremendously important as they are themselves instructional—by reproducing them Drechsler and Barry are emphasizing the lesson itself: self-expression is something you can give to yourself continually and no one can take it away. Self-expression gives you power over your own memory—and over your own sense of self/ subject.

By passing on the lessons that art is liberating should be encouraged and supported, both artists are issuing invitations to participate in artistic self-expression, passing on the emancipatory lessons offered to their child selves, emphasizing a transmission of transformative possibilities. Both Drechsler and Barry offer an aesthetic escape: the working through and rendering of trauma through visuals. However, this escape does not separate mind and body but instead invites the visualization of the body as a form of freeing mental expression. Drechsler says in her interview with *comicsbulletin*, ". . . there are people who know what's what who are making change." Making change, for both Drechsler and Barry, is about inviting others into self-expression; Drechsler has talked about the importance of reimagining the past as a way of moving forward. In a similar vein, Barry teaches writing and drawing classes and gives workshops on accessing the inner storyteller, often describing her work as being about writing

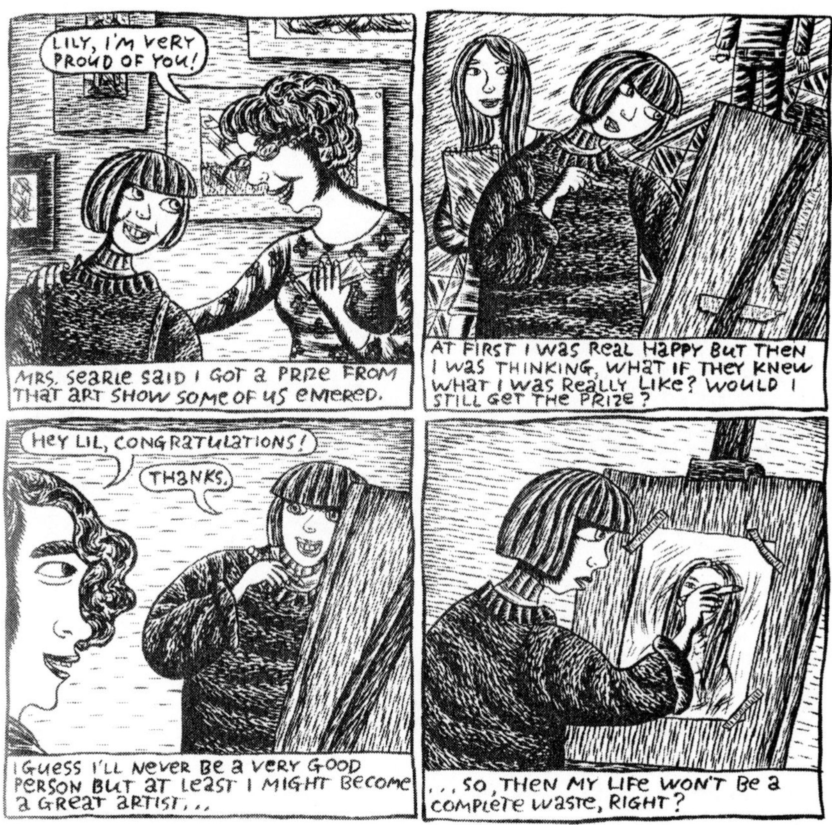

I.8. A lesson about empathy and support is passed on, together with an emphasis on having something valuable of one's own. Debbie Drechsler, *Daddy's Girl*. p. 37.

the unthinkable. Barry has published books intended to draw readers into active artistic participation, *What It Is* and *Picture This*. In "paying forward" the lessons given to their child selves, both artists open up creative, political, and affective possibilities for re-connecting individual and community and moving away from isolation and shame. Ann Cvetkovich's recent brilliant book, *Depression: A Public Feeling*, articulates ways in which the "encounter between feeling and politics is thus open for discussion of forms of activism that can address messy feelings rather than trying to banish them" (110). Such productive and nuanced reimagining of therapy is offered through the works of Barry and Drechsler alike.

Not all the creative writers/artists discussed in this collection are concerned primarily with rendering and confronting demons, of course, but

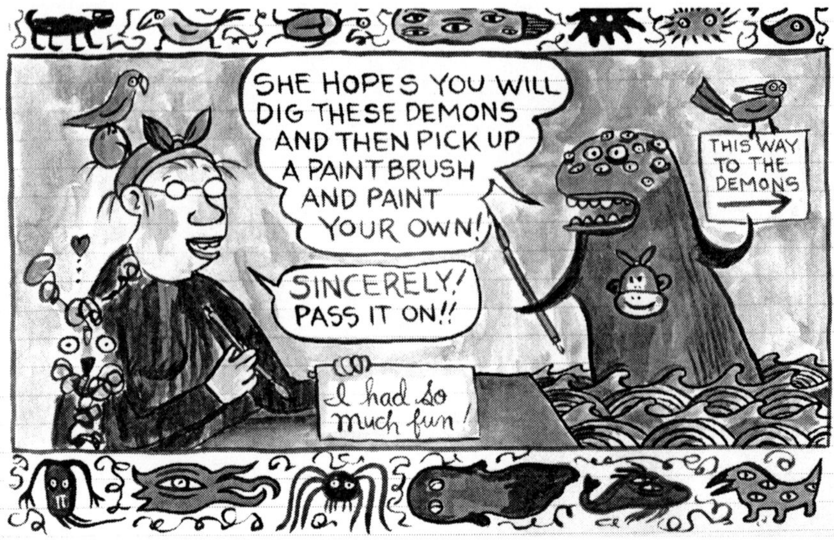

I.9. Here, for once, Barry is the more explicit. Lynda Barry, *One! Hundred! Demons!* p. 13.

all are engaged in active attempts at self-rendering and the remaking and representation of memory. Barbara Christian's word "rememorying" is suggestive, as it implies the active and deliberate reconstruction of memory to void fixed categories (Christian 1990: 48). For indeed, comic rememorying is doing much to unfix, remake, and make us rethink boundaries through the production of "self-regarding art" (Whitlock and Poletti 2008: v). At a recent talk at Queen's University, Glenn Willmott and Bart Beaty talked about the need for comics scholarship to theorize both authorial/creative subject and viewer/audience, much as film theory has done, and it is my hope that the essays in this collection do some of that work.

David Ball and Yaël Schlick begin the analytic work of the collection with attention to self-representation in the comics of Alison Bechdel and Lynda Barry. Ball's work tracks the intertextuality of Bechdel's created self, focusing on the conflation of allusion and confession in *Fun Home*. Ball works with textual genres and canonicity, while Schlick, in a similar vein, approaches the fictionalization of the self in autobiography more broadly, contrasting Bechdel's deployment of the fictional with Barry's refusal to distinguish between fictional and real. While Bechdel's text is obsessively self-reflexive, Barry's work invites reader/viewer participation, reducing the distance between bodies and text.

Michael Chaney's attention is on the body in the text, specifically the animal body. What is it about comics, he asks, that summons the human in bestial form? It is a profound question as animal studies in the humanities is an emerging powerhouse, and one that has not yet engaged fully with comics criticism. Chaney produces a sophisticated analysis of the potential and the dangers of a discourse of animal-human hybridity. In another study of subjectivity located outside the bounds of human form, Jan Baetens offers an examination of Martin Vaughn-James, pointing out that all comic art carries some degree of subjectivity, and working his way through an extended and elegant reading of object-subject relations in *The Cage*. Baetens invites readers to refuse simple conceptualizations of "serious" art and to reject oppositional models for relations between subject/object and subject/abstract.

Benjamin Widiss explores a sort of dialogic subjectivity, in which Chris Ware's relationship(s) with Joseph Cornell inform and inspire Ware's distinctive aesthetic. Cultural dialogues are also at stake in Christopher Bush's analysis of a *nouvelle manga* aesthetic, which incorporates analysis of French and Japanese literary and comics forms, film theory, and literary criticism. Via the *nouvelle manga*, Bush queries connections made between autobiography, self-referentiality, and cultural authenticity. Isaac Cates, too, raises questions about cultural authenticity through his study of the faux memoir and interpretive uncertainty in the collaborations of Neil Gaiman and Dave McKean.

With Lopamudra Basu and Davida Pines, we move into the analysis of trauma, both public and private. These essays focus on autobiographical representations of the events and emotions surrounding 9/11, on acts of recovering, and exploration of pain, grief, and mourning. Focusing on Art Spiegelman, Basu positions comic art as a space of resistance against oppression; Pines, in a similar vein, demonstrates how bearing witness challenges public narratives of unity, triumph, and heroism, referencing Spiegelman, Alissa Torres, and Sungyoon Choi. In contrast, Alisia Chase turns from public to private and calls for a re-engagement with the personal, the messy, and the intimate. Chase works with Phoebe Gloeckner, Debbie Drechsler, and Julie Doucet to expose the importance of quotidian traumas and the emotional confusions of lived experience.

Rachel Trousdale balances the personal and the public in her analysis of Marjane Satrapi's *Persepolis,* unpacking ways in which personal and public rebellions coincide and ways in which bearing witness both engages with universal narratives and produces individuals/individualism. Sharon O'Brien, bringing the collection to an end, looks at ways in which bearing witness to the suffering and pain of others gives voice to bodies and, perhaps, souls, otherwise left out of language. Attentive to emerging work in the medical humanities with her analysis of Brian Fies' *Mom's Cancer*, O'Brien brings us back to the opening premise of this introduction: comics and engagement with embodiment. I chose to end this volume with O'Brien's powerful narrative about hope.

This book has been a labor of love extending over a long period, and it would have been impossible without the careful work and editorial attention given it by Sylvia Andrychuk and Kelly Quinn. I am lucky to have such devoted colleagues and friends. Many thanks to Walter Biggins and Anne Stascavage for their patience, and many thanks to Katie Keene and to all the others at University Press of Mississippi who worked hard on the volume. Thank you to anonymous reviewers. A special thank you to *Tangles* author Sarah Leavitt, who graciously donated her artwork for our cover. Flaws and remaining errors in the book are of course mine.

Works Cited

Barry, Lynda. *One! Hundred! Demons!* Seattle: Sasquatch Books, 2002. Print.

Butler, Judith. *Giving An Account of Oneself.* New York: Fordham UP, 2005. Print.

Christian, Barbara. "The Highs and Lows of Black Feminist Criticism." *Reading Black, Reading Feminist.* Ed. Henry Louis Gates. New York: Penguin Group, 1990. 44–51.

Chute, Hillary, and Marianne DeKoven. "Introduction: Graphic Narrative." *Modern Fiction Studies.* 52:4: 2006. 767–82. Print.

———. *Graphic Women: Life Narrative & Contemporary Comics.* New York: Columbia UP, 2010. Print.

Cvetkovich, Ann. *Depression: a public feeling.* Durham and Longon: Duke UP, 2012. Print.

Drechsler, Debbie. *Daddy's Girl.* Seattle: Fantagraphics Books, 1995. Print.

———. "The Debbie Drechsler Interview." *Comics Journal.* 249: 2002. 82. Print.

Lewis Herman, Judith. *Father-Daughter Incest.* Cambridge: Harvard University Press, 1981. Print.

Rak, Julie. "Introduction: Widening the Field: Auto/biography Theory and Criticism in Canada." *Auto/biography in Canada: Critical Directions.* Waterloo: Wilfred Laurier Press, 2005. 1–30. Print.

Simon, a/k/a. http://www.comicsbulletin.com/nuclear/98705880048391.htm Web. 08 Aug. 2011.

Verstappen, Nicolas. "Interview with Debbie Drechsler." *L'autre bande dessinée.* 2008. http://www.du9.org/Debbie-Drechsler,1018. Web. 08 Aug. 2011.

Whitlock, Gillian. 2006. "Autographics: The Seeing "I" of the Comics." *Modern Fiction Studies* 52:4: 965–79.

——— and Anna Poletti. "Self-Regarding Art." *Biography* 31:1: 2008. v–xxiii. Print.

Woolf, Virginia. *A Room of One's Own.* Harmondsworth, England: Penguin Books, 1975. Print.

Drawing from Life

Allusive Confessions

The Literary Lives of Alison Bechdel's *Fun Home*

—David M. Ball

With its rich and intertwined narratives of a family's history, a father's closeted sexuality, and an artist's coming of age and coming out, Alison Bechdel's 2006 graphic memoir *Fun Home* has quickly emerged as an essential text in the vanguard of contemporary graphic narrative. As scholars incorporate such comics into literary anthologies and course syllabi, this inclusion prompts as-yet-unrealized considerations of the ways in which comics do and do not alter the literary and art historical canons they have begun to enter.[1] Bechdel's work thus proves to be a compelling test case for an integrative approach to the intersections of comics, art history, and literature. *Fun Home* also explicitly theorizes this process by drawing upon, citing from, and transforming genres as seemingly diverse as the coming-out memoir, the *Künstlerroman*, and the graphic novel. In doing so, however, Bechdel's myriad literary allusions perform a degree of the same self-censorship encountered in earlier twentieth-century queer forms of cultural and artistic expression, complicating the confessional frame within which her comics are conventionally appreciated. This singular conflation of the allusion and the confession in *Fun Home* both shields the memoir's revelations from forms of full disclosure while shaping Bechdel's role as craftsman of her own narrative. *Fun Home* thus negotiates its place in literary and art historical canons in a manner exemplified by queer artists and writers before Bechdel, representing an extension of those earlier strategies as much as a departure for lesbian graphic narrative.

Much of the scholarly attention paid to *Fun Home* focuses on the memoir's powerful mode of witnessing and regards Bechdel's meticulous and archival attention to her own life as the primary measure of the text's

"

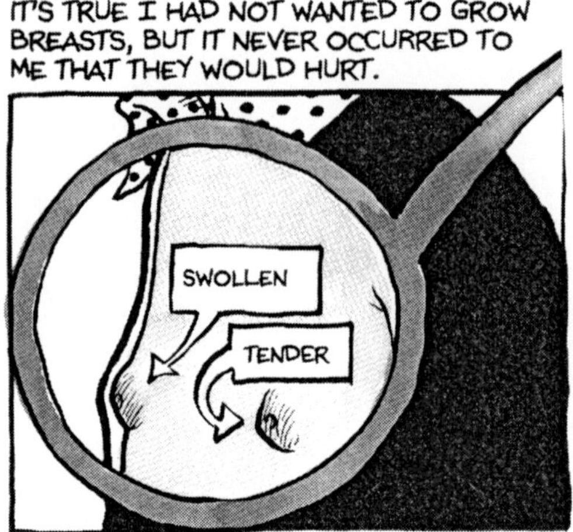

1.1. Alison Bechdel. *Fun Home.* p. 109.

critical import. The graphic memoir plumbs stark and often wrenching truths about Bechdel's ambivalence toward her father Bruce's closeted sexuality, his affairs with young boys, his presumed suicide, and the fractured family life this buried history produces. The parallel narrative of Alison's coming out is tightly imbricated within and mirrored by Bruce's tragedy, complementing and at times competing with her father's story for the center of the memoir's narrative attention. Bechdel's insistence within *Fun Home* upon a visible connection to her father maintains a relationship between her life and his in the memoir that she did not immediately feel during the strained years of their lived lives. Critics have rightly remarked upon the memoir's archival and confessional urges to maintain this tenuous familial bond: journal entries, correspondence, maps, court documents, and family photographs are painstakingly reproduced in Bechdel's panels. Bechdel herself has spoken about this confessional urge in a 2001 *Comics Journal* interview with Trina Robbins: "I don't know, maybe it's because I was raised Catholic. Confession has always held a great appeal for me" (Robbins 82). Additionally, her first book-length autobiographical work is titled *The Indelible Alison Bechdel: Confessions, Comix, and Miscellaneous Dykes to Watch Out For*, which includes a strip labeled "True Confession" (51–54). In doing so, Bechdel participates in what Susannah Radstone has termed confession's "range of narrational strategies to evoke in the reader the experience of the confessant's inward quest for self-transformation" (36).

This confessional urge is exemplified by a panel (fig. 1.1) showing a cut-away image of Alison's adolescent body, a synecdochic scene for the myriad other moments in which Alison literally and figuratively bares her breast—often, as is the case here, while telling narratives of pain—disclosing everything from bedroom scenes to intimate family secrets (109). Read in this light, *Fun Home* unflinchingly participates in a tradition of contemporary lesbian memoir, one which extends an American literary confessional genealogy dating back to Puritan conversion and African-American captivity narratives (Diggs). *Fun Home*, in this account, also staunchly resists the overwhelming invisibility and, to quote Terry Castle, "murderous allegorizing," lesbian characters have been subjected to throughout the course of literary history (7). Among other scholars, Jennifer Lemberg writes admiringly of "the power of graphic narrative as witness" in *Fun Home*, figuring Bechdel as "consistently privileg[ing] drawing as a more direct mode of representation" (129, 133). Similarly, Ann Cvetkovich, while acknowledging the memoir's "power to provide forms of truth that are emotional rather than factual," nonetheless characterizes Bechdel's technique as an "archival mode of witness" ("Drawing" 114), extending her own arguments about the ways in which "lesbian and gay history demands a radical archive of emotion in order to document intimacy, sexuality, love, and activism, all areas of experience that are difficult to chronicle through the materials of a traditional archive" (*Archive* 241).

Given this powerful form of witnessing, however, it would be a simplification to read *Fun Home* as an unvarnished recording of a life history, a narrative unshaped by the literary aspirations and narrative demands of the author. Bechdel is keen to make her readers understand the long-held positions of memoir scholarship: the unreliability of memory, the gulf that invariably separates the speaker of the text from its author, and the multiple ways in which memoirs are ordered and construct narratives that complicate uncritical notions of facticity and testimony. My use of "Bechdel" and "Alison" throughout this essay to refer to the author and her avatar respectively mimics the very distinction Bechdel herself is at great pains to make throughout her memoir. Perhaps more so than any other graphic memoirist, Bechdel carefully draws her readers' attention to these complexities by illustrating imagined scenes to which she has no conceivable access (32, 65, 71), narrating her own "epistemological crisis" as a young diarist (142), willfully altering details small and large in her narrative (41, 185), and establishing an often dramatic distance between the narrative text and her panels' visual content throughout.

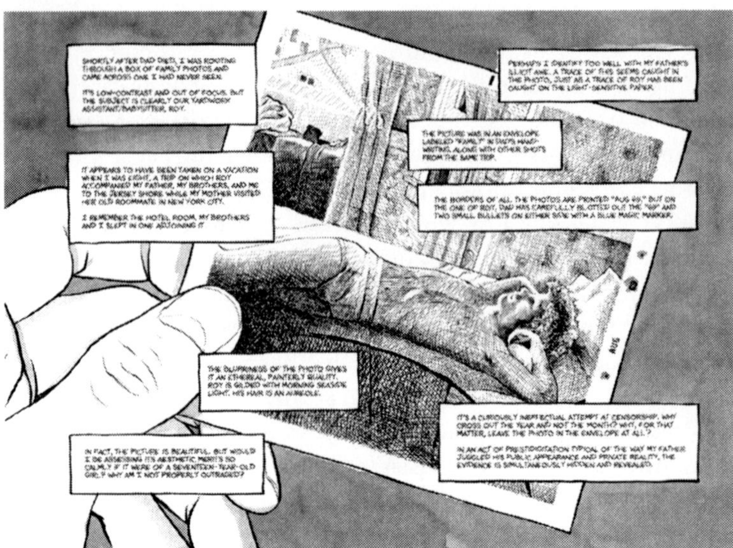

1.2. Alison Bechdel. *Fun Home*. p. 100–01.

Take as a representative example of these disparities the archival "centerfold" of Roy (fig. 1.2), Alison's babysitter and her father's lover (100–101). Bechdel describes the discovery of this photograph as the germ of the entire memoir:

> In many ways photographs really generated the book. In fact the whole story was spawned by a snapshot I found of our old babysitter lying on a hotel bed in his Jockey shorts. [. . .] It was a stunning glimpse into my father's hidden life, this life that was apparently running parallel to our regular everyday existence. And it was particularly compelling to me at the time because I was just coming out myself. I felt this sort of posthumous bond with my father, like I shared this thing with him, like we were comrades. I didn't start working on the book then, but over the years that picture persisted in my memory. It's literally the core of the book, the centerfold. (Chute, "Interview" 1,005–06)

Bechdel uses the language of sudden revelation here, this discovery representing an abiding act of witnessing her father's sexual truth. Likewise, Cvetkovich declares this moment the "visual and emotional kernel out of which the story emerges" (115), and Chute describes this composition as the center of the memoir's "circling, 'labyrinthine' structure [. . .] because it spirals in to the double-spread center of Roy [. . .] and then spirals out"

(*Graphic Women* 183). This splash page is the only one of its kind in the entire memoir; no other single panel in the text even bleeds to the margins. It is also importantly located at the very center of the text, a direct figuration of the leitmotif of revelation and self-discovery striated throughout the memoir. Given all of this—the affective and confessional authority of the photograph, the representational power of Bechdel's art, as well as the central role of these pages in the text—it is easy to forget that images such as this one do not mimetically represent lived experience. For legal reasons such as the protection of the identities of many of the memoir's subjects, as well as a host of other considerations, "Roy" and his likeness are a pseudonym and an avatar respectively. "Roy" is not Roy, and the bodily representation of him reproduced in the text is not as he appears in Bechdel's private archive.

This should not come as a surprise to readers. Roy's careful composition, both in the photograph itself and its appearance within the memoir as a whole, draws upon artistic tropes of the art nude and the *nue couchée* evidenced throughout the text. Bechdel portrays Bruce reading Kenneth Clark's extensive study, *The Nude*, at several points (15, 99), and both he and Alison admire a fashion spread in *Esquire* magazine displaying a similarly recumbent semi-nude model on the page immediately before Roy's centerfold. While more revealing than this advertisement, which somewhat demurely cuts its subject off at the waist, the shadowing and page fold of Roy's spread nonetheless veil the viewer's gaze at the same moment that the body is exposed. The centerfold thus reveals the father's affair while concealing the lover's name and appearance; it is drawn from the family's archive, but registers distance in its conspicuous artfulness and engagement with longstanding artistic practices and archetypes; and it evidences an explicit and corporeal site of Bruce's passions while concealing that very body from our view.

Bechdel withholds information from her readers while concurrently extracting documents, however altered, from the archive of her family's past, even as Alison in the bottom right text box notes her father's "curiously ineffectual attempt at censorship." The panel thus engages, in an oblique fashion, with the very censorship that its text queries. At the very moment she describes her father's "act of prestigidation [*sic*] typical of the way [he] juggled his public appearance and private reality, the evidence [. . .] simultaneously hidden and revealed," Bechdel's composition engages in precisely this unresolved dialectic of withholding and revelation, a preeminent act of mirroring between Bruce and herself that Alison insists upon throughout the text. That Bechdel renders the photographic "evidence" held in her own hand simultaneously brings it to light and holds it at a distance from her readers. It is represented literally under her thumb and drawn, as are all of the memoir's documents, in the artist's hand, a register of the levels of mediation through which both Alison and her readers are dissociated from the events she attempts to narrate and envision on the page. The composition's emotional truth is only achieved through its willful artifice.

The means by which the centerfold of "Roy" embodies this dialectic of revelation and withholding is merely one exemplar of an oscillation that takes place throughout the memoir.[2] This dynamic can be productively understood within a larger history of censorship and self-censorship in modern gay and lesbian visual culture in which *Fun Home* fitfully participates.[3] In his groundbreaking work *Outlaw Representation: Censorship and Homosexuality in Twentieth-Century American Art*, Richard Meyer argues that the "'negative' image of homosexuality—the image of crime or sin, of sickness or stereotype—has constituted an essential part of the pictorial language on which artists have drawn" (8). This "regulation of homosexuality," however, has "provoked unanticipated responses and counterrepresentations, unforeseen pictures of difference and self-conscious stagings of deviance" (10). These selfsame punitive regimes of enforced gay invisibility and compulsory heterosexuality have, according to Meyer, given gay artists the tools for upsetting those very structures of visibility and self-imagining. Meyer views such censorship as a generative device for queer artists, one which:

> compels indirection and "ingenious disguise" on the part of the writer. Censorship produces as well as prohibits writing; it consigns the writer not to silence but to the strategic use of suggestion and metaphor, of submerged meanings and encoded messages [. . .] a dialectical concept of censorship [that] functions not simply to erase but also to enable representation; it generates limits but also reactions to those limits; it imposes silence even as it provokes responses to that silence. (15)

Gay and lesbian visual expression, in Meyer's reading, is thus paradoxically enabled by its very repression. Meyer claims that these forms of censorship and self-censorship are even more powerful in the case of lesbian artists, who have been "restricted from reaching [the] threshold of visibility within American culture" throughout the twentieth century (22).

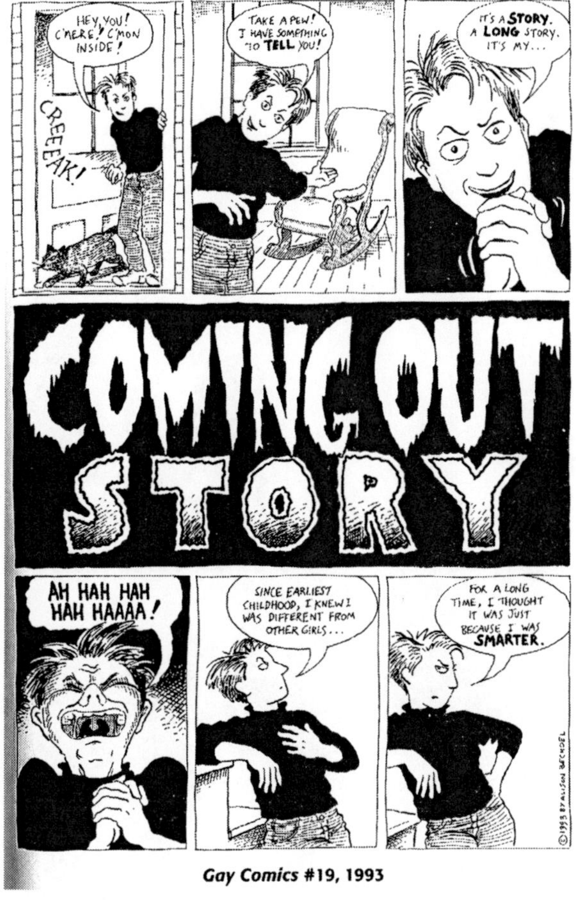

1.3. Alison Bechdel. *"Coming Out Story." Gay Comics* 19 (1993). p. 1.

If anything, we might expect such submerged meanings and encoded messages to have little bearing on a twenty-first-century memoir as "graphic," in every sense of that word, as Bechdel's. The cover of the paperback edition of *Fun Home* celebrates its "refreshingly open" approach to queer autobiography, and Bechdel herself made her early career in the explicitly political and often ribald comic strip *Dykes to Watch Out For.* Her 1993 "Coming Out Story" (fig. 1.3), which is in many respects the urtext of *Fun Home*, mocked reticence in the coming out story with faux horror film iconography (1). Despite one brief, perhaps even obligatory censorship controversy in Missouri, *Fun Home* has met with overwhelming praise rather than vitriol for its depictions of homosexuality.

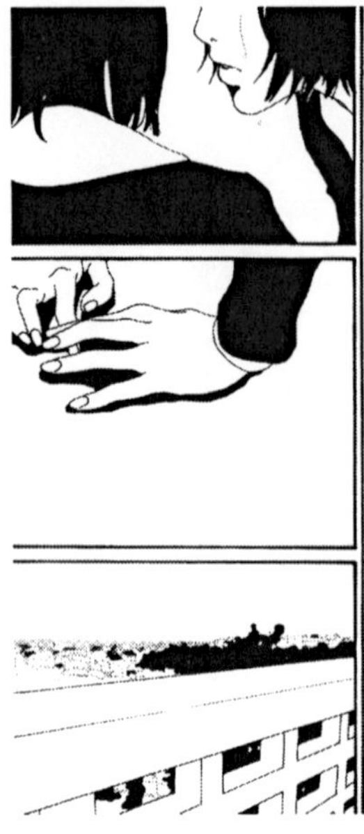

1.4a. Kiriko Nananan. *Blue*. 1997.

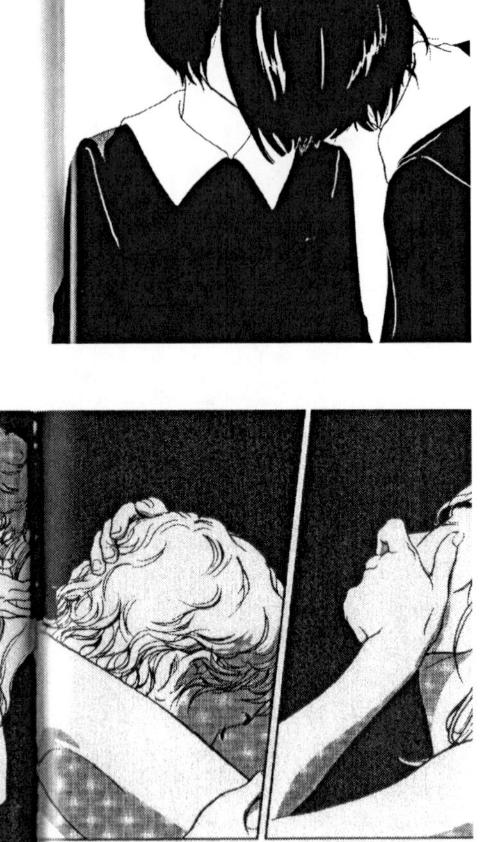

1.4b. June Kim. *12 Days*. 2006.

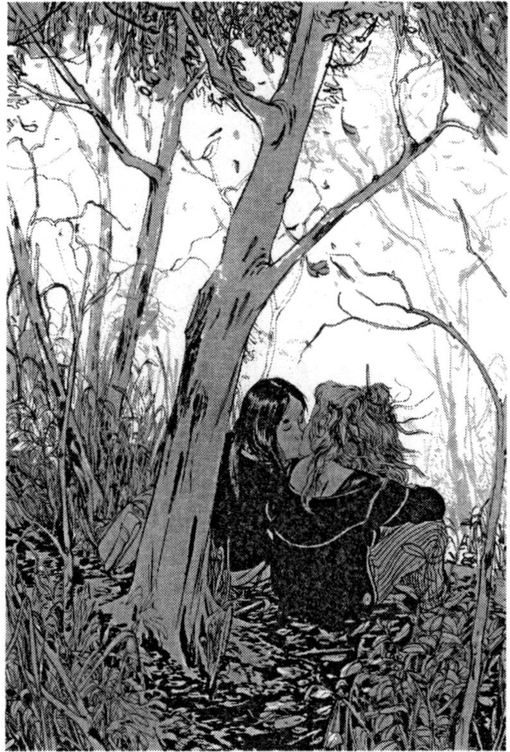

1.4c. Mariko Tamaki and Jillian Tamaki. *Skim*. 2008.

Indeed, compared to figurations of lesbian relationships in many contemporary comics written for audiences outside a gay readership, Bechdel's representations are pronouncedly direct. The panels included here, from Kiriko Nananan's 1997 *Blue* (fig. 1.4a), June Kim's 2006 *12 Days* (fig. 1.4b), and Mariko Tamaki and Jillian Tamaki's 2008 *Skim* (fig. 1.4c) respectively, all draw their visual vocabulary from Japanese *yuri*, a sub-genre of manga that focuses on lesbian relationships, frequently between women of high school age. The dialectic that Meyer describes between self-censorship and counter-representation recurs here in the physical touching of lesbian bodies that also serves as an act of hiding. An image emerges of lesbian attachment that is both aesthetically and emotionally arresting as well as doomed to occlusion and curtailment, often in a violent fashion. In her nouvelle manga *Blue*, Nananan imagines the confession of one girl's love for the other as a "convulsion," with entire panels blacking out as if in a sort of shame reflex (67). When physical relationships between women are figured, they are done so only in brief moments and often abstract forms, the moment of their love's revelation also a simultaneous eclipse of their singularity. Not merely a distinction between American and Japanese comics, this pattern of literally refusing to show the face of lesbian love fully appears throughout a range of works inspired by *yuri* appearing in North America—*Skim* and *12 Days* being written and drawn by Canadian-born artists of Japanese heritage and a Korean-born New Yorker respectively—that adopt a similar course of dialectically revealing and withholding a full depiction of lesbian sexuality.

While seemingly distant from these other contemporaneous portrayals of lesbian love, Bechdel in fact has been criticized as insufficiently radical (Dean, Martindale). While I agree with Cvetkovich that *Fun Home* compellingly complicates homonormative narratives, I am ultimately less interested in such debates about the sufficiency of Bechdel's radicalism than I am in the question of whether Bechdel's pronounced ambivalences in fact make room for the claims and representations she *is* able to draw throughout her work.[4] Nonetheless, the discourse of homosexuality-as-pathology persists in her memoir through Bruce's perceived disease and attempts at therapy, Alison's figuration of her own obsessive-compulsive disorder, and her adoption of the Freudian discourse of "inversion" throughout the text. Indeed, Bechdel has expressed regret for how lesbian iconography has permeated popular culture, evincing a nostalgia for the lost coded language of the minority subculture, as described by Meyer, that generates exactly the "pictorial language" made possible in *Dykes to Watch Out For* and *Fun Home*. One early and particularly prescient example of this assimilation fear is a 1990 episode of "Servants to the Cause"—a monthly strip that ran in the *Advocate* and is reprinted in *The Indelible Alison Bechdel*—which describes gay and lesbian assimilation into mainstream culture as a threat to queer exceptionality and political relevance (191). Even the character who argues that gays and lesbians are fighting for "the right to be like everybody else" in this strip later opines: "Sometimes I miss the furtive, secretive, good old days" ("Coming Out" 36).

One of the most powerful and conspicuous means by which Bechdel negotiates this dialectic in *Fun Home* is through frequent and explicit allusions to other literary works of art, titling each of her chapters with a citation from another text and picturing other works of literature throughout her panels as key visual and narrative registers. These allusions simultaneously sharpen the confessional themes of the text—the concurrent thralls and perils of idealizing a love object, the dramatic and performative nature

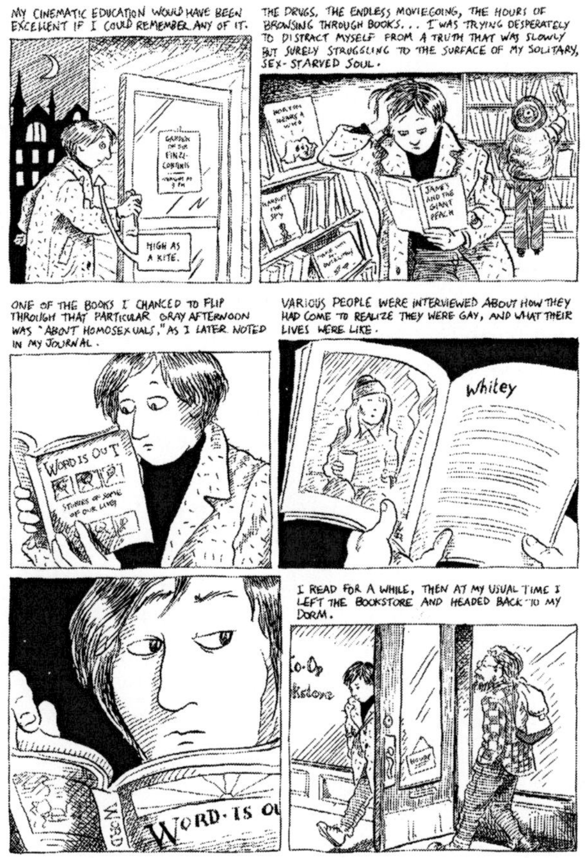

1.5. Alison Bechdel. *"Coming Out Story." Gay Comics* 19 (1993). p. 3.

of everyday life, the human costs of the artist's endeavor—and offer narratives separate from the specifics of the Bechdel family's drama. On the first page alone, Bechdel transforms the child's game of airplane into a layered reference to the Icarus myth while placing a visible copy of *Anna Karenina* open beside her father, both allusions presaging Bruce's suicide. In a supremely metafictional move, both resonances return on the narrative's concluding page; Bruce lies prostrate beneath the Sunbeam bread truck that serves as the memoir's Tolstoyan train, catching Alison in the final iteration of the text's recursive and at times vertiginous allusions to the Icarian fall that cites Greek myth and James Joyce's *Ulysses* alike. This proliferation of literary allusions is also exceedingly germane to Alison's lived life—both her parents were English teachers and she describes her own coming out as a process of reading as much as one of felt experience, as specious as that divide becomes throughout the memoir—and a distancing technique from the often traumatic details of that life.

Taking a longer view, these allusive confessions marked Bechdel's earliest comics as much as her most recent work. "Coming Out Story," first published in the periodical *Gay Comics* more than a decade before *Fun Home*, offers a prehistory and lays bare many of the more subtly refined themes of the finished memoir. On the third page of the short narrative (fig. 1.5) the reader sees Alison "browsing through books [. . .] to distract [herself] from a truth that was slowly but surely struggling to the surface of [her] sex-starved soul" (3). Books and reading here are initially presented as a means to avoid erotic truth, the conspicuous alliteration of the passage itself a distancing technique of the literary. Yet the words are themselves lushly sensuous, conflating the textual and the sexual in ways that will be manifest throughout her later memoirs. Textual study thus both defers self-revelation and prompts Alison's coming out.

This avowal is followed immediately in the next panel by the discovery of *Word is Out*, a 1978 volume that transcribes interviews from a documentary film of the same title. *Word is Out* as a text broadcasts its intent to celebrate gay and lesbian visibility and testimony, an irony heightened by Bechdel as she shows the volume being read in relative secrecy, while also returning to, publishing, and making visible that secret history of reading in her own comics. Indeed, this moment of the discovery of *Word is Out* was later redrawn multiples times in *Fun Home* (74–75, 203) and described as generating "[Alison's] realization at nineteen that [she] was a lesbian [. . .] a revelation not of the flesh but of the mind" (74). The contiguous panels of "Coming Out Story" then show the act of reading to be both irremediably outside of the self and the royal road to that self-realization, both an obstacle to and the ultimate means of sexual awakening. Nonetheless, "Coming Out Story" hews to a stauncher notion of facticity that *Fun Home* eschews. The comic concludes (fig. 1.6) when Alison states: "I've told the true story. My own humble contribution to that epic tale of collective self-revelation that my sisters and brothers have been telling for generations" (12). The tone here is difficult to pin down—part triumphant, part mock-heroic—yet this seemingly bald statement also signals the end of the narrative as such, spoken as it is immediately before the speaker closes the door on her readers. The self is revealed, Bechdel shows us, at the moment the narrative is cut short.

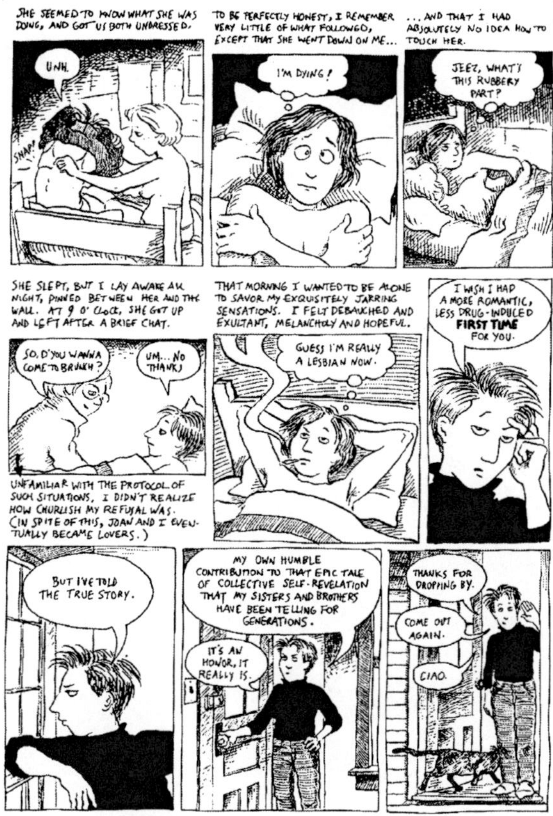

1.6. Alison Bechel. *"Coming Out Story." Gay Comics* 19 (1993). p. 12.

While "Coming Out Story" begins to explore what queer theorists Valerie Rohy and Ann Cvetkovich both deem the "queer archive" in Bechdel's comics, almost none of *Fun Home*'s layered allusions to the more conventional literary canon are present in the earlier text (Cvetkovich, "Drawing," Rohy). With the exceptions of a brief aside comparing Alison's cognitive leap of lesbian self-awareness to Athena springing fully formed from the head of Zeus and the briefest of cameos for James Joyce's *Ulysses*, the most glaring difference between the early "Coming Out Story" and the later *Fun Home* is the relative density of such literary allusions. To chart such allusive confessions in the completed graphic memoir is a near-impossible task; the text is replete with them, from Joyce and Fitzgerald to Wilde and Proust—by my own slightly obsessive-compulsive count, allusions to

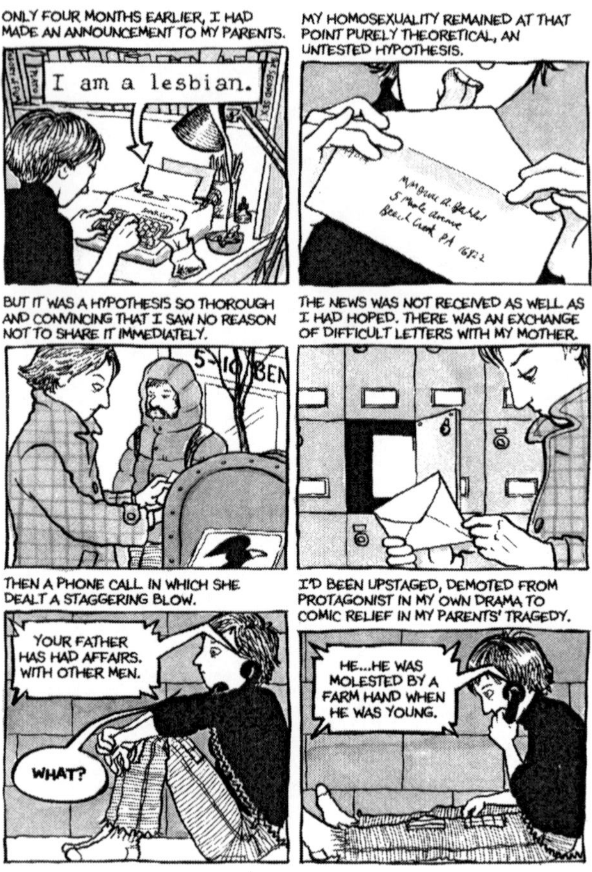

1.7. Alison Bechdel. *Fun Home*. p. 58.

canonical literature appear on 129 of the memoir's 224 pages. In part we can read this increased reliance on the literary as a turn to the father's narrative, and Bechdel herself has spoken in interviews about her dawning revelation throughout the course of the book's composition that she could best explore the lacunae in her knowledge of her father's character by reading his beloved authors, authors about whom she herself was deeply ambivalent. Yet literary allusion enacts a distance from these events as well, an oblique form of the censorship Meyer sees as so central to the discourse of modern gay and lesbian visual culture. Bechdel's projection of the self invariably takes place on the screen of anterior literary archetypes, blending the fictional and the factual, literary and lived experience, throughout *Fun Home*.

Bechdel is most explicit about these stakes of the literary in her third chapter, "That Old Catastrophe," and I would like to explore the implications of Bechdel's allusive confessions through an analysis of this section. While all the chapters share the recursive and chronologically disjointed character of the memoir as a whole, Bechdel's other chapters each hew relatively closely to the central allusion announced in their respective titles. "A Happy Death," the second chapter, explores the absurdity of Bruce's presumed suicide through parallels to Albert Camus's novel of the same title. "In the Shadow of Young Girls in Flower," the fourth chapter, uses Proustian metaphors to explore Bruce's suspect masculinity. By contrast, "That Old Catastrophe" far exceeds the frame provided by the chapter title's reference to Wallace Stevens's poem "Sunday Morning." Allusions to Shakespeare, Hemingway, Fitzgerald, and Henry James proliferate in "That Old Catastrophe," as readers are shown both Bruce's library and Alison's "queer archive" for the first time. In this profusion of allusions, I argue, the work of allusion itself is being negotiated, the structure and syntax of these references providing a model through which to understand the memoir writ large.

Having concluded the second chapter at the foot of Bruce's grave, Bechdel begins the third chapter in his library with Alison looking up the word "queer" in the family's "mammoth Webster," its uncertain etymology of obstruction and obliquity a fitting masthead for the chapter as a whole (58). The following page (fig. 1.7) shows Alison at the moment of her coming out, typing the uncharacteristically direct and prosaic claim "I am a lesbian" in a letter to her parents, only to have the revelation of her father's affairs leave her "upstaged, demoted from protagonist in [her] own drama to comic relief in [her] parents' tragedy" (58). The explicitly theatrical and literary language of this claim, which marginalizes Alison and interrupts her own narrative of coming out, again demonstrates the ways in which allusion occludes as much as inaugurates the coming out story, overwriting the direct and declarative statement of her sexual identity at the top of the page. Alison is left in the fetal position following this revelation, an infantilizing image the memoir returns to insistently (59, 79, 211), her own trajectory forestalled by her father's incursions into the narrative. These intrusions are almost entirely expressed through literature; the very next page begins a tour of her father's library, a place where Bruce's "affectation [was] so thoroughgoing, so authentic in its details, that it stops being pretense . . . and becomes, for all practical purposes, real" (60). Alison ostensibly speaks about her father's projected persona as a Victorian aristocrat and man of leisure here, but the patent subtext throughout the memoir is his suspect performance of heteronormative masculinity as well, as indicated by Roy's introduction on the facing page. In rapid succession, Bechdel then offers an etymology of her and her father's erotic truth and expresses her own in unequivocal terms, only to have her declaration co-opted as Bruce's labyrinthine fictions about his own sexuality take center stage.

This chain of references sets off arguably the most complicated and interwoven sequence of literary allusions in the text, each one revealing new information about the Bechdel family while superimposing the family's narrative onto a dizzying succession of fictional archetypes. Roy and Bruce exchange copies of *The Sun Also Rises* and *The Great Gatsby*—these texts' queer registers and anxieties becoming an unspoken subtext of the sequence as a whole—while Bruce, in the following pages, assumes a heady mix of Fitzgerald's favored themes of failed romance and class minstrelsy in his epistolary courtship of Bechdel's mother, Helen. Helen here is Zelda to Bruce's Scott, as she will subsequently be *Washington Square*'s Catherine Sloper to his Morris Townsend (Helen played the lead in Ruth and Augustus Goetz's *The Heiress*, an adaptation of Henry James's *Washington Square*), *The Taming of the Shrew*'s Katherina to his Petruchio (a production of the Shakespeare play was the occasion of Helen and Bruce's first meeting), and *The Portrait of a Lady*'s Isabel Archer to his Gilbert Osmond (James's novel serving as the template against which the dissolution of Helen's early ideals of independence as well as the unfitness of her marriage takes place) (61–63, 66, 69–70, 70–72). Bechdel, true to form, interrupts this metatextual procession with her own self-conscious claim: "I employ these allusions to James and Fitzgerald not only as descriptive devices, but because my parents are most real to me in fictional terms. And perhaps my cool aesthetic distance itself does more to convey the arctic climate of our family than any particular literary comparison" (67). If this direct, metacritical avowal is a way for Alison to exert control over her narrative, it bears mentioning the distance allusive claims like this one maintain from the bold declaration of her sexuality at the opening of the chapter. Bechdel's legerdemain in these passages, her mature self-awareness of the rhetorical and literary devices of her own narrative, is a version of Bruce's own artful fictions. This final reality is made manifest at the conclusion of this long sequence when Alison is shown literally carrying her father's baggage (73), the mirroring between the two characters here as much a burden as it is a bond between them.

Bechdel then returns her readers to the scene of her earlier, occluded coming out, redrawing similar moments from those first countenanced in "Coming Out Story," namely her dawning lesbian self-discovery through reading the queer archive. *Word is Out, The Well of Loneliness, Maurice,* and at least twenty-three other titles serve as a series of counterweights to the father's library of allusions. At one point, Alison appears behind a wall of these books while on the phone with her parents (76) and she is first shown in bed with her lover Joan surrounded by books from this alternate canon, using their language play as an erotic game between lovers. However, this reimagined relationship to—or through—literature is short-lived. The recursive news of Bruce's self-destruction and eventual death again interrupts the narrative arc of Alison coming into her own lesbian identity. Even Alison's and Helen's grief, what little of it is expressed throughout the memoir, is transacted through books as the interrupted bedroom scene gives way to yet another sequence of panels set in Bruce's library, this time as Helen gives Joan a volume of the titular Wallace Stevens. Literature's possibility for erotic expression is replaced here with its capacity as a register for grief and sacrifice—both the sacrifice of the poem's subject of the crucifixion and Helen's sacrifices throughout her marriage—serving at each instance to forestall Alison's lesbian memoir with the family's tragedy.

It is at the close of "That Old Catastrophe," however, that the tenor of Bechdel's allusive confessions begins to waver. Stevens plays a much less powerful role than many comparable authors alluded to in *Fun Home*; aside from the coincidence of the poem and the father's library sharing images of a cockatoo, the focus is much more on Helen's anguish than it is on Stevens's account of the crucifixion. Bechdel could even be said to flatten the complexity of the poem, opting instead to reproduce verses written by Joan that narrate this scene (fig. 1.8). The reproduced typescript of Joan's poem becomes a visual echo of Alison's opening confession: "I am a lesbian" (82). Images of women predominate here—this being one of the few pages in *Fun Home*, ironically, that passes the so-called "Bechdel test"—and the dense fabric of male literary allusions gives way, however briefly, to a narrative outside of the orbit of Bruce Bechdel and his library.[5] To strictly oppose these lesbian and literary narratives runs the risk of reestablishing a binary distinction *Fun Home* works to complicate. Jane Tolmie rightly argues that "*Fun Home*'s negotiations of a modernist canon do not merely aim to set up a competing discourse of high culture comic books, but also trouble our reliance on

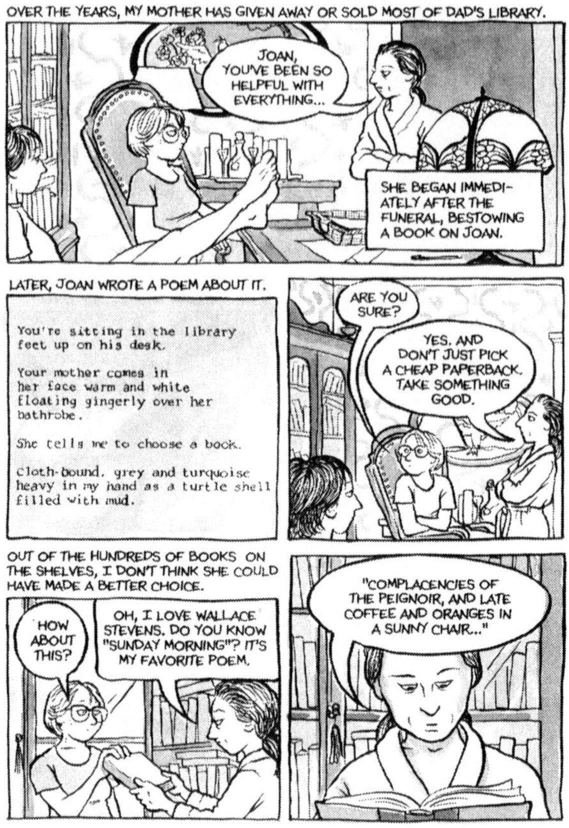

1.8. Alison Bechdel. *Fun Home*. p. 82.

categories of high and low, included and excluded, straight and queer, textual and embodied" (79). In Bechdel's hands canonical literature is in many respects incorporated into the queer archive given the privileged place she accords gay writers in her literary allusions. Yet, having negotiated this elaborate network of allusive confessions in "That Old Catastrophe," we never once return to the father's library in the more than 140 remaining pages of the memoir. Having traversed this dense network of literary allusions, Bechdel intimates a limit to the influence of her father's archive over her narrative.

Rather, Bechdel concludes the chapter with an outside view of the library (fig. 1.9), Alison and Bruce separated by the shutters between twinned windows of the same room (86). She has just asked her father to buy her "some new MAD books," and she is shown writing out a check for

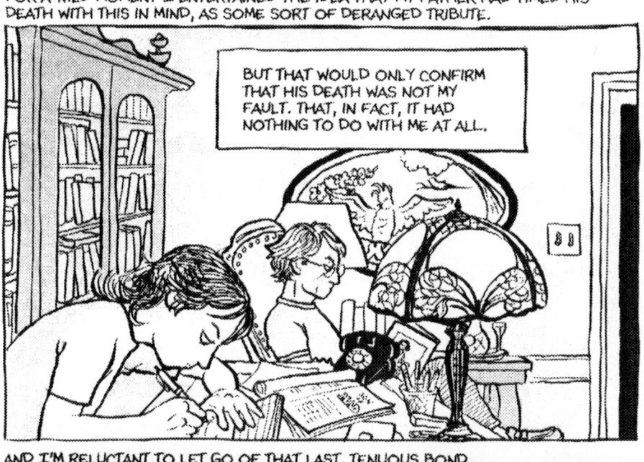

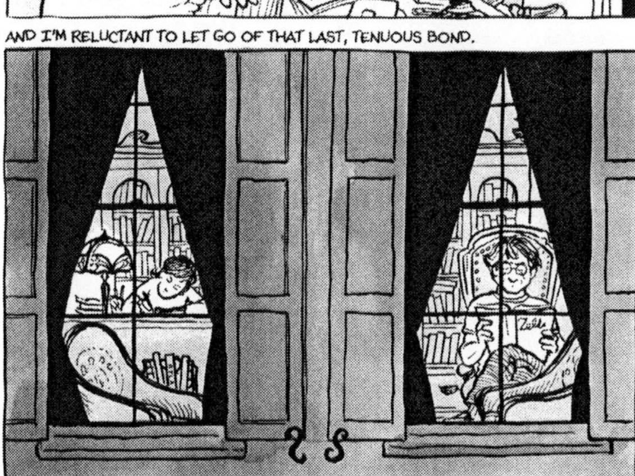

1.9. Alison Bechdel. *Fun Home*. p. 86.

his signature. While she does this, Bruce reads Nancy Milford's *Zelda: A Biography*. In one sense, this is a record of debts owed; Bruce's connection to Milford's biography tacitly acknowledges the familial pain he (as a surrogate F. Scott Fitzgerald throughout the memoir) has caused, while Bechdel's own art, *in utero*, draws on the funds bequeathed to her by her father. As is the case in several renderings of the house that Bruce built, architectural spaces here are shown to encase the separate pursuits of the same family. Though they occupy a shared space, Alison and Bruce are divided in their aims, joined only, in Bechdel's words, by a "last, tenuous bond" she is "reluctant to let go of" (86). Importantly, he is left reading while she is writing, the incorporation of *MAD Magazine*'s antic comics, however briefly, into the otherwise conventional literary canon offering a rare intervention into the traditional literary archive. The canon makes way for comics in this moment, much as the familial narrative makes way for the first stirrings of Bechdel's lesbian memoir.

It is at such moments that we can see Bechdel articulating a place in the father's library for the lesbian graphic memoir. These allusive confessions straddle the personal and the public, the lived and the literary; they recast the generic possibilities of graphic memoir and extend the medium's claims in ways that place Bechdel at the center of our growing appreciation for the possibilities of graphic narrative. In this ambivalent and layered treatment of the literary, Bechdel revises the canon by frequently giving precedence to gay and lesbian writers while simultaneously demarcating a place for herself within that genealogy.[6] This process appears to be both unfinished work and an ongoing project of Bechdel's. In 2008, Bechdel published "Compulsory Reading" in *Entertainment Weekly*, a final, more forceful condemnation of the literature that her father foisted upon her as a child. Structured like a confessional—the first panel reads "Authors, bless me, for I have sinned"—the narrative's lament for books unread quickly becomes a jeremiad against the "coercive paradigm" of her father's expectations for his children's reading (112). Allusions are not abandoned, however, as Alison is shown surrounded by books as various as *The Phenomenology of Spirit* and *The World of Pooh* while researching her next memoir. Nonetheless, the punch line comes when Alison has forsaken appropriately literary texts, and presumably the allusive confessions that come with them, turning instead to "*Harry Potter XXIV*" while averring "I'm just checking out these classical allusions" (113).

That memoir-in-progress was to be titled "Love Life: A Case Study," an explicit treatment of the relationships occluded and interrupted in *Fun Home*. What emerged instead was 2012's *Are You My Mother?*, the undertow of a pathologizing rhetoric in "Love Life's" subtitle expanding out into a psychoanalytic portrait of Alison's relationship with Helen. As in *Fun Home*, Alison's negotiations of her familial relations (the largely literary allusions of *Fun Home* give way to a combination of psychoanalytic and literary citations in *Are You My Mother?*) at times eclipse her accounts of her romantic relations. On one particularly telling page, Bechdel charts the relationships in her life on a graph, including a line for romantic attachments only below lines for both her mother and her therapists (22). This graph is bracketed, like much of the memoir, by scenes in her therapist's office, and the accompanying text centers on her reading of the psychoanalyst Donald Winnicott. As in *Fun Home*, Alison's romantic attachments appear throughout *Are You My Mother?* yet never wholly transfix its narrative attention. How these bonds can be more fully and directly imagined remains an open question, one Bechdel herself continues to negotiate in her ongoing exploration of the possibilities of graphic memoir.

Notes

This chapter has benefited immeasurably by the feedback from audiences at the 2010 ACLA and 2011 MLA conferences as well as from students in my undergraduate courses at Dickinson College. I am particularly indebted to the knowledge, inspiration, and feedback provided by Claire Bowen, Margaret Frohlich, Elizabeth Lee, Wendy Moffat, Sharon O'Brien, Colin Tripp, and Benjamin Widiss across a wide range of fields, graphic narrative, life writing, and sexuality studies among them.

1. Given the recent publication date of *Fun Home*, the critical genealogy of the memoir is excitingly robust. Important critical assessments not treated directly in this chapter include: Gardner, Pearl, Watson, and Whitlock and Poletti.

2. At the risk of what Bechdel would no doubt dismiss as pretension, calling her a dialectical thinker is hardly a stretch. In her short 2008 composition "Compulsory Reading" for *Entertainment Weekly*, she is shown reading a copy of G. W. F. Hegel's *The Phenomenology of Spirit* (alongside children's literature and graphic narratives) as she researches her follow-up graphic memoir, *Are You My Mother?*, all the while dialectically chafing against the notion of compulsory reading so much at the heart of *Fun Home*.

3. In making such an argument about the connections between gay visual culture and Bechdel's comics, I hope to address the disconnect Hillary Chute rightly discerns between comics studies and visual culture studies more generally (*Graphic Women* 221 n.18).

4. Such debates are typified by Rebecca Beirne's trenchant response to Kathleen Martindale's and Gabrielle Dean's critiques of *Dykes to Watch Out For* (169 ff.).

5. To quote from Bechdel's early *Dykes to Watch Out For* strip titled "The Rule," a cultural text passes the test if: "One, it has to have at least two women in it . . . who, two, talk to each other about, three, something besides a man" (22–23).

6. Ariela Freedman makes an analogous point in her essay "Drawing on Modernism in Alison Bechdel's *Fun Home*": "From the beginning, then, Bechdel has juxtaposed the tragic and the comic, the literary and the personal, and established canonical 'high modernist' literature with the emerging graphic narrative. [. . .] Bechdel is clearly staging the legitimacy of the graphic narrative as inheritor of the modernist tradition" (128, 130). For a more detailed argument about contemporary graphic narratives as one afterlife of literary modernism, see my essay "Comics Against Themselves: Chris Ware's Graphic Narratives as Literature."

Works Cited

Ball, David M. "Comics Against Themselves: Chris Ware's Graphic Narratives as Literature." *The Rise of the American Comics Artist: Creators and Contexts*. Ed. Paul Williams and James Lyons. Jackson: UP of Mississippi, 2010. 103–23. Print.

Bechdel, Alison. *Are You My Mother?: A Comic Drama*. Boston: Houghton Mifflin Harcourt, 2012. Print.

———. "Coming Out Story." *Gay Comics* 19 (1993): 1–13. Print.

———. "Compulsory Reading." *Entertainment Weekly*. 27 June 2008 and 4 July 2008: 110–13. Print.

———. *Dykes to Watch Out For*. Ithaca: Firebrand, 1986.

———. *Fun Home: A Family Tragicomic*. Boston: Houghton Mifflin, 2006. Print.

———. *The Indelible Alison Bechdel: Confessions, Comix, and Miscellaneous Dykes to Watch Out For*. Ithaca: Firebrand, 1998. Print.

Beirne, Rebecca. *Lesbians in Television and Text after the Millennium*. New York: Palgrave Macmillan, 2008. Print.

Castle, Terry. *The Apparitional Lesbian: Female Homosexuality and Modern Culture*. New York: Columbia UP, 1993. Print.

Chute, Hillary L. *Graphic Women: Life Narrative and Contemporary Comics*. New York: Columbia UP, 2010. Print.

———. "An Interview with Alison Bechdel." *Modern Fiction Studies* 52.4 (2006): 1,004–13. Print.

Cvetkovich, Ann. *An Archive of Feelings: Trauma, Sexuality, and Lesbian Public Cultures*. Durham: Duke UP, 2003. Print.

———. "Drawing the Archive in Alison Bechdel's *Fun Home*." *WSQ: Women's Studies Quarterly* 36.1 & 2 (2008): 111–28. Print.

Dean, Gabrielle N. "The 'Phallacies' of Dyke Comic Strips." *The Gay '90s: Disciplinary and Interdisciplinary Formations in Queer Studies*. Ed. Thomas Foster, Carol Siegel, and Ellen E. Berry. New York: New York UP, 1997. 199–223. Print.

Diggs, Marylynne. "Lesbian Confession and Case History." *Confessional Politics: Women's Sexual Self-Representations in Life Writing and Popular Media*. Ed. Irene Gammel. Carbondale: Southern Illinois UP, 1999. 133–47. Print.

Freedman, Ariela. "Drawing on Modernism in Alison Bechdel's *Fun Home*." *Journal of Modern Literature* 32.4 (2009): 125–40. Print.

Gardner, Jared. "Autography's Biography, 1972–2007." *Biography: An Interdisciplinary Quarterly* 31.1 (2008): 1–26. Print.

Kim, June. *12 Days*. Los Angeles: Tokyopop, 2006. Print.

Lemberg, Jennifer. "Closing the Gap in Alison Bechdel's *Fun Home*." *WSQ: Women's Studies Quarterly* 36.1 & 2 (2008): 129–40. Print.

Martindale, Kathleen. *Un/popular Culture: Lesbian Writing after the Sex Wars*. Albany: SUNY Press, 1997. Print.

Meyer, Richard. *Outlaw Representation: Censorship and Homosexuality in Twentieth-Century American Art.* Oxford: Oxford UP, 2002. Print.

Nananan, Kiriko. *Blue.* Wisbech, England: Fanfare, 2004. Print.

Pearl, Monica B. "Graphic Language: Redrawing the Family (Romance) in Alison Bechdel's *Fun Home." Prose Studies: History, Theory, Criticism* 30.3 (2008): 286–304. Print.

Radstone, Susannah. *The Sexual Politics of Time: Confession, Nostalgia, Memory.* London and New York: Routledge, 2007. Print.

Robbins, Trina. "Watch Out for Alison Bechdel (She has the Secret to Superhuman Strength)." *Comics Journal* 237 (2001): 80–86. Print.

Rohy, Valerie. "In the Queer Archive: *Fun Home." GLQ: A Journal of Lesbian and Gay Studies 16.3 (2010): 341–61. Print.*

Tamaki, Mariko, and Jillian Tamaki. *Skim.* Toronto: Groundwood, 2008. Print.

Tolmie, Jane. "Modernism, Memory, and Desire: Queer Cultural Production in Alison Bechdel's *Fun Home." Topia: Canadian Journal of Textual Studies* 22 (2009): 77–95. PDF.

Watson, Julia. "Autographic Disclosures and Genealogies of Desire in Alison Bechdel's *Fun Home." Biography: An Interdisciplinary Quarterly* 31.1 (2008): 27–58. Print.

Whitlock, Gillian, and Anna Poletti. "Self-Regarding Art." *Biography: An Interdisciplinary Quarterly* 31.1 (2008): v–xxiii. Print.

What Is an Experience?

Selves and Texts in the Comic Autobiographies
of Alison Bechdel and Lynda Barry

—Yaël Schlick

If, as is likely, all autobiographies can be read as containing (implicitly or explicitly) a theory of autobiography, we might well read Alison Bechdel's comic autobiography *Fun Home* as locating itself at the constructivist end of the spectrum, along a continuum extending from autobiography as a referential practice to autobiography as a practice through which the self is textually constructed, ultimately fictional. Not only does she at one point lament that her father did *not* underline certain lines in Camus's *A Happy Death* (47)—underlining that would have granted both certainty to the interpretation of his death as a suicide, and further elegance to a text that relies so heavily on intertextual references for its skeletal structure—Bechdel also insists that her parents are "most real to [her] in fictional terms" (67), thus reversing the conventional understanding of fact and fiction. Her allusions to texts such as *Ulysses, Portrait of the Artist as a Young Man, A Happy Death, The Myth of Sisyphus,* and *The Great Gatsby* (among others) move us to experience the family drama in textual or even fictional terms, inseparable and indistinguishable from modes of storytelling. Thus the most intimate conversation with her father is dubbed, somewhat anti-climactically, their "Ithaca moment" (222), and heavy-handed, high art references—*Anna Karenina* on the living room rug to designate the conundrums of unhappy families (3) or a CD of Pergolesi's *Stabat Mater* to indicate her mother's troubled response to Bechdel's coming-out letter—appear throughout the text as a means of reminding us how these issues have been thematized already, by others, elsewhere.

Also highly intertextual, Lynda Barry's autobiography *One! Hundred! Demons!* uses stories less as a structuring element and never as allusions to canonical figures. Rather, her work takes as one of its aims the encouragement of readers' ability to generate their own stories or coming to words. Her very text is after all inspired, she says, by a book she found in the library depicting a painting exercise by a sixteenth-century Zen monk. Her reader, she hopes, is the next author. In this avowed "autobiofictionalography," as in Bechdel's text, reading and writing, fiction and reality, are not naively conceived. Barry's text never feels it has to choose between those would-be opposing poles of autobiographical writing—the referential and the fictional. For in evoking the seductive power of narrative and in detailing and demystifying the shift from reading to writing, this autobiography tells us of the power of texts without overshadowing lived experience. It also effectively ponders the ontological status of fictional or imagined characters without ever needing or wanting to draw a final line in the sand. "Why are we moved by stories? Tales of things that never happened told by people we've never met?" asks Barry. "How does a story come so alive?" (150). Her work describes how a text can be a "magic lantern," a "living thing," simultaneously outside of us and a "part of ourselves" (148–50). Thus intertextual references tend to layer rather than mirror lived experience in *One! Hundred! Demons!* They are used, that is, as a mode of creating experience rather than interpreting it. What Barry's mode of telling does, in short, is reduce the distance between bodies and texts, between readers and writers, without one entity superseding the other. The broad range of Barry's intertextual references, furthermore—Filipino folk stories about the Aswang, pop songs, *Charlotte's Web*, "lost and found" ads in the newspaper, and stories in *The Reader's Digest*—democratize creative expression. Indeed, one of Barry's points is that Literature (capital "L") works (in classrooms particularly) as a form of social snobbery and social exclusion, a point she interestingly shares with Bechdel, whose own critique of literary education is equally scathing (and funny). Likely this is the place to ponder the more ironic uses of canonical works in *Fun Home*.

This essay will compare two different modes of deploying intertexutality in autobiographical writing by examining the relationship between textuality and experience in *One! Hundred! Demons!* and *Fun Home*. I will begin by discussing the tensions in Bechdel's sophisticated use of intertextuality, examining first her awareness in *Fun Home* of the way her chosen intertexts work imperfectly as a means of describing and understanding her own experiences. I will then read the epistemological crisis described in chapter 5 of the work as a mise en abyme of the narration, one that offers its reader an apt description of *Fun Home* as a text in crisis despite its intertextual certainties. Finally, I will explore Bechdel's use of textuality in her elaboration of the emergence of the body's sexual truths, the body's truths being that space often diametrically opposed to language, its pleasure and eroticism being beyond words. This discussion will be followed by an analysis of *One! Hundred! Demons!* and its own strategies of depiction, focusing first on Barry's technique when depicting suicide, then on her notion of texts as magic lanterns. Finally, I will discuss her use of intertextuality as a means of interpolating the reader, as a means of modeling textual engagement and turning readers into writers. Barry's introduction tells us just how she herself got started. Her "outro" gives us the tools to create our own texts. I will not only discuss how intertextuality works in each text, but also determine which mode of deploying intertextuality works best to bridge the worlds of experience and expression and to bring about the comingling of lives and texts. I will also ask whether there is a point at which the constructed or fictional end of the autobiographical continuum might not be as problematical as the referential practice of autobiographical writing at the opposite pole.

Intertextual Structure as Compulsion

In an interview with Hillary Chute, Bechdel has noted the evolution of her narrative toward the use of a main text and writer per chapter, a means of thematizing the chapter's content and organizing the text into discrete units (1,004). Thus, as noted by many critics, chapter 1 centers on James Joyce's *Portrait of the Artist as a Young Man*, chapter 2 on Albert Camus's *A Happy Death*, chapter 3 on F. Scott Fitzgerald's *The Great Gatsby*, chapter 4 on Marcel Proust's *Remembrance of Things Past*, chapter 5 on Kenneth Grahame's *The Wind in the Willows*, chapter 6 on Oscar Wilde's *The Importance of Being Earnest*, and chapter 7—circling back to Joyce as it circles back also to the Icarus theme—on James Joyce's *Ulysses*. Many texts by other authors are referred to throughout, particularly ones formative of Alison's emerging lesbian identity. The contents of *Fun Home* are likewise held tightly together, with the airplane/Icarian games of the initial comics page reiterated on the last page like internal bookends to the autobiographical text—doubling the wallpaper that encloses or lines the hardcover edition of the text. The schema is tidy and useful in its ability to hold the complex narrative—not simply linear or chronological in content—together, giving shape to the messiness of lived experience. Indeed, while the organizational logic is seemingly tight, and rather strictly adhered to, Bechdel expresses dismay at points that it is not tighter or tidier still: in chapter 2, the narrator regrets not having borrowed her father's copy of Camus's *A Happy Death*, saying, "I wish I could say I'd accepted his book, that I still had it, that he'd underlined one particular passage" (47). That passage—one that, if the father's act of suicide had been ascertained, would have given further credence to the aptness of *A Happy Death* as a relevant intertext for it—is not in Bechdel's possession; it appears in the text as underlined not by the father but by the daughter who desires closure. It provides the reader with an example of a place in the text where the intertext does not correlate perfectly to the Bechdel family narrative, and, equally importantly, where the narrator is clearly aware that this is so.

Another such instance occurs in the Proust chapter with respect to the theory of inversion as an explanation of homosexuality. "Proust refers to his explicitly homosexual characters as 'inverts,'" writes Bechdel. "I've always been fond of this antiquated clinical term" (97). The image below illustrates this concept's effectiveness in describing the father-daughter dynamic by juxtaposing the father's attentiveness to feminine detail (he is forcing a barrette into his daughter's hair) with the daughter's resistance to feminization, her tomboyishness. The frame here juxtaposes the narrator's awareness of the term's problematic status with its descriptive usefulness, but is followed by another frame, now devoid of images, discussing inversion further: "It's imprecise and insufficient, defining the homosexual as a person whose gender expression is at odds with his or her sex" (97). Here, Bechdel again shows herself as critical, aware of the critique leveled at the inversion trope of homosexuality, discussed, for example, in such well-known works as Eve Sedgewick's *Epistemology of the Closet* and Judith Butler's *Undoing Gender*, where the term is examined for its problematic preservation of an essential heterosexuality within desire itself. It evinces a homosexuality that is itself an effect of the Law. Bechdel's awareness is strongly conveyed when she acknowledges the antiquated nature of the trope, its imprecision, its insufficiency in addressing homosexual desire. As in the reference to Camus's *A Happy Death*, the text simultaneously utilizes the chapter's main, structuring paradigms (the inversion one being read out of Proust's oeuvre) all the while displaying its inadequacy. The inversion model is, furthermore, more than a local issue or understanding, but the text's dominant mode: the trope of inversion and the figure of the chiasmus. This rhetorical figure, itself an instance of inversion, is used to portray the structure of homosexuality as well as the Icarus story, in which the daughter (not the son) and the offspring (not the parent) are shown to be soaring (see 4, 7, 231–32). The figure of the chiasmus also continually functions to depict the extended, narrative trajectories of father and daughter, whose paths cross but do not meet.

Fun Home, in short, is both highly and rigidly structured, yet also implicitly critical of its own structuration. Bechdel has acknowledged her mania for order repeatedly. In an interview she has referred to her archival impulse, saying "I'm the most anal-retentive person I've ever met" (Chute, "Interview" 1007); in the introduction to *The Essential Dykes to Watch Out For* she portrays herself on a ladder in a room of towering filing cabinets reaching for childhood drawings in a file drawer that will reveal her longstanding fixation on masculinity (viii). But a few pages later we see her tossing away texts from her bookshelf decrying how her "tidy schema [of lesbian types] went all to hell in the nineties" (xvi). *Why use a faulty schema?* the reader of *Fun Home* might ask. At stake is not only the intertexts' ability to accurately encapsulate the life, but the central question of whether narrative can adequately describe lived experience. Bechdel's response seems to be that it cannot, but that she wishes it could. The text is both a fabulous tour de force of literary complexity and altogether too neat.

Focusing on the problematics of tidiness, chapter 5, about Alison's OCD crisis, may be a place where the text ponders control schemas themselves—ones that can perhaps manage untamed experience. In that chapter, Alison, the diarist, feels "that gaping rift between signifier and signified" (143) to such an extent that diary entries must finally be crossed off with her curly circumflex, placing doubt amidst even the most ordinary and substantial of her narrative assertions. The OCD crisis is overcome to some extent in that chapter, when Alison no longer wields her pen but gives dictation of her diary entries over to her mother. And yet, *Fun Home* itself is marked by the same lingering question of the adequacy of writing to convey reality, as the narrative questions its own assertions and tests its affinities against some truths potentially diverging from them. As such the epistemological crisis displayed in the diary entries doubles for those of *Fun Home* itself, where the tight organizational schema serves as a means of keeping "life's attendant chaos" (149) at bay.

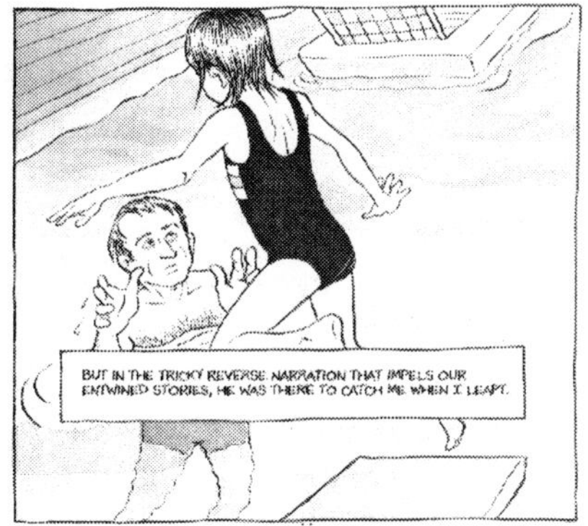

2.1. Alison Bechdel. *Fun Home*. p. 232.

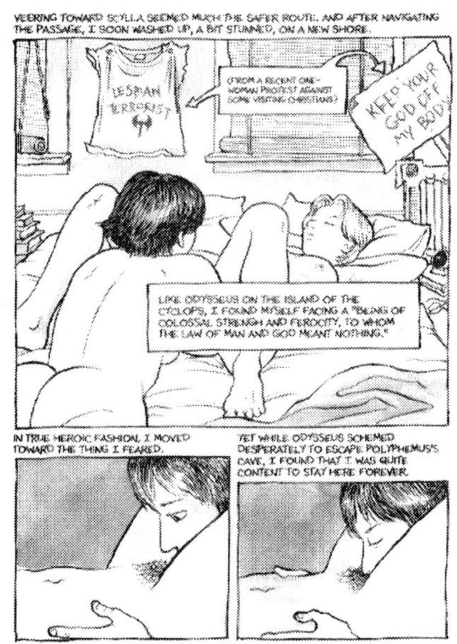

2.2. Alison Bechdel. *Fun Home*. p. 214.

The further image in chapter 5 of Alison reading Dr. Spock is an additional nod to the way we can read this chapter as a mise en abyme of the narrative as a whole. Alison's reading of Dr. Spock, described as "a curious experience in which I was both subject and object" (138), is after all a succinct summary of the autobiographical enterprise itself. In this early meta-autobiographical moment, Dr. Spock seems right on the mark in accurately describing experience. But the relationship of the older Alison to textuality is more complex and more questioning in nature. Bechdel embarks upon the autobiographical enterprise herself through the dual strategies of organizing the chaos while simultaneously acknowledging the inadequacy of doing so (something the Spock text does not do). But still, the text's tidy internal logic—its hall of mirrors—is at times so insistent that we are in danger of either being entirely satisfied with its narrative closure (like dutiful critics, we scurry to explore how the intertextuality reverberates and produces meanings in the text) or overly critical of its simplification of experience. In fact, we always have both in the text itself—structure and chaos, creation and decreation. The intertexts, which are so efficient at organizing experience, are also after all indicative of the impossibility of ever doing so, the intertext gesturing both at the problematical textualization of experience and at the infinity of systems of reference at play. *Fun Home* yearns for elegance and order, for a means of closing the gap "between word and meaning," while knowing the endeavor to be impossible. Its final image, referring to "the tricky reverse narration" of the father's and daughter's stories, says that her father "was there to catch [her] when [she] leapt" (232, see fig. 2.1). But the accompanying image has Alison suspended in midair, emphatically not in her father's arms. The reader is allowed to experience a sense of closure while also sensing an invisible "I think" hovering over the text as a whole. It may be that writing autobiographical narrative itself is an obsessive compulsion, but it may also be a necessary or unavoidable means—like narrative itself—of making sense.

In one sense, then, *Fun Home*'s vacillation between creating and questioning, structuring and unraveling, effectively addresses the challenges inherent in life writing. Its intertextual web or schema means that we are forever lodged in a textual realm where books and selves merge to occupy a single, spatial field, wherein we must own up to that rift between signifier and signified, between chaos and order. Even the body and its sensations inhabit a textual realm in this text. The scene of Alison and Joan having oral sex is so dominated by textual references to *The Odyssey* that all sexual sensation or pleasure becomes oddly displaced (214, see fig. 2.2). Similarly, Alison's masturbation, a moment when she relates her discovery of bodily pleasure, a physical moment akin to the autobiographical act of being both subject and object, takes place under the sign of Gerty McDowell's masturbation in *Ulysses* (207). It is not so much that we expect any longer some simple, bodily expression. Yet there are moments—especially in the last third or so of the narrative—where the narrator seems so intensely wrapped up in the story's intertextual reverberations as to lose sight of lived experience altogether, where the text ceases to dwell on the signified of historical experience altogether (even as an unreachable domain). Texts in this family home become, in Bechdel's own funhouse, both signifier and signified, collapsed onto one plane that no longer distinguishes between their realms. This tendency is most strongly visible in the numerous frames in which texts are both signifier and signified—see, for example, this technique's culmination on page 228 (see fig. 2.3) where the textual rectangles of narrations are superimposed upon a textual image of the last page of *Ulysses*. Julia Watson has referred to such pages as collages that draw the reader's attention to the comic page as an intertextual space (128–29). And there is another, related problem in the insistence on *certain* texts as the lenses through which to filter autobiographical content. While the texts chosen are a useful means of thinking through and

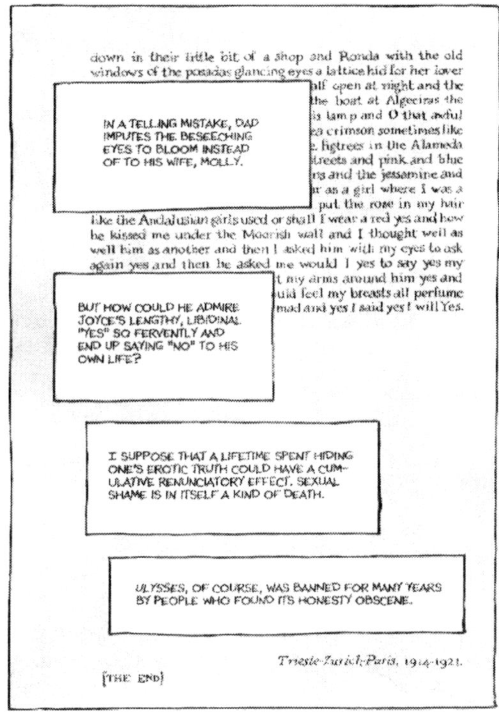

2.3. Alison Bechdel. *Fun Home*. p. 228.

contextualizing the relationship of father and son or father and daughter, they also work to relegate certain characters or issues to the shadows. Might we have heard more about Bechdel's siblings or mother otherwise, with other intertexts in place? Would the mother have emerged as a more fully articulated or interesting character had she not been subjected to playing double to Zelda Fitzgerald or Lady Bracknell or Katherine in *The Taming of the Shrew*? (Bechdel does make her mother the central character in her most recent work, *Are You My Mother?*) The combination of Bechdel's choice of certain, dominant intertexts, coupled with her insistence on their use to structure the narrative, inevitably obscures as well as reveals. The issue of the canonical nature of Bechdel's intertexts—the subject of many critical discussions of *Fun Home*—is less at issue in this respect. With Ariel Freeman, we may acknowledge her gesture as a quest for canonicity in placing both queer narrative and comics on par with the modernist greats. At the same time, we should recognize not merely conformity to a modernist standard, but, following Jane Tolmie, a desire to trouble the very categories that divide texts into high and low cultural objects. Either way, Bechdel's use of intertextuality must be read into and against the text's own signaling of the foundational aporia between language and the real, explored so compellingly in the fifth chapter.

Intertexts as Magic Lanterns

Lynda Barry's story—also one of her emergence as an artist—is more populist in its highlighting of main or important references. The intertextual references in *One! Hundred! Demons!* range widely from a sixteenth-century Japanese Zen scroll to the lost and found ads of the daily paper to *Reader's Digest* stories about body parts. Barry underlines the specifically non-hierarchical tendencies of her narrative with brief references to such texts as *The Bell Jar* and children's classics she never read, such as *The Wind in the Willows* and *Watership Down* (215, 212), although her narrative takes seriously and implicitly—as I will later argue—such famous images as the magic lantern from Proust's *Combray* and the concept of transitional objects from D. W. Winnicott's psychoanalytical writings. It can nonetheless be said that her text refuses to sort its textual web into high and low art or writing, all the while emphasizing the variety of works deemed important in the narrative and their influential role in self-formation. Her references are, furthermore, not predominantly books, and, unlike *Fun Home, One! Hundred! Demons!* does not create a veritable system out of its intertextual references or divide up tidily so as to discretely articulate and separate experiences. The Zen scroll gives her the idea of structuring the text with a different "demon" for each chapter, but these are derived from the autobiographical narrative itself and, while shaping her narrative, leave intact the primacy of her experiences. This structuration, furthermore, is not tidy—the demon standing for, in fact, the various tangles or knots of the past that the text unpacks. Her text, in a word, is still messy, teeming with intertextual life of all sorts—Filipino folk legends, radio hit songs, family stories, TV broadcasts, and "Hints from Heloise" among them—presented without any sense of hierarchy or precedence. Pages are crammed with doodles and scrapbook-type items. As readers, we experience its richness and cacophony.

As Barry makes clear in *What It Is*, a book that is even more of a primer for self-expression than her comic autobiofictionalography, her conception of both life and art is a complex convergence of past and present,

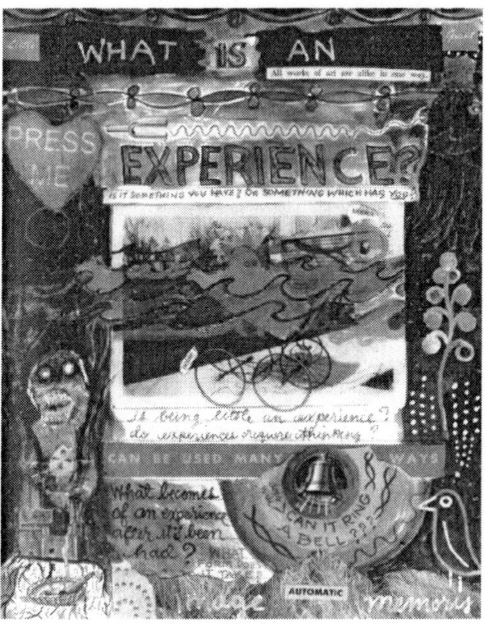

2.4. Lynda Barry. *What It Is*. p. 22.

writing and image, the unconscious and the conscious, the raw matter of life and its formed (but not formalized) products. Her page in that work titled "What Is An Experience?" attempts to include all senses: A cigarette smolders in the lower left corner; "press me" is written on a red heart in the upper left corner; a bell rings in the lower right corner; the page is a crazed fusion of visual elements—ghosts, foliage, bird, dry grass, photo, carriage wheels, swirls, and squiggles. Included in this fusion are, of course, some words, or rather, some questions interspersed throughout the page: "What is an experience?," "Is it something you have? or something which has *you*?," "Is being little an experience?," "Do experiences require thinking?", "What becomes of an experience after it's been had?," "What form does it take?," "Does/Will/Can it ring a bell?" (22, see fig. 2.4). This orchestrated— for it is no less thought-out—messiness of Barry is present also in *One! Hundred! Demons!*, where the narrative is clear enough but attended by so much other visual and textual material in the opening pages of chapters as well as in the introduction and outro that a reader has the sensation of entering a tangled and as yet undigested (perhaps unintelligible) domain. It is a messiness particularly conducive to the writing of experience, of getting as close as we can to it in autobiographical writing, of bridging the rift between experience and its expression, and of questioning writing's ability to capture experience in the first place.

For the text is always reminding us of that morass from which linear narrative emerges, and the rich diet of intertexts provided in this work allows for a rich conception of the relation of art to life. For a sense of how Barry creates a narrative out of this messy tangle while maintaining nonetheless a sense of its ineffability, I will first examine the chapter on suicide. I will then delve into Barry's notion of the magic lantern—a Proustian moment, though not one overtly signaled as such by the text—as a place where the narrative articulates the relations of texts to selves and to self-formation and theorizes it. I will then move on to examine other instances where the sheer fluidity between texts and selves provides a sustained and complex understanding of both experiences and narratives.

It is apt perhaps to begin by examining Barry's depiction of suicide, an event or trauma that presents particular challenges in *Fun Home* as well, where the question of the father's suicide remains suspended and thus haunts the text as a whole. In Barry's work, too, suicide stands at the other extreme from meaning-making, yet is effectively rendered in Barry's "Cicadas" chapter. Actual images of cicadas appear only in the chapter's opening pages and in the last page, but their presence is felt throughout the chapter which refers to their sound, recurring at the end of summer, reminding the narrator of the time of year her childhood friend committed suicide. The "amber husks" of the insect itself are a metaphor for suicide, like summer's end, "brittle ghosts of creatures who call from the tree tops" (166). As in the "What Is An Experience" panel, Barry attempts here to appeal to many senses and to find tangible objects for intangible or indigestible events and feelings. Temporally, the text also creates a complex web—the narration of happy adolescent moments with Bob and of his subsequent suicide in the past are layered with the experience of the recent suicide of another friend. She explains her offer to clean up the room where the latter died, fusing past and present by saying, "It was the unrealness that drove me. The blankness. Bob" (167, see figure 2.5). The room's contents yield that tangibility even as they communicate a sense of unreality, of the person who is no longer living: "I saw the bag from Home Depot that held the rope. I saw the rickety ladder, the spots on the floor. I didn't expect the nectarines. Three pits lined up on a dusty table. Two nectarines still in the paper sack. They were so real. Perishables" (167). The scene is narrated so as to convey that blankness or unrealness through the objects. And the chapter moves from past to present and from literal to symbolic: the

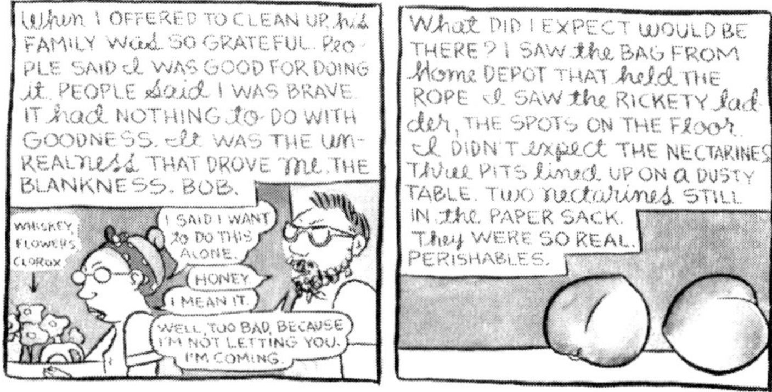

2.5. Lynda Barry. *100! Hundred! Demons!* p. 167.

cicada husks, the perishable nectarines as emblems of absence and presence, and, most centrally, the image of the blank face/mask depicted three times in the short chapter—once as Bob's face, a second time as a recent friend's death, and a final time as the image Lynda is painting at her desk. Like the cicada's husk, this human mask signifies for Barry the person who perished, memory's loss of detail, the blankness of suicide itself, and the artist's difficulty at narrating or filling in the absence of the past.

The final panel of the chapter knits these various strands together: We see Lynda at her desk painting the outlines of a yellow figure against a blue background, and the cicadas are singing as she works, while two nectarines rest at the top right corner of her desk. The past and present merge in this panel also: the caption reads "The 'Dog-Days' cicadas come every year. They are singing as I write this. Invisible to my eye, filling this hour with sound. One year, 17 years, 30 years. I thought I would be over it by now" (168, see fig. 2.6). The merging of the different narrative, imagistic, sensory, and temporal strands in this final panel allows for the blankness of the suicide to remain; the feeling of nothingness lingers because its articulation is full and tangible even though suicide is never depicted directly. Barry evokes the trauma by displaying the edges of events (Chute, *Graphic Women* 95), and her method of elaboration in this chapter is repeated in several textual episodes—elements are introduced and orchestrated without their meaning being encoded. The multiple dimensions of the experiences she relates—sensory, psychological, imagistic, intellectual, physical, and linguistic—are bound together but never flattened out. Often, as in the chapter on the Aswang—like the one titled "Cicadas"—the chapter culminates in the present moment of writing as a moment when the past is

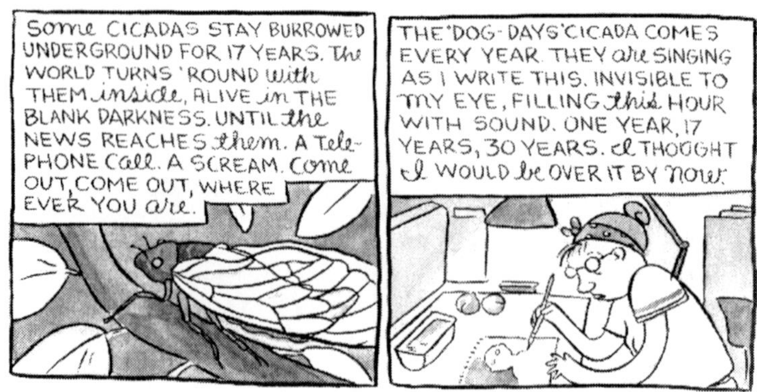

2.6. Lynda Barry. *100! Hundred! Demons!* p. 168.

given form. Yet this form is often the form of questions: "Who was the first aswang in the world?" asks the narrator; "I'm 44 years old but I still don't know the answer" (96). The writer here is a figure through which experience and expression flow without end and without conclusion. Intangibility of experience, like the light hold language has on the real, together with the images depicted, lends a precise—evocative but uncertain, concluding yet not final—rendition of the palpable presence of the past in the present and the narrative struggle to render it so.

The relationship between experience and narrative addressed in the chapter on suicide is reiterated in the text's insistent consideration of the relationship between selves and texts, and is rendered most centrally in the "Magic Lantern" chapter. Barry's attempt to understand how stories come alive in this chapter is a question with obviously larger, self-referential importance. Texts, this work suggests, are just one kind of object that can possess a deep relationship to the self. The "Magic Lantern" chapter in fact traces the way in which one's initial attachment to a stuffed toy or a blanket can become, in later life, an attachment to a text, both potentially objects with which we are so tightly bound that we are bereft without them. There is a part of ourselves, writes Barry, "that lived in the bunny or the bear," a part of that thing "that had a particular sort of aliveness that was different from people or animals" (150). This importance is subsequently granted to books read by the child in the chapter.

What Barry is describing in these pages is what D. W. Winnicott called "transitional objects" or "not-me possessions." In his paper "Transitional Objects and Transitional Phenomena," Winnicott traces the value of these objects and their gradual decathection in a child's normal development.

The attachment to a blanket or stuffed toy endowed with meaning is transitional in two senses: it functions as an intermediary between oral eroticism (the breast, the thumb) and true object relationship (230) and it represents an intermediary territory "between 'inner psychic reality' and 'the external world as perceived by two persons in common', that is to say, over the whole cultural field" (233). The transitional object facilitates this turn to culture because it is neither an internal object nor an external one (237). Like the good enough mother's ability to give the infant the illusion that "there is an external reality that corresponds to the infant's own capacity to create," the transitional object facilitates the child's turn to external reality by sustaining that illusion all the while making room for the acceptance of both difference and similarity. Its intermediary status, its status as a "not-me possession" allows for it to function like a pivot from inner to outer reality and to serve as a step toward "reality-testing" (239). It is not so much that the transitional object is eventually repressed in normal development, but that it eventually loses meaning as transitional phenomena become diffused into the external world, a world of ideas and art that can be shared with others.

In Barry's vision, texts are an important kind of transitional object. They become part of us and in turn represent an alternate world of which we are a part. Like the stuffed toy of the child, a text is something alive: "When we finish a good book, why do we hold it in both hands and gaze at it as if it were somehow alive?" asks Barry (155). Her conclusion to this chapter again gathers the images and narrative strands dispersed through-out it: "A book, a blanket, a cloth rabbit. A place on our bed post we liked to touch as we fell asleep. Each with a magic lantern inside capable of conjuring worlds" (156, see fig. 2.7). Books are an important but not the only type of object that plays a transitional role and forms an inseparable part of personal development. But like those other, previous objects, the experience of a book is crucial in that it is neither simply exterior to the self nor wholly internalized but an object with a complex intermediary status. Barry asks midway through the Magic Lanterns chapter: "Why are we moved by stories? Tales of things that never happened told by people we've never met? How does a story come so alive?" The images show the young Lynda weeping while reading *Charlotte's Web* (154). Texts in *One! Hundred! Demons!* are intertexts not because they are from without—external objects called upon when we need answers or self-definition or a means of organizing the matter of our lives. Here, they are organically fused to the development of subjecthood itself, sources of the self that

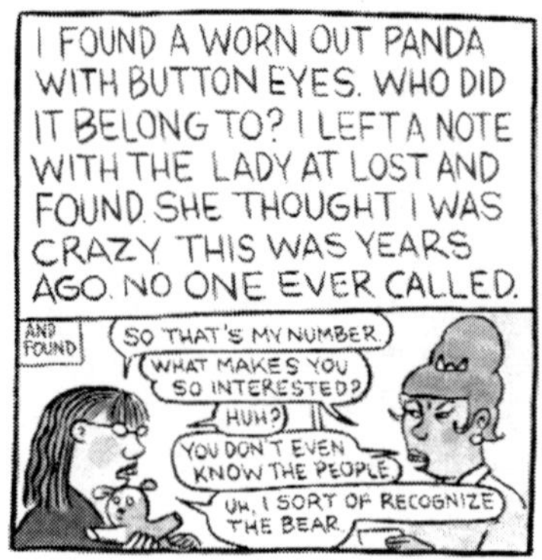

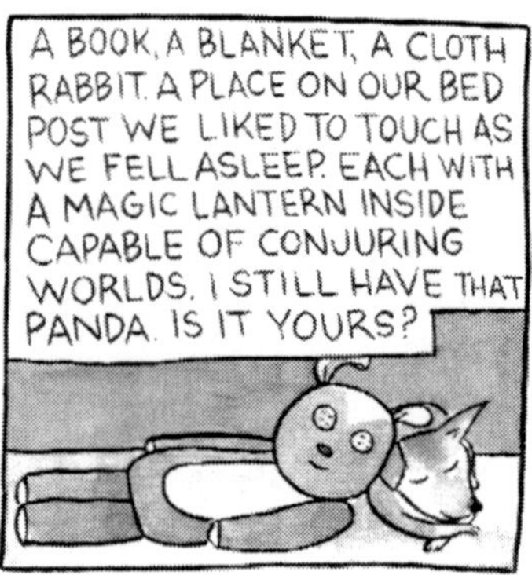

2.7 Lynda Barry. *1oo! Hundred! Demons!* p. 156.

mediate between our inner life and the cultural field at large. And just as one cannot impose a transitional object on a child, so there is no choosing the books that come to play such a role. It may be a pop song or a lost and found ad that means most.

Barry seems to want to make a particular point about those texts that have influenced her by emphasizing their heterogeneity. Her last chapter, "Lost and Found," detailing her own emergence as a comics writer, tells the reader that she did not get into advanced writing classes (214), that she failed to write the kind of literary criticism essay expected in college (215), that her own diary was a pathetic reiteration of romantic adolescent angst supposedly unlike the juvenile writings of famous authors (212). Bechdel too sketches much of this terrain, referring to college courses that left her more puzzled than enlightened and more turned off literature than turned on (200, 206, 208), though her text does emphasize the importance of canonical literature to her particular story and thus, also, implicitly, its ambivalent applicability to lived experience. Literature in Bechdel's text already has a symbolic function mediated by the desire or identity of the father and thus cannot function as a transitional object. I think Barry wants to gesture more broadly at the things that form us and to extend that power to high and low culture both, even emphasizing the low culture spectrum that was—in her childhood home—more accessible and thus more dominant. But she is also trying to make a point about intertexts as transitional objects. The intertexts in *One! Hundred! Demons!* are inevitably derived from the objects Barry had at her disposal, selected by happenstance in the degree to which they responded to the child's or the young adult's needs. Just as a parent cannot choose a transitional object for the child, so, in Barry's work, the intertexts are never ones imposed from without. That is why they are such a mix, or mishmash of sources. We could say they are the self's own canon.

Through her diverse use of intertextuality, Barry is surely also seeking to democratize the creative process. As the "Outro"—a lesson in painting one's own demons—makes clear, the book's desire is to become a magic lantern itself, to enter its reader and to bring about that reader's active participation. "Try it! You will dig it!" we are assured on the last page (n.p.). This gesture, an attempt to urge the reader into creativity, is prefigured in *One! Hundred! Demons!* by Lynda's own modeling of such a response through her own reaction to reading Hints from Heloise or lost and found ads. These lowly forms are shown as starting points for Barry's own formation as an artist: "I snitched envelopes and stamps from my mom and wrote Heloise a couple of times with some hints I'd thought up" (214), confesses Lynda. More productive and elaborate are the stories she makes up about the classified ads she reads (208–11): "They gave me so many weird blanks to fill in" (210). The burgeoning creativity unleashed by these newspaper sections is contrasted with Lynda's failure in other domains, namely her attempts to inculcate high art. She reassures the reader, in other words, that the sources themselves are less important than the beneficial effect they have on the reader. Her own text is a narrative of self-development and a narrative of her formation as an artist as a result of (or even despite) these initial sources of inspiration, but it is also therapeutic in intent, the equivalent of the psychoanalytic setting described by Winnicott: a space for collaborative exchange (Phillips 118). At stake in the Outro, where Lynda provides a tutorial in "painting your demon," is not a kind of "how to get published as a comics artist" approach but a desire—and is this not really part of the function of intertextuality in Bechdel too?—to encourage the expression of trauma and to exorcise it through narration. For this, one need not allude to either Proust's magic lantern, depicting the troubles of Geneviève de Brabant and the evil doings of Golo (Proust 10–11), or to Winnicottian psychoanalysis by name. But they are there, part of that wider cultural field that Barry, as an adult, has been able to access.

"Neither one nor quite two"

Both Bechdel and Barry provide their readers with an explanation of the textual fabric of lived experience—of experience's dialogue with the written word. Texts are not merely objects to be consumed and abandoned, but informative sources for the self and the self's interactions with others. *Fun Home* highlights literature's structuration of life by creating a tight schema or a series of funhouses within which lived experience often becomes subsumed in a mise en abyme, a symbolic chain. A whole range of other texts is there, however—not part of the grand organizational plan—that is wider and wilder in range and equally important even if not in the limelight. Michael Moon, for one, has emphasized the eclectic nature of Bechdel's intertextuality and argued for Colette's centrality to Bechdel's story. Yet regardless of the kind of sources used or the question of which ones are predominant, we can say that when Alison writes "my parents are most real to me in fictional terms" (67), we have reached a (Roland) Barthian moment of the self as the effect of language. Such theorization of autobiography profitably problematizes the distinction between life and art, self and text, but risks flattening these elements into a single surface. Furthermore, the use of intertextuality to systematize *Fun Home* overdetermines the narration or obscures elements of the story. Bechdel is clearly aware of the tendency of the main narratives to overdetermine her own telling, of her tendency toward tidiness. But the critical response to her work has predictably tended to emphasize the text's structuration in seeking out the significance and reverberations of her main intertextual references. Critics have attended less to Bechdel's other insistence on the aporia between signifier and signified, to the "I think" writ large that looms over the narrative as a whole, to the mid-air suspension of its protagonist caught still in that intermediary space between act and word.

Barry's emphasis in narrating, like Bechdel, her artistic development, her coming to be a comics artist, attunes the reader to a wide cultural field. The references it highlights for its readers—those things and texts that make up a self—are both more eclectic and more populist. A child of Filipino immigrants of modest means, Barry does not have a library at home that encloses the great classics of Western literature behind glass cases. But Barry reveals a self just as ravenous to use the world in all its idiosyncratic eclecticism as a means of both self-formation and self-understanding. To the extent that Barry believes in artistic expression as therapeutic (Wachtel), her populism is also a means of demystifying creativity itself as belonging not to a select elite but to anyone who might pick up a pen to doodle and to write. Her "Magic Lantern" chapter need not mention either Proust or Winnicott, but works as a means of opening up the text to a broad cultural field available to any reader. The magic lantern is an image of that space where selves and things, selves and texts, meet—a kind of Winnicottian intermediary territory between interior and exterior reality. Its liminal quality retains the magical force that narratives can project onto our lives and reminds us that there is some middle space or meeting point where selves and texts are "neither one nor quite two" (as John Barth says of the naming process in *Lost in the Funhouse*, 34) but a productive fusion, a space intensely private, broadly cultural, and fully imaginative.

Works Cited

Barry, Lynda. *One! Hundred! Demons!* Seattle, Washington: Sasquatch, 2002. Print.

———. *What It Is*. Montreal, Quebec: Drawn & Quarterly, 2008. Print.

Barth, John. *Lost in the Funhouse*. New York: Anchor, 1988. Print.

Barthes, Roland. *Roland Barthes by Roland Barthes*. Berkeley: U of California P, 1994. Print.

Bechdel, Alison. *Are You My Mother?* New York: Houghton Mifflin Harcourt, 2012. Print.

———. *The Essential Dykes to Watch Out For*. New York: Houghton Mifflin Harcourt, 2008. Print.

———. *Fun Home*. New York: Mariner, 2006. Print.

Butler, Judith. *Undoing Gender*. New York: Routledge, 2004. Print.

Chaney, Michael A., ed. *Graphic Subjects: Critical Essays on Autobiography and Graphic Novels*. Madison: U of Wisconsin P, 2011. Print.

Chute, Hillary. "An Interview with Alison Bechdel." *Modern Fiction Studies* 52.4 (2006): 1,004–13. Print.

———. *Graphic Women: Life Narrative and Contemporary Comics*. New York: Columbia UP, 2010. Print.

Freeman, Ariela. "Drawing on Modernism in Alison Bechdel's *Fun Home*." *Journal of Modern Literature* 32.4 (2009): 125–40. Print.

Moon, Michael. Review. "*Fun Home: A Family Tragicomic*." *Gutter Geek*, Sept. 2006. Web. 9 Mar. 2009.

Phillips, Adam. *Winnicott*. Boston: Harvard University Press, 1989. Print.

Sedgwick, Eve. *Epistemology of the Closet*. Berkeley: U of California P, 1991. Print.

Tolmie, Jane. "Modernism, Memory and Desire: Queer Cultural Production in Alison Bechdel's *Fun Home*." *Topia* 22 (2009): 77–95. Print.

Wachtel, Eleanor. "An Interview with Lynda Barry." *Writers & Company*. CBC Radio. 2 Mar. 2009.

Watson, Julia. "Autographic Disclosures and Genealogies of Desire in Alison Bechdel's *Fun Home*." *Graphic Subjects: Critical Essays on Autobiography and Graphic Novels*. Ed. Michael A. Chaney. Madison: U of Wisconsin P, 2011. 123–56. Print.

Winnicott, D. W. "Transitional Objects and Transitional Phenomena." *Collected Papers*. London: Tavistock, 1958. 229–42. Print.

Animal Subjects of the Graphic Novel

—Michael A. Chaney

Just what is it about comics that summons the human in bestial form? From George Herriman's Krazy Kat to Art Spiegelman's *Maus*, from the animal-human preoccupations of superheroes like Spider-Man and Batman to webcomics variations on the "funny animal" genre in Kean Soo's *Jellaby* or Chris Baldwin's *Little Dee*—comics have theorized the animal by performing it since their incipience and contemporary productions show no signs of flagging. In fact, an examination of representative texts in one of the most acclaimed sub-genres of the medium—the autobiographical graphic novel—confirms that theorizing the animal remains essential to comics narratives of identity. *American Born Chinese* by Gene Luen Yang and *Epileptic* by David B. access identity through very different national, cultural, and ethno-racial contexts, yet each does so by way of an animal identity crisis indicative of the comics' rich tradition of asking a question that many theorists in the humanities pose today: "why is it that our ideas of the animal—perhaps more than any other set of ideas—are the ones which enable us to frame and express ideas about *human* identity?" (Baker 6).[1]

Emerging forays into animal theory are as profuse as those concerning the history of comics, the semiotics of the comics medium, or the new subjectivities (complex assemblages of author, protagonist, and reader) fetishized by the most popular graphic narratives today. Despite the exhaustive sweep of Ian Gordon's or David Kunzle's historical examinations of funny animal comics, however, very little scholarship exists that casts the animal of the comics in the dawning theoretical light of concepts known variously as animality, becoming-animal, or animetaphor.[2] This essay is intended as a preliminary effort toward filling that void. The graphic novels I analyze here have been selected not only for their thematic and theoretical propensities, but also for the way they map the global dimensions of graphic novel production, spanning different national literatures to perform the animal in distinct, yet overlapping sub-genres—humor, trauma, and *Künstlerroman*. It is not my intention to read these genres or the pictorial structure of graphic novels reductively through the prism of animal theory. Rather, I want to cultivate a porous border between the creative texts under discussion and the theoretical lenses used to illuminate them. The result yields a proximate but affectless other—a type of species presence that unmoors the social from those spatial relationalities that dominate graphic narrative. And as species propinquity replaces social norms of anatomical and emotional similarity, the shadow of death looms above each of the animal deployments studied here, haunting the levities of visual exaggeration to remind us that it is always mortality that lurks on the other side of caricature. In this way, the present study ultimately attests to the validity of philosopher Walter Benjamin's description of Mickey Mouse, that in the funny-animal genre of the cartoon "mankind makes preparations to survive civilization [. . . as] Mickey Mouse proves that a creature can still survive even when it has thrown off all resemblance to a human being" (338). As the following examples will show, the perdurable bodies of the exaggeratedly drawn and anthropomorphic creature draws inevitably upon the terminal fragility of the human.

The Animal in the Comics

Before signifying anything so depressing as death writ large, the animal is a clown, a downright virtuoso at playing the ludic cipher of otherness. Its appearance almost always accompanies a strategically parodic veiling of the human. The illustrative style of such comics defamiliarizes visually. An example of such a trick rhythm in the imagistic textures of graphic narrative appears in Ho Che Anderson's *King*, a graphic novel biography of Martin Luther King Jr. At key moments of crisis, Anderson's characters appear feral. They bare their teeth like wild animals or else like skulls, human heads caught in the flash of an X-ray (fig. 3.1). Rarely do these teeth-bared panels exist in sequence. They occur mostly in single panels that disrupt an otherwise normative pattern of, more or less, realistic depictions of the 1960s Civil Rights movement. What is most disturbing about this tic of the illustrator's hand is the deliberate brevity of these moments that obtrude upon the real so as to signal both a *memento mori* and a *memento bestie* of human existence.

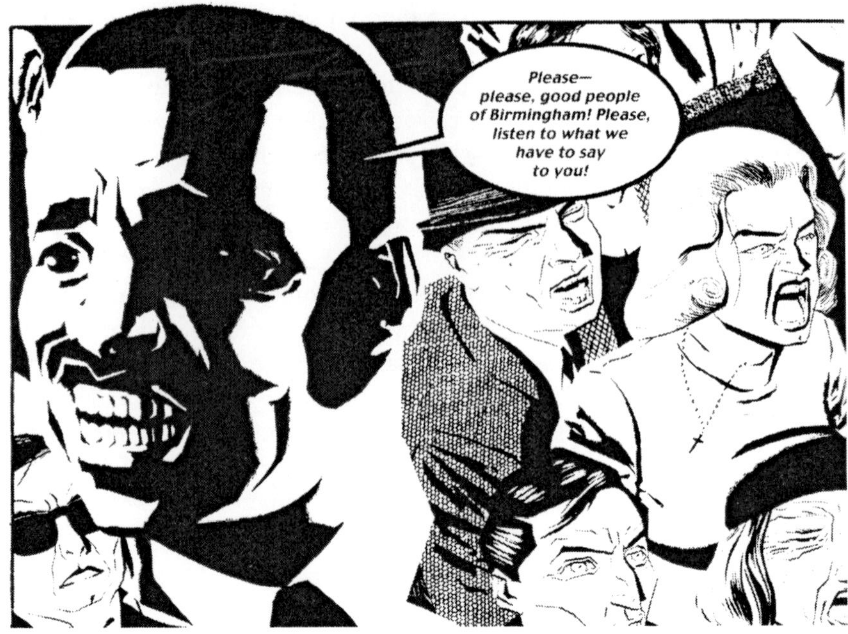

3.1. Bared Teeth from *King*. p. 100.

As if to say, "Remember Thou Art Mortal," the interruptive insertion of these toothy scenes of aggression also beckons, "Remember Thou Art Animal." But toward whom is the warning directed? To King, Anderson's readers, or both? Like some impossible cross between academic biography, Hans Holbein's *The Ambassadors*, and Edgar Allen Poe's "Berenice," *King* reveals dream logics of death and drive in snapshots of the grotesque, yet it does so irresolvedly, as if unreadability were the point. What continues to perplex long after our initial confrontation with these odd scenes of naturalistic expression is a nagging question about the typicality of such moments in sequential art. Is not the animal the semiotic talisman for broaching such questions of representation and its limits in comics? Beyond the comic tradition's fascination with funny animal stories, these eruptions in *King* and other graphic narratives demonstrate how the process of "becoming animal" underwrites even those comics that have seemingly no investment whatever in the fable or its derivatives.[3] And yet comics today seem unable or unwilling to forget their debts to the fabular.

Having always had one figurative foot in the domain of children's literature, comics routinely partake in that fabular preoccupation with talking animals, humans that become animal, and humans that interact with magical animal sidekicks. All of this manifests at the level of the story, that is, in terms of character and plot, but it also occurs at the visual level, where any of the panels of such a comic could be seen individually as representing an animal-human hybridity. Even at this level, where visual markers constituting the human mesh with those that normally constitute the non-human, we should be wary of employing a term so loaded as hybridity. As my point in this essay will be to encourage critical suspicion regarding the seemingly automatic gestures of trans-species democracy in such representations, we should note how rare it is to find an anthropomorphic animal that does not talk or walk erect in the comics. There is a limit to all of this hybridity, in other words, which seizes the animal, not surprisingly, at the vanishing point of the human, but not the other way around. The primacy of human speech and mobility makes the primacy of animal appearance secondary, perhaps even inconsequential. If you look just like a horse, but walk around, wear a cowboy hat, a badge, and carry a side arm, you are more of a sheriff than a hybrid of any kind.

To be sure, rampant visual distortions only make the comics seem indifferent to the totalizing sovereignty usually accorded to the human. Rather than reading the human body as it is, we are often called upon in the comics to imagine it dramatically otherwise. But this reading protocol of inversion is precisely the origin of the potentially conservative politics undergirding distortion. To see, experience, and to some extent to feel the surreal in, say, the bestial tail of the girl in Charles Burns's *Black Hole*, or the dizzying array of background clutter that comes to life in Julie Doucet's *My New York Diary*, is to have to keep in mind a Platonic ideal all the while. It is this visual norm that gets reinforced because it never needs to be visualized. By operating invisibly behind the distortions that we can see, illustration bolsters those negated ideals that we cannot. The animalized human body is visually legible and fictively pleasing, therefore, precisely because it is neither legible nor pleasing in relation to the norm or to the "real" that the comic fantastically suspends yet constantly and invisibly produces as an essential effect of that suspension.

That the animal mask enables the fabulist a measure of distance is a notion that required neither difficult theories of mimesis nor elaborate critiques of the human for early twentieth-century critics and readers to comprehend. What Gilbert Seldes says of George Herriman's Krazy Kat in 1924—that "it is Herriman's bent to disguise what he has to say in the creations of the animal worlds which are neither human nor animal, but each *sui generis*" (23)—continues to be a point of nearly obvious significance to cite regarding the use of animal characters in various literatures. On African oral literatures containing shape-shifting magical animals, for example, Ruth Finnegan explains that such devices portray "human faults and virtues, somewhat removed and detached from reality through being presented in the guise of animals, but nevertheless with an indirect relation to observed human action" (351). A similar interpretation is so common as to be an axiom of children's literature, in which animal representations echo earlier traditions of the fable, myth, and fairy tale. One effect of this hearkening back to primitive culture is that the device of animal representation becomes in itself a signifier of children—those cultural primitives among us for whom Western theology's insistence on the subject-object disparity between man (Adam) and animal does not apply. The point is that children are not simply more like the primitive in our imaginary understanding of those earlier subjects of culture who may have truly believed in shape-shifting animals as part of a pantheistic ideology for instance, but that they are more like the primitive who would have seen him or herself as occupying a more proximate position to the animal as well. And in being only temporarily susceptible to such fantasy, the child further safeguards our fictive certainties regarding the absolute difference between the animal and human. Even so, literature associated with the child and animal representation more generally leaves open the possibility that these certainties have not yet crystallized. To read them is to reserve a space for conceptual amalgamations whose time is figuratively up, but not quite yet.

Those of us who teach comics know all too well how difficult it is for others to associate narratives that tell stories through drawings with anything other than juvenilia of one kind or another. The underground comix of the 1960s, their preoccupation with sex and nakedness notwithstanding, continue to depend upon a juvenile orientation towards the world from this cynically narrow perspective. Thus resistant to maturity, the comics are uniquely suited to representing what early anthropology defined as liminality, the condition of being on the boundary or in the penumbra between youth and adulthood. Of course, we now have so many more sensitive labels for such a condition, and all of its interstitial permutations, which comics are no less apt in conveying. There is the transculturality Rocío Davis sees in *Persepolis*, the post-memory Marianne Hirsch sees in *Maus*, the mestiza consciousness Melinda de Jesús sees in *One Hundred Demons*, and all the forms of hybridity that Hillary Chute and Marianne

DeKoven see in the comics form more generally. All of these concerns with being in-between are themselves articulated at a boundary of identity and representation. That paradox is best expressed in the way comics routinely problematize the human by blurring the ontological boundary between humans and animals according to the same logic that both fuses and separates words and pictures. That paradox is further resonant in another division that ramifies comics, no matter how irksome it is to comics scholars, which imagines the exclusion of child(ish) readers from the domain of serious literature.

Nevertheless, by calling attention to themselves as constructed representations, early comics juvenilia, such as the funny animal comics of Krazy Kat, may be seen as locating being in terms akin to Deleuze and Guattari's notion of becoming—in a zone "that makes it impossible to say where the boundary between the human and animal lies" (273). Herriman's strip in particular accomplishes something along these lines in the way that it troubles conventions (which signal reason and thus the human), replacing clichés of species enmity with radical amity (which could figure in the binary as a kind of animality), and in allowing the framework of its mimesis to come crashing down Babel-like on itself. The deconstructive precocities of Herriman's strip have been noted by critics in its own day and in ours. But I would suggest that within the context of the newspaper as a whole, the weird, unpredictable gags of Krazy and Ignatz and Offica Pup find a conservative closure on the other side of the strip's amazing finesse at articulating the animal. The weird in the strip preserves the serious and the rational that encloses it, making the comic an enclave of inversion that always, to some extent, reinstates the norms it so reliably, yet temporarily, overturns. While this larger betrayal of the comics' fantasy may be leveled against any type of fiction, comics seem particularly haunted by this earlier commercial dependence upon an enfolding regime of popular middle-class notions of the serious that once made them a desirable entertainment of contrast in early newspapers. The animal-human hybridizations prevalent in graphic novels today, in fact, tend to assume a self-conscious air about their visual infractions against the serious, wryly combining the animal and the human visually in such a way as to ultimately (and desultorily in many cases) re-post the human as the undisputed subject of authority. Both because and in spite of its infinitely pliable surfaces, the human is made over in comics as the unmitigated, unadulterated ground of significance and signification. Despite superficial gestures of species combination, the human reigns in the comics as a pure Subject, particularly after the fact of its visual slumming in the comics.

For example, in Charles Burns's *Black Hole* we see again this paradox of subversion via animality's alternative cognition and the eventual cooptation of that subversion through the comics form. Here the paradox plays out against a backdrop of sex according to a familiar binary of vision versus touch, which functions thematically in the graphic novel as dual modes of reading or of knowledge production. Emphasized throughout Burns's weird tale is the idea that the way the central characters, two freakish and libidinal teens, read one another's body in acts of coitus compares with reading comics. Such a connection hangs on the proposition that the eroticized zone of the human's tangible body may be best visualized in a comic through surreal extensions of the body proper. Indeed, the heroine of the text has what appears to be a tail, which doubles as a kind of penis in illustrations of her naked body alongside her male partner, who possesses a vagina with teeth on his chest. The queering of the body thus produced turns away from a notion of knowledge as optic proof so valued by the art-historical tradition of the still-life painting, for example. It represents instead a celebration of protean contingency, available to tenable exploration but never wholly known by perception at all. Nevertheless, the comic is primarily a visual document. It projects its fantasy of a carnal knowledge mediated by touch according to the priorities of visual scripts. The visual finally subsumes any such thing as tactile sensuality into the performance of its own totalizing authority. To kindle the animal therefore as both a new mode of reading (through touch) and as an emergent variation on the human body (the image of the girl's tail) is to stage the animal's failure as author or source of knowledge. The animal in such comics always functions as mere mask or costume, beneath which lies the human, whose universality is reaffirmed and reified in the process. We may attend closely to the way in which this reification happens and to the temporarily radical forms of knowledge that it both supplants and fails to eradicate in two prominent examples of human-animal combinations: Gene Luen Yang's *American Born Chinese* and David Beauchard's *Epileptic*.

American Born Chinese and the Monkey Double

The recipient of five prestigious "Best Book of the Year" awards, Gene Luen Yang's *American Born Chinese* draws on traditional Chinese folklore

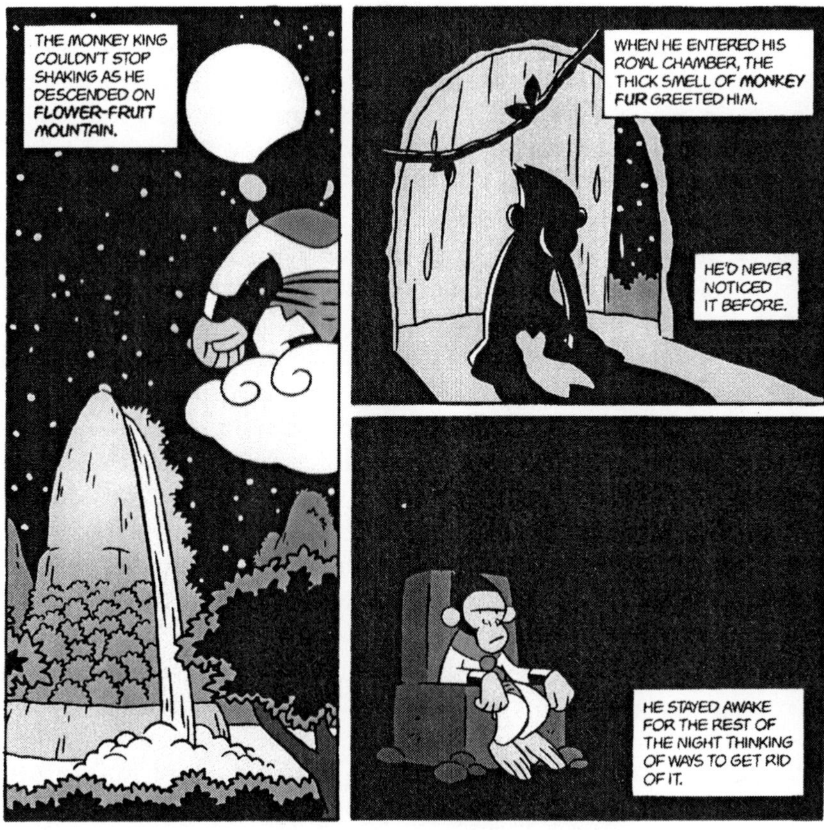

3.2. Panel of Monkey King Brooding from *American Born Chinese*. p. 20.

and contemporary American pop culture for its *dramatis bestiary*: the Monkey King, angsty high-schooler Jin Wang, and Chin-Kee, an incarnation of "Yellow Peril"-era racism. If the "talking animal comic" represents what we might call the primary phase of animal tropology in the comics, Yang's text occupies a secondary phase. This is not a tale told through animal types, but one that finally celebrates transformations of identity by way of creaturely alterity. Put another way, Yang's characters become not simply other than what they are, but the other that they are.

True to its titular play on exiled, split, and doubled identity, *American Born Chinese* theorizes the constitutive interplay of insider and outsider that characterizes the "funny animal" comic strip as well as autobiographical graphic novels. The plot interweaves three initially different heroes, each corresponding to a distinct narrative modality, medium, and milieu:

the Monkey King (Chinese mythology), Jin Wang (coming-of-age, assimilation narrative), and Danny (TV situation comedy in the vein of *The Odd Couple* complete with specialized panel border of "HaHaHaHa"—the comic equivalent of a laugh track). All are embattled outcasts who "transform themselves from self-negation to self-acceptance" (Fu 276).

In keeping with the myth, Yang's Monkey King is a pariah among the gods of Heaven, who snub his brutish nature in spite of his powerful magic.[4] Dejected, the Monkey King returns to his royal chamber (fig. 3.2), where a "thick smell of monkey fur greeted him [that] he'd never noticed before" (20). As with so many other animated characters, the animal mask functions according to a principle of juxtaposition to intensify the pathos of the moment, if only because of the animal's ordinary exclusion from pathos. Is it not central to the juxtaposition inherent to comics that the animal would reinforce, even while countermanding, philosophy's recurring trope of the sadness of animals, poor in this world (*à la* Heidegger) because they are alien to spirit and affect? As with any funny animal comic, this scene tantalizes in part by exacerbating philosophical anxieties regarding the animal's obscure gaze, which, for Agamben, "always seems to be on the verge of uttering words" (113). And similar to the allure of the "funny animal" comic book Joseph Witek ascribes to a "curious indifference to the animal nature of the characters" (109), the Monkey King operates less as an allegorical animal than as a metaphorical minority.

When scenes and characters are at their most cartoonish in *American Born Chinese*, viewers would do well to grow suspicious. Yang's parable of self-acceptance is told through a distorted lens that projects internalized stereotypes as optic truths. Recalling the theme of Toni Morrison's *The Bluest Eye* (1970) and the plot of David Henry Hwang's drama *FOB* (1979), Jin Wang's narrative centers on his attempts at interracial dating, spurred on by an early childhood fascination for Transformer robots (an unsubtle objective correlative) and his emerging friendship with F.O.B (slang for "Fresh-off-the-boat") Wei-Chen. Forlorn because of his unreciprocated crush on the white Amelia, Jin Wang fixates on the curly blonde hair of the boy Amelia frequently accompanies. After Amelia is trapped in an animal storage area of the biology classroom with Wei-Chen, who shares a bizarre affinity with one of the monkeys, the stage is set for Jin Wang and Amelia to date. Jin alters his hair to reflect the curls he believes Amelia admires in others and experiences an arc of electric confidence, ironically visualized by a recurring icon of lightning bolts that curve precisely along Jin's imitation curls.

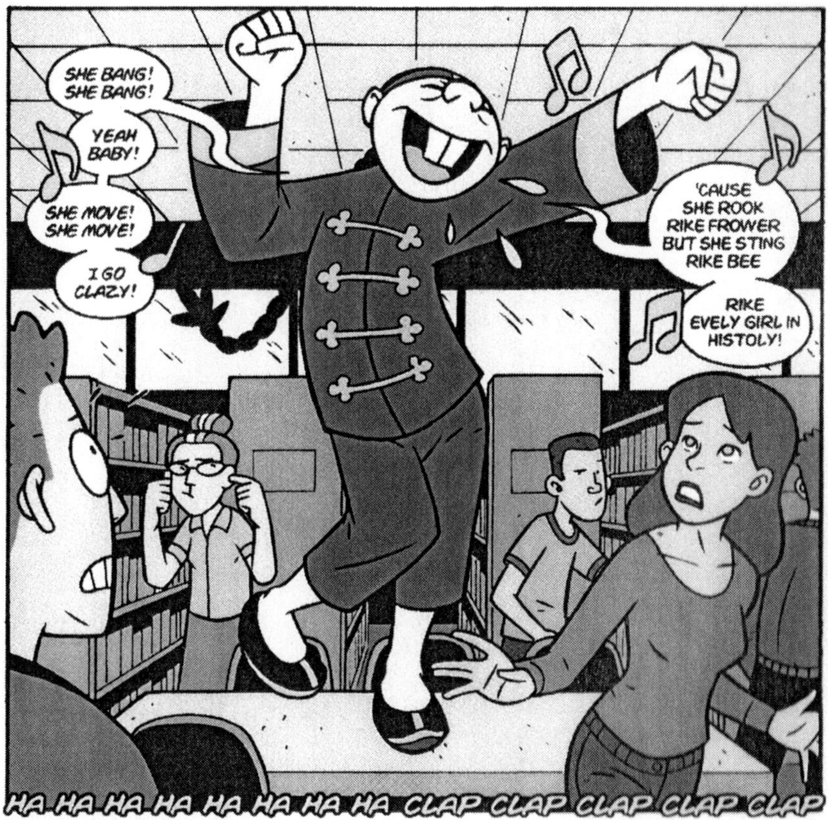

3.3. Chin-Kee as Racist Caricature from *American Born Chinese*. p. 203.

Whereas Jin Wang is drawn, for the most part, so as to reflect the object of his rejection, his Taiwanese identity, Danny is shown in his narrative to be not just white, but to embody the very type of blonde, spikey-haired whiteness elsewhere valorized as an ideal unattainable to Asian characters. Satirizing the television cliché of the wacky buddy scenario, Danny's Asian difference is externalized in the figure of a visiting cousin from China, Chin-Kee (fig. 3.3). Danny's embodied ideal inversely parallels Chin-Kee's hyper re-enactment of racist Asian stereotypes such that both are exposed as pasteboard constructions when all three storylines abruptly converge: Danny has been a psychic projection of Jin Wang's ideal self and Chin-Kee is really the Monkey King, having made flesh exactly what Jin-Wang abjects in himself in order to prompt the youth toward self-reconciliation.

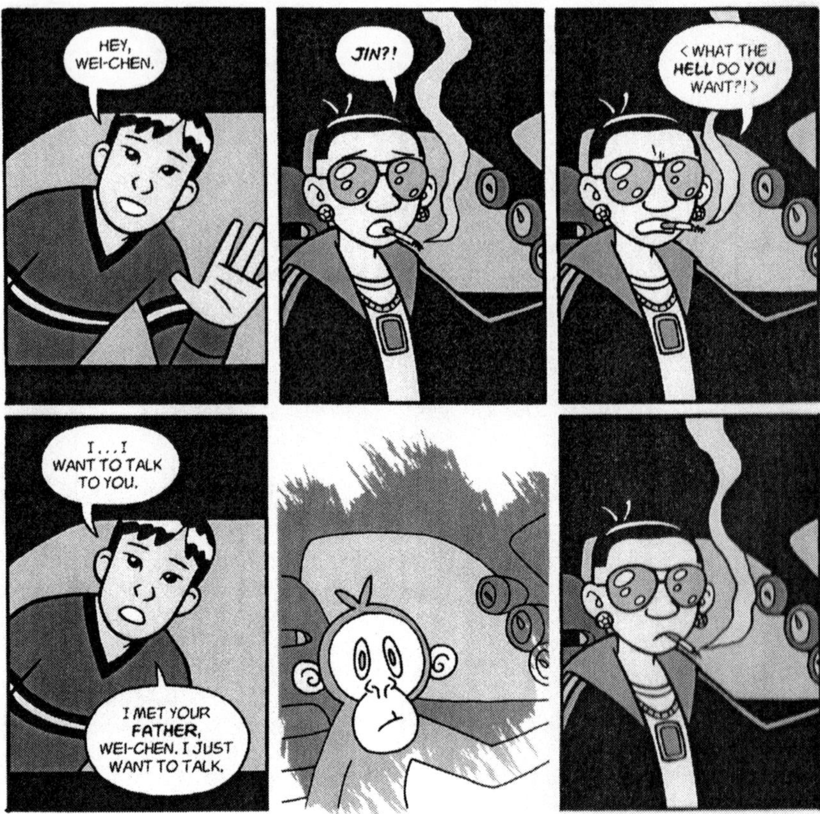

3.4. Wei-Chen's "True" Self from *American Born Chinese*, panels 4–6. p. 229.

American Born Chinese foregrounds animality and race (or animality as race) in its psychic splittings. Among the many turnabouts of identity, Jin learns that Wei-Chen is the son of the Monkey King and has been disguising his simian form to live, as he puts it, "in the mortal world using it for my pleasure" (220). Rereading the graphic novel with this revelation in mind further compounds the bizarre humor of the earlier scene in the biology classroom's animal closet, where a monkey wearing lipstick and mascara constantly reaches out through its bars to seize hold of Wei-Chen. Inexplicably upon the first reading, he is able to detect the animal's male gender with certainty, much to the surprise and repugnance of Amelia who asks: "How do you know? On second thought, I don't really want to know the answer to that" (99). After not having seen Wei-Chen for some time, and eager to confront him about his true identity, the now reformed

Jin Wang encounters Wei-Chen, who has in the meantime modified the Asian features of his human avatar with accoutrements associated with hip-hop culture. At this point, the viewer is granted the vision to see the animal beneath its commodity disguise—the hip-hop regalia as well as the human form (fig. 3.4).

The viability in the panel layout of a recursive, rather than strictly sequential, reading order introduces a paradox.[5] Is the middle panel above merely the reveal in sepia of the true animal body of Wei-Chen, or is it another of Jin Wang's projections? A more expansive semiotic reading—which is always available in such comics—might eschew the mimetic demand that the monkey encode either character's imago. In other words, the monkey may serve to literally mediate Jin Wang and Wei-Chen as doubles of each other. Such a reading complicates the distinction that comics scholars impute to traditional beast fables when differentiating them from funny animal comics. In *Comic Books as History* Witek explains that in contrast to the allegorical characterization of animals in beast fables, which sets up inflexible correspondences between traits and animals that have come to embody such traits in a culture, the "funny animal" comic transcends allegory in its embrace of human typology.[6] For Witek, the animal comic "takes these allegorical meanings as a starting point but then proceeds to ignore, qualify, or reverse them" (110). Yang's inversion of the funny animal comic wreaks havoc with Witek's distinction. Neither anthropomorphic animals who act human nor visual human-animal hybrids, Yang's characters are funny animals disguised as humans, making cameo appearances in a cartoon universe predicated on the human form—a situation more typical of the autobiographical graphic novels under review here. To compound our inquiry of *American Born Chinese*, we might then ask: what do Chin-Kee and the Monkey King have to do with Wei-Chen's optic traversals of identities ethnic, mythic, and animal? Yang's comic clearly has a lesson in mind for reader-viewers at this moment of animal pedagogy, if only we can discern the proper curriculum.

Because the animal in question is the monkey, even the most rigid correspondences of allegorical representation are pressed into the service of substitution, mutability, and other effects associated not only with monkey tricksters but with metaphor as well. Yang's monkey functions, as does the African trickster, to destabilize boundaries between cosmic orders of being and comes to embody, as Henry Louis Gates has famously shown, "the process of interpretation itself" (17). Adapting Gates, John Lowe argues that tricksters based on the myth of the Monkey King serve to "'loosen' knowledge by the way they shake the established order, frequently through their irreverent humor and by the way in which that humor points to the irreconcilable ambiguities of life, which in their absurdity create Freud's classic humor of juxtaposition of opposites" (105–6). Although Asian studies folklorists have observed considerable overlap between African and Asian mythology on this score, the earliest Chinese adaptations of the Monkey King furnish meaningful clues for understanding Yang's most recent contribution to the tradition of Monkey King tales and their implicit meditations on the human-animal relation.

Based on Chinese mythology of Tripitaka's journey to India to bring Buddhism back to China, the story of the Monkey King was published as a novel in the sixteenth century, *The Journey to the West.* Centuries of adaptations, however, have recalibrated focus away from the character of the monk to spotlight his Monkey disciple: "As a cultural icon, Monkey is loved as much for his rambunctious behavior in Heaven as for his maturation into a heroic Buddhist disciple" (Pearson 357).[7] As seen in Maxine Hong Kingston's *Tripmaster Monkey: His Fake Book* (1990), Gerald Vizenor's *Griever: An American Monkey King in China* (1986), and Patricia Chao's *Monkey King* (1997), the Monkey King archetype of Promethean subversion has a long tradition of American adaptation. Many adaptors, like Yang, emphasize the first part of the Monkey's tale, of his profanations and subsequent fall before achieving enlightenment, as "a helpful template for their stories about what it takes to become healthy in the modern world" (Pearson 373). Even Yang's use of the multi-plot narrative mirrors the two-part organization of *Journey to the West* in which the extended prologue of the Monkey King's outrages in Heaven compresses "motifs later developed, in a kind of parody of the enlightenment process" (Plaks 209).

Yang's other intertextual touchstone is the tragic history of assimilation and difference in an American frame, highlighted in Wei-Chen's "gangsta" pose and, of course, in the terrifyingly funny antics of Chin-Kee. Yang himself explains his animal curriculum as a kind of visual matching-exercise in history: "With Chin-Kee, I attempted to tie today's popular images of Asians and Asian-Americans with the more overtly racist imagery prevalent in the late 1800s and early 1900s" ("Printz Award" 12). Even while, as Binbin Fu notes, Chin-Kee represents "the monkey's evil double" (275), he also apes the posture, dress, and even dialogue of various, yet verifiable, antecedents of racist Asian iconography. In interviews Yang pinpoints Long Duk Dong, from John Hughes's 1984 film *Sixteen Candles,* and William Hung's ridiculed performance of "She Bangs" from *American Idol* in 2003 as templates for Chin-Kee, asserting that his comic images "draw on visual cues and shorthand already established in the mind of the audience" ("Printz Award" 13). Even those racialized characters that seem far removed from the signifying mechanics of the funny animal genre are not so different in semantic potential after all. For as the apotheosis of otherness, the animal is also a racial signifier.[8]

Yang's use of the double signifies on other literary works by Asian American authors exploring similar dilemmas of ethnic identity crisis. Sau-Ling Cynthia Wong's analysis of "the double that does justice to the uniqueness of the Asian American experience and its literary expressions" (86) mines the bedrock of denial lying beneath such literary expressions. According to Wong: "The double is symptomatic of a crisis in self-acceptance and self-knowledge: part of the self, denied recognition by the conscious ego, emerges as an external figure exerting a hold over the protagonist that seems disproportionate to provocation or inexplicable by everyday logic" (82). Given Wong's criteria, we might dizzyingly conclude that the double of Jin is Danny, and that Danny's double is Chin-Kee, the double of the Monkey King. And while all these doubled doubles symbolize "that residue of racial difference which dooms Chinese Americans to a position of inferiority in a racist society," the fact that so much of the doubling turns on the figure of the animal exhibits another layer of "psychological disowning" (89). To determine precisely what is disowned by the gaze of the double that is itself doubled by the animal is to pursue a question begged by countless graphic novels, so many, in fact, that the issue ultimately redounds to the visual nature of the medium itself.

American Born Chinese exemplifies the graphic novel's inimitable capacity to articulate visual systems for cognizing the human. And in this regard, the animal as a recurring trope of sequential art opens onto more than, as Witek puts it, "a generic space into a precivilized innocence in which human behavior is stripped down" (111). In Heidegger's phenomenology the animal opens onto a consideration of a world that envelops without directly impacting the animal's sense of Being. Commenting on Heidegger's animal, Jacques Derrida writes: "the property unique to animals and what in the final analysis distinguishes them from man, is their being naked without knowing it" (373). In seeing Wei-Chen's "true" self, the animal's lack of clothing in the second panel betrays a surplus of clothing in the third. If it weren't natural for the animal to be wearing anything other than fur, we may hardly notice how unnatural this surplus appears on Wei-Chen: the gold chains, flashy sunglasses, earrings, and pluming cigarette. The vivid interpolation of the animal prior to the scene of Wei-Chen ensconced in costuming facilitates our ability to see the possibility for and the absurdity in his cross-racial performance of "gangsta" culture. Akin to the racial other but also profoundly (and perhaps problematically) more universal in its claim to otherness, the animal occupies, as Derrida puts it, "a point of view of the absolute other," regarding the human from a position of "absolute alterity" (380). Thus, whereas Wei-Chen's revelation—as Wong might read the scene—measures the "radical dissonance between [his] flattering self-image and the rude reality of [his] inadequate qualifications for full membership in white society" (Wong 96), it also registers, in racial tones, his debarment from human community.

Yang's tripartite tale achieves fairy-tale closure with another of pop culture's infatuations with Asian American assimilative performance taken as comedy: Jin Wang and Wei-Chen singing together on a digital video. The single panel of the last page parodies a parody, a YouTube skit of two Chinese art students spoofing the Backstreet Boys. But how many viewers laughed with, instead of at, the Asian performers? The same question resonates as the last echo of authorial anxiety regarding the comic effects of *American Born Chinese*. For no matter how funny its hypostatizations of anti-Asian sentiments past and present, nor how profound its vehicle for accomplishing parody and parable in the animal, there is yet a danger in the animal metaphor. Stripping persons of that rhetorical costuming we call humanity leaves them open to metaphorical seizure—to animal signifiers that inherently convey an ontological subordination thinly veiled by valorization in the realm of the aesthetic.

Epileptic's Death-Heads and the Significance of Master N

Like *American Born Chinese*, David B.'s *Epileptic* demands that readers experience an ontological change. In thinking about the way *Epileptic* conditions an ideal reader, I am reminded of Leslie Marmon Silko's *Ceremony* (1977), a novel purported to recreate a ceremonial rite for the reader in its organization, plotting, and stylistic effects. *Epileptic* similarly positions the reader to undergo transformation through David B.'s hectic visual rendition of epilepsy. Variously pictured as dragons and serpents, epilepsy takes on a vibrant life of its own in the text, often in menacing pursuit of the adolescent protagonist, Pierre François (David B.'s given name), and his afflicted sibling, Jean-Christophe. Personified as a mythological beast, epilepsy subsumes both physical illness and psychic agon, reconfiguring reading as agony and inducing seizure through surreal details that haunt characters and reader-viewers alike.

The narrative positions readers as epileptics by forcing us to see chaotically, frenetically, wildly. Chapterless like *Ceremony*, the narrative design of *Epileptic* may leave readers feeling overwhelmed by panels teeming with inky, overwrought visual details of marauding samurai and prancing chimera. The urgency of reading is not for the cure, however, but for a stable paradigm (a *sinthome*) that will help us to make sense of and perhaps find pleasure in the disorienting surplus, hyperreal in its signifying yet garbled plenitude. As we strive to distinguish the miniature effects of weapon-brandishing warrior hordes or the yin from the yang elements in various panels, so too must Pierre François (David B.) and his parents labor to distinguish hoaxes from healing, hypocrisy from hope.

Along with the epileptic quality of its graphic style, the symbolic content of the text's dreamwork—its war horses, serpentine dragons, anthropomorphic birds of prey—represents so many death heads of danger and protection. As with *Maus*, only part of the project of this autobiography is to picture the family's struggle in mythical, totemic iconography (which, by the way, gets personalized as David B.'s story, like so many other autobiographical graphic novels that temper the tale of witnessed trauma with triumphant *Künstlerroman*). Partner to this project is a visualization of becoming animal: of becoming human by becoming animal *vis-à-vis* the experience of life and death, the fear of stagnancy and loss, and the hope of vitally expressive becoming—all from the vantage point of the human that cognizes its proximity to the animal. Deleuze and Guattari avail themselves of the animal metaphor to explain such becoming: "Becoming can and should be qualified as becoming-animal even in the absence of a term that would be the animal become. The becoming-animal of the human being is real, even if the animal the human being becomes is not" (238).

To elaborate my unabashedly Deleuzian appreciation for *Epileptic*, let us consider David B.'s graphic animalization of illness in a scene that self-reflexively unveils the text's constructedness. Disrupting a twisting series of family narratives, or mini-biographies, of his mother's grandmother, grandfather, and great-grandmother, David B. interjects a scene that pays homage to Art's discussions with his father in *Maus* about the content of the very story we are reading. Here, the scenes involve the author debating his mother, who protests against his portrayal of his great-great-grandmother

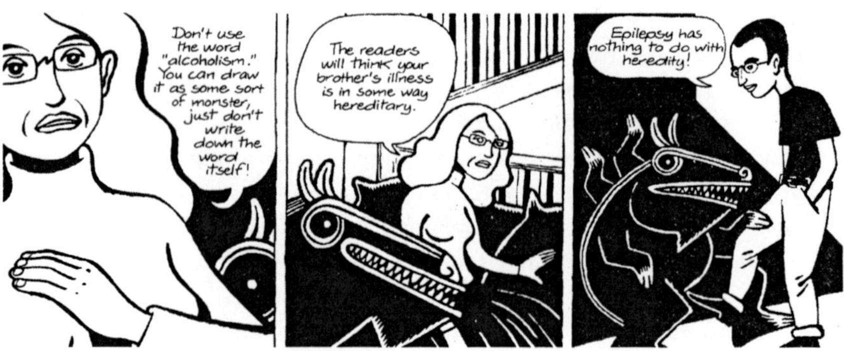

3.5. From David B.'s *Epileptic*, panels 6–8. p. 94.

as an alcoholic. In step with Matthew T. Jones's suggestion that self-reflexivity yields demystification—"the act of revealing the mechanisms of production responsible for creating the particular text" (276)—the scene makes clear the struggle of author and text, man and monster, past and present to approximate the subjective verities and flights of fancy that constitute existence. However, the mechanism of this demystification, let's say, of the animal core of *Epileptic*, is achieved through a reiteration of the text's primary vehicle of mystification, the monster or shadow beast, which this scene simultaneously invokes and exorcises.

As the mother pleads with Pierre François while holding a draft in her hand (presumably of the panel we have just viewed) and insists that he depict the alcoholism as "some sort of monster" (94), he replies, "But it's all true" (fig. 3.5). As if to verify the full symbolic scope of his notion of truth, a monster stands behind the mother unseen by her in a subsequent panel (96). Thus, despite the fact that the verisimilitude of the story as construction is on one level questioned, its textuality demystified, the signature element of David B.'s textual style—what I call the shadow beast—is on another level manifestly present. The demystifying, non-diegetic narrative, in other words, is hereby engulfed with mystifying, diegetic elements: that which is demystified in a moment of metacritical revelation is present during the scene. As with the iconic effect of the dragon-like rendering of epilepsy, the shadow beast of alcoholism is by no means limited to representing the affliction, but encompasses the rupture of discourse and epistemology entailed by the affliction as well.

Aside from referencing *Maus*, David B.'s illustration strategy of the animal here retroactively acts as a substitute for the allegedly shameful illustration of a foremother whose debauchery has already been rendered.

Like the mouse masks in Spiegelman's text, the shadow beast also demarcates that rupture of memory and representation that together attempts to bring closure to an implacable trauma. As an icon of trauma the animal in *Epileptic* yokes divergent domains of affective response to the past, haunting the present with an alterity of being-with-the-past in the face of objections to its proper telling in the present.

Thus *Epileptic's* animals function as psychic indices of becoming in the Deleuzian sense, but the text as a whole is far too magisterial in scope and complexity for me to do justice to it here. By way of working toward a conclusion, however, I want to focus on one of the text's pictorial and animal anomalies. In its bewildering characterization of Master N (fig. 3.6), *Epileptic* discloses the dark underside of an otherwise jubilant surrealism of animal figures seen only by the author-protagonist. Representing a middle ground between the racist overtones of the funny animal comic and the animal reader of the trauma narrative, Master N is the only animal character to interact with other more realistically illustrated characters—aside, that is, from his son Julian and his double, another Master N who briefly appears later, also in the form of a cat. Drawn as a hybrid tiger-human, Master N is atypical in this book, but characteristic of "the estranging effect of the hybrid animal characters, which constantly alerts one to the artificiality of visual representation, [and] offers a more radical destruction of the illusion of realism than does the stylized minimalism of the comics in general" (Orbán 63). Of course, the "estranging effect" in this case takes on an even deeper level of estrangement relative to the rest of the comic, since Master N is one of the only hybrid figures in the work to occupy a diegetic space of addressability—he speaks to and is heard by other characters, regardless of whether he is seen by them in the same animalized way that David B. has depicted him or not. What is special about Master N then is that he is the only animalized character shown interacting with others, as opposed to the beastly entourage of humanoid creatures that regularly attend Pierre François, which represent externalizations of his own warped interiority, but that interact only with him in spaces of shadowy depth and wooded mystery that visually announce them as more psychic than realistic. Master N, on the other hand, is shown in spaces coded as ordinary, speaking with other members of the family, seemingly unabashed by his outward felinity and wholly oblivious to its difference. Thus, if, as Andreas Huyssen in another context has argued, the materiality of the drawn animal figure disrupts "the very pictoriality of the animal comic" (134), and seeing as *Epileptic* resists giving itself completely

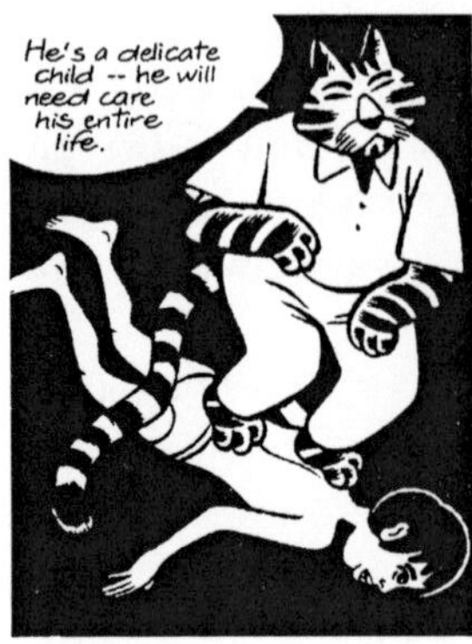

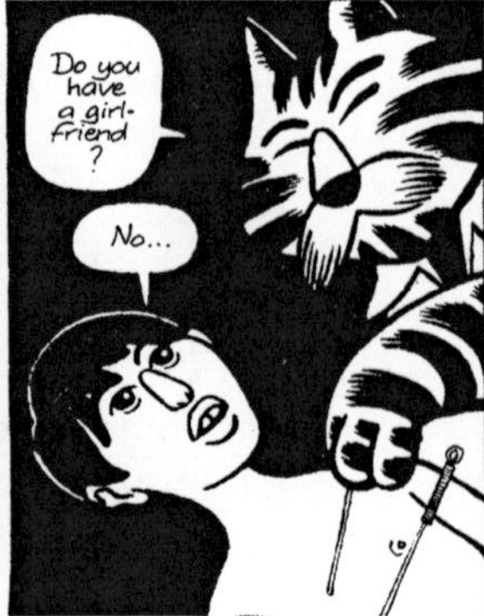

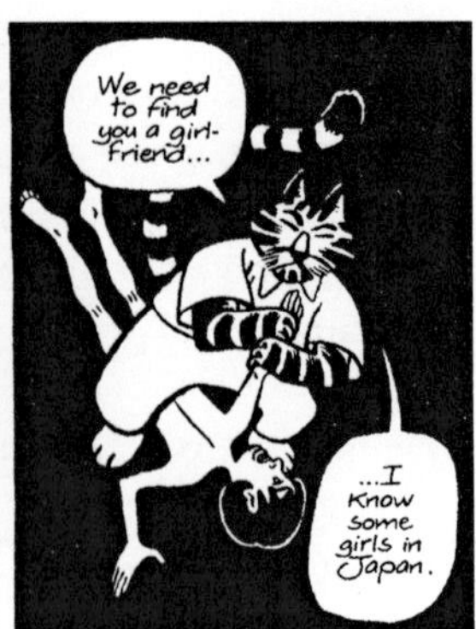

3.6. Master N from *Epileptic*, panels 3–5. p. 54.

over to the animal comic genre, then we must assume that some *other level of pictoriality* is disrupted by it. And given our prior lessons in animal pedagogy, it should come as no surprise that this other level yields residual ideological tensions in the text's questioning of race and illness (or moribundity) as twin afflictions of the body proper.

Recalling Jean-Christophe and Pierre François's racist name-calling of the Algerian ("raghead") and emblematic of the book's sustained treatment of Asian-influenced lifestyles, the animalized appearance of Master N, an aikido master with dubious healing powers, is more than comical. The very uniqueness of his body in brute interaction with other human bodies opposes the phantasmatic—or shall we say, merely pictorial—display of similar hybrid bodies in the text, which never interact with other bodies marked as real. Indeed, these others inhabit a space of fantasy and fear, death and imagination, but this one explicitly, and oddly, does not. So what is it about the Japanese exoticism and intense physicality of Master N that yields him such anomalous status? His foil, Klim Y, who runs the commune the family joins, is also Japanese. He also bears the single letter surname, yet he is not depicted as an animal. Is it therefore Master N's willing proximity to the infirm body—which everywhere in the text is shadowed by animal monstrosity—that transfers this honorific animal coding?

In response, let us recall Deleuze's insistence on the strange reality of the condition of becoming-animal, in which "[t]he becoming-animal of the human being is real, even if the animal the human being becomes is not" (238). Aptly, the animal in *Epileptic* never signifies beyond the symbolic. In its panels, the animal is always the emblem of something else, from the child-protagonist's embrace of Anubis, dog-headed god of the dead, to his materialized hallucination of his dead grandfather transformed into "goony-looking bird" (75) with an elongated beak in the shape of the Grim Reaper's sickle, the animal becomes the grotesque icon of the terrible becoming of the human, its proliferating transpirations and expirations. Thus unreal animals or monsters provide Pierre François a refuge from threats embodied in the real and in the normative. More importantly, however, they authorize varieties of his becoming relational: in relation to his brother's transformation through illness, to his family's struggle to accept that illness, and to his own intractable separation from both. In other words, these animals, ghosts, and monsters allow David B. to pose himself in conceptual equality to his brother. Only in the pages of this book can the two occupy a commensurate position with respect to the unseen and its intrusions upon the real.

Although the two feline Master N's mark David B.'s becoming animal project with inextricable entanglements of race, they nevertheless suggest a protection from threatening encroachments of the real in terms of physical alterity as well as the inability to ensure such protection. The second Master N, who is drawn as an enlarged housecat, loses all of his astounding skills at aikido after a car accident and refuses to help Jean-Christophe; he is resolved instead to watch over the death of his ailing father (another wizened cat). Ultimately, *Epileptic* suffers from a schizophrenic disorder of iconographic display; it neither accepts nor abandons completely the mother's faith in the enchantments of mysticisms marked as exotic, arcane, animal—by turns distinguished at the level of the drawing, but sometimes lumped together into a pictorial cacophony of all things Buddhist or Oriental. But like David's ghostly retinue and all the animals studied in this essay, the Masters N are rendered as animal not simply because they are otherworldy, but because they signify the enabling conditions of art in, and as, life. We might observe, as a final point, that the narrative proper is less about the failure of the family's quest to cure Jean-Christophe's epilepsy than it is about the triumph of Pierre François's maturation as an artist—his becoming, in other words, a master. And what better way to announce this successful promotion than to change his name to David B., in fitting tribute to his animal exemplar, Master N?

As Katalin Orbán contends, the hybrid animal-human body of the comics is "a body that does not settle what is and is not human but keeps asking this question—quietly but constantly" (68). And even as physiognomy haunts the human in such comics with monstrous excesses, it also produces the body as a horizon of infinite translatability, capacious in symbolization, halting in its unreadability. Indeed, like the oblivion of the animal's face as recounted in theoretical speculations, the stylizations of the normative human in the comics is never too far removed from the cartoon animal's prevarications of it. And yet, it remains for us to ask, even as the comics relentlessly prod us to the question: what does the comic animal think and what, in thinking it, are we permitted to see in ourselves?

Notes

An early version of this essay appears as "Animal Subjects of the Graphic Novel." *College Literature* 38.3 (2011): 129-149.

1. Although Baker poses the question succinctly, his work contrasts contemporary animal studies by aligning the animal with the real that transcends discourse, thus fleeing via the animal from postmodern and poststructuralist conceptions of reality.

2. For a thorough bibliography of comics studies scholarship on the funny animal genre and the larger "world upside-down" tradition from which it derives, consult Kunzle. See also Groensteen.

3. For Deleuze and Guattari, any notion of becoming is available to a productive review whereby all "Becoming can and should be qualified as becoming-animal" (238). More than any specific reference to their notion of "becoming animal," which entails a radically non-linear, non-traditional conception of cognitive and psychological organization, I am here referring to the way in which even realistic comics, still being primarily illustrated rather than simply written, bear evidence of that visually obvious impress of the illustrator's subjective treatment of whatever the subject is, so that eruptions of a non-typical, unrealistic visual representation appear sporadically. Whether deliberate or accidental, whether intended by the illustrator or merely perceived by the reader, such eruptions tend to define themselves as divergences from a code already established in the text for representing human physiognomic typicality in which divergence is almost always coded as a type of animality.

4. For more on the origins of the Monkey King myth, see Lai 39.

5. Comics theorist Thierry Groensteen stresses that this recursivity is made available by the precondition of pictorial co-presence in comics, pinpointing "the relational play of plurality of interdependent images as the unique ontological foundations of comics" (17).

6. Like Witek, Miles Orvell sees the animal metaphorically in *Maus*, as "the reader comes to forget that these are cats, mice, pigs and soon begins to view them instead as human types" (119).

7. Other animal disciples in the story include Pigsy and the White Horse.

8. See Singer 109. Eric Lott also includes cartoons among popular texts underwritten by blackface structures of feeling: "From 'Oh Susanna' to Elvis Presley, from circus

clowns to Saturday morning cartoons, blackface acts and words have figured significantly in the white imaginary of the United States" (4–5).

Works Cited

Adorno, Theodor. *Minima Moralia: Reflections from Damaged Life*. Trans. E. F. N. Jephcott. London: Verso, 1974. Print.

Agamben, Giorgio. *Idea of Prose*. Trans. Michael Sullivan and Sam Whitsitt. Albany, NY: SUNY P, 1995. Print.

Anderson, Ho Che. *King: A Comics Biography of Martin Luther King, Jr.* Seattle, WA: Fantagraphics, 2005. Print.

B., David. *Epileptic*. Trans. Kim Thompson. New York: Pantheon, 2005. Print.

Baker, Steve. *Picturing the Beast: Animals, Identity, and Representation*. Manchester: Manchester UP, 1993. Print.

Benjamin, Walter. *The Work of Art in the Age of its Technological Reproducibility and Other Writings on Media*. Cambridge, MA: Belknap/Harvard UP, 2008. Print.

Deleuze, Gilles, and Félix Guattari. *A Thousand Plateaus: Capitalism and Schizophrenia*. Trans. Brian Massumi. Minneapolis: U of Minnesota P, 1987. Print.

Derrida, Jacques. "The Animal That Therefore I Am (More to Follow)." Trans. David Wills. *Critical Inquiry* 28.2 (2002): 369–418. Print.

Felman, Shoshana. "Camus' *The Plague*, or A Monument to Witnessing." *Testimony: Crises of Witnessing in Literature, Psychoanalysis, and History*. Shoshana Felman and Dori Laub. New York: Routledge, 1992. 93–119. Print.

Finnegan, Ruth. *Oral Literature in Africa*. Oxford: Oxford UP, 1970. Print.

Fu, Binbin. "Review of *American Born Chinese*." *MELUS* 32.3 (2007): 274–76. Print.

Gates, Henry Louis. *The Signifying Monkey: A Theory of Afro-American Literary Criticism*. Oxford: Oxford UP, 1988. Print.

Groensteen, Thierry. *The System of Comics*. Trans. Bart Beaty and Nick Nguyen. Jackson, MS: UP of Mississippi, 2007. Print.

Hirsch, Marianne. "Surviving Images: Holocaust Photographs and the Work of Postmemory." *The Yale Journal of Criticism* 14.1 (2001): 5–37. Print.

Huyssen, Andreas. *Present Pasts: Urban Palimpsests and the Politics of Memory*. Stanford, CA: Stanford UP, 2003. Print.

Jones, Matthew T. 2005. "Reflexivity in Comic Art." *International Journal of Comic Art* 7.1 (2005): 270–86. Print.

Kunzle, David. "Gary Larson and the World Upside Down." *International Journal of Comic Art* 11.1 (2009): 135–57. Print.

Lai, Whalen. "From Protean Ape to Handsome Saint: The Monkey King." *Asian Folklore Studies* 53.1 (1994): 29–65. Print.

Lott, Eric. *Love and Theft: Blackface Minstrelsy and the American Working Class.* New York: Oxford UP, 1993. Print.

Lowe, John. "Monkey Kings and Mojo: Postmodern Ethnic Humor in Kingston, Reed and Vizenor." *MELUS* 21.4 (1996): 103–26. Print.

Orbán, Katalin. "Trauma and Visuality: Art Spiegelman's *Maus* and *In the Shadow of No Towers.*" *Representations* 97 (2007): 57–89. Print.

Orvell, Miles. "Writing Posthistorically: Krazy Kat, *Maus*, and the Contemporary Fiction Cartoon." *American Literary History* 4.1 (1992): 110–28. Print.

Pearson, J. Stephen. "The Monkey King in the American Canon: Patricia Chao and Gerald Vizenor's use of an Iconic Chinese Character." *Comparative Literature Studies* 43.3 (2006): 355–74. Print.

Plaks, Andrew. *Four Masterworks of the Ming Novel: "Ssu-ta ch'i-shhu."* Princeton, NJ: Princeton UP, 1987. Print.

Seldes, Gilbert. "The Krazy Kat that Walks by Himself." *Arguing Comics: Literary Masters on a Popular Medium.* Eds. Jeet Heer and Kent Worcester. Jackson: UP of Mississippi, 2005. 22–29. Print.

Singer, Marc. "'Black Skins' and White Masks: Comic Books and the Secret of Race." *African American Review* 36.1 (2002): 107–20. Print.

Spiegelman, Art. *Maus.* 2 vols. New York: Pantheon, 1986. Print.

Witek, Joseph. *Comic Books as History: The Narrative of Jack Johnson, Art Spiegelman, and Harvey Pekar.* Jackson, MS: UP of Mississippi, 1989. Print.

Wong, Sau-Ling Cynthia. *Reading Asian American Literature: From Necessity to Extravagance.* Princeton, NJ: Princeton UP, 1993. Print.

Yang, Gene Luen. *American Born Chinese.* New York: First Second, 2006. Print.

———. 2007. "Printz Award Winner Speech." *Young Adult Library Services* 6.1: 11–13. Print.

Uncaging and Reframing
Martin Vaughn-James's *The Cage*

—Jan Baetens

Objectivity, Lorraine Daston and Peter Galison argue, is inextricably linked to our ideas, our practices, our history of subjectivity. This claim does not only hold for science but also for (popular) culture, and it also goes the other way round: subjectivity in culture cannot be thought of outside our stances on objects, objecthood, and objectivity. In this chapter I would like to advance a reading of "subjectivity through the object," by applying it to one of the great missing links in the history of the graphic novel: Martin Vaughn-James's (1943–2009) cult-album *The Cage*, started in 1968, first published in Toronto in 1975, and currently only available in its French edition (Vaughn-James 2010).

Individuality and Subjectivity in Comics

The shift from "commercial" to "serious" comic art—a shift that partially coincides with the emergence and increasing success of the term "graphic novel"—has been strongly characterized by the "subjective" and even "autobiographical turn" in the medium (for a critical assessment, see Wolk). True, classic forms of graphic storytelling are all but deprived of subjective elements, whether direct or indirect, and it is now common knowledge that a superhero comic such as *Superman* can after all bear many traces of the individual lives, dreams, and desires of its makers, *in casu* Jerry Siegel and Joe Shuster (Jones). Yet the revolution in comics achieved by later generations working for an adult audience, from the underground *comix* authors to today's graphic novelists (even if some of them, such as Marjane Satrapi, continue to discard the notion of graphic novel as elite and snooty), implies quite different and more complex forms of subjectivity.

Broadly speaking, one might say that these new forms of subjectivity penetrate the various aspects and levels on which subjectivity can be localized in a work of art. First, serious comic art always has an author, that is, a specific individual in charge of the final result and no longer an often anonymous studio artist hired to realize, as in a factory line, part of a work in progress that is commissioned and controlled by business executives (see Eisner for a *roman à clef* representation of this environment, which of course describes only the dark half of the truth, for creativity and personal initiative are certainly not absent from the comics trade). However, what defines the new type of author put forward by serious comics is the complete character of his or her work, namely the ambition to elaborate both drawing and scriptwriting (Peeters). Second, serious comic art also discloses a strong narratorial presence. The story is no longer seemingly telling itself: it is presented and filtered through a narrative voice or tone, which can be made directly visible in the work. Third, this emphasis on author and narrator frequently determines specific content matters: serious graphic storytelling has a strong tendency towards either documentary or autobiography or semi-autobiography—and both aspects are clearly not mutually incompatible (Chute). Finally, although this dimension is perhaps less explicitly thematized in reflections on subjectivity in comics, serious comic storytelling also features specific, strongly individualized ways of drawing. Serious artists may not always be the most technically gifted from a traditional point of view, but they all have a style that is unmistakably theirs.

Thanks to the work of the Belgian theoretician Philippe Marion (1993; Baetens "Revealing Traces"), we now have an instrument at our disposal to better describe the formal dimension of subjectivity. Marion's concept of *graphiation*, the visual or graphic counterpart of verbal storytelling, helps make useful distinctions between an objective pole of graphic storytelling in which the "hand" of the maker aspires to maximal transparency (the typical example being the "Clear Line" aesthetics as developed by Hergé in *The Adventures of Tintin* or the minimalist style of Schulz in *Peanuts*) and a subjective pole of maximal opacity in which the act of drawing and the individual style of the author/storyteller are foregrounded at the expense of the objects represented in the drawing itself (a good example of this stance would be George Herriman's *Krazy Kat*). Of course, it should be noted that aspiring to maximum transparency does not mean that it is actually possible not to draw attention to the presence of the hand. As argued by Jared Gardner, comics is probably the medium that best matches Walter Benjamin's description of the storyteller's actual physical connection to the artisanship of storytelling:

> In fact, alone of all of the narrative arts born at the end of the nineteenth century, the sequential comic has not effaced the line of the artist, the handprint of the storyteller. This fact is central to what makes the comic form unique, and also to what makes the line, the mark of the individual upon the page, such a unique challenge for narrative theory. We simply have no language—because we have no parallel in any other narrative form—for describing its narrative work. In comics alone the promise of Benjamin's looked-for 'moving script' continued to develop throughout the twentieth century. Here the act of inscription remains always visible, and the story of its making remains central to the narrative work (. . .). (Gardner, "Storylines" 56–57)

Although the concept of *graphiation* is a tool to measure the degree of subjectivity in comics, its relationship with other aspects of subjectivity is not always unproblematic. Its emphasis on formal aspects can diminish the attention paid to content matter and therefore to the possible autobiographical dimension of the work. The recent interest in abstract comics (Molotiu, Baetens, "Abstractions") exemplifies quite convincingly how the craving for subjective *graphiation* tends to put the narrative and biographical content between brackets. From that point of view it implies a reduction of subjectivity.

The graphic novel on which I shall focus in this chapter, Martin Vaughn-James's *The Cage*, is a paradoxical case as far as the expression of subjectivity is concerned (fig. 4.1a, fig. 4.1b, fig. 4.1c). The book itself has achieved a cult status, as demonstrated by the existence of extensive scholarship, mainly in France and Belgium (Groensteen, "La construction"), where the book has been translated successfully and where the author spent the last part of his life. (At the end of his life he lived in Brussels. The book was translated in Paris—the company later moved to Brussels—whereas he was living in Belgium already.) In the American context, the book is quite unusual as well, given its blatant—and in the eyes of an American readership perhaps slightly elitist—claim to literary legitimacy, which makes it very difficult to give it a clear (and politically correct, or at least acceptable) position in the ongoing dialogue between popular and literary

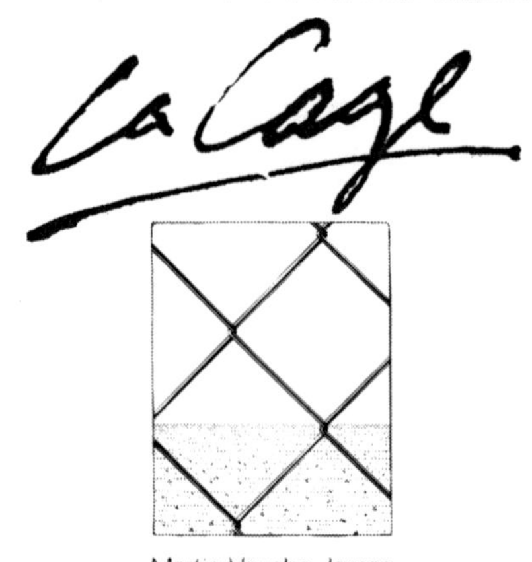

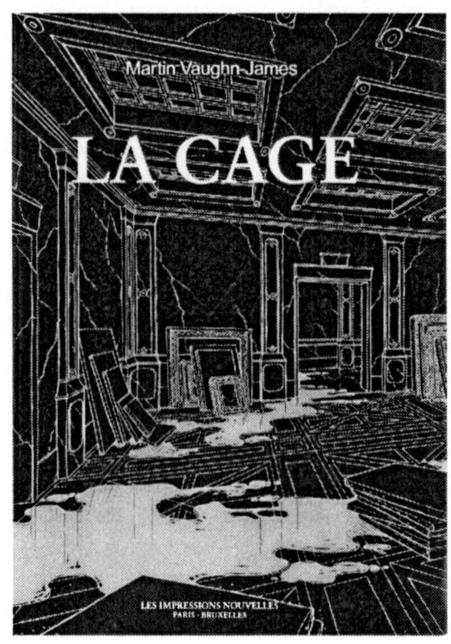

Martin Vaughn-James

LA CAGE

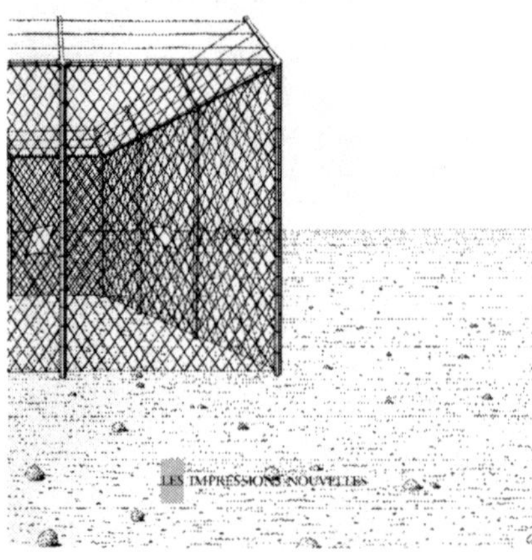

4.1. (a, b, c) Covers of three different editions of the French edition of Martin Vaughn-James' *The Cage* (1985, 2002, and 2010). Copyright Les Impressions Nouvelles, Brussels, 2010.

culture that is so characteristic of the comic format, as very convincingly argued throughout Gardner's book *Projections*.

Yet what matters most from the perspective of memory and subjectivity is the distance kept from the models of multilayered subjectivity that underlie the paradigm of serious comics of which *The Cage* is undoubtedly a major example. Published initially in the then-dominant large A4 album format (its present reprint is closer to the currently hegemonic graphic novel format of 17 cm x 24 cm), *The Cage* immediately became famous for offering a story breaking all the written and unwritten laws of the genre: each page contains only one panel (the format of which can vary), captions instead of word balloons (although some pages remain totally wordless), its length of some 180 pages is quite unusual, and, most strikingly, it is a story with no characters, containing only images of objects and places. In addition, its graphic black-and-white style is astonishingly cool, if not cold: *The Cage* is light years away from the expressionist transformations of traditional drawing techniques that can be found in many innovative works of the post-*comix* period.

In light of *graphiation* theory, *The Cage* is a book one is not spontaneously tempted to label as subjective. Today, we know, moreover, that the slices of text that run underneath some of the drawings have only been added afterwards, and that in a sense one does not lose much by simply ignoring them. Hence the question that is at the heart of my analysis: can one also read *The Cage* as an example of how subjectivity, autobiography, and memory work in comics? Such a reading will obviously have to stretch or redefine the articulation of the subjective and objective pole of graphic storytelling, as I will suggest that the apparently objective style of Martin Vaughn-James exemplifies a different idea of subjectivity. It is of course this difference I am interested in.

A Dynamic Approach to Graphiation

Martin Vaughn-James's ink drawings seem to resist any analysis in terms of subjective *graphiation*. Each is made in an impersonal style and even when chaotic or anarchic details enter the fictional world, the key word remains stylization. This unsettling strategy can take the appearance of inkblots and stains that pop up within panels. From the very first pages (non-paginated in the book), the image is disrupted by the sudden arrival of such an external element, which at first sight looks like a bomb or a fire in a French garden. In narratological terms, the blot in question is a *metalepsis*:[1] it reveals the labor of an extradiegetic author whose body invades—by (calculated) accident—the imaginary world of *The Cage*, a little as if one were to find a painter's fingerprints or thumb traces on a painted canvas. However, this metaleptic intrusion of the author's body in the clean drawing world of *The Cage* is so overstylized that its rhetorical and hence bodily effect is strongly attenuated, if not actually becoming non-existent. The ink stain is so well balanced, so craftily executed that it no longer appears as a stain, but as the perfect imitation of the ideal stain or the perfect look-alike stain, so that even this extreme case of a possible encounter between the objective and the subjective is perfectly neutralized. In retrospect, the current interest in abstract comics may invite us to reread this blot as one of the first examples of a tendency or subgenre that has been acquiring a real presence in the contemporary comics field. However, such an interpretation has a serious risk: that of detaching "pure" abstract qualities of the work from what is key to the understanding of *The Cage*, namely the permanent conflict between its figurative and its nonfigurative horizon.

Subjectivity is present, however, but not in the way that traditional *graphiation* theory would have it. In order to localize and identify the subjectivity of *The Cage*, one has to follow a different path, one that exploits a crucial aspect of medium specificity in graphic storytelling: the role of the gutter (in this case of the margins, for there is only one panel per page in Vaughn-James's book). The importance of ellipsis in comic storytelling supposes that panels do not produce one or more continuous animated sequences, but a chain or string of units that maintain their independence and that are always looked at in relationship to what preceded as well as to what is still to come. From that essentially discontinuous point of view, the objective drawings of Martin Vaughn-James almost immediately achieve a high degree of subjectivity. As a matter of fact, the leap from one image to the next is never smooth or linear. Even if style, theme, content matter, and so on, do not change, each panel always brings something dramatically new, not only because so much information remains hidden in the gutter, but also because very often the changes cannot be rationally explained. Things grow older or younger in the transition from one panel to another, settings are altered, props come and go, identical forms such as squares, triangles, spheres, pyramids, and so on, return in totally different thematic constellations: a pyramid becomes a ziggurat, a frontally shown pyramid metamorphoses into a bird's-eye view of a Western megapolis, a cage becomes a grilled window, a hospital bed, a tiled floor, and so on. It is this pulse—a rhythmic category that does not depend on the action or lack of action contained within the images, but on the cuts between the panels—that becomes the very locus of subjectivity in *The Cage*. It is the often extraordinary shift from one representation to another that lays bare the subjectivity underneath the objective style of each panel. Such an approach to subjectivity no longer has anything to do with the traditional analysis of drawing details, features, and styles as informed or distributed by the individual hand of the maker. What one observes here is thus a sequential appropriation of *graphiation* in which the subjective dimension is the un-shown but dramatically present pulse that determines Martin Vaughn-James's way of narrating in *The Cage*.

Considered from this perspective, the expression of *Fremdkörper* within the drawings, as with the appearance of the dots and stains that have been "dropped" on the page or the sudden cracks that disfigure the surface of objects, signifies not the realistic representation of aging or decay, but the symptom of a deeper tension between conflicting drawing styles. In that sense, these foreign objects symbolize the difficulty of containing the heterogeneity of the drawing process within the limits of a neat, cool, Clear Line-like drawing technique. According to such a reading, all fictional elements of the book suddenly acquire a metanarrative aspect: instead of building an autonomous fictional universe, they become a symptomatic after-effect of the artist's subjectivity. The objectivist style tries to domesticate these impulses, but they remain visible even in the technically most perfect ink drawings. This metafictional understanding also makes room for a global reinterpretation of the book, including its title. A superlative version of the typically modernist grid, the cage can be seen as the thematic expansion or translation of the basic elements of objectivism: the line and its expanded form that is the Clear Line technique; the surface and the subsequent emphasis put on the square angle, as all objects tend to become grids (even the clouds in the sky!) in which all other forms are trapped or locked; the volume, here thematized by the cage but also by the factory, the hospital, or the prison.

The impossibility of keeping it all together, of sticking to one type of representation only, produces a new way of inscribing the artist's subjectivity in the final result of his drawings: a temporal-metonymic process highlighted by ruptures between images that do not themselves display traces of subjectivity. This dynamic approach is a plausible correlative of the difference between a drawing and a comic. The former can be seen, in the tradition of Lessing, as belonging to the paradigm of the arts of Space; the latter tends towards the arts of Time. In this regard, the dynamic and sequential analysis of subjective *graphiation* does not differ radically from the equally temporal analysis (of the dynamic analysis) of the comic-page layout proposed by Thierry Groensteen in his *System of Comics*. Rather than describing the relationships in which panels and page are involved in a static way, Groensteen gives full priority to the either stable or unstable character of these relationships through time. The analysis of subjectivity follows similar theoretical lines: objectivity and subjectivity are not properties of the drawings and panels themselves—on the contrary, they concern the stable or unstable repetitions of the plate layout as it can be discovered in the successive pages. Stability here becomes a motor of "objectivity" and distance (even in those cases where, at panel level, the drawing style seems to be very subjective), while instability hints at subjectivity and proximity (even if, as in *The Cage*, the visual style of the work seems very non-subjective, if not slightly impersonal).

Comics as Change, and the Invention of the Object

If comics is an art of repetition and change, it can be fruitful to ask where the representations of *The Cage* actually come from and how the impact of the artist's gesture intervenes in the process of their transformation.

The Cage brings to the fore a homogeneous world, with an apparent continuity in all its graphic dimensions: dot, line, angle, grid, cube—all traced with the same pencil. In addition, one easily observes how each abstract geometrical unit or component is translated into thematic and fictional forms that naturalize its material basis. The clouds in the sky, for instance, with their dotted contour lines, the absolute rectilinear form of their bottom lines and the regularity of their dispersion over the implicit lines of the page, are so stylized that one almost feels the mechanism that has invested the form with meaning. Moreover, there is an almost perfect symmetry between these clouds and the rows of pebbles in the desert, among many other comparable items, so that one can almost immediately decipher these iconic figures as equivalent to letters and words on the page (fig. 4.2a, fig. 4.2b). Each fictional object present within the dehumanized world of *The Cage* can be explained this way and turned back into its abstract components. The cage itself, a quadrangular fence surrounding a wide set of smaller buildings or constructions, refers both to

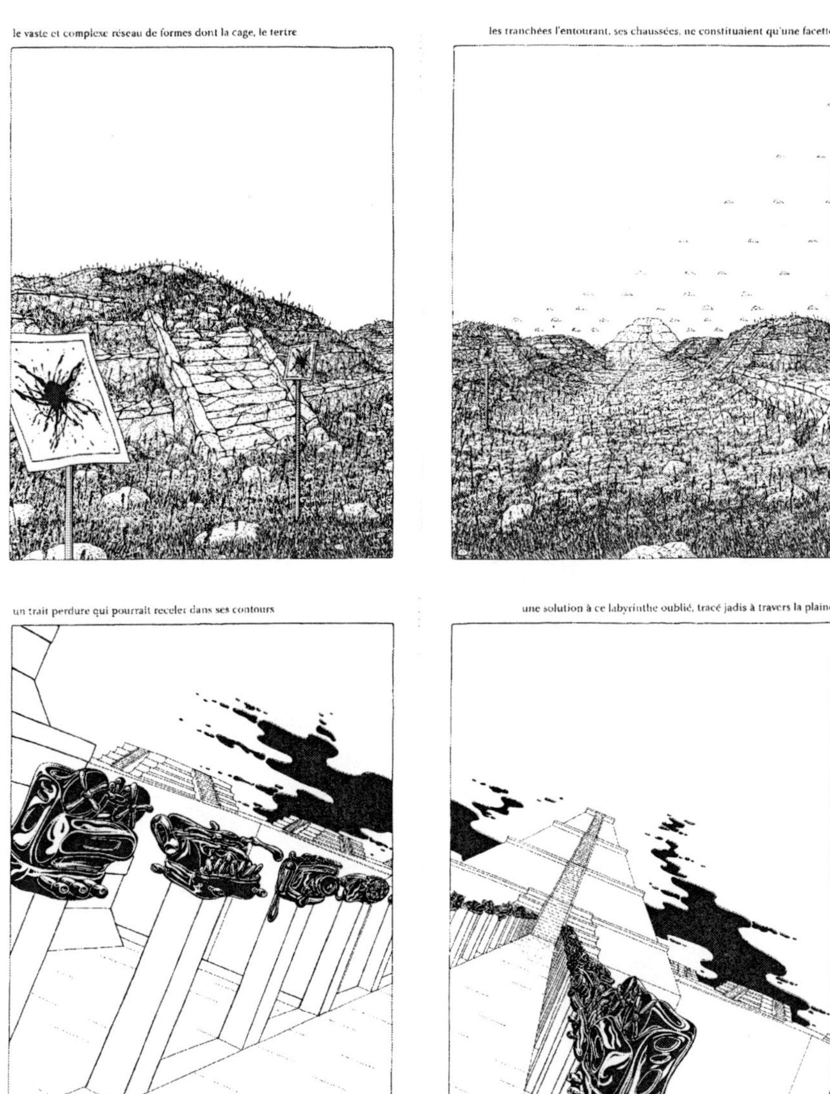

4.2. (a, b) Fragment of the opening sequence (nonpaginated)

the book as a container (in case one reads the fictional world as a transfer of written signs into a visual world) and the white cube of the exhibition space (in case one focuses on the iconic dimension of the work). Words become things, pages become walls, covers become cages, and vice versa.

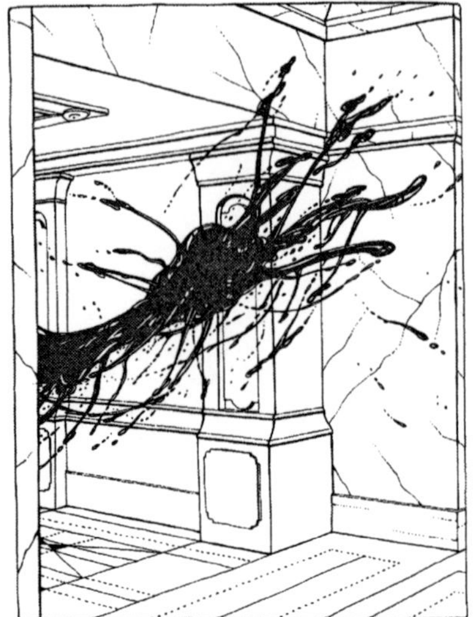

se jetant contre l'immuable façade, l'éclaboussure figée, en
suspens, ou condamnée à se répéter maintes fois elle-même
au ralenti, de telle sorte que chaque minuscule ondulation
pourrait être arrêtée dans sa trajectoire, observée

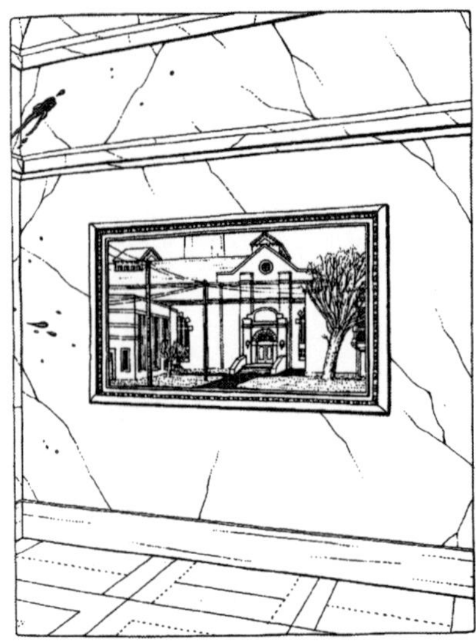

son vol méticuleusement enregistré dans l'espoir qu'une
fois rassemblées ces observations fluctuantes serviraient
en quelque façon à reconstituer et finalement à éclairer
cette chose dont la nature même défiait l'examen

4.3. One of the many examples of the "ink blot" (nonpaginated)

Yet this oscillation between abstract forms and their figurative translations—almost a textbook example of what in Greimasian semiotics is meant by the *generative trajectory* (Wolde)—is never mechanical. The relationship between both forces is never symmetric. If there is symmetry, it is symmetry with a difference, in the same way as the transfer or translation puts a strong emphasis on creative adaptation and even on drift. In this regard, it is certainly not by chance that behind the fence one finds a power station, the very symbol of the shift from (static) *form* to (mobile) *force*. The generative force of the power station—a symbol that represents among other things the work of the author—is less that it is repetitive and virtually endless, than that it produces gaps, ruptures, in short, a *clinamen*.[2] It is true that starting from a line one can draw a grid and then a hospital room and eventually a full-fledged city (although still a city with no inhabitants, no traffic, no noise), but this generative dynamic is at the same time jeopardized by the appearance of cracks. The dots can refuse to fall back into dotted lines and break out as uncontrollable—yet meticulously drawn—and free-floating—yet carefully positioned—elements, such as the already mentioned inkblots that prevent the restless and infinite reduplication of visible objects and visual patterns (fig. 4.3). Elsewhere, the inkblots become blood stains, floods of sand, and whirlpools of debris, although never with a visible source. We see the after-effect of an imaginary explosion, but never the explosion itself. More precisely, we see the objects being blown up by the hypothetic blast, but not the resulting wreckage, for here as well time is always on the move, with no known direction. What the jump cuts between the pages disclose is less a play of before and after than a transformation that is never teleologically oriented. Readers of *The Cage* can never know whether the fictional world is moving backwards or forward, whether the things seen are in decay or under construction, whether the next page represents the future or the past.

In *The Cage*, new forms of objecthood come into sight. Just as the apparent objectivity appears to lose its non-subjective character once replaced by the broken-up sequences that make the eye of the observer and the hand of the artist visible, so the status of the very objects changes dramatically. Objects in *The Cage* are always in-between; they are liminal objects that move from one state to another, but never in a linear way. Their nature is change, and the curious mix of science fiction and historical fiction is a plausible effect as well as a metaphor of their essential temporal indeterminacy.

Martin Vaughn-James's Rewriting of the New Novel: The Aesthetics of the Object and Beyond

The world of *The Cage* is a changing one. Objects metamorphose ceaselessly, while the subjectivity that lies beneath the alleged objectivity of their Clear Line *graphiation* becomes apparent through these changes. It would be a mistake, though, to consider *The Cage* a world closed in on itself, to see it as a mere dialogue or struggle between an enunciated and enunciation, between a graphic style and a process of *graphiation*. Martin Vaughn-James's book is indeed deeply marked by a cultural and historical context I will now discuss. This broadening of the analysis will help enhance the complexity of the object in *The Cage*.

Narrativity as explored by *The Cage* bears a strong likeness to the writing techniques of the French New Novel. The story is clearly *self-generating*; it does not build upon the idea of representing a given world outside the book nor upon that of giving voice to the interior life of the artist (the two inseparable but commonly *reproductive*, i.e., *non-self-generating* orientations of traditional writing). As we have seen, this self-generation starts with a pool of material data, the materiality in case always being a verbal one, and it is then performed on these data through a series of measurable and programmable interventions. Yet in the years that Martin Vaughn-James was working on *The Cage* and that he was biographically very close to the New Novel scene, for instance via the illustrations he created for works by Samuel Beckett and Robert Pinget, this literary movement was undergoing a thorough alteration related to the question of the *object* (and hence of *subjectivity*), on the one hand, and to the question of the *image* (and hence of *textuality*), on the other.

The first generation of New Novelists revolutionized post-war French writing that was dominated at the time by political and ideological issues as in the *littérature engagée* of Jean-Paul Sartre. The New Novelists' phenomenologically inspired works were conceived through the marriage of two already existing yet until then completely separated stances: first, the appropriation of behaviorist and objectivist methods of writing, which produced a home-grown version of American *camera eye* literature; second, the integration of the formally sophisticated constructions of poetry (a type of writing that was moving heavily toward free verse) in the prose work of the novel (a genre defined as defying all genre rules or formats).[3] So extreme was the obsession with descriptive purity—only objects, no subjects, only objectivity, no subjectivity—and so absolute the craving for a perfect verbal architecture of the fictional world, that the first New Novels can easily be considered examples of Greenbergian modernism, that is, an attempt to strip down the whole text to its most elementary, most typical, and hence purest elements: letters, words, syntax, composition. *The Cage*, though a good example of New Novel techniques, challenges these modernist assumptions. True, it is clearly built on the combination and thematization of its underlying material elements—dots, lines, angles, grids, and cubes—but at the same time it is shamelessly figurative. True, it adopts rigorous compositional techniques, but at the same time its meticulously shaped world is torn apart by savage disfigurations. This challenge of modernist purity and order is symptomatic of the fizzling out of a certain kind of modernity, as corroborated by the transformations of the first New Novel. Exactly as was the case for the abstract paintings praised by Greenberg, the works of the first New Novelists were always (already) distorted by their censored opposite: words could not do without images, and the New Novelists proved unable to put between brackets the images they tried to convert into strictly linguistic components in a desperate endeavor to block the visual imagination of the reader, forcing a return to the words on the page. (The impossibility of achieving such a purely verbal reading is of course a way to undermine the ideal of medium-specificity in literary texts.) Moreover, the objective style the first New Novelists aspired to proved destabilized by subjective and unconscious emotions so violent and aggressive that it no longer even took a psychoanalytical lens—as in the readings by Bruce Morrisette—to disclose their presence (and this revelation was of course a slap in the face to those who had attacked the "humanist" subjectivity of traditional narrative). *The Cage* showcases all these tensions very explicitly.

A closer reading of the notion of object highlights the particular position of *The Cage* with regard to the cultural history of the New Novel. In Vaughn-James's graphic novel, the objectifying approach of the New Novel, with its thematic preference for "things" on the one hand and its choice to stick to a non-subjective description on the other hand, is still dominant, but at the same time the book already mirrors the dismantling of its objectivist approach by making room for all sorts of uncanny representations.

The Cage is not dissimilar to *Jealousy* by Alain Robbe-Grillet. In this book, the story is told by a jealous husband whose presence is only revealed through the biased perceptions that transform the most neutral objects and descriptions into hallucinatory scenes. Vaughn-James's erasure of all human characters in *The Cage* can be compared to Robbe-Grillet's radical device, but in the former case the clues are less hidden: the progressive disruption and eventual destruction of the hard-edged fictional world is apparent from the first pages of *The Cage*. What we see in Vaughn-James's work is a world of objects, machines, places, and buildings deprived of human existence, in which the sudden shifts from one image to another reveal all the more the haunting presence of an observing eye that behaves in increasingly delirious ways. The progressively resounding tone of the captions forms supplementary proof of this obsession. One does not even need to read the pseudo-objective texts to realize that the whole fiction is seen as well as narrated through an unreliable narrator incapable of keeping up appearances and whose utterances eventually break down into shaky screams: *"the cage, the cage, the cage, the cage"* (Vaughn-James, *La Cage*: no pagination, italics in original).[4]

However, the internal transformations of the New Novel not only concerned the position of the object. They also affected the nature of the image, which provoked a discussion that was part of the broader issue of medium-specificity. Although highly descriptive and therefore utterly visual, the first New Novel tended to frown upon any kind of illustration as well as on any kind of literary image, such as metaphors and comparisons (see Robbe-Grillet). The image had to be kept outside the text in the name of a certain idea of medium-specificity (and here too it would be too obvious to stress the relationship with Greenbergian modernism). Authors could move from one medium to another, as did for instance Robbe-Grillet when he started making movies, provided they agreed not to "repeat" or "reduplicate" or "illustrate" their literary work by way of images, and vice versa. A New Novel description is not a description that aims at making us see the object; it is on the contrary a description that aims at making us aware of the gap between words and things (Ricardou, *Problèmes* and *Le nouveau roman*). This craving for medium-specificity in Ricardou's theory, whose ideas on illustrations and word and image relationships were a blatant remediation of Lessing's premodern defense of the separation of the arts of time and the arts of space, would soon be questioned by the blurring of the boundaries between text and image that timidly started in the '70s (Baetens and Van Gelder). Vaughn-James's contribution to this debate was less the transfer of the New Novel to a visual medium (after all, others had done so before) than the willful embrace of what had been an absolute taboo: the illustration. His decision to mix words and images and to present the visual story as a quasi-equivalent of what could be found in a typical New Novel was not only new, it was most of all something that went against the grain. Moreover, what made his case even worse was the fact that during those years, besides the reappropriation of the New Novel universe in *The Cage*, Vaughn-James also proposed various examples of blatantly classic illustrations of New Novel-authors such as Samuel Beckett[5] and Robert Pinget.[6]

From a cultural-historical point of view, *The Cage* testifies to the temporal complexities of these tensions. In transposing New Novel elements to the genre of the graphic novel, Vaughn-James was looking backwards and as well as looking ahead of his time. He was still coping with issues of objectivity and subjectivity that newer forms of the New Novel, strongly influenced by the radical experiments of *Tel Quel* and other avant-garde groups, had already abandoned, but he was already performing what even these newer forms were still very afraid of doing: erasing the frontiers between words and images. In that sense, Vaughn-James's book arguably illustrates a well-known lesson in intermedial exchanges and influences: techniques and viewpoints becoming obsolete in one medium or genre can nevertheless still prove to be revolutionary in another. *The Cage* has from the very beginning been read as a real avant-garde book, while also customizing for the field of the graphic novel a set of ideas and devices that had been abandoned many years earlier in favor of other forms within the New Novel. At the same time, *The Cage* also points to a broader phenomenon, that of the fundamental heterogeneity of culture in which, to follow Raymond Williams's terminology, it is always the case that different "structures of feeling" interfere: *residual*, *dominant*, and *emergent* frames are mixed (Williams; for a modern rereading, see McConachie). Williams's cultural theory helps in understanding why an avant-garde artist such as Vaughn-James was still struggling with outdated problems. This is, unless of course, following the even more challenging suggestions made by William Marx and others, innovation is not incompatible at all with the defense of apparently more conservative policies. But this is of course another story.

Things That Tell

Before addressing a final question regarding the treatment of objects in *The Cage*, I would like to recapitulate the essential steps of my argument. Given the impossibility of separating issues of objectivity and subjectivity, I have tried to examine the role played by the object in the construction of a historically rooted subjectivity. First, by showing, through the analysis of *graphiation*, that objective drawings can prove very subjective provided one does not limit the analysis to the images themselves, but agrees to expand the analysis to their transformations. Second, by suggesting that objects are not only images referring to a given world, but ways of coping with the possibility of transforming material aspects of a given medium (in this case drawing) into fictional elements. Third by demonstrating that all these questions (objectivist style, medium-specificity, word and image relationships) were characteristic of the cultural period and background in which Martin Vaughn-James was preparing, in utter solitude, his groundbreaking work.

In the last section of this chapter, I will examine the role of objects in a more general way. As argued by Sherry Turkle, recent social and cognitive research in science studies has turned away from the distinction between abstract and concrete thinking. Taking up the thread initiated by Claude Lévi-Strauss's interest in *bricolage* and Jean Piaget's study of the intellectual development of children, but leaving behind the division these two thinkers still accepted between primitive, inchoative forms of thinking and complete, rational thinking, contemporary science studies have overturned the wall between concrete and abstract practices and methods of thinking. They therefore pay great attention to the role of simple objects in creative thinking. Turkle rightly stresses the abolition of the concrete/abstract distinction as well as the fading of the difference between emotion and intellect: "*Objects bring together thought and feeling. In particular, objects of science are objects of passion*" (Turkle 9; italics in the original). Physical sensation and intellectual comprehension may not be the same, but they are systematically intertwined.

For the reader of comics, the most interesting aspect of Turkle's line of thinking is however not just the object's usefulness in daily life—a usefulness that has been demonstrated by Henry Jenkins in his use of childhood superhero comics in adult daily life judgments—but the narrative dimension of the object. Things occupy the center of associative networks, half-retrieved from memory, half-elaborated through creative musing and projection, and the most efficient objects are those that prove capable of taking strong narrative forms. Such objects are not only objects of thought, they are thinking objects and, by corollary, such objects are not only objects of telling, they are telling objects as well. Following Lorraine Daston, who edited a great collection called *Things That Talk*, it should be possible to speak here of "things that tell."

A graphic novel is undoubtedly an example of such a storytelling hybrid in which object and subject (the author, but also the reader!), genre, medium, ink, image, and so on intermingle in a process that bestows all the initiative upon the telling transformation of the object. In one of the rare critical comments he has made on his own work, Vaughn-James confirmed what all readers of *The Cage* can see without knowing anything about the genesis of the book: *The Cage* was written with no previous plan; it obeys a program of self-generation, instead of relying on a preexisting script, whatever form this script might have taken (Vaughn-James, "Le non-scénario"). In this regard, Vaughn-James, whose graphic style may seem astonishingly classic, is definitely a forerunner. His objectivist drawings may remind us of what the New Novel was doing one or two decades earlier, but in surrendering to the work's "productivity" (a term coined by Julia Kristeva to refer to the infinite creative possibilities of a text's self-engenderment, as theorized in the most radical years of Tel Quel's ideology of *écriture*) he was clearly ahead of his time, at least in the field of the graphic novel, where many believed that the necessary condition of the cultural upgrading of the medium was to be found in the adoption of literary screenplays and the more or less faithful adaptation of literary source material.

Vaughn-James unleashes completely different powers. Although literary influences are present in the book (after all, *The Cage* is a graphic New Novel), the reappropriation of the intertext is very free and the author takes advantage of his objectivist rewriting of the comics world to propose a vibrantly subjective, personal, idiosyncratic story world. This is a world in which objects come to life, not in the magical, anthropomorphic sense of fairy tales and other kinds of fantasy, but through the machinations of the avant-garde devices of montage, jump cut, and ellipsis. A world in which things hint at secret feelings, those of the author as well as those of the reader, since both have to collaborate in order for it to—ironically—materialize. Object, objecthood, and objectivity give birth to new forms of subject, subjecthood, and subjectivity in which the frontiers between reader and writer disappear. Deconstruction and critical theory emphasize (and popularize) this point when electronic literature came into sight around 1990 (Landow), yet in 1975, *The Cage*, with its subtly paradoxical title, was already clearing the ground for this radical message.

Notes

1. According to Genette, a *metalepsis* (a rhetorical term whose actual meaning is broader than the one used in narratology) is a breaking of the boundaries that separate distinct levels of a narrative.

2. The term of *clinamen*, which has its roots in antique natural philosophy, has been appropriated by contemporary theoreticians of constrained writing in order to qualify the production of a deflection or an anomaly that helps create a more complex structure within a system.

3. The best description of this astonishing change, with poetry imitating the freedom of the novel and the novel adopting some constraints better accepted in the poetic field, is given by Roland Barthes in *Writing Degree Zero*.

4. A clear parody of Mallarmé's famous outburst of desperation and longing at the end of his poem *L'azur*: "Je suis hanté: l'azur, l'azur, l'azur, l'azur", where the most significant transformation is of course the deletion of the first-person voice. The quadruple repetition of this word was probably inspired by the similar use of this rhetorical figure in Edgar Allan Poe's "The Bells."

5. The link between Beckett and the New Novel may seem a little surprising to Anglophone readers, but in the French context of the '60s and '70s it would not have been as unusual to claim such a relationship, mainly based on the fact that Beckett's

work was published by the same company that hosted most of the "official" New Novelists and that, moreover, the concrete definition of the New Novel group (who was in and who was out) was only fixed at the famous Cerisy conference of 1971, to which Beckett had been invited (see Ricardou, *Le nouveau roman*).

6. Published in the journal *Minuit*, a laboratory journal that served as a launching pad for young authors of the publishing company that had established the New Novel, these images were (partially) gathered in Vaughn-James's *Après la Bataille*).

Works Cited

Baetens, Jan. "Revealing Traces: A New Theory of Graphic Enunciation." *The Language of Comics: Word and Image.* Eds. Robin Varnum and Christina Robbins. Jackson: Mississippi UP, 2001. 145–55. Print.

———. "Abstraction in Comics." *Substance* 40.1 (2011): 94–113. Print.

Baetens, Jan, and Hilde Van Gelder. "Petite poétique de la photographie mise en roman (1970–1990)." *Photographie et romanesque.* Ed. Danièle Méaux. Caen: Lettres Modernes Minard, 2006. 257–271. Print.

Barthes, Roland. *Writing Degree Zero.* 1957. Trans. Annette Lavers and Colin Smith. New York: Hill and Wang, 1968. Print.

Chute, Hillary. "Comics as Literature? Reading Graphic Narrative." *PMLA* 123.2 (2008): 452–65. Print.

Daston, Lorraine, ed. *Things That Talk. Object Lessons from Art and Science.* New York: Zone Books, 2004. Print.

Daston, Lorraine, and Peter Galison. *Objectivity.* New York: Zone Books, 2007. Print.

Eisner, Will. *The Dreamer.* 1986. New York: Norton, 2008. Print.

Gardner, Jared. "Storylines." *Substance* 40.1 (2011): 53–69. Print.

———. *Projections: Comics and the History of Twenty-First Century Storytelling.* Stanford: Stanford UP, 2011. Print.

Genette, Gérard. *Métalepse. De la figure à la fiction.* Paris: Seuil, 2004. Print.

Groensteen, Thierry. *The System of Comics.* Trans. Bart Beaty and Nick Nguyen. Jackson: UP of Mississippi, 2007. Print.

———. "La construction de *La Cage.*" Martin Vaughn-James. *La Cage, suivi de 'La construction de La Cage' par Thierry Groensteen.* Brussels: Les Impressions Nouvelles, 2010, I-L. Print.

Jenkins, Henry. "Death-Defying Superheroes." *Evocative Objects: Things We Think With.* Ed. Sherry Turkle. Cambridge, Mass.: MIT P, 2007. 195–207. Print.

Jones, Gerard. *Men of Tomorrow: Geeks, Gangsters, and the Birth of the Comic Book.* New York: Basic Books, 2004. Print.

Kristeva, Julia. *Le texte du roman.* The Hague: Mouton, 1971. Print.

Landow, George. *Hypertext 3.0.* Baltimore: Johns Hopkins UP, 2006. Print.

Marion, Philippe. *Traces en cases.* Louvain-la-Neuve: Académia, 1993. Print.

Marx, William, ed. *Les arrière-gardes au XXe siècle.* 2002. Paris: PUF, 2008. Print.

McConachie, Bruce. "Toward a Cognitive Cultural Hegemony." *Introduction to Cognitive Cultural Studies.* Ed. Lisa Zunshine. Baltimore: Johns Hopkins UP, 2010. 134–50. Print.

Molotiu, Andrei. *Abstract Comics.* Seattle: Fantagraphics, 2009. Print.

Morrisette, Bruce. *The Novels of Robbe-Grillet.* Ithaca: Cornell UP, 1975. Print.

Peeters, Benoît. *Case, planche, récit.* Paris: Casterman, 1998. Print.

Ricardou, Jean. *Le nouveau roman.* Paris: Seuil, 1973. Print.

Ricardou, Jean. *Problèmes du nouveau roman.* Paris: Seuil, 1967. Print.

Robbe-Grillet, Alain. *Jealousy.* 1957. Trans. Richard Howard. New York: Grove, 1987. Print.

Robbe-Grillet, Alain. *Pour un nouveau roman.* Paris: Minuit, 1963. Print.

Turkle, Sherry, ed. *Evocative Objects. Things We Think With.* Cambridge, Mass.: MIT P, 2007. Print.

Vaughn-James, Martin. *Après la bataille.* Liège: atelier de l'Agneau, 1982. Print.

———. "Le non-scénario de *La Cage.*" *Revue de l'Université de Bruxelles* 1/2 (1986): 235–40. Print.

———. *La Cage, suivi de 'La construction de La Cage' par Thierry Groensteen.* Brussels: Les Impressions Nouvelles, 2010 (first publication: Toronto: The Coach House Press, 1975).

Williams, Raymond. *Marxism and Literature.* Oxford: Oxford UP, 1977. Print.

Wolde, E. J. "Greimas and Peirce. Greimas' Generative Semiotics and Elements from Peirce's Semiotics United into a Generative Explanatory Model." *Kodicas* 9.3/4 (1986): 331–66. Print.

Wolk, Douglas. "Comics." *New York Times* 6 Dec. 2009: BR14. Print.

Comics as Non-Sequential Art

Chris Ware's Joseph Cornell

—Benjamin Widiss

One of the elements of Chris Ware's artistic biography most frequently attested to is his affinity for the work of Joseph Cornell, but it is also one of the least analyzed. The scholarly archive is nearly silent on the topic, the massed media deeply and unreflectingly reiterative. Dozens of websites offer the same observation that, complementing the obvious influence of cartoonists like George Herriman, Winsor McCay, Frank King, and Charles Schulz, "Ware has found inspiration and a kindred soul in artist and sculptor Joseph Cornell, both men sharing the need to capture items of nostalgia, grace, and beauty within 'boxes,'"[1] while an even greater number reduce this minimal elucidation to the yet simpler affirmation that Ware "has spoken about finding inspiration in the work of artist Joseph Cornell."[2] The origin of this intelligence, the alpha and ambivalent omega of extended discussion on the topic, is almost certainly Daniel Raeburn's writings. His 2004 Yale University Press monograph indicates that Ware "reveres" the older artist and has built a wooden curio cabinet loosely based on his example *(Chris Ware* 50), while true cognoscenti might have learned as far back as 1999, through a short side-note in Raeburn's 40,000-word Ware fanzine, that "Ware has fashioned in his living room a shrine of sorts to honor Joseph Cornell and the unique, inventive, private life that Cornell shared through his art" ("Smartest" 16). Raeburn reads this installation as "a box of sorts"—"a wooden bookcase filled with books about Cornell, aging photographs, and Cornell-inspired pieces given Chris by fellow admirers . . . arranged . . . so that they touch each other, just so, almost as carefully as Cornell arranged the ephemera with which he composed his own, three-dimensional collages" (16). Once he's recorded these visual and behavioral homologies, though, Raeburn resists actually theorizing the relationship between the two artists, or even drawing "explicit comparisons" (16). He concludes that "Cornell's influence . . . is easy to see and is best grasped wordlessly" through exposure to the Art Institute of Chicago's holdings. "Visit the . . . collection," Raeburn exhorts his reader, "and see [Cornell's] inner world for yourself. When you do you will see exactly what I am not talking about" (16).

I begin with this conflicted two-step of invocation and refusal because, in spite of himself, Raeburn provides a good deal of assistance in working out the relationship between the artists. The tension he notes between the private and the shared, the importance of invention as a mediating force, and the implication of the second-person ("you will see") as an endpoint to the discussion: all these are crucial attributes of Ware's borrowings from Cornell. So, too, is the emphasis on silent contemplation that yields an awareness of correspondences and kinship. But the embrace of contemplation itself—sustained reflection on an object, and the elastic capacity for that reflection to rebound inward toward the self—is perhaps the deepest stake of all, and the one that most clearly requires of Ware models from outside comics' teleological rush. Ware avers that he learned from Herriman and King techniques for over-all page composition, possibilities for conveying emotion not through words or images but through "the way the story itself [is] structured" (quoted in Raeburn, *Chris Ware* 13). These approaches feature a mode of storytelling in which the story is preceded and subtended by a minimally narrative or even non-narrative synthetic visual apprehension, productive in itself of a certain readerly "mood" and stance (13). To go yet further in the direction of pure meditation, however, Ware turns to Cornell and other sources beyond the comics canon. He waxes rhapsodic, for example, in an "appreciation" of painter Philip Guston's "genuinely revolutionary" profiles of a disembodied head with a solitary staring eye— "a long, single white orb, pushing out of a pink gash bisecting a lumpy, potato-shaped mass of flesh"—which Ware casts as "decidedly contemplative" in the most profound sense: "picture-memor[ies] of something felt," "paintings . . . not [of] what it looks like to see a human being, but what it *feels* like to *inhabit* one" (Ware, "Philip Guston" 89).[3] Ware's work does not much dwell in such raw phenomenology, but an interest in creating a certain number of pages and objects that solicit "seeing" as much as "reading,"[4] and that encourage protracted meditation as a result, characterizes Ware's output at every stage of his career.

The pages that follow trace instances of that meditation over the first decade of Ware's output, stretching from his college years cartooning for UT Austin's *Daily Texan* in the late 1980s and early '90s, through the initial issues of his sporadic periodical *The ACME Novelty Library* (1993–), and then to the aftermath of the breakout success of his first complete graphic novel, *Jimmy Corrigan* (2000), which allowed him to reintroduce a selection of the *ACME* material—itself often first published even earlier in the *Daily Texan* or elsewhere—as *Quimby the Mouse* (2003). Throughout this period, Ware avails himself of an array of formal syntaxes traceable to Cornell in order to yoke veiled autobiographical reflections to implicit commentaries on the capacities of the comic strip and book, as they exist on the page and as they circulate in the world.

Adapting the enthralling force of Cornell's singular constructions to new ends requires some changes, of course, for Ware's comics would seem in fundamental ways to be almost perfectly opposed to Cornell's combinatory aesthetic. While Ware sometimes toys with a notional or latent third dimension through the inclusion of figures the reader is invited to cut out and assemble, his comics are by definition fundamentally bound to the flatness of the page. His mature style, with its minimal shading, almost unvarying line, and frequent repetitions, accentuates that flatness enormously. But even the early work, for all its aggregate demonstration of Ware's astonishing ability to channel myriad graphic vocabularies from the full arc of comics history, rarely ventures on individual pages beyond a careful counterpoint of contrasting approaches to foreground and background. Ware thereby eschews the more radical juxtaposition of manifold disparate materials that gives Cornell's work its surrealist frisson. What's more, Cornell's iconoclastic curatorial endeavor—his active staging of these disjunctive assemblies in individual pieces that circulated according to his dictate and whim—further differentiates his output from Ware's, which is designed for and defined by mechanical reproduction.

But Ware's adoption of Cornell's model also constitutes a powerful intervention in the mechanisms of comics as usual. If Ware half-springs the mystical enclosure of the Cornell box through a practice of physical flattening and reproduction, the metaphysical depths he brings to the comic page also cut powerfully against the process of "closure" connecting each "box," or frame, to the one that follows in the standard comic. Scott McCloud, in his extremely influential *Understanding Comics*, adopts from Gestalt psychology the principle of closure—"observing the parts but perceiving the whole" (63)—to characterize the work readers do to bridge the gaps between frames in a comic strip, work that he proposes as at some level the very essence of comics.[5] "Comics panels fracture both time and space," McCloud writes, "offering a jagged, staccato rhythm of unconnected moments. But closure allows us to connect these moments and mentally construct a continuous, unified reality" (67). For all its formal complexity, Ware's work generally does commit the reader to this work of narrative suturing and to the resulting production of a coherent "reality."[6] In an interview from 2006, though, he argues that a central "esthetic hurdle" for contemporary comics is "the novelist's problem 150 years ago: namely, to take comics from storytelling into . . . 'writing,' the major distinction between the two . . . being that the former gives one the facts, but the latter tries to recreate the sensation and complexities of life within the fluidity of consciousness and experience" (Bengal). At points in the works I will discuss here, Ware all but dispenses with inciting his readers towards closure, or pushes a much more abstract notion of closure to non-narrative ends. In these instances, echoing his enthusiasm for Guston's disembodied heads, he subordinates the diegetic representation of "the fluidity of consciousness and experience" to actually eliciting that very flux. Rather than engaging the reader fully in sequential progress from one part of the page to the next, Ware solicits instead a process of association and reflection only partially dictated by narrative prompts. Psychological continuities—both within the reader and between the reader and Ware—take precedence over, at the same time as they undergird, more localized narrative ones. Indeed, I suggest calling this a strategy of "overture," on the strength of the etymological opposition with closure, and in our current sense of an approach or gesture toward a relationship with another party.

The vector of narrative is also supplanted, in these instances, by a logic of display, and with it an imagined depth of field, both of which we can trace back to Cornell. Like Ware, Cornell worked in multiple media, ranging from collage to magazine layout to avant-garde film, but he is best known for what we have come to call his "shadow boxes," although they bear only a limited resemblance to the mundane glass-fronted display cabinets for which we generally employ the term. Cornell's handmade wooden boxes house elaborate assemblages of pages from nineteenth-century novels and twentieth-century periodicals, aged prints and astronomical charts, metal rings and coins and clock springs, and all manner of thrift-store finds: goblets and bottles both whole and broken, plastic ice cubes, maps and stamps, corks and clay pipes, seashells and birds' nests and stuffed birds, blocks and jacks and marbles and balls, dolls and other children's toys. The art lies in the combining of these disparate components; Cornell claimed no skill as a draftsman or painter, and critics have agreed with his self-assessment, but they also concur that the finished works bespeak their singularity incessantly, testifying through assemblage alone to the artist's hand. The traces of that hand also help underscore the boxes' idiosyncratic physicality; their depth relative to the picture plane they first present functions metaphorically as well as literally. The layers and recesses and moving parts we can see, and of which we can intuit the operating principles but that we literally cannot grasp, surely contribute to the hushed and awed metaphysical language that Cornell's artwork routinely elicits.

But that language begins with Cornell's own account of his work's personal value. Cornell lived all but his prep school years in his mother's house, spending much of his time and energy caring for a younger brother with cerebral palsy. He worked as a salesman in his twenties and thirties, and as a designer in the following decade, only beginning to sell his pieces for significant sums as he neared the age of fifty, remaining nearly as reclusive in the face of growing recognition as he had been before. His principal form of recreation was trolling the bookstores and second-hand shops of New York City for the materials out of which he made his art, which then frequently served as a substitute for further worldly interactions. The search for materials yielded, when it was most successful, objects that Cornell thought of as carrying with them some of the "lift," "juice," or even "transcendence" of the finest among the fleeing interactions and impressions his peregrinations produced.[7] Combining these bits into artistic wholes was, then, a process of preservation and communication—a protracted ritual in itself (individual pieces, despite their small size, sometimes occupied Cornell intermittently for years), prelude to an extremely fraught system of exchange. Certain boxes were destined for the objects of Cornell's erotic fixations: shopgirls met or glimpsed on his rounds, famous ballerinas, Hollywood figures. He appears to have had almost no actual sexual relations;[8] rather, as Mary Ann Caws writes, "Many of his boxes were made for the starlets and models whose charms he wanted to salute and capture—as if imprisoning them in boxes were his sole way of partaking of the experience he was never to have" (34).[9] More often, though, Cornell gave the boxes to local friends and artists, letting them speak volumes in his stead, and then sometimes requesting the boxes' return when friendship faded. This redefinition of what had been taken to be a gift as, instead, a loan often shocked the recipient asked to return the piece, but it underscores the boxes' function as personal stand-ins communicating

Cornell's presence in the recipients' lives, stand-ins to be called home when that presence had diminished or was no longer desired.

One can hear echoes here of numerous elements of the persona Ware adopts in many interviews, particularly before the arrival of his daughter in 2005: the lonely and sexually maladroit artist intensely devoted to his craft, to superannuated cultural ephemera, and to his birth family.[10] Cornell seems to have lived the life that Ware alternately espouses and fears; their multiple affinities might be seen as explaining Ware's reverence for the older artist in psychological and behavioral terms alone, were one to stumble over the obvious divergences in their artistic practices. But I want to argue instead that these affinities provide the grounds for Ware's canny repurposing of Cornell's model, his harnessing of the intense solitude out of which Cornell fashioned his pieces and the equally intense interpersonal cathexes they gave and continue to give rise to. For Ware, this constitutes an intellectual puzzle as well as an emotional one—or even an intellectual puzzle as an avenue toward solving the emotional one—for which his personal shrine is only the beginning of an answer. In his role as a working artist rather than a private connoisseur, Ware faces the task of translating Cornell's accomplishment—the exquisite distillation of singular experience into gnomic symbol—to the mass-produced medium of comics.

One response to this challenge is formal iteration. In the single-page strips that constitute the bulk of *Quimby the Mouse*, with their frequently recurrent narrative arcs, the guiding spirit is George Herriman's *Krazy Kat*, its punch line essentially repeated daily for thirty years. *Jimmy Corrigan*, on the other hand, works via Joycean expansion and interconnection, an intricate web of references and resonances quietly organizing a sprawling tale. In both cases, repetitions confer legibility by constructing a world with what come to be predictable qualities, however idiosyncratic they might initially seem. But a second response, counter to this elaboration of an intensely personal aesthetic, is to look for broader societal patterns and repetitions in which the self is merely one among countless other participants, and to distill these repetitions in such a fashion as to make them newly recognizable, apprehensible, and at length meaningful, to others. Ware pursues this second strategy by producing a common currency out of the very experience of isolation, an isolation so profound as to seem not only physical or emotional but almost temporal—the experience of feeling passed over by narrative itself. Where Cornell captures moments and respites, Ware explores troughs and sloughs. His model here might be the sad irony of the dinner party that closes the first half of Virginia Woolf's *To the Lighthouse*, in which the repeated mantra is each character's inward fear that he or she alone does not partake of the fellow-feeling uniting the others; all are united, unbeknownst to any of them, in their perceived solitude. Ware's overture highlights the way private experience—even the swamp of despair—is always already shared, autobiographical specifics no more than a distraction from the common human predicament.

The particular grace of his solution arises from its being articulated through comic books, making them not just his medium but also his implicit subject—the ground of experience and the material of psychic drama—and then insisting that this immersion in a world defined by comics is not his alone. Charles Simic memorably refers to Cornell's practice as "dime-store alchemy": the production of singular, talismanic pieces through the transmogrification of the cultural detritus found in the low-rent districts of New York City. Ware brings a related set of techniques to bear in a "comic-store," or more simply "comic-book," alchemy. Here, the variegated world constituted by New York's thrift shops and antiquarian bookstores, its five-and-dimes and perfume counters and cinemas—all the myriad appeals structuring Cornell's rambles through the city and providing the material and psychological terrain for his art—is supplanted by the world found in mainstream comic books: the vaunted narratives of heroism and wish-fulfillment, the heavily gendered expectations, and the hectoring voices massed in the advertisements on the back pages. For Cornell's profoundly idiosyncratic itinerary Ware substitutes an emblematic one, a generic circuit he employs to trump the very binary between self and other.

We can trace the developing conception of this circuit from unique physical constructions obviously reminiscent of Cornell's to the printed comic page, and thus from objects conceived of as private to work destined for the public. At the same time, we will move from Ware's employ of literal comic books to their mere invocation (albeit within a comic book), and from a material record of personal history to abstract reflections on the medium. In the Yale monograph, Raeburn cites Cornell as the inspiration for a traditionally styled shadow box Ware has crafted to house various curios and miniature comics of his own design, and implicitly ties Cornell's example as well to the homemade "ACME Book Dispenser" on the facing page. These and other complex wooden mechanisms pictured on the surrounding pages date from 1988–93, embracing Ware's tenure at the University of Texas and his first years in Chicago: the interval in which he fully took up the mantle of a comic-strip artist, and also the interval in which he aggressively rethought what that mantle might entail and might mean in the wake of his quickly repudiated science fiction satire, *Floyd Farland: Citizen of the Future* (1987). Ware soon dismissed *Farland* as an unthinking pastiche of dystopian fiction and adolescent anti-establishment impulses—"*Blade Runner/1984* stuff from high school"—material that needed simply to be "evacuated" from his "mental bowels" (Groth 126). The discussion that follows will bring us back, at length, to high school, but in the form of Ware's imaginative reconstruction of his younger sensibility and even more imaginative recuperation of its energies. In his post-*Farland* undertakings, Ware rejects the doubled displacement—both temporal (citizen of the future) and figuratively physical (far-land)—in favor of opening up the stakes of the personal, seeking to negotiate between his own history and that of his medium, between the world as he finds it and as he desires it to be, and between the possible isolation of autobiography and the common ground of generational consciousness.

We begin, though, with Ware's shadow box, its variegated contents making reference to the mixture of mass-produced ephemera and labored art pieces, curios and repurposed household objects found in Cornell's boxes, but with the singular and radical difference that all the elements in Ware's box are his own constructions rather than thrift-store finds (fig 5.1). Indeed, all are either miniature comic books (including the one on offer in the Book Dispenser) or related paraphernalia—paper models of his early recurring characters Sparky and Quimby along with accompanying props, zoetrope-like contrivances built to animate cartoon sequences, an even smaller rudimentary shadow box filled with marble-like Sparky heads, and so forth. The striking heterogeneity of the objects sutured together in Cornell's shadow boxes is replaced by a collocation of comics and more comics. We might explain this discrepancy away through an appeal to the differing status of the two men's shadow boxes—Cornell's are his art, Ware's is a mere ancilla—but I want to suggest that another equation lurks within this divergence: that Ware here proposes comics as his essential mental furniture, the building blocks of his world as well as its yield.[11]

The complementary suggestion made by the Book Dispenser is that Ware's readers might be served by and through this model. The dispenser looks like a particularly elegant cross between an armoire, a pinball machine and a guillotine (this last resemblance might be dismissed as accidental if not for the prevalence of decapitations in *Quimby*'s pages), but it delivers a comic book rather than a beheading (fig 5.2).

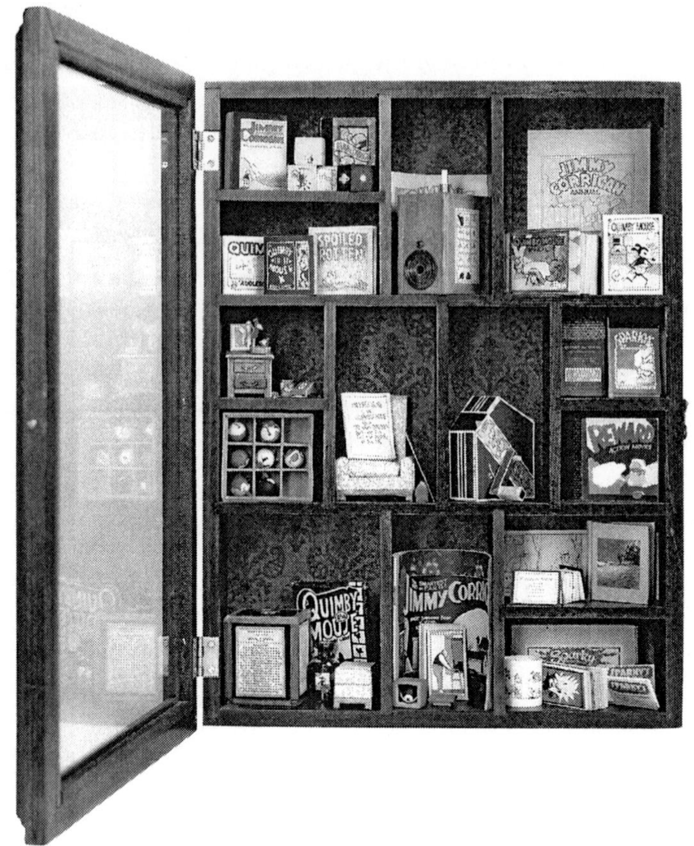

5.1. Daniel Raeburn. *Chris Ware.* p. 50.

"Dropping any house key into the slot in this contraption," Raeburn explains, "produces a miniature 60-page comic book containing the very first version of the Jimmy Corrigan 'island story', unavailable elsewhere" (50). The "island story," as published subsequently in *The ACME Novelty Library* 10, is a narrative of insurmountable isolation: Superman saves Jimmy from a shipwreck but then strands him on a deserted island and violently scuttles rescue attempts; months or years later he returns Jimmy to his mother, but the result is only that Jimmy finds himself trapped alone in his bedroom while his mother cavorts with her lover, consigning Jimmy once again to the emotional alienation with which the story begins. But the Book Dispenser obliquely countermands the story's defeated nihilism through a functionality that oversteps its own forbidding appearance and

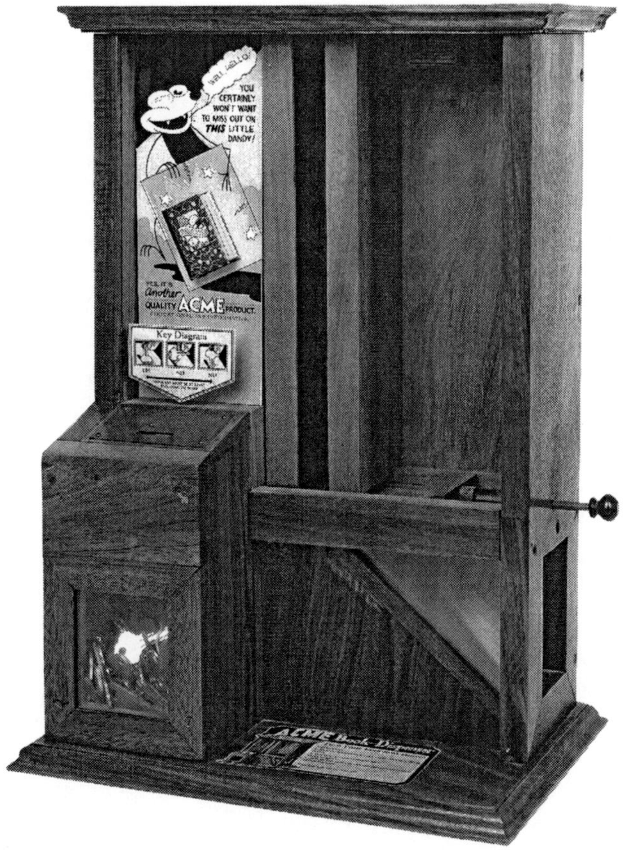

5.2. Daniel Raeburn. *Chris Ware*. p. 51.

that fosters interpersonal connections. Ware's redeployment of a house key opens into rich metaphorical territory: a key stands against Jimmy's solitude and for threshold- or boundary-crossing, at the same time as it connotes the core or essential aspect of an object or situation, the means of control or possession. A house key in particular offers access to the interior of an especially large and enduring externalization the self—or, if not the key to one's own domicile, bespeaks significant intimacy with another. On the other hand, an expendable key—as to a residence one is no longer inclined or permitted to enter—is worth even less than the quarter it operationally replaces here.

Ware seems to have both these valuations in mind, and with them the tenuous status of his art form, when he proposes that appropriate recompense for the sacrifice of a key might be a small Jimmy Corrigan comic book. The suggestion made, with mathematical simplicity, is that a comic might run the same emotional and functional gamut as does a key: that what seems expendable junk in the aggregate or abstract might constitute a personal treasure in the particular. "Turn your keys into stories," crows the label on the machine's base, another alchemical promise that might suffer under pressure—apparently there is only one story on offer here, and it's already been written—or that might open up into a further mode of magical transformation. Just as a key is a mass-produced item that, through minimal tooling in a factory or at the hands of a local locksmith, acquires unique contours and enormous individualized importance, so too might a mass-produced comic book prove unexpectedly hospitable to personal investments not just by its maker but also by its reader.

Ware's suggestions, then, are both that the landscape of the mainstream comics he grew up with might provide an avenue by which to articulate his psychology, and that this articulation might prove sufficiently elastic and hospitable to serve his readers as well. We can trace this pivot through key pages in Ware's early post-*Farland* oeuvre, as they make their way from the *Daily Texan* to the first issues of *The ACME Novelty Library* and then on to *Quimby the Mouse.* I have written elsewhere on the autobiographical narratives more or less deeply submerged in these materials, finally articulated with greatest clarity in *Quimby.*[12] Here, I want to focus instead on non-narrative moments, on sites of display and the internal thought processes they both reflect and provoke. I'll do so by reference to the pages as they appear in *Quimby*, but with consideration of the change and supplementation they undergo on their way there, emendation that I think reveals much regarding Ware's developing sense of his chosen métier and its potentials.

The shadow box surfaces explicitly one more time. Midway through the run of Quimby cartoons that make up the first half of *Quimby the Mouse*, Ware begins experimenting with increasingly baroque and ostentatious frames for his strips, highlighting his mastery of page-layout and accentuating his work's amenability to display alongside its facility with narrative. In one of these strips, the panels are actually bounded by the representation of two tall columns of shadow-box shelving, filled with a mixture of household scrap (a paperclip, a coin, a bit of string), bits of nature such as a child might collect (a leaf, an acorn, two snail shells), and items that might be more personally fraught (a tooth, a key, a ring) (fig 5.3). Meanwhile, at the strip's heart stands a single image of Quimby, drawn as

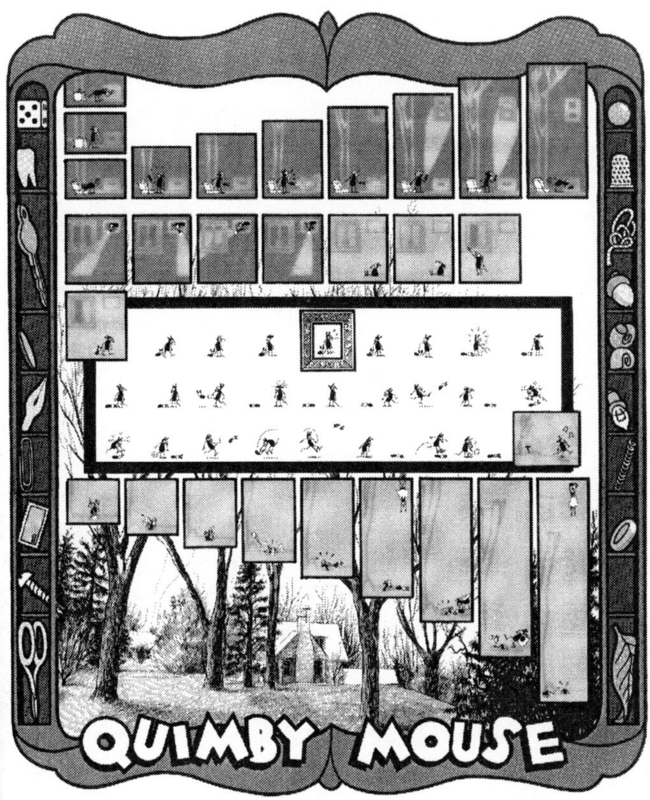

5.3. Chris Ware. *Quimby the Mouse*. p. 19.

if in an actual ornate, three-dimensional carved wooden frame (19). The interplay between these two aesthetic registers, the homely and the high, nods to Cornell (as do several of the items nested in the shelves), while the specifics of the representation speak to the use Ware makes of this artistic legacy. The comic's story again turns repeatedly on questions of accessible and inaccessible spaces, property and confinement, alienation and belonging, and concludes quite negatively: Quimby's head is kicked from his trunk by a caped superhero mouse. But the story's momentum is counterbalanced by the quiet company of its borders, the shadow box's compartments like two ranks of panels that refuse to participate in the nearby depravity. And, as with the Book Dispenser, the image of violent bodily dis-integration is countered by a detail opposite in the shadow box, where a screw displayed in one of its compartments breaks through the box's inner wall and into the space of the strip, even as the position of the screw's head (flush against the opposite wall of its compartment) and the shading of its thread (darker on the top side, suggesting that the head leans into the box rather than out of it and into the light) make it difficult to imagine how the screw might have achieved its current placement. The apparent physical impossibility of this construction speaks to metaphysical possibility, to what may be accomplished through two-dimensional depiction and reproduction as opposed to that which singular objects do. The artistic liberties Ware takes in this representation presage the emotional ones to follow, and both oppose the thematics of constraint in the strip that the shadow box—only literally—bounds.

Delivering on this promise requires Ware to shift the axis of approach to comics, though, moving not just as an author but also as a reader from a "storytelling" perspective to a "writing" one, digging from manifest content to the deeper psychological terrain that both grounds that content and at length is susceptible to being structured by it. Bodying forth that terrain, rather than suggesting it elliptically, means supplementing the inheritance from Cornell, and its mystical hold on individual consciousness, with a more expansive and explicit account of contemplation, albeit still one predicated on a remove from immediate experience. For this, Ware turns to the novelistic tradition in the wake of its mid-nineteenth-century representational impasse. He takes up Henry James, in particular the famous Chapter Forty-Two of *The Portrait of a Lady* in which Isabel Archer sits alone in her drawing room "far into the night and still further, . . . haunted with terrors" (354–55) at the course her life has taken—the uses to which she has put her finances, the cruel marriage she has entered into and the manipulation of her fortunes by malevolent parties, the impostures she has unwittingly demanded of her friends—in the "extraordinary meditative vigil" that James called "obviously the best thing in the book" (14–15). Ware's storytelling/writing binary is anticipated in James's proud attempt to capture "all the vivacity of incident" in "a representation simply of [Isabel] motionlessly *seeing* . . . without her being approached by another person and without her leaving her chair" (14–15, emphasis James's). Ware's work in *Jimmy Corrigan* and since is dotted with incident-less passages of mental perception and association, and indeed he appears to reference Chapter Forty-Two in the "General Instructions" on comics-reading in the novel's endpapers, recalling to his reader the experience in which one has "simply sat, unclothed, in an easy chair in one's living room in the middle of the night, and, quite unsuspectingly, been seized by the horrible, gnawing sense of all that has led up to this one point in their life, the hopefulness of their childhood, the friends lost, the trysts unrealized, the hearts broken." But his closest approach to Isabel's protracted "vigil of searching criticism" (James 14)—in which the play of her emotional investments and her illusions, the long-term repercussions of her decisions and indeed of her very character, all suddenly become painfully clear—may well be on a single page in *Quimby*.

The book opens with a dense, extended autobiographical essay, elaborating on the conditions in which the comics that make up the volume were first created and implicitly providing interpretive keys elucidating the hidden personal stakes to the book's predominantly surreal episodes. The essay fills the book's first page, recto and verso, and then spills over in a small way onto two more, including something less than a column inch in the lower-right corner of a page of faux advertisements two-thirds of the way through (fig. 5.4), before squeezing into the white space of a cutout Quimby and Sparky diorama at the close (42, 68). The choice to carry the essay onto these later pages is not forced—room could easily have been made at the start by eliminating one or two images—and the choice to make the middle stop of the itinerary page forty-two seems to me not just equally contingent, but pointedly willful. Reading the page number as an allusion to James's chapter number clarifies how Ware interweaves the stakes of autobiography and advertisement, how the collagist impulse (still a ghostly presence in the aggregation of the ads) opens up to provoke a more pointed mode of reflection. This welter of ads of Ware's own design emerges with the strips' migration from newsprint to bound form, first in the *ACME* volumes and then here in *Quimby*, where the ads offer an account of Ware's thinking about the greater circulation and endurance thereby conferred on his work, and by extension his thinking about the comic-book medium.

The ads read most obviously under the sign of parody. They reproduce in yet more glaring form the noisy onslaught of their avatars in the back pages of mainstream comic books, substituting for the real advertisements' gee-whiz promises a more caustic knowingness. Ware's ads rely on a particularly queasy mix of insinuating questions and daunting imperatives in their banner headlines, and draw on the same knot of adolescent male desires and anxieties that gives rise to X-Ray Specs, switchblade combs, and come-ons from Charles Atlas, only to promise not so much that the products they offer will assuage the trials of puberty as that these difficulties will prove to be intractable, ineradicable. Thus, for example, "The De-Luxe Library of Mistakes" in the top-left corner provides a "complete

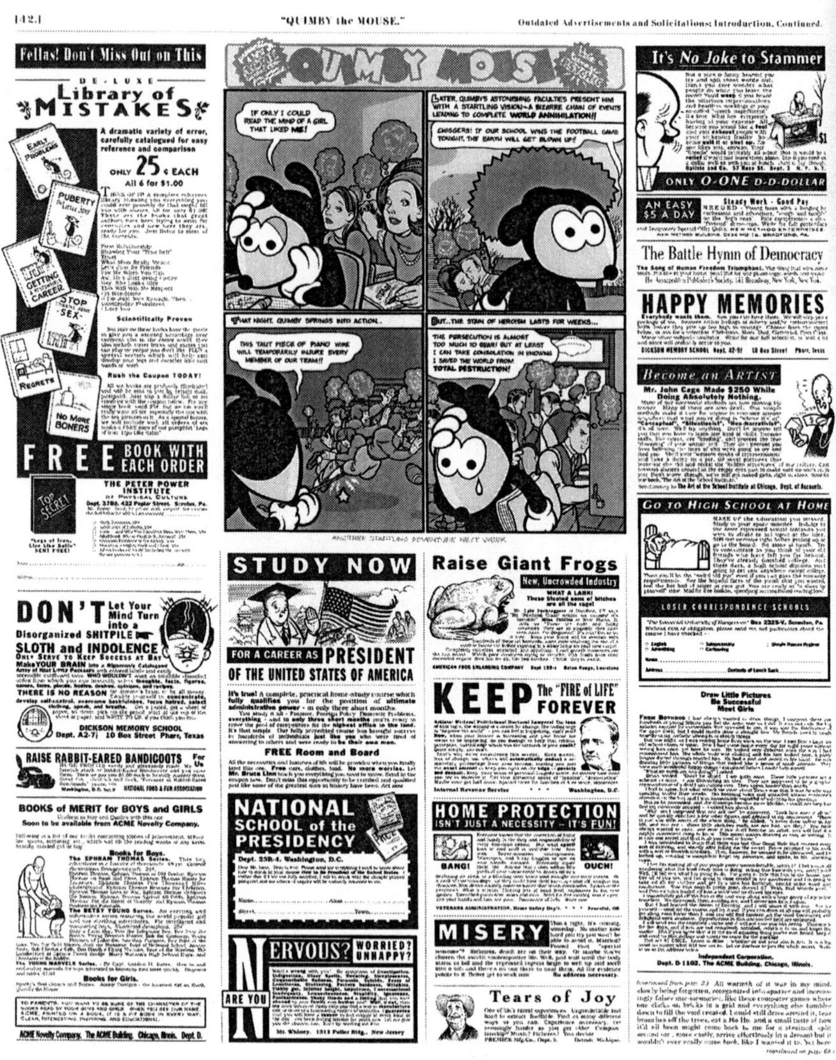

5.4. Chris Ware. *Quimby the Mouse.* p. 42.

reference library showing you everything you could ever possibly do that might fill you with shame" from the onset of sexual awareness to the grave, its varied titles offset by reiterative cover illustrations suggesting that the continuing underlying issue is unwanted erections. Likewise, in the opposite corner, a headline promising the enticing sequence "Draw Little Pictures / Be Successful / Meet Girls"[13] devolves into a description of the accomplished cartoonist as a "loud crazy man" who trumpets on the city bus his intention to head home and "smoke some weed and masturbate" in the tub.

But Ware's parody does not content itself with producing a mocking critical distance from the gullible lad he may once have been. Instead, the skepticism that every reader learns as a mode of self-protection over the course of sustained exposure to comic-book ads—"that can't really work," "it won't actually look like that," "I'm sure it's not that easy"—here is turned against that protected self and veers into a more corrosive cynicism, such that the solidity and satisfactions of adult life are construed as so much veneer that can be peeled away, revealing the old fears and insecurities still very much in play. The Internal Revenue Service, for example, observes in a pitch to the successful white-collar professional that increased income and improved home life are likely to produce a loss of "that critical, perceptive, hateful edge which was the earmark of . . . youth" and a resultant "waning of the desire for change." The organization therefore offers its assistance in depleting one's coffers so as to place one continuously "right on the edge of poverty and despair," one's "sense of personal tragedy acute" and undiminished. A nearby ad segues quickly from an opening invocation of signature bodily anxieties of male middle age ("Pattern baldness, Wrinkles, Flabby gut, Inferior Height, Impotence") to behaviors perhaps equally representative of teenagers ("Conversational inadequacy, Loquaciousness, Stupidity, Ignorance, Foolhardiness, Shaky Hands"), finally suturing the two via the "feeling that you were abused by your family," (all references from ads, *Quimby*, 42).

There are enough specifics sprinkled through the page to reinforce the sense that the group as a whole reflects Ware's personal experience and sensibility: the boy being offered a "Book of Merit" by a benevolent superhero figure in one ad appears to be a young Jimmy Corrigan, and the National School of the Presidency candidate being sworn into office in another bears a distinct resemblance to the men of the Corrigan line;[14] the language and imagery in the pitch for Dickson Memory School, depicting the brain as "an infallible, classified index" with "colored labels and easily accessible cardboard tabs," anticipates Ware's characterization of his own "mental file drawers" in the autobiographical essay's conclusion (68), while the con artists hawking "Conceptual," "Situationist," and "Neo-Narrativist" aesthetic strategies (as substitutes for "skills," "talent," and "western myths of representation") at "The Art of the School Institute at Chicago" clearly invoke Ware's experience at—and resistance to—the School of the Art

Institute of Chicago, mentioned in the introduction's first page (1). Too, the four brightly colored blocks of the Quimby strip at the top of the page, positioned as if they had just fallen into the black-and-white world of the double-page spread, seem like concrete instantiations of Ware's description (in the snippet of his essay in the page's bottom-right corner) of his brain's contents as "like those computer games where one clicks on bricks in a grid and everything else tumbles down to fill the void created."[15] But the overall force of the page, as with the real advertisements it mimics, is to generalize its claims through the interaction of numerous capacious abstractions with enough sticky particulars to encourage specific points of identification. Ware plays this game at a microcosmic level as well, making the strategy all but explicit through minor grammatical parapraxes. The "Draw Little Pictures" ad, the last on the page, contains multiple apparent typographical errors, dropping the letter "i" in two words in its final sentences, and substituting "you" for "who" near its start, at the same moment as it first asserts a similarity between its speaker and its readers: "I suppose there are hundreds of young fellows you feel the same way as I did."

It will not have escaped the reader's notice, though, here and throughout the page, that this is a universal tilted heavily toward the masculine—reflecting the assumption (or the cliché) that comic-readers are themselves an almost uniformly male population. Ware invokes this stereotype elsewhere, too, most famously in the multiple-choice quiz in the endpapers of *Jimmy Corrigan*. The exam begins by asking whether the test-taker is male or female, and instructs those who answer the latter to ignore the remainder of the test. The presumption, based on the questions that follow, appears to be that females will have no connection with the emotional quandaries and ineptitudes the novel explores, or will be so alienated from its medium as to find the whole unintelligible. But Ware complicates this premise in *Quimby*. The "Books of Merit" ad in the bottom-left corner of page 42 proposes that boys take up various tales of adventure and sexual conquest, while girls are directed towards nothing but Ware's own work: *Jimmy Corrigan, Quimby,* and *Sparky's Best Comics and Stories.* In light of the metric of heterosexual accomplishment in many of the individual ads on the page, this segregation would seem to denigrate Ware's work, presenting him as incapable of producing a comic book that would appeal to the medium's own natural constituency. Such a reading would be consistent with Jimmy Corrigan's fate in the one comic strip on the page as it appeared in *The ACME Novelty Library* 2 in 1994 (fig. 5.5). In the central panel, "Superman" throws open the door to Jimmy's apartment, calls him

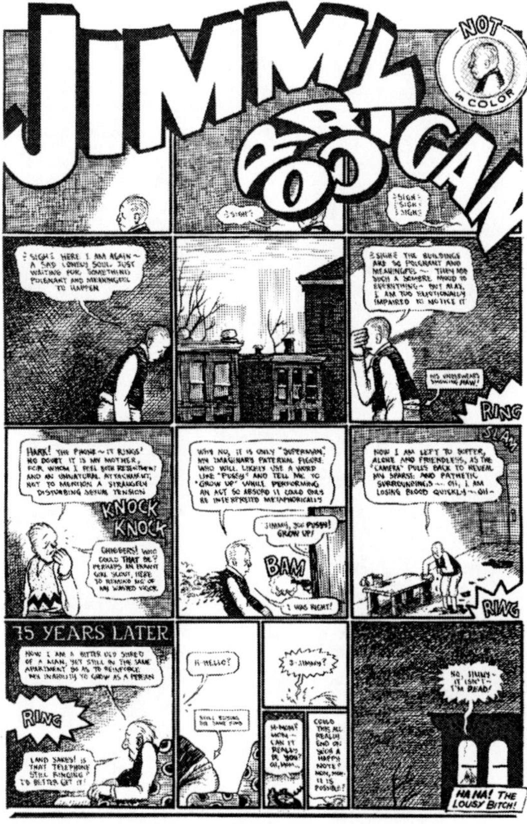

5.5. Chris Ware. *The ACME Novelty Library* 2. p. 24.

a "pussy" and tells him to "grow up," and then shoots Jimmy in the chest in what Jimmy recognizes as "an act so absurd it could only be interpreted metaphorically" (24). The quintessential representative of traditional comics, and of a hyperbolically heroic masculinity, thus both verbally and figuratively asserts his potency and derides Jimmy's at the same time, leaving Jimmy still crying for his mother "75 years later" in the final panels. Irrespective of its satirical gloss, this narrative affirms traditional gender norms and measures Jimmy's failure to live up to them in wholly negative terms.

In the reissue of this material as *Quimby the Mouse* in 2003, Ware removes this strip. The four-panel comic that takes its place presents us with a Quimby who is at once both superhero and alienated nerd (fig. 5.6). Possessed of "astonishing faculties" of clairvoyance and prophecy hitherto unmentioned, this Quimby teeters between male and

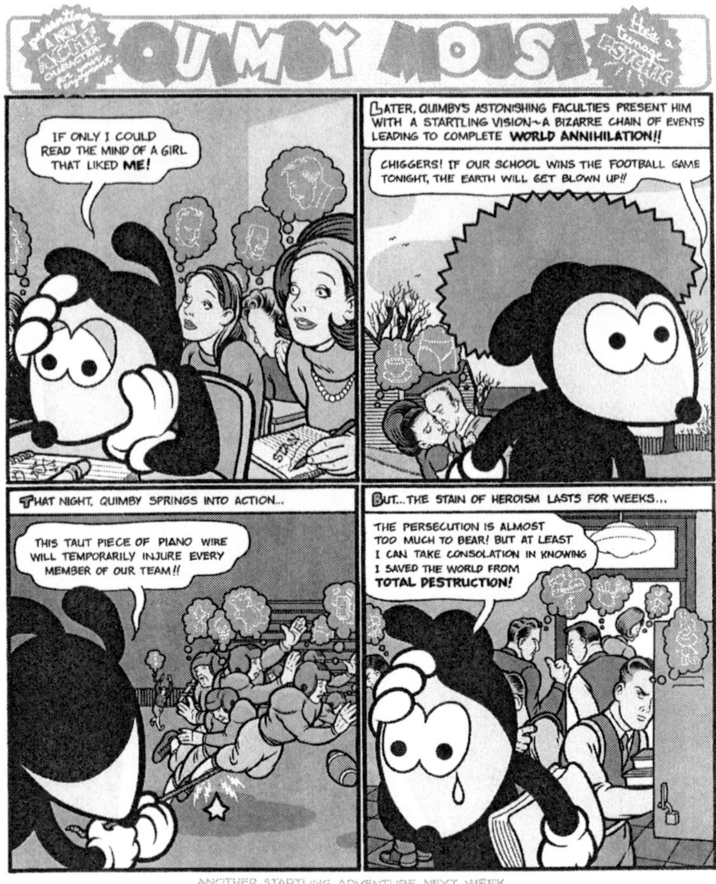

5.6. Chris Ware. *Quimby the Mouse*. p. 42. (detail)

female identifications. He begins the strip dejectedly reading the minds of the girls in his high school class, wishing that one of them might be thinking warmly about him but finding instead that each is caught up in dreamy reverie of one or another clean-cut hunk. But in the second frame, Quimby has "a startling vision" in which he learns that if the school wins that evening's football game, "the earth will get blown up!!" Quimby averts this disaster by stringing a taut piano wire across the playing field, "temporarily injur[ing] every member of [the] team." But, as his motives remain secret, he receives only opprobrium and disdain—the particulars of which he can't help but read in the minds of his classmates—for his pains. There may be a passing moment of comic-geek wish-fulfillment here, in which the spindly introvert not only saves the world but also simultaneously trips up the school's entire football team, but Quimby can take no lasting pleasure in the accomplishment precisely because his thoughts remain wholly opaque to his peers. No one suspects the selfless rationale for his actions; many of his classmates imagine cutting his head off or blowing it up, and one mentally replaces it with a steaming pile of shit. Thus, while Quimby is ambiguously gifted with immediate access to the thoughts of his peers, those very thoughts are violently dismissive of any gesture of reciprocity. Rather than inquire into what might have been going on in Quimby's mind at the game, his schoolmates would rather deny him a mind (indeed, a head) entirely.

One girl participates in these fantasies of dismemberment, but the overall force of the strip is to code them as masculine, in contradistinction to a feminine "dreaminess" that Quimby pointedly shares in the first and last panels. The consistency of his posture and of the layout helps the intervenient world-saving action effectively to drop away, subordinated to what thus appears to be an ongoing "meditative vigil" absorbing Quimby equally before the strip begins and after it ends. The cant and orientation of his body in these outer panels mirror those of the girls in the opening frame, and both he and the girl to his left doodle in their notebooks—she writing the name of her inamorato, he apparently anticipating his classmates' thoughts later in the strip. At the same time, the first panel anticipates the strip itself, and the whole of the book: the parallel compositions and color schemes of the first and fourth frames suggest that the very "furniture" of Quimby's reflection at the start, his bright orange chair, is transmuted to the similarly positioned and likewise gently convex bright yellow book at the close. Into this metaphorical book disappear, then, both the doodles from the start: the beheaded Quimby and the dreamy "Stan"—distillations of the "male" genre of action and the "female" one of romance, respectively, and more abstractly simple distillations of self and other.

This synthesis allows for a different response to the assertion—or even the aspiration—that Ware's comics might appeal to a female audience, a response that confers a positive valuation on Ware's exceptional status vis-à-vis the segregation that the page suggests is a hallmark of the comics medium. By this light, Ware's self-inscription in the Jamesian tradition highlights the possibilities for crossing gender boundaries both at the level of form (as with James's effort to remake the novel as a high art; Ware of course would be reversing this trajectory, making comics safe for a female audience instead of masculinizing the novel) and at that of character

(James's ability to inhabit and bring forth a female consciousness so fully, a challenge Ware sets himself subsequently in *Building Stories*). As with the shadow box and the Book Dispenser, the stakes are played out in the disjunction between the comic and that which surrounds it; once again, the comic portrays isolation while the frame belies it, belies in some sense the very notion of a frame. For the failure in this comic lies in the unidirectional nature of its represented mode of intersubjectivity; Quimby shares everyone else's thoughts, but no one shares his. Except, of course, for the reader of the strip, who is privy to Quimby's ongoing monologue explaining his actions, as well as to snippets of third-person narration and to the images Quimby sees in the minds all around him. What the reader does not see, however, is the contents of Quimby's own thoughts before they have been translated into his monologue—the premonition of Doomsday, for example, is simply represented as a jagged-edged, hot-pink penumbra encircling his head—and nor, obviously, does Quimby have access to the reader's mental landscape. If this brief comic constitutes—through what it does not deliver as well as through what it does—an exhortation and a step or two towards intersubjective reciprocity, the false advertisements filling the rest of the page are dedicated to a fuller realization of this goal. The drama of consciousness comes to the fore here, as narrative gives way to anticipation and reflection, and the clear inflection of emotion through a fictional character is replaced by the foggier atmospherics of second-person address—the "you" constructed by the advertisements serving both to limn Ware's psyche and to hail and prod the reader into a complementary self-recognition.[16]

Quimby's drawing of himself signals the importance of the autobiographical for Ware's endeavor, at the same time it winkingly underscores the autobiographical nature of Quimby comics themselves. But its layers of indirection are crucial. Autobiography is clearly an ambivalent prospect for Ware. A great deal of his work—especially that from the 1990s—has obvious autobiographical origins, a fact he has increasingly acknowledged in the years since. But there are also manifold differentiations between material explicitly treating his own life—for example, the daily comic diary he keeps, which he tends to recapitulate in both style and layout in straightforwardly autobiographical venues such as the introduction to the *ACME Datebooks*—and the more ambiguously refracted pieces that make up the bulk of his published output. Personal details routinely impinge on the latter, but it remains a far cry from the transparently autobiographical narratives constituting a large portion of the independent comics scene today. Ware has been faulted for prioritizing this latter work, with its commitment to the mundane and the mimetic, in his selections as editor/curator for *The Best American Comics 2007* and *McSweeney's*.[17] His more idiosyncratic undertaking in *Quimby's* fine print cannot fully answer this critique, but it does suggest how capacious his own sense of the autobiographical might be. He construes the mode here as prognostic as well as retrospective, abstract as well as particular, communal as well as individual: an avenue for reaching out as much as for burrowing in. Perhaps yet more radically, he produces autobiography as an ideational cluster, a collage, that only sometimes or obliquely yields a discernible narrative. The substitution of the Quimby strip on page 42 for the earlier Jimmy Corrigan one, for example, functions primarily to illustrate how significantly a new juxtaposition can redefine old material, recasting the imputation that Ware's oeuvre is "books for girls" from self-denigration to unheralded potential.

Only secondarily, with an archivist's eye, can we read the shift from the page as constituted in *The ACME Novelty Library* 2 to its construction in *Quimby* as implicitly recounting a profound shift in Ware's thinking and his self-conception, tracking his emergence from a ghetto of wonky testosterone into more mainstream precincts and legitimized high-art aspirations. This interpretive possibility suggests, though, how much we might be able to read out of the decisions Ware makes as he collates work first published piecemeal in myriad venues into the more-or-less annual installments of *The ACME Novelty Library*, and then repositions some portion of it again in the even more infrequent stand-alone volumes like *Jimmy Corrigan*, *Building Stories*, and *Rusty Brown*. If these books are most eagerly awaited for what they promise in what Ware calls the "storytelling" mode—offering a coherent presentation of the narrative "facts" over a continuous or at least an apprehensible chronological arc—we may yet also look to them as a deeply layered form of "writing" relating "the fluidity of consciousness and experience" not just in Ware's characters' minds, but also in his own. Cornell, as I noted early on, often held onto pieces for years, slowly refashioning them according to his whims or needs, bestowing them on others and then sometimes repossessing them when he saw fit. For all the nuance of the making, then, the significance of which largely remained cloaked in Cornell's gnomic private vocabulary, the life of the pieces outside Cornell's hands reduced itself at one level to a simple binary of presence or absence. Ware's method of publication and republication, with the fresh juxtapositions and recontextualizations it affords, allows him to keep a finger on his mass-produced artwork even after he has launched it into the world to circulate in fashions over which he otherwise has no control, allows him to gloss and re-gloss it at will. The overture thus continually restructured and renewed, Ware's presence in the work is repeatedly redefined, and with it the reader's as well.

Notes

1. See, for example, http://www.biographicon.com/view/b8qp0.

2. At one point, this language appeared on Ware's own (unauthorized) Facebook page; at the time of this writing it remains on the Wikipedia page dedicated to Ware. A more stable site might be: http://www.enotes.com/topic/Chris_Ware.

As I revised this piece, a blog posting by Kirstie Gregory appeared, exploring consonances between Ware's work and that of several sculptors, beginning with Cornell. She observes "both formal and thematic connections" between the two artists, including "a notable drive for experimentation, as well as a marked interest and influence back and forth between popular culture and fine art, the junk shop and the art object, the toy shop and the vitrine." She goes on to cite Carter Ratliff's suggestion that "each of Cornell's works is joined by its image-chains to other works," and reads what Ratcliff calls Cornell's "obsessive desire for series" as tying him more generally to comics and sequential art. Gregory's first set of connections seems exactly right to me, but (as will become clear) I take any serial links between Cornell's sculptures to be much less important for Ware's purposes than the captivating gravity of each individual piece.

3. Guston's bodiless heads would seem to be an important but generally unacknowledged intertext for Ware's early, somewhat phantasmagorical comics, before his adoption of the more mimetic (if streamlined) style for which he has become best known. We might cite the "Potato Guy," whose shape echoes that of Guston's heads and also Ware's vocabulary describing them; Quimby the Mouse, whose head is frequently severed from his body by various individuals and machines; and Sparky the Cat, never more than a disembodied head, often one posed face-down on the floor in the posture adopted by the head in the first Guston painting reproduced in Ware's article (86–87). (These strips are collected in *The ACME Novelty Library* 2–4, and, in Quimby and Sparky's case, in *Quimby the Mouse*.)

4. Here I am keying off a further statement in Ware's elucidation of Guston's significance, in which Ware argues that Guston's "cartoony" style "straddles" the "fundamental difference between comic strips and painting (or, for that matter, practically all visual art)"—that "comics are made to be read, and paintings are made to be seen" (87).

5. "If visual iconography is the vocabulary of comics, closure is its grammar. And since our definition of comics hinges on the arrangement of elements—then, in a very real sense, comics is closure!" (67).

6. See, however, Bredehoft and Cates for earlier discussions of non-narrative elements in Ware's fiction.

7. See Vine 39 for this specific language, and more broadly for his take on the religious implications Cornell, a devoted Christian Scientist, built into his work.

8. Or at least none until very late in life; see Solomon 293–94 and 355–56, and Roche.

9. Also see Tashjian.

10. The three most thorough and enlightening are probably Gary Groth's in the *Comics Journal*, Ware's lengthy on-stage colloquy with Ira Glass (Bridwell-Bowles), and the many statements and confidences woven into Raeburn's issue of *The Imp* devoted to Ware.

11. Jennifer Gonzalez recommends considering shadowboxes, home altars, and the like as "autotopographies"—"a syntagmatic array of physical signs in a spatial representation of identity" (133)—a suggestion I find quite congenial. Again, what is striking in Ware's case is just how autotelic this landscape is.

12. See my "Autobiography with Two Heads."

13. An equation only very rarely drawn by actual Art Instruction, Inc. ads, e.g. http://wheezersociety.blogs.com/wheezer/2006/07/index.html.

14. Ware is relatively frank regarding the autobiographical elements of *Jimmy Corrigan*'s plot, both in the paratext to the book itself and in subsequent interviews. See, for example, his colloquy with Ira Glass (Bridwell-Bowles), in the course of which the moderator asks, "How do you deal with the inevitable conclusion that Jimmy Corrigan is really you?" and Ware responds, "Well, it's fair enough, I guess, I mean. Um, I mean, I guess it was more me when I was a bit younger, or something like that. I mean, I met my real dad, and um . . . I don't know, I guess, I mean, it's a fair enough accusation, or something like that. I hope I'm not that weird looking, but I guess I sort of am" (62).

15. The game referenced would seem to be GameHouse's *Collapse!* See, for example, http://www.shockwave.com/gamelanding/collapse.jsp.

16. That this intersubjective potential rises in tandem with a loosely autobiographical appeal to female readership is perhaps no accident. Jared Gardner's *Projections* reads the trailblazing 1972 *Wimmen's Comix* anthology as foundational in the importance it accords to "collective identities . . . forged through personal autobiography" (126). Group identity in this case was a gendered reaction against the "almost inevitably white, male, and straight" protagonists in the LSD comix of the years just previous, but Gardner sees multiple vectors of identification as the broader stake in the anthology's dedication to comics autobiography: an "emerging form . . . that would profoundly influence the next generation of comics" (126). Ultimately he defines the very medium through "its invitation to the reader to project herself into the narrative and to project the narrative beyond the page" (193). Ware's particular contribution, as I have been arguing, is to expand or even explode our sense of what comics narrative might mean, and thus also to extend the possibilities for projection and more abstract forms of "contemplation" beyond the momentary pauses "between the panels" that Gardner too sees as the complement to comics' more obvious demands for closure (154).

17. See Worden and Singer.

Works Cited

Bengal, Rebecca. "On Cartooning." Interview with Chris Ware. *P.O.V.* PBS, 2006. Web. 15 July 2011.

Bredehoft, Thomas A. "Comics Architecture, Multidimensionality, and Time: Chris Ware's *Jimmy Corrigan: The Smartest Kid on Earth.*" *Modern Fiction Studies* 52 (2006): 869–90. Print.

Bridwell-Bowles, Lillian, ed. "Glass/Ware: New Media for Writing American Lives." *Speaker Series* (The Center for Interdisciplinary Studies of Writing, University of Minnesota) 20 (2002). Print.

Cates, Isaac. "Comics and the Grammar of Diagrams." *The Comics of Chris Ware: Drawing Is a Way of Thinking.* Eds. David M. Ball and Martha B. Kuhlman. Jackson: UP of Mississippi, 2010. Print.

Caws, Mary Ann, ed. *Joseph Cornell's Theater of the Mind: Selected Diaries, Letters, and Files.* New York: Thames & Hudson, 1993. Print.

Gardner, Jared. *Projections: Comics and the History of Twenty-First-Century Storytelling.* Stanford: Stanford UP, 2012. Print.

Gonzalez, Jennifer. "Autotopographies." *Prosthetic Territories: Politics and Hypertechnologies.* Eds. Gabriel Brahm, Jr. and Marc Driscoll. Boulder, CO: Westview Press, 1995. Print.

Gregory, Kirstie. "Sculpture and Comic Art #2: Chris Ware: Cabinets, Cardboard and Joseph Cornell." *Comics Forum.* Thought Bubble, 28 June 2011. Web. 15 July 2011.

Groth, Gary. "Understanding (Chris Ware's) Comics." Interview with Chris Ware. *Comics Journal* 200 (1997): 118–71. Print.

James, Henry. *The Portrait of a Lady.* Ed. Robert D. Bamberg. 2nd Ed. New York: W.W. Norton, 1975. Print.

McCloud, Scott. *Understanding Comics.* New York: Harper Collins, 1994. Print.

Raeburn, Daniel. *Chris Ware.* New Haven: Yale UP, 2004. Print.

———. "The Smartest Cartoonist on Earth." *The Imp* 3 (1999): 1–19. Print.

Roche, Joanna. "Performing Memory in *Moon in a Tree*: Carolee Schneemann Recollects Joseph Cornell." *Art Journal* 60 (2001): 6–15. Print.

Simic, Charles. *Dime-Store Alchemy: The Art of Joseph Cornell.* Hopewell, NJ: Ecco, 1992. Print.

Singer, Marc. "The Limits of Realism: Alternative Comics and Middlebrow Aesthetics in the Anthologies of Chris Ware." *The Comics of Chris Ware: Drawing Is a Way of Thinking.* Eds. David M. Ball and Martha B. Kuhlman. Jackson: UP of Mississippi, 2010. Print.

Solomon, Deborah. *Utopia Parkway: The Life and Work of Joseph Cornell.* New York: Farrar, Straus and Giroux, 1997. Print.

Tashjian, Dickran. *Joseph Cornell: Gifts of Desire.* Miami Beach: Grassfield Press, 1992. Print.

Vine, Richard. "Eterniday: 'Metaphysique.'" *Joseph Cornell: Shadowplay Eterniday*. Ed. Robert Lehrman. NY: Thames & Hudson, 2003. Print.

Ware, Chris. *The ACME Novelty Datebook*. Montreal: Drawn & Quarterly, 2003. Print.

———. *The ACME Novelty Datebook, Volume Two*. Montreal: Drawn & Quarterly, 2007. Print.

———. *The ACME Novelty Library 2*. Seattle: Fantagraphics, 1994. Print.

———. *The ACME Novelty Library 10*. Seattle: Fantagraphics, 1998. Print.

———. *The ACME Novelty Library Final Report to Shareholders and Rainy Day Saturday Afternoon Fun Book*. New York: Pantheon, 2005. Print.

———. *Floyd Farland: Citizen of the Future*. Forestville, CA: Eclipse, 1987. Print.

———. *Jimmy Corrigan: The Smartest Kid on Earth*. New York: Pantheon, 2000. Print.

———. "Philip Guston: A Cartoonist's Appreciation." *McSweeney's Quarterly Concern* 13 (2004): 85–91. Print.

———. *Quimby the Mouse*. Seattle: Fantagraphics, 2003. Print.

Widiss, Benjamin. "Autobiography with Two Heads: *Quimby the Mouse*." *The Comics of Chris Ware: Drawing Is a Way of Thinking*. Eds. David M. Ball and Martha B. Kuhlman. Jackson: UP of Mississippi, 2010. Print.

Worden, Daniel. "The Shameful Art: *McSweeney's Quarterly Concern*, Comics, and the Politics of Affect." *Modern Fiction Studies* 52 (2006): 891–917. Print.

Yukiko's Spinach and the *Nouvelle Manga* Aesthetic

—Christopher Bush

First scene: a cinematic sequence of "shots," twenty-one narrow vertical panels spaced evenly over seven pages, fading in from black and out to white. Amid the play of electric lights blazing in the dark, fragments of numbers and letters appear, lit and neon signs giving just enough information to indicate the setting: Tokyo, Shibuya district. The images are accompanied by what it is tempting to call a voiceover, five phrases spaced evenly across the five central pages of the scene, separated by ellipses: "Damn you're pretty to look at . . . Your neck . . . Your shoulders . . . Your stomach . . . Your spinach . . ." (8–12).[1]

The second scene is not quite a scene, unless it is a scene of writing: a single page from a French-Japanese date book, presented as a bit of *realia*, a document of an encounter. The page is dated Saturday, April 8 (hence 2000). Atop the page is written the location and time of an evening event: an exhibition on the French New Wave, Bunkamura, 6:00 p.m. The remainder of the page is filled with notes about and sketches of people at the exhibition. These include a series of hands and, in the bottom right corner, a more finished drawing (with an ink wash) of a young Japanese woman smiling warmly. To the right her name is written in Japanese: Yukiko. And to the left a note in French: "Met Yukiko *Hashimoto*. She *smiled* at me!! Gave her telephone number to me, and to Horiguchi, who gave us a ride in his car." A love triangle, then, one that will not end well for the narrator, a conclusion already hinted at by a two-character phrase that appears discreetly next to the word "Saturday" in the Japanese date: ?? *shyakkō*, an unpropitious day on which no new ventures should be undertaken.

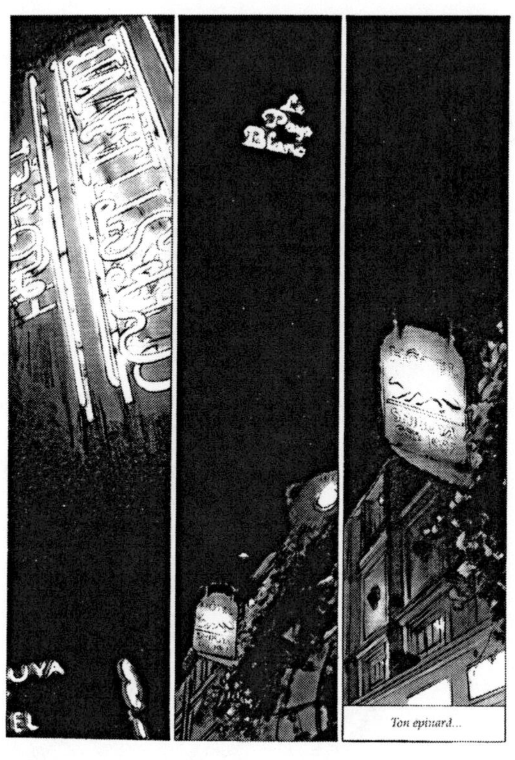
Le Pays Blanc
Ton epinard...

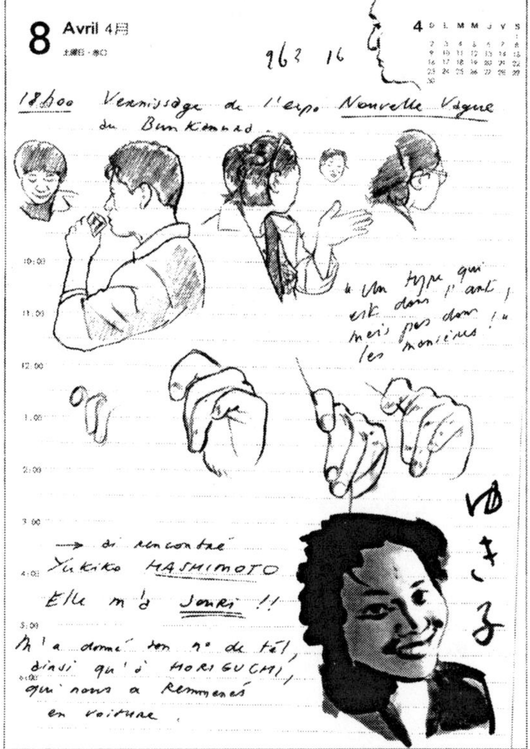

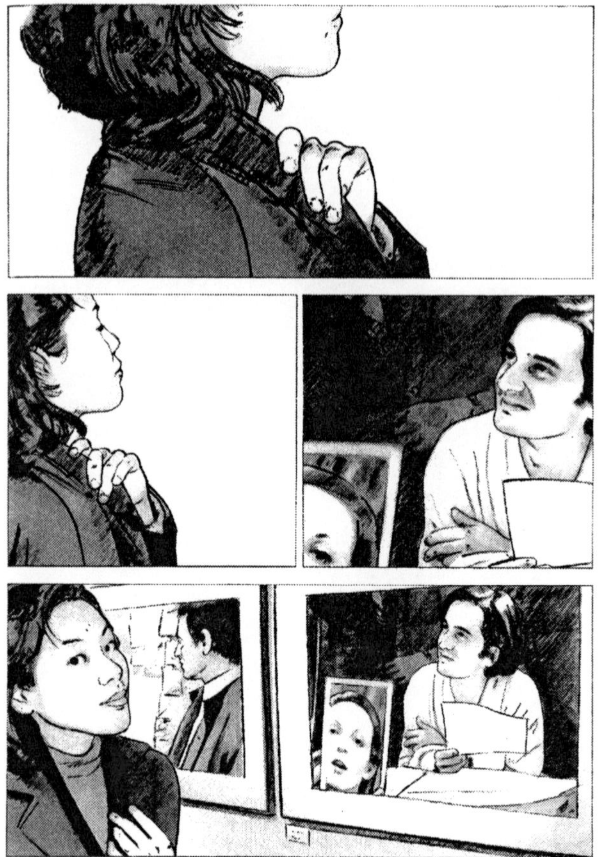

Third scene, also a single page: a crisscrossing of gazes and media. In the first of the four panels we see a close-up of Yukiko's hand (the hand from the date book sketches) resting on the lapel of a raincoat. In the second a slightly wider angle reveals the side of her face as she looks to the right, out of the panel. Next we see a European man (perhaps he seems familiar?), smiling as he looks leftward out of his panel, up at Yukiko (or so the eyeline match would suggest). In the lower-left corner of this panel we see the corner of a photograph, revealing a European woman's eye. The man is looking up from a piece of paper he is holding. Another photograph? In the fourth and final panel, a wider angle still: the man is looking out from a photograph hung on the gallery wall. It is Jean-Pierre Léaud, the most iconic actor of the French New Wave, and the woman whose eye we saw in the previous panel is actress Claude Jade, best known for her role as Léaud's wife, Christine, in three of François Truffaut's Antoine Doinel films. An adjacent photo on the wall shows actor Charles Denner in Truffaut's *The Man Who Loved Women*.[2] Yukiko has now turned away from the photos on the wall and with a slight smile looks straight toward . . . the camera? "Us"? The man whose gaze we have been sharing . . . but should we call him the "narrator"? "Boilet"?

This opening series of scenes functions as a kind of overture to what will gradually unfold as the love story that is Frédéric Boilet's *Yukiko's Spinach* (*L'épinard de Yukiko*, 2001). Individually and together they establish the thematic and formal elements of the story to follow. The visual style establishes a cinematic visual language, a composite of what seems to be a first-person perspective and a looser kind of "camera" work in which the point of view fluctuates more freely. The specific list of body parts will be repeated later (Yukiko's beauty is in many ways the central character of the story), but more importantly it establishes a leitmotivic structure in which images and words are repeated, often out of sync with one another, drifting freely from their original contexts. The date book page suggests an almost documentary mode, as if we were being given access to the raw materials of a story that took place just so: down to the addresses, dates, and even the times. But the following scene's overt cinematic allusions immediately put into question this documentary effect. To what extent do we interpret the exhibition scene as in some sense the "real" event, of which the date book page is the document (the picture of Yukiko must have been *finished* after the event)? To what extent is the date book page the script on which this scene is based (a scene that is, we must not forget, *drawn*)? The gallery scene also presents the essential dynamics of the relationship to come: the *mangaka* observing Yukiko; Yukiko aware and interested but keeping a certain distance; unstated feelings mediated by films, photographs, the displacements and substitutions of other people's love stories, and of course the art of comics itself.[3]

A blurb on the cover of the American edition of *Yukiko's Spinach* announces it to be "The Defining Work of Nouvelle Manga," a claim that has generally been accepted in mainstream and scholarly discussions.[4] With the work now translated into nine languages there is strong evidence that it has, at a minimum, become the most internationally well-known *nouvelle manga*. Although the term has come to be associated with a number of different authors, then, it is first and foremost identified with Boilet, in large part because of his active advocacy of the term, most apparent in his 2006 "Nouvelle Manga Manifesto."[5]

As the term itself implies, *la nouvelle manga* straddles two cultures, but also two (or more) media. On the one hand, we have the Japanese term *manga* (a loanword now at least as domesticated in French as in English), invoking a tradition that Boilet's manifesto praises largely at the expense of the Franco-Belgian *bande dessinée*.[6] On the other hand, we have the French adjective *nouvelle*, which not only tells us that we are dealing with something new, but also self-consciously echoes the cinematic *nouvelle vague* (New Wave film of the 1950s and 1960s). To this must be added the primarily autobiographical *nouvelle bande dessinée* of the 1990s and, perhaps, the *nouveau roman* (roughly contemporary with the cinematic New Wave).[7] Without defining a "movement" in any strict sense, *la nouvelle manga* both named an existing phenomenon and created a retroactive unity among, for example, the diverse group of French and Japanese artists and writers who in the fall of 2001 participated in the "Nouvelle Manga Event" in Tokyo. These artists have subsequently engaged in various collaborations, but their commonalities and differences are most concisely on display in *Japan as Seen by 17 Authors*, which includes such French artists as Aurélia Aurita, François Schuiten, Joann Sfar, and Fabrice Neaud, and such Japanese artists as Kan Takahama, Jirō Taniguchi, and Little Fish.[8] The *nouvelle manga* thus represents a significant and still-evolving event in the history of comics: an actively promoted, self-conscious crossing of national traditions characterized by a wide range of formal innovations.

While the *nouvelle manga* often engages with the autobiographical mode that has been so important to the recent cultural legitimization of comics in a number of different national contexts, the *nouvelle manga*'s formal inventiveness in many ways undermines any direct appeal to autobiographical authenticity. The opening sequence of scenes in *Yukiko's Spinach* blends or juxtaposes cinematic effects and the craft of drawing by hand, narrative voice and written document, a simple story and complex narrative temporalities. The question then arises of how the work's invocations of autobiographical, even documentary realism, confront its formal inventiveness. What might this confrontation teach us about the broader significance of the *nouvelle manga* as a culturally and mediatically hybrid form?

This essay attempts a multifaceted analysis of *Yukiko's Spinach* that can account for the interplay between its autobiographical mode, its innovative formal language, and its art-sociological position.[9] I begin with the art-sociological context of the *nouvelle manga* as successor to the *nouvelle bande dessinée* in particular and to *bande desinée* and manga more generally. I then turn to the ways in which *Yukiko's Spinach* plays with the form of autobiography, focusing on how the hybrid visual-linguistic field of comics vexes standard ways of locating a "first-person" narrator. The following section then revisits Scott McCloud's classic typology of transitions to analyze Boilet's visual syntax, which is derived from, but also differs from, that of manga. My concluding section interprets the *nouvelle manga*'s relationship to literature and film in terms of Jacques Rancière's account of aesthetic modernity as characterized by a mixing of the visual and the literary (rather than by the pursuit of medium-specificity, as in Clement Greenburg's influential model).

The *Nouvelle Manga* Manifesto and Its Contexts

Boilet's manifesto asserts its aesthetic values in the context of a polemical overview of the recent history of comics.[10] Contrasting American *comics*, the Franco-Belgian *bande dessinée*, and Japanese *manga*, Boilet uses these terms less as translations of one another and more as distinct names for distinct forms. Although critical of a number of different aspects of each, Boilet is largely dismissive of *comics*, saving his praise for certain manga, and his more nuanced criticisms for the *bande dessinée*.

Boilet takes the Franco-Belgian *bande dessinée* to task for two major faults. First, that its stories have been directed primarily toward adolescent boys. To the extent that other audiences have been sought, these have been other niche audiences rather than a broader reading public comparable to that of the novel or cinema. Second, that the *bande dessinée* has emphasized drawing at the expense of story, with the result that it has never really developed the latter art. (This is not to say that plot is not important to any given *bande dessinée*, but simply that the *bande dessinée* as a whole has not developed as a narrative art in ways comparable to the novel or film.)

This situation began to change in the 1990s with the development of a *nouvelle bande dessinée*, whose stories were oriented toward adult readers, often focusing on the everyday rather than the fantastic. Within this current, the small press L'Association, founded in 1990, was "the most important single industrial player in this transformation and [. . .] the model for much of what would transpire" (Beaty 9). Often emphasizing autobiography, such L'Association artists such David B., Jean-Christophe Menu, and Lewis Trondheim announced, "[W]e are above all authors [*auteurs*]" (qtd. in Beaty 30).

Alongside L'Association, another widely influential press was the future home of the *nouvelle manga*, ego comme x, founded in 1994 with a strong emphasis on autobiography.[11] As Bart Beaty explains: "Ego Comme X was started by students from the Atelier Bande Dessinée at the Ecole Régionale des Beaux-Art[s] d'Angoulême. Their stated desire was to highlight the importance of 'the real' in contradistinction to the dominant comics aesthetic of escapist fantasy" (Beaty 148).[12] The press published, and continues to publish, a wide array of critically acclaimed authors, including Fabrice Neaud and Frédéric Poincelet, as well as Frédéric Boilet himself.

The subject matter of this *nouvelle bande dessinée* was not wholly restricted to autobiography, but "recollections of childhood and a recounting of intimate or sexual encounters" were prominent topics (Beaty 147). While perhaps not representative, certainly the most widely known work from this milieu is Marjane Satrapi's *Persepolis*, published by L'Association from 2000 to 2003, and selling almost a half-million copies worldwide by 2004. Naturally, these comic autobiographies by comic artists tended to include the writing and drawing of comics, as in Satrapi's work. What was perhaps less predictable was that this "narrativization of comic book production [became] a central signifier of *authenticity* in the contemporary European small-press scene" (141; emphasis added). That is, rather than being read as, for example, "postmodern" (entirely possible in the France of the 1990s), self-referential autobiography "becomes a mode which foregrounds both realism (as opposed to the traditions of fantasy) and the sense of the author as an artist demanding legitimacy (in contrast to the view of the cartoonist as a cultural hack slaving away to turn out mass-mediated product)" (144). In sum, "autobiography has become the genre that most distinctly defines the small-press comics production of Europe in its current revitalization" (140–41), but the genre tended to be used in such a way that it self-reflexively foregrounded its own production and medium-specificity, rather than claiming to provide a transparent window into the life of an artist.

Beaty further argues that autobiography was not just a prominent mode in an alternative comics sales boom, but was in fact central to the cultural legitimization of comics in France during this period, a tendency that "stems at least in part from the renewed importance of the genre in the field of French literature in the 1970s and 1980s" (142).[13] Comics artists participated in and benefited from a general pushback against the "death of the author," seeking legitimacy precisely in an author function that the literary avant-garde had previously declared to be outmoded.[14] As Beaty emphasizes, "An important precursor in this regard was cinema, a medium in which the development of auteur theory had created the social conditions under which film could come to be regarded as a legitimated art form" (143).[15] Taking this one step further, I would claim that the reassertion of the author principle by the *nouvelle manga* should be seen as intimately bound up with the intermedial character of its aesthetic. That is, the appeal to a model of authorship borrowed from film reflects the *nouvelle manga*'s more general exploration of the still-indeterminate place of comics in relation to the other arts, both sociologically and formally.

This is the immediate historical context in which Boilet situates the *nouvelle manga*, explicitly citing the importance of both L'Association and ego comme x. Describing artists from both presses as working "close to the spirit of French cinema and the French novel," Boilet asserts that their works have in fact found a wider international audience than have the ostensibly more "commercial works" of traditional Franco-Belgian *bande dessinée*. Three interrelated principles thus emerge as central to his manifesto's program: 1) the pursuit of a general, adult public comparable to that of cinema or the novel; 2) a privileging of the "everyday" as subject matter; and 3) a valorization of story against the *bande dessinée*'s traditional emphasis on the art.

How does manga enter into this picture? After all, does manga not represent precisely the mass-produced commercial products against which Boilet defines his *nouvelle manga*? When Boilet wrote his manifesto, the manga boom underway in France for almost twenty years now had already begun. Throughout the 1990s, "the translation of Japanese comics (manga) throughout Europe [. . . was] inarguably the most important economic driver of the comics industry" (Beaty 15). Initially, the major publisher of these works was Glénat, which translated Katsuhiro Otomo's *Akira* in 1989, followed by *Dragon Ball* in 1991, before entering the translation business in full force in 1993.[16] By 2002, 377 Japanese comics were released in France, by 2004 at least 600, the most popular of which were selling more than one million copies. Sales increased dramatically during the 2000s, with the number of translated titles rising 567 percent between 2000 and 2008. During this time, France became the European capital of manga: "whereas as recently as 2000, the total number of new manga titles published each year in Italy had been five times higher than in France," by

2010, researchers report, the hexagon "seems to be the leading European importer of manga" (Bouissou et al. 254–55).[17]

Boilet is interested in a very different kind of manga, namely works by such alternative *mangaka* as Yoshiharu Tsuge, Kiriko Nananan, and Kan Takahama, whose recent popularity in France has in part been fostered by Boilet himself. The work of Jirō Taniguchi has been of particular importance. Boilet first read Taniguchi's *Walking Man* (*Aruku hito*) in Japan in 1993, recognizing a kindred spirit: "It was a story about the everyday, the kind I like" (Bastide). Beyond Boilet's personal tastes, however, the French translation of Taniguchi's book as *L'Homme qui marche* (Casterman, 1995) was a significant event for the French *bande dessinée* world as a whole. As Beaty writes, Taniguchi, along with Tsuge, "became the Japanese faces of the European small-press comics revolution" (113). During 2003–2004 there was a wave of major translations from a variety of presses, small and large: Tsuge's *L'Homme sans talent* and Kazuichi Hanawa's *Dans la Prison* (both ego comme X, 2003), Taniguchi's *Au Temps de Botchan* (Seuil, 2003), as well as Nananan's *Blue* and Takahama's *Kinderbook* (both Casterman, 2004).[18] Boilet would collaborate with a number of these authors or be involved in translations of their works.

As Boilet himself explains, his sense that these works share some common aesthetic values with French cinema is well founded. The Japanese alternative manga tradition has long been engaged with French (although not just French) cinema, perhaps the most famous instance being manga pioneer Yoshihiro Tatsumi's "gekiga" ("dramatic pictures").[19] According to Boilet, not only do such now-classic New Wave directors as Bresson and Godard maintain a strong presence, but contemporary directors such as Jacques Doillon, Cédric Klapisch, and Leos Carax are more appreciated than anywhere outside of France. Indeed, Japan is today the second-largest market for French film, after France itself.[20] French-language *bande dessinée*, by contrast, have not been embraced. Following Boilet's claim about the *bande dessinée*'s emphasis on drawing, the draftsmanship of artists like Moebius and Enki Bilal is appreciated by professional artists in Japan, but the *bande dessinée* has, with the exception of *Tintin*, found only a small audience.

The "Nouvelle Manga Manifesto" therefore seeks to identify, for a non-Japanese audience, an existing trend within Japanese manga and to transform it into a conscious aesthetic program to "present to the readers of these two countries manga of quality rather than of commerce, and this in the universal register of the autobiographical, documentary, or fictional everyday." This invocation of an ostensibly universal "everyday" seems to have something particularly *French* about it, as Boilet himself recognizes: "When it speaks of the everyday, the BD not only becomes more universal [. . .] it also becomes, in the eyes of foreign readers, more 'French.'" It should come as no surprise that Boilet's own work has received a culturally divided reception: "whereas the French remember the 'Japanese' side, it is the very 'French' tone of my stories that strikes Japanese readers."[21]

What exactly is this "everyday" and how is it manifest in the actual works? Given Boilet's account of the *nouvelle manga* as emphasizing story over drawing, one might well imagine very "literary" works: dialogue-driven, with complex plots, perhaps full of literary allusions. But the opposite is generally the case. Boilet's works tend to have few characters, to tell very simple stories, and to have relatively little dialogue and almost no narration. *Yukiko's Spinach* in particular is full of silence. The turn to story, in other words, involves a sense of story that is not literary in any obvious sense. Indeed, it might sooner be described as cinematic, although there is something off about this comparison as well since the very *auteurs* Boilet evokes as models so often assert the medium-specificity of film. Literature or film, then? Neither, of course, but then what? Comics in their specificity, even *medium* specificity? That cannot be the answer either, I will argue, because even for Boilet himself the references ("the spirit of French cinema and the French novel") seem unavoidable, as if such comparisons were not so much symptoms of the failure of medium-specificity as its necessary foundation.

Yukiko's Spinach: Realism and Autobiography

The basic plot of *Yukiko's Spinach* is easy to summarize. A French *mangaka* living in Tokyo falls in love with a Japanese woman he meets at a film exhibition. She returns his affections, but is also in love with a Japanese man, Horiguchi, who, in turn, is already in a long-term relationship with another woman. While Horiguchi is making up his mind, the *mangaka* and Yukiko engage in an affair. There are a few meals and walks, a few love scenes. These scenes are artfully structured as repetitions, variations, foreshadowings, and recollections whose exact chronological sequence is unclear upon first reading. In the end Horiguchi (whom we never meet) chooses Yukiko and Yukiko chooses Horiguchi. Throughout the book the *mangaka* sketches and photographs Yukiko and with the end of the relationship he has some of the raw materials, and the basic story, for his next book. In a brief coda of sorts, the *mangaka* meets a young woman named Mariko on a train. The scene and the conversation echo past scenes with Yukiko and we are led to believe the two will have a relationship.[22]

Is the story autobiographical? The single-word answer must be "no," but *Yukiko's Spinach* is nonetheless a work that plays with the autobiographical mode, that is, that often looks and feels like an autobiographical text, but we should not conclude from this that it is or tries to be an accurate record of its author's life. On the one hand, the basic facts of the *mangaka*'s life and loves broadly parallel those of Boilet. We are encouraged to believe that the work is scrupulously documenting the times and places of its events, both verbally ("Kissed at 11:15!!") and visually (the drawings are all based on actual people and places, with Boilet himself serving as the model for the *mangaka*).

On the other hand, the book foregrounds its own techniques of representation and of reconstructing the past. As the earlier-discussed juxtaposition of the date book page and the gallery scene suggested, Boilet consistently complicates our efforts to read the more naturalistically rendered scenes as somehow real or primary and the re-presentations (that is, those images that appear *as images* in the world of the story) as secondary. This is true in a number of subtle ways throughout the book, but it is most strikingly and extraordinarily apparent in a simple fact that I have yet to mention: about halfway through the book the character of Yukiko is, without explanation, suddenly based on a different model, namely Mariko, to whom we are first introduced (so to speak), only in the book's final pages.[23] The effect is particularly striking given the extent to which the *mangaka*'s praise of Yukiko's beauty focuses on precisely those things that register the history of a unique body: a scar on her forehead in the shape of Bora Bora, bruises on her thighs, a crease on one eyelid, her belly button. "What I love about you," he tells Yukiko *in a scene for which Mariko is the model*, "is everything that isn't perfect . . . Everything that's you and that's hard to draw" (103). *Yukiko's Spinach* might be real, then, but it is not particularly true.

To say this is not to criticize Boilet (he never promised us an autobiography), but rather to delineate the specificity of his project, namely, the pursuit of an "everyday" that must be *real* or, perhaps better, *realist*, but in a sense that must be further clarified. French writer and film critic Domonique Noguez has declared, "Boilet's originality is due to his

having decided, once and for all, to produce nothing, whether it be information, text or a finished drawing, that is not directly *a trace of reality*"
(6).²⁴ Noguez specifically allies Boilet with a tradition of *literary* realists
who, "descending from both Stendhal and Flaubert, love nothing so much
as the intoxicating scent of the true, and do not present a single face,
word, blade of grass, stone, or bolt in a scene that is not *drawn from life*"
(6). Accordingly, Noguez describes Boilet's work as representing a "kind
of autobiographical novel" (6). The qualification is appropriate because
of Boilet's already-noted affiliation with a tradition of *novelistic* realism.
Noguez remarks that the numerous faxes passing between Boilet and
Peeters as they collaborated on *Tokyo is My Garden* remind him of "Flaubert begging Maupassant to find a cliff whose description will match the
beginning of a paragraph in *Bouvard et Pécuchet*" (7). Boilet's works might
all be drawn from life, but they are not necessarily based on *his* life. To be
a bit more precise: they are not necessarily based on his "life" in a strictly
biographical sense. We can be fairly certain that Boilet shows us what he
has seen, but not necessarily only things that happened, or that happened
to him, or that happened in precisely the way we are shown them.

Boilet recognizes the temptation to read his works autobiographi-
cally, a temptation already offered by such earlier works as *3615 Alexia*
(1990) and his first collaboration with Peeters, *Love Hotel* (1993). In interviews, however, he is quite explicit about the sense in which his works are
about their author: "I am not the subject of *Yukiko's Spinach*. An actor
who looks like me plays his part, is involved in it, but he's just an actor.
And it's only a supporting role! If my books turned, at a certain moment,
in a certain direction, rather than the personal or the autobiographical, I
would sooner say that it was toward the everyday and *a transposition of
this everyday* [. . .] Comics always seemed to me an ideal means of expression for reconstruction of the everyday" (Boudet; emphases added). Boilet
might make use of what I have been calling an autobiographical mode
and even draw on personal raw material, but these are means (if perhaps
privileged means) used to the end of reconstructing and "transposing" the
everyday. Boilet's work is autobiographical in the sense that it is *by means
of*, but not particularly *about*, himself:

> I don't try to describe what is deep inside me, even less what is deep inside
> the other, and think I usually remain, when I draw, distinctly on the surface.
> In this sense, I did not feel that *Yukiko's Spinach*, for example, was a 'personal'

> [*intime*] work. With this book I simply tried to reconstruct attitudes, situations, in other words, appearances . . . What do we know in the end about the deeper motives of these characters? Very little, it seems to me. (Boudet)

Boilet's works are all *eye* and very little *I*. The desire to remain "on the surface" would suggest a visual rather than a literary project, but we should recall that modern literature is full of experimental efforts similarly to remain on the surface. The *nouveau roman* is perhaps the most obvious example, if only because it clearly constitutes one of Boilet's direct inspirations, but the literary discipline of remaining on the surface can be traced back to the very pioneers of novelistic realism just discussed.

I will reprise the question of the *nouvelle manga*'s relationship to other artistic forms in my conclusion. Here, however, I would like to describe in greater detail the ways in which *Yukiko's Spinach* formally constructs its pseudo-autobiographical subject. That is, I will specify how Boilet uses words and pictures together both to suggest an autobiographical form and to displace the subject of that would-be autobiography. The slipperiness of Boilet's work is revealed by the difficulty of locating it on the now-classic grid of biographical narrative positions Philippe Lejeune proposes in *On Autobiography*, according to which a "classic autobiography" would be a first-person text in which the narrator is the principal character.[25] Bracketing the question of the work's veracity, we can say that the basic form of *Yukiko's Spinach* fits this definition: the "grammatical person" is first (in the sense that the story is related from the *mangaka*'s perspective) and the narrator is, in certain respects, the principal character.

And yet there are two immediate complications to even this thoroughly hedged formulation. First, there is the fact that the "grammatical person" is visual rather than linguistic, a difference that fundamentally undermines many of the very qualities of first person-ness that makes the category meaningful in literary analysis. What we find in *Yukiko's Spinach* is a kind of depersonalized subjectivity, as if we were looking not through someone's eyes but through the lens of a camera (being operated, to be sure, by a specific individual).[26] That is, what we see is largely guided by the embodied perspective of the *mangaka*, directed by his desires, the limits of his bodily location, and so on, but the images are far more photographic or cinematic than "subjective," an effect made explicit when the image goes *out of focus* at a moment of emotional intensity (see, for example, 113). Similarly, the visual field we encounter routinely exceeds what could be taken in by any given moment of consciousness. A first-person literary narrator cannot say things of which he or she is unaware, but a simulated first-person camera *perspective* can show things the person looking through that camera is not noticing. Hence the need for the very photographs and sketchbooks that are the basis of the book. In sum, the narrative perspective is a composite of third- and first-person qualities: we see what *he* sees as much as we see what (his) *I* sees.

Second, this visual narrative position is syncopated with a verbal narrative position that is similarly difficult to pin down. There is no extradiegetic "narrator" who speaks directly to the reader. The words occupying the place traditionally held by a narrative voice are directed not to the reader but to Yukiko: even when the words are not *shown* being spoken between characters, they are to be understood as being spoken by one character to another, and thus constitute a form of dialogue. That is, if we consider as the narration the boxed text that represents the *mangaka*'s voice, then the narrator speaks almost exclusively in a form of second-person address, as in the opening "voice over." (There are two exceptions to this: 1) the notes in the date book pages, which are sometimes in the first person, but effectively have the form of a self-address; 2) diegetic dialogue, in which the *mangaka*'s speech is presented in word balloons.)

Putting these all together, we have a mostly first-person visual perspective characterized by third-person effects, accompanied by a verbal narrative position that is neither first- nor third-person, and at times assumes a form of second-person address. Where, then, would we locate the work on Lejeune's grid? The grammatical person of *Yukiko's Spinach* is decidedly multiple. What of the principal character? According to Boilet himself, it is not the *mangaka* but rather Yukiko! The narrator thus both is (for most readers) and is not (according to the author) the principal character. In sum, Boilet's book effectively touches all the squares on Lejeune's grid, and it is able to do this because of its syncopated word-image interplay.

This non-coincidence of the verbal and the visual can sometimes, as in the opening sequence, produce a kind of cinematic effect. But a foundational precedent for such effects can be found within the comics medium itself, namely in the language of manga. As Aarnoud Rommens notes, the "'doubling' of narrative information through textual description is not to be found in any manga [. . .] In manga, interpretation is achieved through the succession of visual cues, *with the significant exception of dialogue*" (Rommens; emphases added). In the case of *Yukiko's Spinach*, this exception is, as we have seen, significant indeed in terms of the ways it complicates efforts to understand the work as a kind of autobiographical narrative. The Lejeunian grid is, of course, based on literary texts, whereas the *nouvelle manga* clearly calls for an approach that reckons with the complexities and ambiguities of word-image interplay. To that end, I will now consider in greater detail the visual language of *Yukiko's Spinach*, specifically in terms of its debt to manga.

The Language of Manga and *Nouvelle Manga*

If Boilet's manifesto makes fairly explicit what about the *nouvelle manga* is supposed to be *nouvelle* (at least with respect to the *bande dessinée*), it is less explicit about what it takes from manga (beyond general references to quality and the everyday). In this section I will sketch out a contrast and comparison of manga and *nouvelle manga* as formal languages. Throughout I will reference a number of the basic analytic distinctions introduced by Scott McCloud's now-classic *Understanding Comics*, especially his typology of transitions.[27]

To begin with the ways in which the *nouvelle manga* is *not* like manga, let us consider Neil Cohn's account of the latter, which argues that there exists a standardized Japanese Visual Language (or "JVL") "unconnected to any particular author's manner of drawing" (189). Indeed, manga are often drawn by multiple artists. "This 'style' is so schematized," Cohn continues, "that often characters' faces cannot be distinguished from each other, leading to authors' use of other features to allow readers to differentiate them" (188–89). In terms of McCloud's range of representational possibilities—ranging from a photorealistic image suggesting the uniqueness of its subject to an iconic smiley face that represents no one in particular—the visual language of manga is fairly far toward the latter, iconic end of the spectrum (McCloud 27–59).

If the generic manga image could be by and of a wide range of people, the *nouvelle manga*, by contrast consistently asserts the value of the author function and often emphasizes the distinctive appearance of its main characters. Indeed, in the case of Boilet's work we often have recognizable portraits.[28] More important than the images' accuracy *per se*, however, is their realism *effect*, an effect that is based in a visual style but reinforced within the stories, when, for example, we see the *mangaka* making a drawing based on a "photograph" (i.e., a drawing that represents a photograph).[29] However fictionalized or artfully manipulated, Boilet's characters are not presented through a visual language that renders them as *types*. On the contrary, we are consistently offered the temptation to believe that we are looking at (relatively) precise visual records of actual people.

Such stylistic distinctions between manga and *nouvelle manga* images correspond to specific syntactic differences. Fusanosuke Natsume has claimed of manga that "using a consistent visual vocabulary allows readers the freedom to focus on the content of the expressions rather than on the expressions themselves" (Cohn 190). If conventional manga rely on a standardized and caricatural visual vocabulary, this is all the better to whisk readers through the story rather than encouraging them to pore over details of individual images. Studies suggest that expert manga readers pay more attention to images than words, smoothly moving through the sequences, while amateurs focus more on the words and have more erratic eye movements (199). Unlike Euro-American comics, manga tend not to pack as much narrative information as possible into a minimal number of pregnant images accompanied and often explained by captions and dialogue. Instead, manga tend to use a much larger numbers of panels, with a minimal linguistic element, allowing for narration through a more purely pictorial *language*. That is, experienced manga readers focus on the images not in the sense that they *look* rather than read, but in the sense that they *read the images*. Boilet's images, by contrast, do foreground their own qualities as (often quite beautiful) images. To recall McCloud's realism-iconicity spectrum: Boilet's images would be located further toward the realistic end of the spectrum than would standard manga images. Moreover, the meta-formal play of Boilet's work encourages and rewards attention to detail and even rereading (generally not the case in standard JVL).

As McCloud writes, whereas cartoons "tend to flow easily through the conceptual territory between panels [. . .] realistic images have a bumpier ride" (90–91). More iconic drawings allow us to experience a sequence as "a continuous series of moments," while more realistic images are experienced "more like a series of still pictures" (91). McCloud concludes that "A good rule of thumb is that if readers are particularly *aware* of the art in a given story, then closure [i.e., the reader's construction of the narrative connection between panels] is probably not happening without some effort. Of course, making the reader work a little may be just what the artist is trying to do" (91). Such is the case with Boilet.[30]

Despite these numerous differences, the *nouvelle manga* remains indebted to and builds on manga's visual syntax, particularly in the area of transition types. McCloud's typology posits five kinds of panel-to-panel transitions. The first is the moment transition, in which there is very little change from one panel to the next, suggesting a very brief passage of time. (One of McCloud's examples is an image of a woman's face, followed by the same face but with the eyes now closed). The second type, the action transition, involves a single subject engaged in an act that demonstrates a distinct progression in time: in one panel we see a car speeding along and in the next panel we see it crashed into a tree. The third type, the subject transition, involves a change of subject but stays within a given scene or idea, as when panels move between headshots of two characters engaged in a dialogue. The fourth category is the scene transition, which "transport[s] us across significant distances of time and space" (71). Finally, McCloud posits the idea of an aspect transition that "bypasses time for the most part and sets a wandering eye on different aspects of a place, idea, or mood" (72).[31]

The critical payoff of these rather broad categories comes when they are applied in a quantitative analysis of different forms of comics. McCloud argues that action, subject, and scene transitions (in that order) constitute the whole transitional repertoire of standard American comics. An analysis of a 1966 *Fantastic Four* by Jack Kirby, for example, contains 65-percent action, 20-percent subject, and 15-percent scene transitions. An analysis of Hergé's *The Black Island* shows similar proportions, if with fewer scene transitions. An analysis of a fair number of European and American works reveals that all contain roughly similar proportions. "If we choose to see stories as connected series of events," McCloud concludes, "then the predominance of types 2–4 [i.e., action, subject, and scene] is easily explained" (76).

Japanese works, by contrast, use fewer scene transitions and considerably fewer action transitions. More significantly, they also include two kinds of transitions virtually absent from Euro-American comics, namely moment and aspect transitions. With the former—still relatively uncommon even in Japanese works—a short amount of time passes from one panel to the next, too little to constitute an "action" in any conventional sense. With the latter, we have little or no temporal development, but a shifting point of view on the same moment from one panel to the next. Such aspect transitions are relatively common in Japanese works, constituting approximately 15 percent of all transitions. McCloud's analysis of a range of Japanese works, starting with those of Osamu Tezuka, reveals a basic pattern: the three types familiar from Euro-American works are still quite prominent (if with a decrease in action transitions), but to this must be added moment transitions (sometimes) and a substantial percentage of aspect transitions. Indeed, in some cases the percentage of moment transitions is equal to or even greater than that of subject or scene transitions (77–80).

Relating these transitional categories to *Yukiko's Spinach*, we find a dramatic increase in the categories specifically identified with the language of manga, namely moment and aspect transitions, especially the latter.[32] By my own count (which can only be approximate, for reasons I will detail below), the percentages for Boilet's book would be as follows: 18-percent moment, 24-percent action, 10-percent subject, 4-percent scene, 36-percent aspect.[33] Three things are immediately striking about these numbers. First, the work does not have that many scenes. Second, it does not have that many subjects. Third, the large number of aspect transitions suggests that we spend a lot of time seeing different aspects of a given scene or subject. Putting these together, we get the outlines of a narrative structure: a limited number of scenes in each of which we see many different facets of a very small number of subjects. And indeed the book is, in effect, a handful of scenes in which Yukiko is the central figure.

A closer examination of these categories' applicability to Boilet's book gives a far more precise sense of its specific aesthetic. The percentages given above would not quite add up to 100 percent. The missing 8 percent is accounted for by two kinds of transitions that do not fit into any of McCloud's categories. At about 3 percent, the first, which I will call "symbolic transitions," is relatively minor. For example, Yukiko has on her forehead a scar whose shape recalls, for the *mangaka*, Bora Bora. Thus there are two moments in the book in which we suddenly see a single panel of Yukiko on a beach in Bora Bora. This is not exactly a "scene" transition in that she is not in reality in Bora Bora, and for the same reason it seems pointless to ask about the temporal relation of such panels to the ones surrounding them. These are not non-sequiturs because they make thematic and psychological sense, but they function in ways that render normal spatio-temporal categories of transition inapplicable.[34]

At almost 5 percent, the second new category I propose is not quantitatively much greater, but it does play a more significant role. These "mediatic transitions," as I call them, are from one medium or representational level to another, as when transitioning from a room to an image of what is on the screen of a television in that room, or from a room to a blueprint of that same room. So, for example, in the scene with the Léaud photo what at first looked to be a subject transition might retroactively be understood as a scene transition (if we think of the "photo" as a representation of another location), or perhaps still as a subject transition, but now with the understanding that the new "subject" is a thing (a piece of paper on a wall) rather than a person. However, thinking of this transition as "mediatic" brackets these complexities, while also allowing for a distinction that would not otherwise be possible ("picture of Leaud" rather than "Leaud"). Another important example of this kind of transition would be the date book pages that appear throughout *Yukiko's Spinach*.[35] The causal and spatio-temporal relationship of such pages to the panels surrounding them does not follow the normative guidelines of action-driven narratives. For example, many of the date book pages include multiple drawings and notes added at different times. These notes and pictures can have a prospective *and* retrospective relationship to the panels that follow. To return to the example with which we began: the time and location of the film exhibition were presumably written *before* the *mangaka* attends, while the notes about Yukiko were written *after*.[36] In sum, because we are switching from one representation to another, the spatio-temporal distinctions that seem so natural if we think in terms of *what is represented* quickly lose their relevance.

To give an extreme example of how Boilet's book challenges the transitional categories: in the previously mentioned photo booth scene we see a series of twenty-four identically sized, horizontally oriented panels (three per page), all of which are from the perspective of the photo booth camera. The visual field is cluttered with captions and animations (added by the anime-themed photo booth). A handful of these panels are drawn with a flash-effect that indicates a photo is being taken. The last six panels in this sequence are (visually) exact repetitions of the last one of these "photos." The characters, however, continue their conversation! How would we describe the transition from one of these panels to the next? Visually, we have what might be described as a series of zero-degree aspect transitions in which no time passes. In another sense, however, time clearly does pass because a conversation is taking place (an important one no less: this is the moment Yukiko agrees to have an affair with the *mangaka*). The visual and linguistic dimensions of the text thus obey not only different but conflicting temporalities.

Such exceptional scenes aside, Boilet's work regularly strains the limits of McCloud's transitional categories because it pushes the limits of what constitutes an action, or even a moment. Because the actions are often so minimal, it may be difficult to decide what constitutes a moment and what an action transition. Following one of McCloud's own examples, we should define as moment transitions the numerous scenes in which, from one panel to the next, we have substantially similar images in which Yukiko smiles or turns her head a bit. And yet because such moments are so much what the story is about, it is tempting to think of them as rising to the level of an "action," at least occasionally.[37]

Just as the inflation of moment transitions blurs their distinctiveness from action transitions, so too the hyperinflation of aspect transitions blurs their distinctiveness from subject transitions. For example, should we understand a transition from Yukiko's face to a close-up of her hand as an aspect or a subject transition? To the extent that we understand the different parts of Yukiko as different facets of the same thing (namely, Yukiko's body), then we are dealing with an aspect transition. But to the extent that we are dealing with body parts that have become objects of aesthetic contemplation in their own right, the different body parts achieve a kind of relative autonomy and we are, arguably, dealing with a subject transition: that is, we are not looking at a different facet of the same thing, but at something else. Here McCloud's categories are strained because of the ways in which Boilet's images are bound to a pseudo-subjective perspective. Unlike the examples McCloud uses, Boilet's transitions cannot be defined exclusively in terms of *what they represent*. In many of Boilet's scenes, the spatio-temporal relations among the panels become inseparable from issues of consciousness and intentionality because little or nothing, beyond the roaming of the *mangaka*'s eye, is happening. The change of emphasis from action to moment transitions, and from subject to aspect transitions is, in short, a formal embodiment of the *nouvelle manga*'s aesthetic agenda. As we have seen, the *mangaka*'s wandering "eye" is not so much personal as cinematic, that is, the first-person perspective is less about helping us get inside the *mangaka*'s head and more about using his localized perspective to register a series of transpositions of the everyday.[38]

Comics and the Aesthetic

In conclusion, I would like to sketch out a number of compelling parallels between the *nouvelle manga* aesthetic and Jacques Rancière's efforts to rethink the history of modern art (since Romanticism) as an "aesthetic regime."[39] The first of these concerns the function of what I have been calling the autobiographical mode, "the life of the artist as work"

(*Discontents* 4), but only in a specific sense. According to Rancière, the "aesthetic" often privileges a first-person perspective, not so that a self can express itself, but as a form through which literature can come to be a registration of the sensuous. Flaubert's style, he writes, is exemplary in its efforts "to affect the passivity of the empty gaze of reasonless things in its exposition of everyday actions," such that style "itself became passive, invisible [. . .] painstakingly effac[ing] the difference between itself and the ordinary prose of the world" (*Fables* 8). He thus reads Stendhal's *Vie de Henry Brulard* (1835) as establishing "what was to become the exemplary form of new fictional narration: the juxtaposition of *sensory microevents*," (*Discontents* 4–5; emphases added).[40] Rancière thus sees what many might consider a "modernist" or even specifically cinematic aesthetic as dating back to precisely the early- to mid-nineteenth century authors Noguez references in his efforts to define Boilet's distinctive realism.

The second parallel concerns the fact that such a focus on "sensory micro-events" disarticulates plot. According to Rancière, with the advent of the aesthetic regime "fictional arrangement is no longer identified with the Aristotelian causal sequence of actions 'according to necessity and plausibility' [. . .] It is the identification of modes of fictional construction with means of deciphering the signs inscribed in the general aspect of a place, a group, a wall, an article of clothing, a face" (*Politics of Aesthetics* 36–37). Whereas works created under the "representative" regime had sought above all to represent the coherent unity of an action, those of the aesthetic regime are not held together by a preexisting logic. While the former regime effectively begins with a whole that defines and governs the relations among the parts, the latter begins with parts (often "sensory micro-events") that the artist must interpret or construct into an arrangement that will constitute a work.[41] In his "Preface" to *Tokyo is My Garden*, Noguez writes that, despite the work's fragmentary origins, "there is a story line. Reality, yes, but one that is adjusted. What Aristotle called *poiesis*, the alteration whereby, keeping the future audience in mind, fiction is rendered less obscure, less abrupt, less improbable, less meaningless than life" (7). Rancière's and Noguez's common reference to Aristotle brings into focus what might seem a contradiction that in fact represents two aspects of the same process. On the one hand, Boilet opens comics up to the sensory microevent, to the passivity of the sensuous impression and the consequent disarticulation of plot. On the other hand, Boilet brings order to an otherwise incoherent realm of mere facts and indexes. These tendencies are not so much contradictory as complementary. The latter presupposes the former: only if one has first committed to recording and gathering what is obscure, abrupt, improbable, or meaningless ("life") can one subsequently organize it.

Boilet might undo any ordinary sense of plot by restricting his raw material to what he can draw from life, behaving like a note-taking reporter or even an impersonal camera, but he must then subsequently arrange this primarily visual (indeed, often silent) material in such a way that it acquires meaning. While the former gesture undoes the "literary" dimensions of the work (character and plot), making it more essentially visual, the latter makes a kind of story out of what might otherwise be but a collection of pictures. This is how *Yukiko's Spinach* is *like* a documentary film or an autobiography, but with the important caveat that it does not claim to be true and it is not about its author.

Although initially helpful, the literary/visual distinction I have just made is also somewhat misleading. The passages I have so far cited from Rancière might suggest that the aesthetic regime is defined by a passive registration of sensory microevents and, therefore, that the indexical media of photography and cinema would automatically achieve this ambition. This is because I have so far concentrated on *literature*'s place in the aesthetic regime, but that place is itself defined by a movement to which that of cinema is complementary: "Literature, to thwart the arrangement of incidents and the conflict of wills, let itself be infiltrated by the great passivity of the visible. The addition of the image to literature amounted to a subtraction of sense. Cinema, for its part, can only appropriate this power by reversing the game and hollowing out the visible with the word" (*Fables* 14).[42] It is not pure passivity *per se* that defines the aesthetic regime, but an economy of "image" and "word," of non-sense and sense that constitutes what Rancière calls a "distribution of the sensible," (*Aesthetics and Its Discontents* 24). Rancière's account of cinematic aesthetics thus illuminates the *nouvelle manga* aesthetic's double movement of subtracting and adding sense.

The temptation to describe certain aspects of Boilet's aesthetics as in some sense cinematic is, accordingly, similarly helpful but misleading. Rancière emphasizes that much of what we today think of as cinematic did not have to wait for the invention of the camera: "[T]he aesthetic revolution is first of all the honor acquired by the commonplace, which is pictorial and literary before being photographic or cinematic" (*Politics of Aesthetics* 33). He specifies elsewhere: "[T]he camera's fixing on the hand that pours the water and the hand that holds the candle is no more particular to cinema than the fixing of Doctor Bovary's gaze on Mademoiselle

Emma's nails, or of Madame Bovary's gaze on those of the notary's clerk, is particular to literature" (*Future* 5). If Boilet's work is "cinematic" in its simulation of a passive registration of the world, its aesthetic is not *properly* cinematic in any strong sense: it predates cinema; not all cinema features it; and it can be deployed in other media, even and perhaps especially at a time when the "death of cinema" is routinely discussed. The fact that all this is explored in an art whose most basic means of production is anything but automatic (drawing) only serves to highlight the extent to which medium specificity is of limited explanatory value here.

The fourth and final point I would like to take from Rancière thus concerns his critique of the notion that artistic modernity can be understood as a pursuit of medium-specificity, an idea perhaps most widely associated with Clement Greenberg, but also central to a wide range of theoretical accounts of film (an early formulation of which would be Jean Epstein's notion of "photogénie"). For Rancière, one of the defining features of the aesthetic regime is its singularization of art; that is, beginning around the time of what we generally call Romanticism there are no longer *arts* that pursue their specific techniques, but instead *art* defined by its relationship to a new sensorium. Any specific art is thus condemned to (or, if one prefers, has the freedom to) borrow from the others, thereby constituting its "distribution of the sensible" only in relation to something other than itself. For Rancière "an art is an idea of art" (*Fables* 24), an idea that might justify itself in terms of medium specificity, but that is in fact utterly dependent on other arts both in concept and in execution. The modern age's undoing of *ut pictura poesis* does not place image on one side and words on the other: "It means quite the opposite: the abolition of the principle that allocated the place and means of each, separating the art of words from that of forms, temporal arts from spatial arts. It means the constitution of *a shared surface* in place of separate spheres of imitation" (*Future* 105; emphases added).

This is relevant to Boilet's work in two ways. First, it provides a theoretical framework for my claim that we might better understand Boilet's "cinematic" effects less as a kind of *borrowing* from film and more as one facet of a general contrapuntal relationship between image and narrative that is as much akin to Flaubert as to Bresson. This helps explain the above-described double movement of Boilet's works: his unraveling of story by allowing passive visibility into the literary, but also his construction of a world of characters and plot from this material. Thus it is precisely Boilet's prioritization of "story" that draws him toward an increasingly silent and plotless visual field.

Rancière writes that "like painting and literature, cinema is *the name of an art whose meaning cuts across the borders between the arts*" (*Fables* 4). The same is true, I want to suggest as a conclusion, of comics, as the *nouvelle manga* makes more apparent than do most forms. To put this claim in a more provocative form: comics become art in becoming like novels or films, but only to the extent that novels and films were also already like comics. That is, comics do not so much *combine* arts as reveal the composite character of all aesthetic art (singular), defined by a common "shared surface" of which comics might be understood as a singularly literal figure.

The question of medium specificity has been a perpetual headache for theoreticians of comics. McCloud, for example, imagines comics as torn between two forms of medium specificity, that of literature and that of art: "Our need for a unified language of comics sends us toward the center where words and pictures are like two sides of one coin! But our need for sophistication in comics seems to lead us outward, where words and pictures are more separate" (49).[43] The Rancièrean model I have sketched out above would reframe the terms in which "sophistication" and cultural legitimization might be understood. The question should not be "Can comics be added to the list of arts (plural)?" but rather "What particular kind of constellation is 'comics' within art (singular)?" If it is not the case that literature is word and painting image, but rather that all are composite, then comics' own more overtly composite character stands in need not so much of justification as of explanation. Comics do not need to define their specificity in terms of a set of qualities unique to it, but rather in terms of its being one family of visual-verbal arrangements among other such families of arrangements. In historiographic terms, this might mean that determining the (relative) specificity of comics should involve not so much tracing the unfolding of a medium-specificity since Rodolphe Töpffer or *The Yellow Kid*, for example, but rather analyzing the place of comics within the broader landscape of arts at any given moment: "abstraction" in painting, the coming of sound in cinema, the birth of television, the "death" of cinema.

Today we see comics acquiring new levels of social and artist legitimacy that are frequently described in terms of either the literary (perhaps above all various forms of autobiography) or the cinematic. Surely it cannot be a coincidence that this is occurring precisely at a time when mainstream cinema is becoming more and more like "comic books," not simply because of the explosion of films in genres traditionally associated with comics, but more essentially because of digitalization, which has undermined traditional accounts of film's medium-specificity, above all the notion of film's *indexical* character.[44] Comics represent one of the most prominent ways in which the *author* has lived on in the present, years beyond reports of his (and at the time it was *his*) death. The *nouvelle manga* suggests that comics might be one of the ways in which *film* (as a certain idea of art) will live on as well.

Notes

Where only an English title appears in the Works Cited, that translation is being cited. In cases where the work is listed in French, translations are my own.

1. The culmination of this blason—perhaps an allusion to the opening sequence of Jean-Luc Godard's *Contempt* (*Le mépris*, 1963)—is far less indecent than it might seem: the narrator had meant to say "belly button" *(o-heso)*, but pronounced it "spinach" (*hōrensō*). We learn this, however, only much later. The pronunciation of initial Hs is presented as a trap for French speakers of Japanese (later in the book, one of the narrator's friends calls Yukiko "Miss Ashimoto" rather than "Miss Hashimoto"). Le Duc suggests the connection to the Godard film.

2. While the Denner film has an obvious thematic resonance with Boilet's work, the Léaud and Jade images might also refer to in *Bed and Board* the Doinel character falls in love and has an affair with a Japanese woman shortly after his marriage to Christine.

3. I will use the Japanese term *mangaka* (manga artist/writer) throughout to refer to the main male character in *Yukiko's Spinach*. This follows Boilet's usage in two ways: first, it allows me to avoid identifying this character with Boilet the author (in interviews Boilet refers to the character as "the *mangaka*" precisely in order to distance himself) and, second, it allows me to avoid distinguishing between "manga artist" and "manga writer."

4. See, for example, Arnold, Cha, Le Duc, and Paugam.

5. Boilet's manifesto is available on his website in French, English, Spanish, and Japanese. There are no page numbers.

6. And, to a lesser extent, of U.S. *comics*, from which he understandably feels less need to distinguish his own work.

7. The conscious choice of the cinematic echo is surely one motive for the choice of a feminine gender for the adjective. *Manga* is ordinarily a masculine word in French, an issue Boilet discusses at some length in his manifesto. The word was in fact feminine in nineteenth-century French usage (Edmond de Goncourt, for

example, had written of "*la* manga de Hokusaï") but the largely forgotten word would be masculinized in the 1980s.

8. *Le Japon vu par 17 auteurs* (Casterman, 2005). The majority of these stories (about two-thirds) are at least *presented* as autobiographical. While some of the stories occasionally drift into a kind of magic realism, they are generally rooted in everyday life, with a penchant toward stories about childhood, travel, and love affairs. The collection appeared more or less simultaneously in English, Spanish, Italian, and Dutch, in addition to French and Japanese.

9. It is my hope that some of this analysis will apply, *mutatis mutandis*, to other *nouvelle manga* works, but that corpus is too broad and varied to deal with in a short article of this scale. Aurélia Aurita's work, for example, is closely connected to Boilet's in a number of ways and yet would not seem to conform to many of the generalizations one might be tempted to make based on *Yukiko's Spinach* alone.

10. I will use the term "comics" to refer broadly to what has variously been called, in English, comix, sequential art, the ninth art, narrative art, and so on. That is, I use the term globally for the sake of internal consistency, not in order to give any special privilege to the American forms. My usage is therefore *not* consistent with Boilet's own in his manifesto. For a recent scholarly account of the differences between European, American, and Japanese art comics, see Couch.

11. Even today the website reminds potential contributors, "please do not forget that ego comme x publishes almost exclusively AUTOBIOGRAPHICAL STORIES" (capitalization in original).

12. As my numerous citations make clear, this account of the *nouvelle bande dessinée* is heavily indebted to Beaty's.

13. For a more general account of this issue, see Groensteen, "Why Are Comics Still in Search of Cultural Legitimization?"

14. The fundamental texts of the "death of the author" debate remain those of Barthes and Foucault. For a more general sampling of texts from the *auteur* debate in cinema studies, see Caughie.

15. Beaty's account of the *nouvelle bande dessinée*'s legitimization seems to go against Boilet's emphasis on story over drawing: "The 1990s [. . .] reversed the polarity of the comic book. Without entirely abandoning the well-written tendency, comic book artists of this era increasingly drew inspiration from the visual arts [. . .] No longer would comic book artists seek legitimacy in relation to literature, but in relation to the visual arts" (7). The contradiction is, however, only apparent: Beaty is writing about social institutions rather than the formal qualities or thematic emphases of the works.

16. Up to and during this period, the majority of manga translated into French were retranslations of American editions. French ideas about manga were therefore necessarily based on a subset of the American market. In part because of this mediating influence, the manga available in France were for a long time largely those directed at adolescents.

17. See also Boissou in the same volume. These numbers are provided by the research group Manga Network, whose very existence under the umbrella of the prestigious

Institut d'études politiques (a.k.a. "Sciences Po") suggests the importance of manga in contemporary France. For more information about the Manga Network, see http://www.ceri-sciences-po.org/themes/manga/.

18. I give the French titles here. Many of these works have subsequently been translated into English, almost exclusively by the English- and Spanish-language small press Fanfare/Ponent-Mon. In addition to works by Boilet, these include Kan Takahama's *Monokuro Kinderbook*, Kazuichi Hanawa's *Doing Time*, Jirō Taniguchi's *The Walking Man*, Kiriko Nananan's *Blue*, and four volumes of Jirō Taniguchi and Natsuo Sekikawa's *The Times of Botchan*.

19. The origins of *gekiga* are a central subject of Yoshihiro's autobiographical *A Drifting Life*.

20. This Franco-Japanese cinephilia is explicitly thematized in *Tokyo is My Garden*, a collaboration between Boilet, Taniguchi, and Benoît Peeters.

21. In a less generous vein, the cover of the American edition of *Yukiko's Spinach* reproduces a blurb from the website *Fanboy Planet* that ends its highly favorable review with the exclamation "damn Boilet for making the French likeable again!"

22. And indeed this Mariko will be Boilet's principal model for a number of years, most extravagantly in *Mariko Parade*.

23. The new-look Yukiko does, in the scene in which she first appears, mention her "new haircut," but this is certainly not intended to fool the reader, at least not for long. Whatever practical necessities might have compelled Boilet to switch models, it is nonetheless difficult not to see in this overt switch an allusion to Luis Buñuel's *That Obscure Object of Desire* (1977), in which the character of Conchita is famously played by both Carole Bouquet and Angela Molina.

24. Page numbers are to the English edition of *Tokyo is My Garden*, to which Noguez's essay appears as a preface, but the translations have been modified. The French text is available at: http://www.boilet.net/fr/noguez.html.

25. Lejeune posits three columns, one for each of the grammatical persons of enunciation: first, second, and third, a.k.a. I, you, and she/he. Under each of these lie two rows, one for those cases in which the narrator is the principle character, one for those in which he or she is not. The result is a six-square grid, with each square representing a different possible biographical form, some, naturally, more common than others. A text written in the third person in which the narrator is not the principal character would be a "classic biography" (very common), whereas a text written in the second person in which the narrator is the principal character would be what Lejeune calls, quite simply, an "autobiography in the second person" (not very common).

26. On the camera as a locus of "impersonal subjectivity" see Banfield. This is of course all simulated: a drawing is not an index; it is always mediated by consciousness as well as the artist's skill.

27. I am implicitly agreeing here with Neil Cohn's claim that "manga" must be understood as not simply a type of book (defined sociologically or thematically), but also a kind of visual *language* (187). Although now somewhat dated, the standard

English-language introduction to manga remains Schodt. For a more recent, brief historical overview of manga, see Bouissou.

28. This can be confirmed both by the accounts we have of Boilet's method and by the photos of himself and his models that are sometimes included in the works.

29. This value is similarly confirmed in the epilogue to *Yukiko's Spinach*, which stages the *mangaka's* first meeting with Mariko. When she looks at the sketch he has been making of her, she exclaims, "That really looks like me! You're not bad" (136). The implicit realism of the style is also indirectly confirmed when, for example, the *mangaka* notices that Yukiko is wearing the same outfit as on one of their previous dates and he jokes, "You would make a good manga character!" (45). Numerous ironies attend this remark: not only has Yukiko indeed become a (nouvelle) manga character by the time we have read this remark, but he makes the joke precisely when the two are having their pictures taken, copies of which will be included in the book itself. That is, at precisely the moment that the possibility of Yukiko being a type is raised, her realism and singularity are asserted.

30. Guillaume Paugam suggests that over the course of Boilet's career we can trace "a progressive weakening of the narrative with respect to the drawing, an ever more tenuous relationship to autobiography," a weakening that might be described as "the passage from a self-presentation [. . .] to a pure and simple diary" (Paugam). While I do not disagree with Paugam's notion that one can trace such a trajectory over the course of Boilet's career, I would describe these differences less in terms of an "evolution" (Paugam's word) over time and more in terms of productive tension that can be found within each of the works.

31. McCloud also lists a sixth kind of transition, the non-sequitur, in which there is "no logical relationship between panels whatsoever" (72). However, he thinks this kind of transition is not strictly possible, so I do not include it here.

32. McCloud's findings about the differences between Japanese and Euro-American comics are echoed in the compositional aspects of manga. Cohn introduces a terminology of micro, mono, and macro panels, roughly corresponding to close-up, medium, and long-range shots in cinema. Cohn concludes that manga uses micros and especially monos at significantly higher rates than do American comics and they do so at the expense of macros (197–98). That is, he writes, "JVL seems to focus on individual *parts* of environments more often than on larger scenes that show the environment outright (macros)" (198). This is another similarity between manga and the *nouvelle manga*.

33. While Rommens may be correct that Boilet's "page layouts follow a certain regular pattern and can therefore be termed 'European,'" my own analysis suggests that the arrangement of the panels is not a sufficient indicator of how "European" or "Japanese" the syntax of Boilet's work is.

34. Ingulsrud and Allen reference a similar idea in Jessica Abel and Matt Madden's *Drawing Words and Writing Pictures*.

35. Boilet's use of these mediatic transitions contributes significantly to the lower percentage of scene transitions noted above. Looking at the scene transition percentage

in isolation, one would imagine a book with no more than four or five scenes, but the various mediatic transitions add retrospections, repetitions, and other forms of interruption that provide a sense of narrative complexity that would otherwise be lacking. These mediatic transitions almost always involve what I call "returns," that is, a transition back to the previous diegetic level. In the percentages given above I counted these returns as mediatic transitions.

36. One could no doubt develop numerous subcategories of mediatic transitions. My goal here is not to provide a comprehensive sub-typology, but simply to identify a category of transition that is absent from McCloud's typology and plays an important role in Boilet's work.

37. The other difficulty with defining moment transitions stems from the fact that Boilet spatially manipulates his images in ways whose diegetic status is not always clear. Indeed, the diegetic/extra-diegetic distinction is itself regularly destabilized throughout the book: when we watch the *mangaka* in the story manipulate an image, then this is diegetic, if in a complex sense. But when we have no sign of the *mangaka*'s hand and see slightly different versions of an image, is this the work of Boilet the author or of the *mangaka*? For example, we see Yukiko sitting at a table and then in the next panel we see the same image of Yukiko, but closer. How are we to interpret this? Are we looking through the character's eyes and we have leaned in? Or is this an image frozen in time on which our spatial perspective has changed because the *mangaka* has cropped the image?

38. This is not to say that the formal techniques have *no* psychological content (after all, it is not just any "object" that is the privileged focus of all that dilated attention!), but simply that the *mangaka*'s psychology is not the work's primary topic, despite the first-person perspective.

39. Rancière's is a multifaceted and complex argument put forward in series of works over the past approximately fifteen years, an argument that in turn develops several decades of original political-philosophical thought. Needless to say, I do not here attempt anything like a comprehensive summary of this argument, nor do I wish to suggest the *nouvelle manga* speaks to the full range of Rancière's thought, which is ultimately a philosophical exploration of equality. Rather, I simply wish to highlight a series of interrelated facets of the aesthetic theory that have direct relevance to the issues *nouvelle manga* raises about comics and aesthetics.

40. This first-person perspective can be *indirect* in the sense that the grammatical person of the text might be primarily third person, for example, but through a kind of sensory free indirect discourse the implicit perspective is nonetheless necessarily first.

41. Rancière's three "regimes" (ethical, representational, aesthetic) are not strictly historical in their range, but for the sake of simplicity one might say here that the representational regime was in force from the sixteenth through the eighteenth century, the aesthetic from the early nineteenth into the present. See especially *The Politics of Aesthetics*.

42. For a valuable introduction to the stakes of Rancière's writings on cinema, see Conley.

43. McCloud gives a thumbnail history of modern art that explicitly relies on the very notion of artistic "modernity" of which Rancière is so critical, namely as a movement toward abstraction: "Impressionism sent Western art toward the abstract vortex, but in a way that clung to what the eye saw" (146). With modern art, "the main thrust was a return to meaning in art, away from resemblance, back to the realm of ideas" (147). He continues: "Meanwhile, the written word was also changing. Poetry began turning away from the elusive, twice-abstracted language of old toward a more direct, even colloquial style. In prose, language was becoming even more direct, conveying meaning simply and quickly, more like pictures" (147). The visual and linguistic arts were thus "headed for a collision!" (147). This "collision" in some ways anticipates Ranicère's "shared surface": "the fact that the modern comic was born just as art and writing were preparing to change direction is at least intriguing. And perhaps this common thread of unification did grow out of a shared instinct" (149). For accounts of definitional problems, see Groensteen "The Impossible Definition" and Heer and Worcester's editorial notes, especially their introduction to the section "Craft, Art, Form."

44. See, for example, Dudley Andrew's recent book, which opens with a contrast between a Bazinian-Truffautian tradition and Jean-Pierre Jeunet's hugely successful *Amélie.*

Works Cited

Andrew, Dudley. *What Cinema Is!* Sussex: Wiley-Blackwell, 2010. Print.

Arnold, Andrew. "Manga Mon Amour." *Time* 11 Nov. 2004. Print.

Aurita, Aurélia. "Je peux mourir, maintenant!". *Japon vu par 17 auteurs.* Ed. Frédéric Boilet. Paris: Casterman, 2005. Print.

———. *Fraise et chocolat.* Brussels: Les Impressions nouvelles, 2006. Print.

———. *Fraise et chocolat 2.* Brussels: Les Impressions nouvelles, 2007. Print.

Banfield, Ann. "L'imparfait de *l'objectif*: The Imperfect of the Object Glass," *Camera Obscura* 24 (1990): 65–87. Print.

Barthes, Roland. "The Death of the Author." *Image-Music-Text.* New York: Hill and Wang, 1977. 142–148. Print.

Bastide, Julien. "Conversation avec Boilet et Taniguchi." *Neuvième art. 2.0* Cité internationale de la bande dessinée et de l'image, 2004. Web. 08 Aug. 2012.

Beaty, Bart. *Unpopular Culture: Transforming the European Comic Book in the 1990s.* Toronto: University of Toronto Press, 2007. Print.

Boilet, Frédéric. *L'épinard de Yukiko.* Angloulème, France: ego comme x, 2001. Print.

———. "Manifeste de la Nouvelle Manga." Frédéric Boilet, n.d. Web. 08 Aug. 2012.

———. *Mariko Parade.* Paris: Casterman, 2003. Print.

———. *L'Apprenti japonais.* Brussels: Les Impressions nouvelles, 2006. Print.

Boilet, Frédéric and Benoît Peeters. *Tokyo est mon jardin.* 1997. Paris: Casterman, 2003. Print.

Boudet, François. "Entretien avec Frédéric Boilet, à propos de Love Hotel." Éditions Ego Comme X, 1997. Web. 08 Aug. 2012.

Bouissou, Jean-Marie. "Manga: A Historical Overview." Johnson-Woods 17–33. Print.

Bouissou, Jean-Marie, Marco Pellitteri, and Bernd Dolle-Weinkauff with Ariane Beldi. "Manga in Europe: A Short Study of Market and Fandom." Johnson-Woods 253–66. Print.

Caughie, John, ed. *Theories of Authorship: A Reader*. London: Boston: Routledge & Kegan Paul, 1981. Print.

Cohn, Neil. "Japanese Visual Language: The Structure of Manga." Johnson-Woods 187–203. Print.

Conley, Tom. "Cinema and its Discontents: Jacques Rancière and Film Theory." *SubStance* 34:3 (2005): 96–106. Print.

Couch, N. C. Christopher. "International Singularity in Sequential Art: The Graphic Novel in the United States, Europe, and Japan." Johnson-Woods 204–20. Print.

Foucault, Michel. "What is an Author?" *The Foucault Reader*. Ed. Paul Rabinow. New York: Vintage, 1984. 101–118. Print.

Gardner, Jared. *Projections: Comics and the History of Twenty-First Century Storytelling*. Stanford, California: Stanford UP, 2012. Print.

Groensteen, Thierry. "Why Are Comics Still in Search of Cultural Legitimation?" Heer and Worcester 3–11. Print.

———. "The Impossible Definition." Heer and Worcester 124–31. Print.

Hanawa, Kazuichi. *Doing Time*. Wisbech, England: Toptron/Fanfare, 2006. Print.

Heer, Jeet, and Kent Worcester, eds. *A Comics Studies Reader*. Jackson: UP of Mississippi, 2008. Print.

Ingulsrud, John, and Kate Allen. *Reading Japan Cool*. Lanham, MD: Lexington, 2009. Print.

Johnson-Woods, Toni., ed. *Manga: An Anthology of Global and Cultural Perspectives*. New York: Continuum, 2010. Print.

Kunzle, David. "Rodolphe Töpffer's Aesthetic Revolution" Heer and Worcester 17–24. Print.

Le Duc, Dominique. "La Nouvelle bande dessinée: L'épinard de Yukiko." *Belphégor* 6:2. Dalhousie University Electronic Text Centre, 2007. Web. 08 Aug. 2012.

Lejeune, Philippe. *Le pacte autobiographique*. Paris: Seuil, 1975. Print.

McCloud, Scott. *Understanding Comics: The Invisible Art*. 1993. New York: Harper, 1994. Print.

Nananan Kiriki. *Blue*. Paris: Casterman, 2004. Print.

Noguez, Dominique. "Tokyo mon amour." Boilet and Peeters 5–7. Print.

Paugam, Guillaume. "Boilet et l'envers de la BD: Nouvelle manga ou dernier avatar du japonisme?" *Labyrinthe* 25:3 (2006): 83–96. Web. 08 Aug. 2012.

Rancière, Jacques. *Aesthetics and Its Discontents*. Trans. Steven Corcoran. Cambridge, UK: Polity, 2009. Print.

———. *The Politics of Aesthetics: The Distribution of the Sensible*. Trans. Gabriel Rockhill. New York: Continuum, 2004. Print.

———. *Fables of Cinema*. Trans. Emiliano Battista. Oxford: Berg 2006. Print.

———. *The Future of the Image*. Trans. Gregory Elliott. London: Verso, 2007. Print.

Rommens, Aarnoud. "Manga story-telling/showing." *Image and Narrative*. 1 (2000). Web. 08 Aug. 2012.

Shamon, Deborah. "Cinematic Narrative in Gekiga." *Mangatopia: Essays on Manga and Anime in the Modern World*. Eds. Timothy Perper and Martha Cornog. Santa Barbara, California: Libraries Unlimited, 2011. Print.

Schodt, Frederik. *Manga! Manga!: The World of Japanese Comics*. New York: Kodansha America, 1986. Print.

Takahama Kan. *Monokuro Kinderbook*. Wisbech, England: Toptron/Fanfare, 2006. Print.

Taniguchi Jirō. *The Walking Man*. Wisbech, England: Toptron/Fanfare, 2006. Print.

Tatsumi Yoshihiro. *A Drifting Life*. Montreal: Drawn and Quarterly, 2009. Print.

Memory, Signal, and Noise
in the Collaborations of
Neil Gaiman and Dave McKean

—Isaac Cates

Neil Gaiman is best known for his novels and for writing *The Sandman*, one of the foundational titles of the DC Comics Vertigo imprint. The novels and *The Sandman*, along with a number of Gaiman's other works, occupy a recognizable genre, somewhere between fantasy literature and the contemporary gothic: Gaiman's protagonists are often, for example, fallen gods; his characters pass into alternate dimensions; their dreams are magically real. But Gaiman is not only a fantasist, and with his frequent collaborator Dave McKean he has also created a handful of short, intensely subjective but realist graphic novels, two of which work mainly within the conventions of the memoir. Gaiman himself has described these two books, *Mr. Punch* and *Violent Cases*, as "essentially . . . autobiography full of lies,"[1] and taken together they present a compelling argument about the uneasy interpretive position of children, the ambiguity of memory, and the fundamental fictiveness of memoir itself.[2] Neither of the books directly claims to be autobiographical fact, but since they employ the procedures of memoir, it is reasonable to consider the ways in which they engage and comment upon that ostensibly nonfiction genre. If memoir often promises to shed light on early mysteries or incompletely understood events, however, both of these books relish their obscurity, in places even deliberately feigning ignorance where the narrator later reveals knowledge. This artful occlusion mainly serves to recreate the interpretive position of the child, glimpsing but incompletely understanding the problems of adults. Gaiman and McKean develop their deliberate obscurity in all of the semantic fields available to comics: text, image, and even the relationship between text and image. By inviting the reader to resolve these ambiguities, Gaiman and McKean create an atmosphere of dense interpretive potential, charging details with the sense that they might mean more than is initially apparent. This surfeit of possible meaning, typically associated with genres like the gothic or the fantastic, is also, as Gaiman argues, an integral part of childhood experience, an aura around childhood memory that these faux memoirs would rather represent than resolve.

Violent Cases, Gaiman and McKean's first collaboration, may not engage these questions of interpretation and ambiguity as directly as *Mr. Punch* does, but the small trauma that opens *Violent Cases* is remembered with the same suggestive lack of clarity: "I would not want you to think I was a battered child," begins an adult narrator who looks a great deal like Gaiman, "However [. . .] when I was four years old my father did something to my arm. I no longer remember, if I ever knew, exactly what it was. He dislocated it, or sprained it."[3] This ambiguous injury leads to a series of visits to an osteopath, who apparently treated the gangster Al Capone on a regular basis decades earlier. In the conversations during their appointments, the young protagonist confides that he doesn't like parties, and the osteopath reveals his own history and a bit about his association with Prohibition-era gangsters. Later, without explanation, the osteopath appears again, in the bar of a hotel where the young narrator is attending a birthday party for the daughter of one of his parents' friends. After another conversation about Capone, the boy watches a trio in trenchcoats, carrying baseball bats, escort the osteopath out of the bar, presumably to his execution, though the narrator never confirms this fate nor gives a clear indication of why the osteopath would have been in danger. This climax arrives while the other children at the birthday party scuffle during a game of musical chairs, locating violence or the potential for violence in both child and adult worlds, in both private and public space. The secret that *Violent Cases* seems to be skirting is that the young narrator's father (and his father's friends) are connected to organized crime: the corpulent bald magician that appears at all the children's parties seems also to have, in his business life, a powerful position in the mob.

An even more sinister secret circulates through *Mr. Punch*, in which the narrator, as a boy of eight—possibly the same character who was four years old in *Violent Cases*, though McKean's rendering style changes enough both within and between the books that it's impossible to be certain—spends a summer with his paternal grandparents while his grandfather closes his failing seaside arcade. As he meets the employees of the grandfather's arcade, particularly the woman who sings as a mermaid in a tank and the "professor," Swatchell, who arrives to perform the Punch and Judy puppet show in the arcade's final days, the young boy is shuffled from the care of one adult to another, catching snatches of conversations he is probably not meant to overhear. Although the adult narrator never acknowledges it directly, these fragmentary conversations reveal that the grandfather is also terminating an affair he has been having with the mermaid, that she is pregnant with his child, and that, after she refuses to abort the baby, the grandfather beats her with a wooden board and she miscarries. The boy's grandfather subsequently goes mad, and the final memory in the book takes place while he is on day-leave from an asylum. Interspersed throughout the story, scenes from the Punch-and-Judy puppet play suggest correlations between the Punch puppets and the adults in the fictionalized memoir. The mermaid visually resembles the puppet of Punch's illicit girlfriend (his "little bit of stuff"—"But you won't never see her any more," Swatchell mutters, because the puppet has been retired from most performances of the show[4]). Both the grandfather and the hunchbacked Uncle Morton are symbolically connected to Punch himself at various points, as is Swatchell. These shifting allusive parallels contribute to the uneasy sense of invisible significance that permeates *Mr. Punch* and, as Gaiman argues, much of childhood.

For a child, as Gaiman's narrators explain, the world of adults is perceived just incompletely enough that its sense, adults' intentions and meanings, cannot be trusted. The narrator of *Mr. Punch* points out that behind the teasing threats and jibes of adults—"I'll eat you all up" or "I'll put you into the rubbish-bin"—is the anxiety that in this case the threat might be a true one: "no matter how much you tell yourself that they're lying, or teasing, there's always a chance. Maybe they are telling the truth. . . . Adults lie. But not always" (25).[5] Later, offering to hire the little boy, Swatchell simultaneously suggests that he is not sincere: "he laughed when he said it, in the way adults do, to show you that they don't mean what they're saying" (32). In both of these passages, as in most of the rest of the narration, the speaker positions both himself and the reader as children, or at least as outsiders to the world and the ways of adults; he explains adult behavior in order to make it strange again, to remind us how it looks through a child's eyes. "Adults do what adults do," he remarks. "They live in a bigger world to which children are denied access" (33). In *Violent Cases*, this division between the world of adults and the world of children is presented spatially and thematically rather than in the narration: the young boy peers at his distant parents through a crack in the door (13), or passes through a closed curtain from a child's birthday party to a hotel bar (22); when the osteopath is taken away by mobsters the boy watches from the other side of the curtain (40). In all of these cases, the effect for the young protagonist is a multiplicity of incomplete and unresolved meanings—"Adults lie. But not always."—that places mystery and interpretation at the center of both faux memoirs.

Further interpretive uncertainty is created, both in *Mr. Punch* and in *Violent Cases*, by the distance of these childhood memories, and by the acknowledged imperfections of memory itself. The narrator in *Mr. Punch* addresses this problem directly: "The path of memory is neither straight nor safe," he writes, "and we travel down it at our own risk" (10). Conversations with other family members, conducted years later, seem to contradict what the narrator remembers from his boyhood, and in the end he can only conclude, "I don't know what the truth was" (80). He is frequently explicit about being unable to remember things, or having only recently remembered things long forgotten. Early in *Mr. Punch*, he makes an effort to remember his great-uncle Morton's face, and pieces it together from details (hair, brow, grin, nose, eyes); accompanying this narration, McKean shows a silhouette that more accurately belongs to the Punch puppet (10) than to the images of Uncle Morton that appear later in the book. (In the previous panel, this silhouette seems to be the shadow of the boy, still young, brooding over the family photos on the mantel.) Over and over again, Gaiman's narrator calls attention to the shifting and uncertain quality of memory, particularly the private hearsay of recalled childhood, in a way that makes memoir seem a dubious if not impossible enterprise: "I wish with all my heart, now, I could go back and talk to them, ask questions, illuminate the darkness of the past. But these people are dead, and will not talk. Now that I want to go scrabbling around in the past, I cannot" (59).

The story in *Mr. Punch* takes place when the narrator is eight years old. The protagonist of *Violent Cases*, however, is only four, and his memories are even less complete, less precise, more shadowy and ambiguous, than those in *Mr. Punch*. *Violent Cases* is full of admissions of fragmentary or absent memory, but the one that stands out most prominently is forced onto the narrator by the comics medium: although the character must be presented visually, the narrator cannot clearly remember what the osteopath looked like. "I asked my father the other day," he tells us, and the fragments and combinations of details that his father remembers coalesce in a page of strikingly collaged images: "He had a big nose. An eagle's nose," the narrator's father recalls, over an image of an eagle's head, with the beak highlighted by a circle and a scribbled label reading "hook." The father continues: "He had a full head of hair—a good head of hair for such an old man. He spoke English with an accent—middle European. Not American." In the same panel of imagery, a doodle of a mustached man in spectacles with a hooked beak covers an enlarged photocopy of the dictionary entry for *English* and a faint, reduced map of Europe, with the Adriatic Sea at its center. "He looked like a red Indian chief,—a Polish red Indian chief," the father concludes, and an image of a Native American completes the collage. There is no mustache this time, but there is a marginal note reading "lots of hair" where no hair is drawn in (6). This nonsense concatenation of images leaves the narrator unsatisfied: "I am not sure that his description agrees with my own memories," he writes. "I remember an owl-like man, chubby and friendly, peering at me over thick spectacles." Rather than rejecting either of these images, the narrator "synthesize[s] the two pictures into a third, undoubtedly imaginary" (7) that is then used as the face of the osteopath for most of the book. Given McKean's protean approach to cartooning, however, the osteopath's image isn't entirely stable; mostly he can be recognized by his mustache and his glasses, or by the narrative context that leaves him as the only adult in the conversation.

A little over halfway through the book, however, during the scene in the hotel bar, Gaiman's narrator interrupts himself to correct the images of the osteopath. "I suppose I should intrude here," he says, "in the interests of strict accuracy,—and point out that the picture I have of him at this point is neither the grey haired Indian—nor the tubby doctor,—nor the amalgam of the two I remembered earlier in this narrative." Instead, he writes, he remembers the osteopath in the hotel bar looking "much younger," and "like Humphrey Bogart's partner in *The Maltese Falcon*." At this point and for the rest of the book, the osteopath's appearance changes radically, to a bespectacled portrait of the actor Jerome Cowan, a halftone photograph of whom is also collaged into the page (29). This redefinition or revision of a character's appearance partway through a comic flouts the medium's conventions of panel-to-panel continuity and may in fact seem more suitable to the logic of dreams than to any memories of lived experience. The ordinary reading experience of comics, like the navigation of the waking world, requires that people appear recognizably the same from moment to moment.[6] Although Gaiman's narrator makes this surprising alteration in the name of "strict accuracy," its overall effect is to blur even further the notion of accurate memory, to the point that even the things and people actually perceived by the child protagonist begin to behave like the figments of a dream.

Overall, both books seem to be making use of an approach to meaning and memory that approximates the genre or literary mode[7] that Tzvetan Todorov calls the *fantastic*. For Todorov, the fantastic operates by suspending the reader (and usually the protagonist as well) between two possible but mutually exclusive explanations for peculiar or unsettling events: either the events can be explained rationally by improbable but natural physical forces and human actions, or supernatural powers are responsible. As long as the phenomena remain unexplained, as long as the two possible explanations remain mutually suspended, the reader is in the uneasy position of "hesitating" between the explanations,[8] unable to assign meaning with any surety to the various "clues" that the narrative has presented up to that point. This hesitation or suspense is, for Todorov, the defining characteristic of the fantastic. The fantastic mode is therefore not merely defined by plot logic and missing explanation; it must also be a question of interpretation and interpretive alternatives, in that the uneasy atmosphere of the fantastic derives from problems of *reading* the unsettling phenomenon and its causes. Fantastic events are not merely unexplained; rather, they have at least two potential and mutually contradictory explanations. Because the fantastic relies in this way on the interpretation of evidence, Todorov must rule out instances of "poetic" or "allegorical" unreal events, which are only metaphorically present in the "evoked world" of the fiction and require a different approach to interpretation or comprehension.[9] If the events aren't depicted as "really" happening within the fiction, or if their primary value is understood to be symbolic rather than literal, then they will not carry the eerie charge Todorov associates with the fantastic. An event for which the correct interpretive paradigm is unclear, on the other hand—an image that might be literal or might be allegory—will participate in at least some of this fantastic uneasiness, at least until its significance (or at least its type of significance) resolves more clearly.

For Gaiman, it seems, the experience of childhood is inescapably fantastic in Todorov's sense of the word. The epistemology of childhood, handled honestly, must thus warp the genre of childhood memoir into something less rational, more interpretively suspended, and more spooky. The ways of the adult world are so obscure to Gaiman's child protagonists that they are constantly unsure about how to interpret what they perceive. In fact, each book also contains some supernumerary strange phenomenon that goes totally unexplained. In *Violent Cases*, the narrator describes seeing a star brightening until it illuminates the night with "a freezing white light," and then fading again into its place in the night sky, never seen or noted by anyone else (39). He sets the image aside as a memory "that simply [does] not work" in relation to the rest of his world (37). *Mr. Punch* opens with a scene that takes place about a year before the rest of the book, in which the boy is off for an early-morning fishing expedition with his maternal grandfather and finds an empty Punch-and-Judy tent on the gray beach. Although the boy (and the reader) can see that the puppet tent is empty, a performance begins, and the boy watches until Punch hurls his baby off of the little stage (3–7). No explanation is offered for the impossibility of either of these events, and no other witness corroborates either narrator's visions. Either the bright star or the haunted puppet tent could be a quirk of incomplete memory, a hallucination, or a dream remembered as real; either could be a supernatural occurrence: they are therefore phenomena in the realm of Todorov's fantastic. In fact, these events, ancillary to their main storylines, seem to be introduced mainly to conjure the queasy atmosphere of unknowing that accompanies the fantastic. The potential for paranormal explanation is not, however, the books' main source of this uneasiness; rather, it arises from the young protagonists' uncertainty about how to parse more ordinary events, and from an epistemology that views anything shadowy or ambiguous with the same creeping fear associated with the fantastic. Both books make a point of the way children easily believe things that adults can discard as impossibilities: the nursery-school theory that "there were miles and miles of snakes and worms inside a person [and] when you died they all came out" (*Violent Cases* 10), an aunt's claim that her dress conceals a tail (*Mr. Punch* 25), or the possibility that a badger mask (from a performance of *The Wind in the Willows*) might "whisper secrets" or "vast truths" (*Mr. Punch* 12–13). Since children live "in a land of giants," as the narrator of *Mr. Punch* puts it (13), something as ordinary as an undisclosed secret suggests shadowy possibilities akin to those of the fantastic.

Gaiman and McKean take pains to extend this atmosphere of interpretive fecundity throughout both books, chiefly by writing or making visible a kind of deliberate obscurity that invites close scrutiny while making any perfectly clear reading a challenge. This inscrutability is at work in all of the structural components of their comics: in Gaiman's text, in McKean's images, and even in the correlation between word and image. In this way,

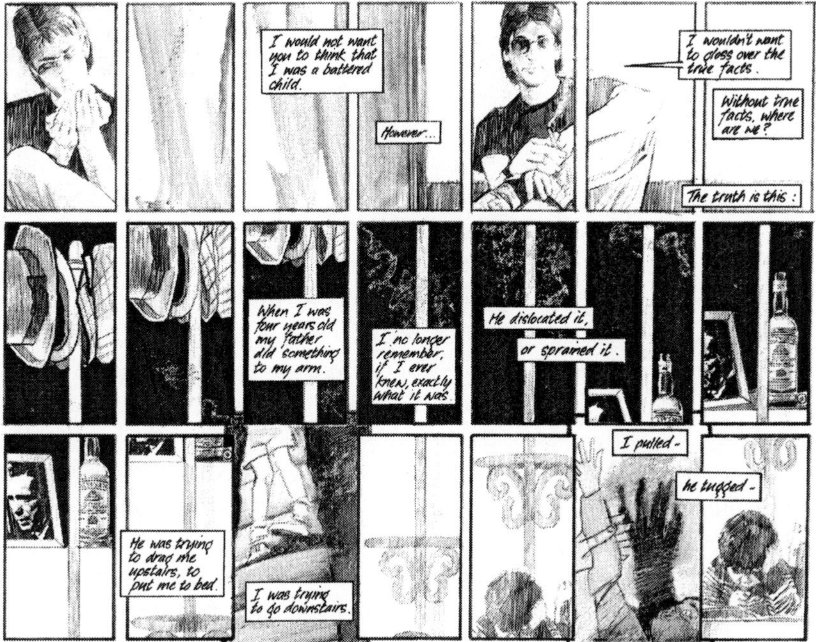

7.1. Occluded imagery on the first page of Gaiman and McKean's *Violent Cases*.

the collaborators are able to exploit the semiotic density of the comics page, which delivers information in several ways at once, by temporarily occluding one or more of those channels. In the momentary absence of a clear signal, the reading mind attempts to parse noise, however foggy or scruffy it seems. McKean's images, particularly in *Mr. Punch*, are often so distorted or so out-of-focus that they can be difficult to decipher. The first page of *Violent Cases* is a grid of thirty-five small vertical panels, eleven of which are bisected by the stem of a hat rack the same width as the panel gutters (the notional "camera" is slowly panning down from the hats to the boy reading at the base). These split panels create the illusion of twice as many panels, even narrower, each containing even more fragmentary information. Blurring, collage, and distortion are so common in both books as to appear on nearly every page. *Mr. Punch* makes extensive use of photo-collage, using photographs of actual Punch-and-Judy puppets, or of sculptures and assemblages McKean built for the book (often in turn incorporating fragments of photographs), double exposures, inverted or distorted photographs, photos that have been painted on or digitally lettered over, torn fragmentary photographs collaged together, and so forth.

The primary "reality" of the memoir is depicted in painted cartoon images (ink drawings photostated onto acetate film, viewed over a layer of opaque paint—the color for the ink cartoons and the white of the word balloons—applied to a blurred photo that serves as the background);[10] the other photographic manipulations listed above represent dreams, flashbacks, imagination, and a variety of other parallel framed representations, as well as the Punch-and-Judy puppet show itself. Learning to navigate these layers of representation is one of the challenges the book presents, and the unstable terms of its visual representation contribute to the creepy aura of hidden significance that permeates the book.

In fact, the half-seen or out-of-focus images are often but not always legible, as in one case when the boy narrator has wandered into the "Looking-Glass Hall" at the end of the labyrinth in his grandfather's arcade. The cartoon image of the narrator is, once he has reached this room, flanked by four distorted and orange-tinted photographs of a real boy, recognizable from other photographic representations of the narrator in earlier scenes. He is impressed for the first time with the fact that mirrors (like adults) can lie, and then realizes that "there [is] someone standing next to [him]. A huge head: beady wooden eyes." In the next panel, the boy turns to look over his shoulder, and in the third panel we see Swatchell, the Punch-and-Judy professor, looking back at him with narrowed eyes. In the second panel, however, before we see Swatchell, a different face is "reflected" in the blurry orange photographic background: the creepy Punch puppet from the recurring inserted scenes relating the puppet-show narrative (62).[11] This legible obscurity suggests, briefly, that Swatchell and Punch are at some level one and the same, though of course this is a room of distorted and not faithful reflections. Making the violent puppet the reflection of the puppeteer recalls Swatchell's warning that, as Punch is always on the puppeteer's right hand, once the puppet goes on, "he stays on" (40), or "once you bring Mr. Punch to life, there's no getting rid of him" (41). In the same scene where he delivers these warnings, however, Swatchell asserts that he is himself the Crocodile (one of the puppets), or that he "used to be" (38). Whatever conclusions may be drawn from the vision of Mr. Punch in Swatchell's reflection, the legibility of this blurred and obscured background photo both suggests a rationale behind the book's graphically mad surface and suspends multiple interpretations of the image. Imagery like this, at once potentially rich with meaning and resistant to complete understanding, occurs frequently in both *Mr. Punch* and *Violent Cases*, inviting the reader to pore over pages that cannot in the end be fully explained.

Gaiman's narration, furthermore, will often leave some detail vague or unspecified when it is clearly known to the narrator and understood by the reader. In the scene in the hall of mirrors, for example, the narration briefly withholds the identity of the person standing next to the young boy—"*someone* standing next to me"—rather than acknowledging that Swatchell is the other person in the room. At one point, earlier in *Mr. Punch*, the young boy approaches the back part of his grandfather's arcade, where the mermaid would be singing. There, "a small hunchbacked man [is] talking to the mermaid, who [is] sitting on the rock" in her artificial lake (57). On the following page, after the boy walks close enough to overhear the conversation (clearly about the boy's grandfather and his affair with the mermaid, though the boy doesn't realize it), he identifies this "small hunchbacked man" as his Uncle Morton, whom we have seen several times already. There is no other hunchbacked man among the cast of characters, except perhaps the puppet of Punch. The only reason for the narrator to be so indirect in describing his first sight of Uncle Morton in this scene is to summon a momentary illusion of uncertainty about Morton's identity, raising the question of whether this is a stranger, or whether Morton could have a double. In fact, one of the family mysteries that the narrator cannot resolve is whether either Uncle Morton or his brother, the boy's grandfather, had a lost twin (60, 80). The briefly sustained ambiguity contributes a charge of mystery to the conversation that follows. A similar moment of pointed non-identification occurs in *Violent Cases* as well, when the birthday-party magician, now dressed in a suit but carrying his starry robe, appears in the hotel bar where the boy protagonist is talking to Al Capone's osteopath. At this point, the narrator does not acknowledge that this bald man is the magician, initially naming him only with pronouns: "He smelt of fireworks,—and his head was as bald as a billiard ball. He asked for a pint of lager" (28). Later, after another story about Al Capone and the melee that ends the children's game of musical chairs, this bald man is called "the conjuror" (40), so the narrator clearly knows his identity even at his first appearance in the bar. Again, the text's obscurity invites interpretation and briefly sustains improbable alternative readings that turn out not to be true.

The most prominent of these moments of deliberately ambiguous writing is in the climax of *Mr. Punch*. Having entered the shuttered arcade at night to find a toilet, the boy accidentally eavesdrops on an altercation between "three men I recognised, and a woman that I didn't" (71). The narrator never identifies these three men, but since Morton, Swatchell, and his grandfather are virtually the only three male adults in the book, the reader can readily infer who they are. The images on these pages focus on the boy's face (a series of small sculpted masks that resemble his painted cartoon visage) peering out from under a scrim of burlap onto which shadows of the adult figures are cast. One of the men (likely the boy's grandfather) picks up "a slat of wood" and assaults the woman, "once in the stomach" and "once across the face" (73). She pulls herself to her feet and flees: "As she ran past me, blood dripping from the side of her face like red paint, panting and sobbing and clutching her swollen stomach," the narrator says, "I recognised her" (75). But his narration gives no indication of the woman's identity. Looking back at the previous two panels, which show her face without the blood he specifies, and her short brown hair, it is possible to recognize the mermaid without her long blond wig (74), whose "swollen belly" has been the object of rumor and speculation earlier in the book (57). (On the other hand, McKean's designs for the characters' faces are abstract enough that it's possible to misread this as a woman heretofore unseen in the book.) The panels that follow this moment of unexplained recognition hint at the consequences of her beating. The puppet of Mr. Punch's baby, the one he throws out the window, has been wrapped in white cloth and tucked up under the burlap wall all along, unnoticed, and in a sequence of four silent panels it falls away from the boy's hand: a metaphorical representation of the mermaid's miscarriage, never addressed or acknowledged by the narrator, but painfully visible to the reader thanks to McKean's images. Again, although the narrator states that he has recognized her, neither the text nor the images is explicit about this being the mermaid. The purposes of deliberate vagueness or obscurity here may go beyond conjuring that aura of the fantastic, suggesting perhaps the suppression of traumatic memories or a momentary slide into the interpretive paradigm of metaphor, but its main function seems still to be an invitation to interpretation, analysis, and careful scrutiny. This is, after all, the moment when the book's central secret is indirectly revealed; at this moment the reader must be primed to read with special attention. Although the narrator does not tell us whom he has recognized, he implies that a careful reader will be able to determine who, in fact, she is. Thus, like McKean's challenging images, the deliberate omissions in Gaiman's narration suggest there is more beyond the explicit—that the narrator's words, like McKean's images, must be interpreted.

Along these same lines, Gaiman's scripts also favor double meaning, double entendre, and suggestions of symbolism. These can be fairly straightforward instances of adults talking over the boy's head, as when his grandfather tells the mermaid, early in the book, "You come down to the office later, we'll reckon up" (26). This reckoning, literally the mermaid receiving her pay and possibly a scheduled sexual liaison, also foreshadows the violent, sorrowful reckoning that will come to the mermaid in the book's climax. Similarly, as Swatchell and the boy leave the mirror labyrinth, a final mirror on the floor reads, "Ladies beware" (65). In the preceding panel, Swatchell has described the mined beaches of World War II, so the mirror's warning underfoot (though most obviously about the mirror's capacity to give a view up a passing skirt) could refer back to that subject, though given the book's brutal conclusion it is clearly also foreshadowing another sort of warning as well. Even the title of *Violent Cases* makes extra significance out of the boy's malapropism for the violin cases in which gangsters of Capone's era carried their tommy guns (11). In a text that so favors double (or triple) meaning, the reader may be encouraged to construct additional meaning around incidents or lines of dialogue that are merely functional to the plot on the one hand or resolutely mysterious on the other hand. Soon, vague clouds of potential meaning circulate around almost every textual or graphic detail, justified by the winking hints and riddles that the reader has already solved. A pun that is a mere joke in its context can, in this atmosphere of symbolic potential, easily lend itself to dark foreshadowing; the offhand choice of a Dickens novel may suggest complex and fraught allusions.[12] In many ways this aura of interpretive potential is similar to the child's position, from which all statements might have a coded, secret, additional meaning never quite within the child's reach.

Gaiman's double-meanings and aporia are familiar literary devices, common both in prose and in verse, but a third sort of obscurity or complexity in his collaborations with McKean makes use of a semantic area particular to comics. Most of the panels in *Violent Cases* and *Mr. Punch* exhibit a relatively straightforward relationship between narration and image. In most cases, the image chiefly illustrates or elaborates on the text; at times, McKean's images are abstract enough or disconnected enough that they clearly "illustrate" tone rather than plot. But McKean also sets up sequences in which the connection—or what he has called the "counterpoint"[13]—between word and image is more difficult to define. In *Violent Cases*, for example, some panels illustrate ambiguously. During a story about Capone murdering a series of underlings with a baseball bat, a panel's narration states that one man "is trying to threaten Capone. The police chief is crying." McKean's image shows only a single male face, teeth exposed in a grimace and eyes squeezed tightly shut (33). This could be a depiction of either the man threatening Capone or the crying police chief; it can't be both. Another panel, near the book's conclusion, shows only a flare of light under the caption "He tipped his hat to me" (41). This could be a flash of light from the gangster's diamond-studded tooth, or it could be the inexplicably bright star that is described just two pages earlier. In *Mr. Punch*, whole sequences of panels occasionally come untethered from the narrative line. On one early page, for example, six panels show the boy protagonist being led by the hand away from his parents' home by his paternal grandfather, then looking up at his grandfather, who returns his glance and smiles. The narration on this page covers a great deal more time, including statements that might be difficult to illustrate. The boy is being sent away from home to protect his soon-to-be-born sister from "one of the routine childhood diseases—chicken pox, or mumps" that he has recently recovered from; the narration describes the way his other sister would tease him about not having been there to meet his new sibling, and the final panel reveals that the visit to his grandparents "was shortly before my grandfather went mad" (14). Perhaps only the third panel, where the narration discusses his having been sent away, has a direct illustrative relationship between text and image. In the others, however, one can't help looking for and discerning a resonance between the words and the picture. In the final panel, one might see a subtle sign of incipient madness in the grandfather's smile. In the first panel, where the caption reads "There's no getting away from the dead," the stakes of a picket fence slightly resemble tombstones and may suggest that the grandfather, his arm leading off past the right edge of the panel, will not survive until the boy is old enough to tell this story. As with the other deliberate obscurities of *Mr. Punch* and *Violent Cases*, this peculiar relationship between text and image does not offer so much an obstacle to interpretation as an invitation to more careful consideration of its details, a heightening of the reader's attention. When this augmented attention makes every detail potentially significant, however, and every blurred background or narrative vagueness potentially legible, then the reader's scrutiny begins to approximate that of the pensive children who are Gaiman's protagonists. Most memoirs of childhood offer, by means of the adult narrator's reflection and reassessment, some attempts to dispel the heady atmosphere of childhood half-knowledge; in this way, Gaiman and McKean leave the procedures of memoir incomplete, offering autobiographers who still cannot or will not resolve the mysteries of their upbringing.

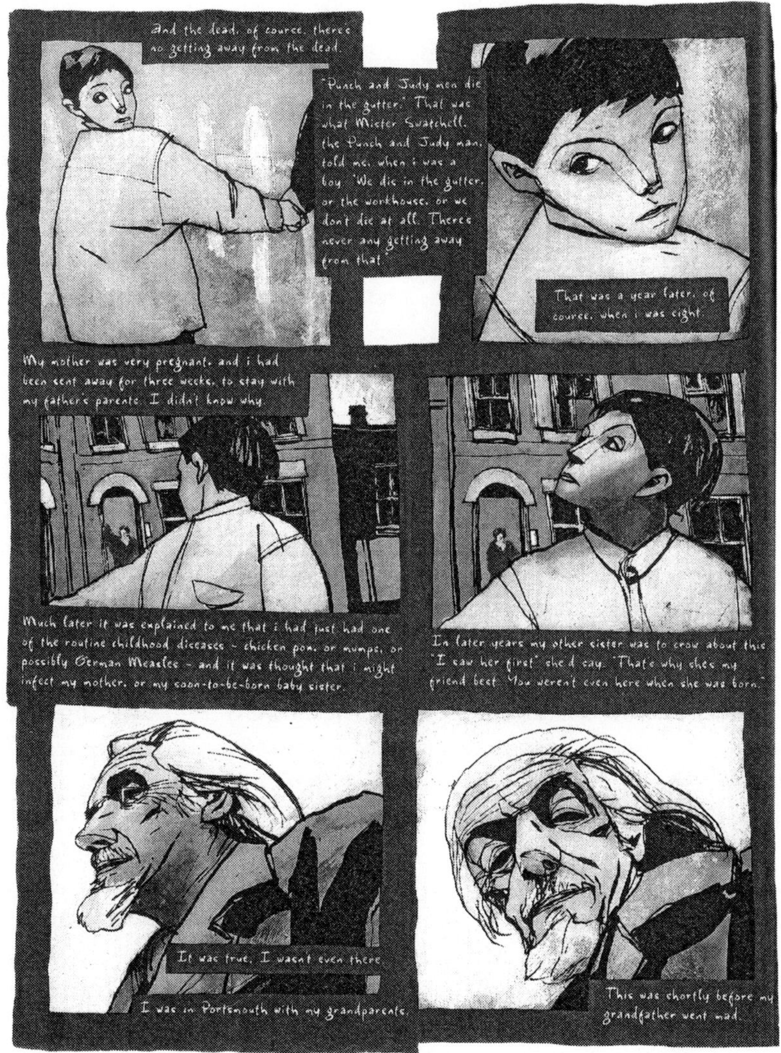

7.2. Text and image relate ambiguously in a sequence from Gaiman and McKean's *Mr. Punch*.

One of the most charged dissociations between text and image appears in the final panel of *Mr. Punch*. In the final scene, the narrator, after watching a Punch-and-Judy performance in a festival in Covent Garden "last May," sees (or thinks that he sees) Swatchell again, through the shifting bodies of a crowd, although he acknowledges that Swatchell could not still be alive. "Nobody lives forever," he says, "not even the Devil. Everybody dies but Mr. Punch, and he has only the life he steals from others" (85). Of course, if any credit is given to Swatchell's earlier stories about following Mr. Punch around as a dragon "in the dawn days" (39) or being harassed by "some busybodies, in the last Queen's day" (37)—that is, before Victoria's death in 1901—he may in fact be supernaturally long-lived; as in the tales Todorov labels fantastic, this question is never resolved. After this sighting or imagining of Swatchell, the narrator meets a puppet salesman who offers him two things. The first, a small device that the puppeteer holds in his mouth to make Mr. Punch's voice, is revealed for the first time in the book to be a *swatchell* (or, in more common terminology, a swazzle), suggesting that Swatchell's name may have been an alias, or (if he is in fact supernaturally superannuated) that he may have been the device's eponymous inventor in the "dawn days" of his profession. The second item is a Mr. Punch puppet, which the narrator dizzily and vehemently refuses to try on, even though (or perhaps because) it "would have whispered its secrets to [him], explained [his] childhood, explained [his] life" (86). He then sees a nearby Punch-and-Judy performance coming to its conclusion, as Mr. Punch defeats the devil and announces that "everybody is free to do whatever they wish" (88). A bottler (the puppeteer's assistant) asks him for money, and the narrator then leaves the churchyard, "shivering in spite of the May sunshine, and [goes] about his life" (89). This is the narrative caption in the final panel, which shows an inert Punch puppet half-buried by a sack of coins in front of a closed curtain. This Punch, the same puppet that has been photographed for nearly every Punch-and-Judy show in the book, is clearly not inhabited by a hand, but his bulging small-pupiled eyes and his leering grin suggest a kind of perpetual, sinister life. Although the puppet's unsettling visage might be enough to stir the shivers mentioned in the caption, the narrator is explicitly not reacting to this particular puppet. This Punch puppet's interminable stare, however, lingering as the book's final image, undermines the narrator's final claim that he is moving on with his life. Yet although they may undercut each other's apparent assertions, text and image have no direct relationship here. Although the coins suggest some sort of symbolic, almost allegorical, reading—violence and madness tied up with, or perhaps overwhelmed by, greed—nothing about this panel confirms either that specific interpretation or that allegorical approach to reading. Instead, the book concludes with a dissonant tension between what we see and what we are told, appropriate again to the interpretive position of the small child.

The deliberate obscurity of the faux-memoirs *Violent Cases* and *Mr. Punch* is less common in Gaiman and McKean's other comics collaborations, mainly because of matters of genre and tone. *Black Orchid*, their second collaboration, is a superhero story (albeit one with a twist) written for DC Comics; Gaiman and McKean take several steps to invert the standard superhero tropes, most notably resolving the book's final confrontation without any impressive display of super-powers, but their storytelling innovations are mostly limited to *Watchmen*-style ironic juxtapositions of (plot-driven) images with (quoted) text. *Signal to Noise*, a much more ambitious project that followed *Black Orchid*, has a good deal less narration and no interest in the creepiness that Gaiman and McKean seem to associate with childhood. In *Signal to Noise*, a fifty-year-old movie director discovers that he has terminal cancer and begins work on a final screenplay he knows he can never film. Although the book makes substantial use of abstract or non-literal images, in line with its thematic concerns with the legible and the illegible, there seems to be less confusion as to how these sequences should be read: McKean's images here are either representationally consistent with the text or abstractly removed from it. Though photographic images are manipulated and distorted in *Signal to Noise*, their lines are almost alienatingly crisp, and none of them is blurred by soft focus. When he narrates, Gaiman's film director is neither mysterious nor withholding. Given that the technique of deliberate obscurity appears prominently only in Gaiman and McKean's first and (so far) last comics collaborations, it seems deliberately linked with the heady atmosphere of half-knowledge that these works associate with recollected childhood. At eight years old, *Mr. Punch*'s narrator says, "I believed in what I could see and was scared of anything I couldn't. Scared of things in the darkness, of things invisible to see" (26). The central epistemological tenet in the child's position is that there *are* invisible things wherever none can be seen: adults' secrets, frightening histories, half-forgotten traumas, lurking crocodiles, or the hands of a hidden puppeteer. In these two books, Gaiman and McKean are careful to cultivate a reading atmosphere that encourages this epistemology, a suspicion that both the words and the images mean more than we can see.

One of the unarticulated tensions in comics criticism is in the contrasting claims about the power of comics to carry dense or rich information, and therefore about the sort of communication that should be prized in comics memoir. Writers and cartoonists as different as Scott McCloud and Art Spiegelman have argued that comics as a medium relies on a streamlining of information, or an abstraction by simplification, that approximates the diagram rather than the photograph. On the other hand, cartoonists—particularly cartoonists whose concerns run close to the documentary, either in journalism (like Joe Sacco's *Footnotes in Gaza*) or in the memoir (like Alison Bechdel's *Fun Home*)—are frequently praised for the capacity of their images to contain and organize information densely; writers like Alan Moore are celebrated for complex "multi-track" information in comics where several strands of text or image occur simultaneously, as if in a fugue. These two approaches to comics are not mutually exclusive, of course: almost any *Where's Waldo?* page, for example, will demonstrate that drawing can be both diagrammatically simplified and visually dense. What the schools of simplification and density share, however, is a celebration of the clarity of expression that Gaiman's collaborations with McKean instead call into question. If a memory is hazy, incomplete, or uncertain, they argue, it should not be represented with clarity, but with an occluded surface, full of ambiguities that, like the plots of Todorov's fantastic, resist explanation or classification. That these sorts of obscure textures can occur in works that are still unambiguously comics is a testament at once to McKean's commitment to a comics avant-garde[14] and to the still-unsounded potential of the medium.

Notes

I would like to offer my gratitude to Charles Hatfield, David Rosen, and Mike Wenthe, conversations with whom underlie much of my thinking about this material. I would also like to thank my colleagues Sarah C. Alexander and Jennifer Sisk, who offered useful feedback and assistance during my final round of revisions.

1. Neil Gaiman, interview by Kim Thompson, *Comics Journal* 155 (Jan. 1993) 71.

2. By this phrase I do not mean to invoke the role of memoir in self-discovery, self-creation, or the constructions of identities as discussed by life-writing critics like Paul John Eakin (in *Fictions in Autobiography: Studies in the Art of Self-Invention* (Princeton: Princeton UP, 1985) and in *How Our Lives Become Stories: Making Selves* (Ithaca: Cornell UP, 1999), for example)—but the obverse of this coin: the way that memoir is by its nature a made thing, pressed into structure by an author's inherited sense of narrative, including fictional narrative. In other words, even though its materials are factual, memoir uses not only the structures but also the shaping imagination required by fictional narrative. In *fiction*'s original etymological sense of a made or fabricated thing, memoir is also *fictional*.

3. Neil Gaiman and Dave McKean, *Violent Cases* (Northampton, MA: Tundra Publishing, 1992) n.p. Further citations of *Violent Cases* will appear parenthetically by page number in the body of the text. The pages of *Violent Cases* are not numbered, but I have numbered them in my copy; this opening narration is on p. 1.

4. Neil Gaiman and Dave McKean, *The Comical Tragedy or Tragical Comedy of Mr. Punch* (New York: Vertigo / DC Comics, 1995) n.p. As with *Violent Cases*, I have hand-numbered the pages in my copy; this exchange runs from p. 37–38. Future citations of *Mr. Punch* will occur parenthetically in the body of the text.

5. This confusion is not precisely the "interplay between 'meaning it,' not meaning it, and not *not* meaning it" that a savvy adult can detect in hyperbolic or ironically delivered threats and curses (Claude Rawson, *God, Gulliver, and Genocide: Barbarism and the European Imagination, 1492–1945* (Oxford: Oxford UP, 2001) 251). Gaiman depicts the child as unable to absorb different degrees of intent simultaneously, except as uncertainty and unresolvable mystery. At best, the child can *suspect* what an adult means by one of these teasing lies.

6. In this way, reading several images in a comics sequence really does resemble the psychological "closure" that allows the mind to assemble and complete the fragmentary information taken in by the senses. See Scott McCloud, *Understanding Comics: the Invisible Art* (Northampton, MA: Kitchen Sink Press, 1993) 63. McCloud quickly, in a bit of rhetorical sleight-of-hand, expands this sort of "closure" until it is a less precise and less useful term.

7. Todorov, in Richard Howard's translation, refers to the fantastic as a *genre*; Christine Brooke-Rose has argued convincingly that we should regard the fantastic as an *element* rather than a genre, since the fantastic can seem to exist within a work and then evanesce into either the uncanny or the supernatural. See Christine Brooke-Rose, *A Rhetoric of the Unreal: Studies in Narrative and Structure, Especially of the Fantastic* (Cambridge: Cambridge UP, 1981) 62–65.

8. Tzvetan Todorov, *The Fantastic: a Structural Approach to a Literary Genre*, trans. Richard Howard (Cleveland: Press of Case Western Reserve University, 1973) 33.

9. Todorov, 58–63.

10. This cumbersome multi-stage process of layering was, as McKean points out, "pre-computer." (Dave McKean, tweet to the author, 1 Aug. 2012.)

11. In truth, the reader probably sees and reads these two panels simultaneously. Even though there is a panel of uncertainty before Swatchell is revealed, his face is easily legible upon first glancing at the page, and much clearer in the reader's peripheral vision than the blurred face of Mr. Punch in panel two.

12. In fact, *Mr. Punch*'s narrator, while waiting for his grandfather to retrieve him, takes up *The Old Curiosity Shop* (68)—which features a mad grandfather, honest children deceived and betrayed, and a malicious hunchback.

13. Dave McKean, interview with Leo John De Freitas, *Comics Journal* 155 (Jan. 1993) 58.

14. See for example Dave McKean, interview with De Freitas, 58.

Works Cited

Brooke-Rose, Christine. *A Rhetoric of the Unreal: Studies in Narrative and Structure, Especially of the Fantastic.* Cambridge: Cambridge UP, 1981. Print.

De Freitas, Leo John. "Dave McKean Interview." *Comics Journal* 155 (Jan. 1993): 54–62, 65. Print.

Eakin, Paul John. *Fictions in Autobiography: Studies in the Art of Self-Invention.* Princeton: Princeton UP, 1985. Print.

———. *How Our Lives Become Stories: Making Selves.* Ithaca: Cornell UP, 1999. Print.

Gaiman, Neil and Dave McKean. *The Comical Tragedy or Tragical Comedy of Mr. Punch.* New York: Vertigo/DC Comics, 1995. Print.

Gaiman, Neil, and Dave McKean. *Violent Cases.* Northampton, MA: Tundra Publishing, 1992. Print.

McCloud, Scott. *Understanding Comics: the Invisible Art.* Northampton, MA: Kitchen Sink Press, 1993. Print.

McKean, Dave (DaveMcKean). "@SatisfactComics They were drawn on paper, then photostated onto acetate overlays, painting on photos underneath (pre-computer)." 1 Aug. 2012, 1:46 a.m. Tweet.

Rawson, Claude. *God, Gulliver, and Genocide: Barbarism and the European Imagination, 1492–1945.* Oxford: Oxford UP, 2001. Print.

Thompson, Kim. "Neil Gaiman Interview." *Comics Journal* 155 (Jan. 1993): 66–71, 73–82, 85. Print.

Todorov, Tzvetan. *The Fantastic: A Structural Approach to a Literary Genre.* Trans. Richard Howard. Cleveland: Press of Case Western Reserve University, 1973. Print.

The Graphic Memoir
in a State of Exception

Transformations of the Personal in
Art Spiegelman's *In the Shadow of No Towers*

—Lopamudra Basu

Trauma across Generations

This essay explores the graphic memoir *In the Shadow of No Towers* by Art Spiegelman as an example of autobiographical recording in graphic form of the very public national tragedy of 9/11. Unlike Spiegelman's previous foray in deploying the graphic memoir form for the memorializing of the public trauma of the Holocaust in *Maus 1* and *Maus 2*, this particular memoir is a commentary on immediate American foreign and domestic policies of the Bush era, rather than an attempt to recover and resolve the traumatic experiences of his ancestors. Spiegelman experiences and records his personal memories of the tragedy, but more significantly, he opts to voice his outrage at the co-optation of this national tragedy for the purposes of American military retaliation. In a climate of increasing censorship and the shrinking of the public sphere as a space for democratic protest, Spiegelman's graphic memoir oscillates between a polemical critique of the political administration and the parallel task of reproducing an archive of comics of the early twentieth century. Like the poetry readings referred to as therapeutic acts in the aftermath of 9/11, this is a self-reflexive act of recovering as a graphic memoirist by reconnecting with an older artistic tradition. It is also an act of harnessing the autonomous space of art to initiate resistance against the "state of exception" created in the U.S. after the events of September 11, 2001.

Spiegelman's memoir negotiates the role of art as polemic while also being autonomous from the political sphere. This graphic memoir is a significant testimony memorializing the national tragedy of September 11, 2001, by an eyewitness and graphic memoirist. It also contributes to the debate about American retaliatory wars in Iraq and Afghanistan abroad and the curtailment of domestic freedoms within the territory of the U.S. under the auspices of the Patriot Act, which inaugurated a state of exception to the constitutional safeguards of the U.S. This is done in the graphic memoir in a popular form rather than in the genre of a debate on political theory. Nevertheless, it is an important contribution to the archive of testimony and analysis of the collective national trauma. The personal memoir in graphic form fuses the immediacy of the autobiographical voice with the visual images of the tragedy. The personal eye-witness testimonial lends credibility to the critique of the political situation. The graphic images in the memoir evoke visual memories of the tragedy obtained from television, but the comic art form of the work defamiliarizes the images and invites alternative perspectives to rethink and re-evaluate the trauma in ways that do not repeat the prevailing narrative of American national victimhood and recuperation through an imperialist war.

Although critical responses to *In the Shadow of No Towers* have been varied, I consider this memoir to be a record of Spiegelman's personal encounter with the trauma of the destruction of the Twin Towers, which triggers in his psyche the traumatic memory of the Holocaust experienced by his parents. This graphic memoir can be read as a continuation of his previous memoirs, which exclusively focused on his parents' experiences. In *Unclaimed Experience: Trauma, Narrative, and History*, Cathy Caruth provides a definition of trauma with an example to clarify it:

> In its most general definition, trauma describes an overwhelming experience of sudden or catastrophic events in which the response to the event occurs in the often delayed, uncontrolled repetitive appearance of hallucinations and other intrusive phenomena. The experience of the soldier faced with sudden and massive death around him, for example, who suffers this sight in a numbed state, only to relive it later on in repeated nightmares, is a central and recurring image of trauma in our century. (11)

Not only is repetition a characteristic of personal trauma, repetition of traumatic memory seems to be recurring in the psychic lives of the next generation. In this sense, the Holocaust (and the anti-Semitism producing it) resurfaces not only in the lives of Spiegelman's parents, influencing his mother's suicide, but the painful memory revisits Spiegelman too. In the aftermath of 9/11, the fear, confusion, and disorientation produce a recurrence of Holocaust memories. Spiegelman draws many explicit connections between his earlier exploration of trauma in *Maus* and the present memoir.

In a relatively small panel on the second broadsheet of *In the Shadow of No Towers*, Spiegelman connects his traumatic experience and its effect on his artistic sensibility to Samuel Taylor Coleridge's "Rime of the Ancient Mariner" by drawing himself as a bearded, middle-aged, bespectacled intellectual with an albatross tied around his neck. Although this panel parodies the great Romantic poem about suffering and art, this allusion traces a distinct genealogy of the integral connection of traumatic memory with art and underscores once again the repetitive and recursive nature of trauma. Like the suffering of the ancient mariner, precipitated by his wanton act of violence in killing the albatross, the memory of which revisits him periodically and for which the only available release seems to be in the telling of his story, the traumatic family history of surviving the Holocaust is a burden that Spiegelman inherits and has to grapple with often in his own life. The past traumas of the Holocaust seem to fuse with the present horrors of surviving the destruction of the Twin Towers in 2001. The image of the albatross around Spiegelman's neck is symbolic not only of the burden of the family trauma of the Holocaust but of his own self-chosen vocation of the historian/memoirist of that trauma through works like *Maus 1* and *Maus 2*. According to David Hajdu in a *New York Times* review, "*Maus* and its Pulitzer elevated comics in the public eye, much as they lifted Spiegelman out of the realm of mere comic-book people and up a few tiers in the cultural hierarchy to the sphere of serious, respected authors and artists." In writing a memoir of September 11, 2001, Spiegelman has to contend with the burden of his own fame as serious comic artist along with the similarities of the two violent and traumatic experiences, without conflating the two. The protagonists of the two memoirs are contrasted by their differing personalities. Hajdu notes the contrast between Vladek and Art: "The elder was a man of unceasing action and confidence, the younger a reflective sort haunted by impassivity and doubt." This reflective personality identifies Art Spiegelman with the figure of the suffering mariner in Coleridge's poem.

Spiegelman experienced this incident personally; as a long-term resident of Lower Manhattan, he spent the first few hours in the aftermath of the attacks trying to find his daughter and son at their respective schools, which were close to the site of the burning towers. Unlike his Pulitzer award–winning *Maus 1* and *Maus 2*, which chronicle the experience of the Holocaust that his father underwent, this encounter with trauma is experienced directly and its recreation through the graphic memoir takes place in the immediate aftermath of the traumatic event. There is no luxury of time or generational distance to provide a healing perspective on this corrosive material that he must grapple with as an artist. In the opening lines of the preface in *In the Shadow of No Towers*, Spiegelman invokes his familial connection with trauma, through the specific invocation of his parents' survival of the Holocaust during the Second World War. He admits in the preface that his own ill-preparedness for coping with trauma, along with his excitable and nervous temperament, had not equipped him for "coping with the sky when it actually falls." Spiegelman notes in the preface that he finds himself "on the fault lines where World History and Personal History collide—the intersection [his] parents, Auschwitz survivors had warned [him] about when they taught [him] to always keep [his] bags packed." In this opening statement, Spiegelman is highlighting the intersection of this graphic memoir with personal trauma as well as contemporary public events, necessitating reflection on public and foreign policy. He also situates his personal experience of 9/11 in the family history of surviving trauma by specifically invoking his parents' experience of Auschwitz.

Incidentally, the title of the preface is "The Sky is Falling Down" and it appears in boldface on one side of the book and the letters are inverted in the same title in boldface on the page on the other side. At the center of the narrative preface is a circle with images of two petrified men in close up against the backdrop of the twin towers rendered in orange and red colors. On the opposite page there is an even larger circle, where the faces of the two men have been blown up further, accentuating their terror-stricken expressions. However, the image on this page is not a self-contained circle; the image has been lightened to form the backdrop on which the text appears in the foreground. This circle recurs in the first of the comic broadsheets, with the figures of the men drawn in more detail. This time the circle is captioned "Waiting for that Other Shoe to Drop" and also includes the photograph of a giant shoe suspended above the heads of the fleeing human figures. Spiegelman's comic art is literalizing the metaphor for impending disaster.

The textual connection with Spiegelman's earlier graphic memoirs *Maus 1* and *Maus 2*, mentioned in the preface, is expanded through graphic images in the third broadsheet of *In the Shadow of No Towers*.

In this section, Spiegelman reverts to the representation of himself as a mouse, just as he had drawn his father and other Jewish relatives as mice in the earlier graphic memoirs. In this sequence, it is not Spiegelman's father but he himself who is represented as a mouse as he reflects on the physical environment of Lower Manhattan after the destruction of the towers and finds the odors of this carnage unbearable. He makes an explicit comparison between the air of his neighborhood with the toxic air of Auschwitz that his parents had described as "indescribable." He uses the term "witch's brew" to describe the amalgam of "asbestos, PCBs, lead, dioxins, and body parts" that pollute the air of Manhattan (3). In the lower half of this broadsheet, we witness Art Spiegelman literally taking over his father's nervous and paranoid persona. Not only does he represent himself as a mouse, he also depicts himself as organizing a protest against the air quality of the city, which he claims is unfit for children. He also represents himself as a nervous wreck, smoking endlessly and declaring that in a post-9/11 world, he may not live long enough to be killed by cigarettes.

Spiegelman connects his family's experience and the surviving memory of the Holocaust with his personal paranoia, stemming in part from the continuation of anti-Semitism in the U.S. This anti-Semitism becomes immediately apparent in the popular rumors circulating in the city after the disaster. In the sixth broadsheet, Spiegelman recreates his harrowing personal encounter with anti-Semitism, directed at him from a homeless "Crazy Lady." In spite of Mayor Giuliani's attempts to purge the city of its poor and homeless population in his campaign against crime, somehow the Crazy Lady had not disappeared. Prior to 9/11, she had uttered "incoherent invective" at Spiegelman (6). In the post-9/11 city, somehow her invective transforms from Russian to English and her tirade is directed at Spiegelman's Jewish identity as she threatens to hang all Jews from the posts, one by one. This episode is a reminder to Spiegelman that even though anti-Semitism has become relatively less prevalent in contemporary New York, it is still present, in fringe groups, and these old and buried animosities can be ignited and released into the open in unpredictable ways. However, Spiegelman in the next panel vociferously retaliates against the invective of this Russian woman by stating "Damnit Lady! If you don't stop blaming everything on the Jews, people are gonna think you're crazy!" (6). This seems to be Spiegelman's response to the conspiracy theories subscribed to by many traumatized Arab Americans that 9/11 was a Jewish plot. Spiegelman refers to these theories in the preface and in this sequence he lashes out against it. Once again, the Crazy Lady episode opens old wounds and perpetuates the trajectory of generational trauma. However, Spiegelman does not cast himself as a victim here, but angrily rebuts these unfounded conspiratorial rumors about Jewish involvement in the tragedy.

Spiegelman's emphasis on his personal experience of the traumatic event of 9/11 and his effort to link this with the historic trauma his family experienced as Nazi concentration camp survivors helps to establish his credibility as a political commentator. His political intervention in the debate on American policy in the aftermath of 9/11 cannot be easily dismissed as a response prompted by his left-wing ideological leanings or an abstract, intellectual response of someone who has not been affected by the immediacy of the attacks. The personal relationship with the tragedy also affects the form of the graphic memoir and the unique aesthetic it develops, which, while being thoroughly engaged politically, relies on the logic of its aesthetic for its success rather than on the polemic of its content.

Cartoons and Politics

Critical responses to *In the Shadow of No Towers* have spanned the range of enthusiastic admiration to harsh dismissal of its merits. I explore some strains of the debate in the reception of this graphic memoir to provide an overview of reader responses to the memoir. However, my greater emphasis in this section is to situate the memoir in the context of political debates about 9/11 and its aftermath. In the concluding section, I attempt to examine Spiegelman's aesthetic as something that goes beyond the polemical focus of the work.

David Hajdu's review of *In The Shadow of No Towers* locates it in the tradition of family memoir begun with *Maus* and focuses on explicit connections between the two. Michiko Kakutani's review, while tracing the memoir's connection with the *Maus* books, sees in it an aesthetic break from the earlier works. For Kakutani, "*No Towers* is ultimately a fragmentary, unfinished piece: brilliant at times, but scattershot, incomplete and bizarrely truncated." Kakutani expresses her dissatisfaction with many artistic and literary works that have attempted to memorialize 9/11; she thinks that many of them attempt to forcefully impose an aesthetic closure on content that defies such an attempt and often feels "hollow and forced." She believes that time and distance are needed to produce the best artistic works on traumatic events and that not enough time has elapsed between the tragedy of 9/11 and the production of Spiegelman's memoir. However, she is appreciative of the fragmentary, disjointed, and hybrid form of the work as "a harbinger of artistic works to come." For Kakutani, the memoir's "frantic, collage like juxtaposition of styles; its repudiation of traditional narrative; its noisy mix of images and words; [. . .] all recall the most innovative works to come out of the Vietnam War, works like Michael Herr's *Dispatche* and Tim O'Brien's *Going After Cacciato.*" In spite of Kakutani's hesitation about the unfinished quality of the work, she is already attempting to secure a place for this graphic memoir in the canon of literary representations of 9/11.

Not all early reviewers were so positive about *In the Shadow of No Towers*. Adam Begley's review in the *New York Observer* accuses Spiegelman's work of narcissism. Begley's criticism can be summarized in his statement: "In short, *No Towers* is interesting, provocative, even amusing—but not compelling." Begley believes that the over-emphasis on the author and his paranoia and the lack of an ability in the narrative to keep the reader engaged ultimately compromise the artistic merit of the work. In a similar vein, Noah Berlatsky in a review originally published in the *Comics Journal* launches a scathing attack on Spiegelman's work. The main reasons Berlatsky cites for his dislike of the book include the lack of a plot or suficient autobiographical material, the hybrid and fragmentary nature of the drawings, and the lack of a strong connection between the reproductions of old comics and Spiegelman's own drawings. Ultimately, like Adam Begley, Berlatsky also accuses Spiegelman of narcissism, and like David Hajdu, Berlatsky accuses Spiegelman of nostalgia for the early-twentieth-century world in which comics began. Berlatsky goes a step further and criticizes Spiegelman for a limited understanding of the historical origins of imperialism and global capitalism, which were flourishing in the early twentieth century.

A scholarly article which takes into account these varied early reviews and critiques and provides a convincing defense of Spiegelman's artistic strategies is Kristiaan Versluys's essay "Art Spiegelman's *In the Shadow of No Towers*: 9/11 and the Representation of Trauma," published in a 2006 issue of *Modern Fiction Studies*. In this essay, Versluys offers two reasons for the fragmentary style of the graphic memoir and its "random pile up of material," both of which have provoked a negative reaction from some reviewers. Given the background of the commodification of 9/11 memorialization, Versluys believes that Spiegelman must have felt "the pressure to avoid an easy, unproblematic rendering of historical facts" (989).

Therefore, it is Spiegelman's choice to avoid complete transparency of meaning in the memoir. Versluys argues that the fragmentary nature of the narrative also serves as "objective correlative for the author's scrambled state of mind" (989) and that the memoir is a "direct, in-your-face impression of extreme confusion and perplexity" (989). Versluys does not read the introduction of early twentieth-century comic characters as an escapist or nostalgic move, but rather as an attempt to work through the trauma by using a strategy of defamiliarization, similar to the use of animal characters to represent trauma of the Holocaust. He also sees the early comic characters as allegorically connected to contemporary events. Versluys concludes that the "cartoon characters account for both distance and resistance" (991). In my personal reading of the graphic memoir, I extend Versluys's insights and examine how the appendix of cartoons is not extraneous, but instead is connected integrally to the political and aesthetic preoccupations of the graphic memoir.

Much of the reader response to Spiegelman's memoir has focused on whether the aesthetic form is effective. The political content of the memoir has not always received sufficient attention. I think the aesthetic and the political questions raised in the memoir are intertwined. It is important not to diminish either. This graphic memoir is a serious political comment on post-9/11 American foreign and domestic policies. I examine some dominant currents in the theoretical analysis of American wars in Iraq and Afghanistan, in order to argue that *In the Shadow of No Towers* contributes to this discourse, even though it is rendered in a popular comic art form. Even though Spiegelman's memoir has elicited a variety of critical responses, there seems be a broad consensus that it is a serious attempt to record and represent the traumatic events of 9/11, as well as admiration for its attempt at fashioning a new aesthetic to accomplish the complex task of memorializing trauma and articulating a strong political critique.

Spiegelman's representation of the post-9/11 U.S. seems to be closely related to the characteristics of a state of exception as theorized by Giorgio Agamben. Agamben's explicit connection between the Afghanistan detainees/prisoners of war and the Jews in Nazi concentration camps resonates powerfully with Spiegelman's own identification of the loss of civil liberties for American citizens and the parallel loss of universal human rights for prisoners in Iraq and Afghanistan with the erosion of democratic freedoms his Jewish family members experienced during the Second World War, which culminated in the horrific experience of Auschwitz.

Agamben uses the Carl Schmitt's 1922 definition of the sovereign as "he who decides on the state of exception" as a launching pad to explain a condition of "juridical measures that cannot be understood in legal terms" (1), and he goes on to describe the state of exception as "the legal form of what cannot have legal form" (1). Agamben's classic example of a state of exception, derived from Schmitt, who is considered the theorist of the Nazi state, is the example of Hitler's Germany. Hitler's "Decree for the Protection of the People and the State" suspended the Weimar Constitution. Agamben identifies the Third Reich with the "state of exception":

> The decree was never repealed, so that from a juridical standpoint the entire
> Third Reich can be considered a state of exception that lasted twelve years.
> In this sense, modern totalitarianism can be defined as the establishment, by
> means of the state of exception, of a legal civil war that allows for the physical
> elimination not only of political adversaries but of entire categories of citizens
> who for some reason cannot be integrated into the political system. (2)

Although Agamben provides a condensed history of the emergence of the state of exception in history, his immediate inspiration for the theorization of the state of exception is the USA Patriot Act of 2001. He does provide previous examples of the state of exception that is the suspension of usual laws for the state, posited as necessary to the interest of survival of extraordinary situations. Positive examples of prior states of exception, where American constitutional safeguards against excessive presidential powers were suspended, include Abraham Lincoln's Emancipation Proclamation and Franklin D. Roosevelt's New Deal legislation, which coped with the extraordinary circumstances of Civil War and the Great Depression respectively. However, for Agamben, the USA Patriot Act of 2001 is qualitatively different from these two previous examples of the state of exception and more similar to the "spectacular violation of civil rights (which) occurred on February 19, 1942, with the internment of seventy thousand American citizens of Japanese descent" (22). American laws already allowed for immigrants suspected of compromising American national security to be taken into custody. According to Agamben, the new feature of the state of exception created by the Bush administration is that

> it radically erases any legal status of the individual, thus producing a legally
> unnamable and unclassifiable being. Not only do the Taliban captured in

> Afghanistan not enjoy the status of POWs as defined by the Geneva Convention, they do not even have the status of persons charged with a crime according to American laws. Neither prisoners nor persons accused, but simply 'detainees,' they are the object of a pure de facto rule, of a detention that is indefinite not only in the temporal sense but in its very nature as well, since it is entirely removed from the law and from juridical oversight. The only thing to which it could possibly be compared is the legal situation of Jews in Nazi *Lager* (camps), who, along with their citizenship, had lost every legal identity, but at least retained their identities as Jews. (4)

The similarity of perspectives shared by Agamben and Spiegelman is revealed in numerous images depicting the infringement of civil liberties, as well as newspaper headlines collected in the last broadsheet, one of which reads: "War is Hell (On Your Civil Liberties)." However, the most visceral connection with the Holocaust is made when Spiegelman draws himself as a human with a mouse face and compares the air quality of lower Manhattan to "what the smoke in Auschwitz smelled like" (3), underscoring the physical and psychic feelings of oppression produced by the political ideologies underpinning each historic event.

Agamben's theory of a state of exception has attracted considerable scholarly attention and debate. Among his detractors, John Brenkman in *The Cultural Contradictions of Democracy* interprets Agamben's theory of sovereignty as it emerges from Carl Schmitt as a "deceptively appealing criticism of the modern state and a symptom of the malaise of contemporary 'radical' political thought" (20). Brenkman goes on to cite the 2006 Supreme Court ruling in the case of *Hamdan vs. Rumsfeld*, which held that the Geneva Convention provisions applied to "enemy combatants." According to Brenkman: "Congress and Democrats remained fairly timid and acquiescent even after the Supreme Court in effect overturned the Bush administration's understanding of executive power, largely because the public's commitments to rights and international law seemed far less intense than its craving for a sense of security and invincibility" (55)" Brenkman emphasizes the limits to the unbridled power of the Bush administration exerted by the Supreme Court and public opinion. He maintains that "presidential power is not absolute, even under what are widely perceived as wartime conditions" (55). Brenkman critiques Agamben for his tendency to club all kinds of limitations of civil liberties under the umbrella of the state of exception, without offering some analysis of the structures within modern democratic states that deter absolute transformations into autocratic regimes.

Unlike Spiegelman, who is very attentive to the imperialist underpinnings of the post-9/11 American retaliatory wars and the oil interests that these wars are supporting, Brenkman's line of argument does not address the question of the imperialist rationale for spreading democracy, a project that has had dubious results. Recent examples of pro-democracy movements in Tunisia and Egypt suggest that indigenous struggles towards democracy are far more likely to succeed than western-backed wars of liberation. Secondly, Brenkman's analysis pays very little attention to the American materialist interests in the Iraq campaign and the lure of oil money that lies at the heart of this American adventure, camouflaged by the overt rhetoric of democracy and freedom.

Spiegelman's observations and insights about the Iraq war resonate with Naomi Klein's trenchant critique of the war as an enterprise serving the aggressive capitalist interests of the U.S. In *The Shock Doctrine: The Rise of Disaster Capitalism*, Klein does not accept the general consensus in the establishment that "the invasion was a 'success' while the occupation was a failure" (331). She argues instead that "the invasion and occupation were a part of a unified strategy—the initial bombardment was designed to erase the canvass on which the model nation could be built" (331). The invasion of Iraq created conditions of sensory deprivation, similar to methods described in CIA torture handbooks, by the deliberate destruction of phone lines, so that Iraqis would be unable to get any information about the survival and safety of their relatives after brutal and incessant bomb blasts. In addition, American forces made no attempts to save the artifacts of the National Museum, which are some of the oldest artifacts of human civilization, and no steps were taken to guard the art treasures from mob violence. Klein argues that these were concerted attempts to strip Iraqis of their sense of nationhood, pride, and culture. With that accomplished, the American caretaker government in Iraq under Paul Bremer proceeded to sell and whittle away the assets of the Iraqi state. Bremer auctioned off many state assets, opened the borders to the free flow of cheap goods, and stopped food and fuel subsidies to Iraqis. These economic reforms imposed unprecedented hardships on Iraqis and bred tremendous hostility against the American occupation. It escalated unemployment and it decimated state-run industries, public schools, and a free public health system. All these parts of the Iraqi state were auctioned off to corporations like Halliburton, bringing about a reverse of the Marshall Plan. Unlike the original Marshall Plan, which provided assistance to Germany and Japan and helped to develop their economies by including Germans and Japanese people in the process of wealth creation, Paul Bremer's methods only facilitated profits for American companies and impoverished the Iraqi people. This, Klein claims, was the root cause of the insurgency, which exacerbated the old ethnic divisions between Shias, Sunnis, and Kurds. The disenchantment of Iraqis with the sham in the name of nation building, their economic desperation, and shame in losing their rich historical national identity spurred the growth of more groups of Islamic militias. Spiegelman's concluding page tabulating various newspaper headlines makes several references to dubious "weapons of mass destruction" as the rationale for the Iraq War. These ironic headlines include "Forget Osama, Says Bush—But Look out Saddam!" and "Weapons of Mass Disappearance. *Time* 6/09/03." This collection of black-and-white newspaper headlines in the last page of the memoir suggests that Spiegelman is deeply skeptical of the official information on the war and rationalizations for the military intervention being offered in the mainstream media. Like Naomi Klein, Spiegelman seems to be acutely aware of the commercial interests of companies such as Halliburton determining the course of the Iraq War.

Donald E. Pease, in *The New American Exceptionalism*, weaves Agamben's theories of a state of exception (as that in which normal juridical privileges are suspended) with the older idea of America's exceptionality as a nation. This older idea of American exceptionality emerges from foundational myths of American nation building like the idea of America's manifest destiny, its status as a chosen nation, and a nation destined to lead other nations. Pease goes on to argue that at different moments in American history, governments have created elaborate fantasies of American exceptionality, and the citizens' relationships to their homelands have been mediated by these constructed fantasies. Pease uses a psychoanalytic framework to argue that it is the task of fantasy to "construct a vision of society that is not split by internal division, a society in which relations among parts appear organic and complementary" (15). Pease asserts that 1950 ushered in the first prolonged state of exception, in the sense invoked by Agamben, since it marked the beginning of the Cold War with the Soviet Union. During this era, the fantasy of the threat of communism to the survival of the state was deployed to limit free speech, trade unionism, and a host of other freedoms previously permitted. The fantasy of a state at war or facing imminent attack from communism successfully preempted any protests against the limitations to these fundamental democratic rights. Pease traces the events of the Vietnam War, particularly the figure of the traumatized survivor of Vietnam, as the image that was able to disrupt the totalizing narrative of the Cold War state fantasy. The Gulf War, with its televisual representation of American might conquering Iraq, was meant to usher in the fantasy of American triumph and superpower status after the end of the Cold War. However, the abject figure of Rodney King being beaten by LAPD in March 1991 disrupted this mythology of American nationalist pride and produced instead a sense of shame and outrage at the continued inability of the nation to protect the rights of its minorities. After 9/11, George W. Bush tried to reinvigorate the fantasy of American exceptionalism by reworking the myth of a virgin land of the Puritans with a deliberate presentation of Ground Zero as virgin land that had been violated by foreign attackers. The attacks were followed by the Patriot Act, which severely limited the civil rights and liberties of Americans for the sake of securing the state in a pattern not very different from the logic of the Cold War. Pease points to the manner in which the Virgin Land fantasy transformed citizens to spectators of the violence perpetrated by the state in its wars abroad: "These spectacles of violence encouraged the public's belief that it participated in the state's power because it shared in the spectacle through which the state gave expression to its power. But the people were also the potential targets of the shows of force they witnessed" (173). The visual images that disrupt this trajectory of American citizens' consumption of the spectacle of war are the photographs of Abu Ghraib. Pease claims: "Abu Ghraib's significance resided in the restoration of a history of national shame that met with the disapproval or condemnation of the entire political spectrum. [. . .] The Abu Ghraib photographs exposed the Homeland Security State as the cause of the traumas it purported to oppose" (190). Pease concludes his book with images of homeless men and women after Hurricane Katrina and of the figure of Cindy Sheehan, the mother of a soldier killed in Iraq who became an anti-war activist, as images that radically disrupt the fantasy of the homeland security state. Pease is very sensitive to the power of visual images in creating state fantasies and also to the power of alternate images that disrupt these totalizing state narratives. Although Abu Ghraib, Cindy Sheehan, and Katrina do not appear as images in *In the Shadow of No Towers*, Spiegelman is consciously engaged in the task of deconstructing official narratives of American retaliatory wars and deploys a whole range of comic techniques to provide alternative images of 9/11 and its aftermath.

In developing images of American society after 9/11, how does Art Spiegelman interrogate the fantasies available to a world overloaded with visual stimuli and images of the trauma? Spiegelman's representation of American democracy seems to express a despondent and even cynical attitude, rather than positing any faith, as Brenkman does, in the system's ability to correct itself from excesses by its own internal system of checks and balances. He refuses the rationale for wars as humanitarian interventions against autocratic regimes and hints at pecuniary reasons for the military campaign. The memoir does not offer us images of destruction of Baghdad, but there is a profound sense of identification with the victimization of Iraq.

Agamben's comparison of the targets of the USA Patriot Act with Nazi concentration camp prisoners is relevant to an analysis of *In the Shadow of No Towers*. This is precisely the political insight of the memoir, and the repeated references to Spiegelman's parents' survival of Auschwitz resonate not only with Spiegelman's personal encounter with the destruction and decay of Lower Manhattan, but also with the general attack on civil liberties for all citizens as a result of this "exceptional" legislation. Spiegelman encounters this attack on American civil liberties personally in the de facto code of censorship ushered in by the Bush administration, which severely limited the public sphere of free speech and democratic exchange of ideas. Any dissent or disagreement with the Bush administration's policies was either directly censored, or the dissenters were quickly labeled as "unpatriotic." It is not a coincidence that public intellectuals and entertainers such as Susan Sontag and Bill Maher faced a great deal of criticism and Maher faced the cancellation of his show on network television for daring to attribute a certain perverse courage to the perpetrators of the World Trade Center bombings. It should be emphasized that this particular graphic memoir too was first published in Germany, rather than the U.S., since the audience in the U.S. at that time and the conditions in the publishing industry were not conducive to its publication within the U.S. In his preface Art Spiegelman mentions his good fortune in having his friend Michael Neumann offer to publish his 9/11 cartoons in the German weekly broadsheet newspaper *Die Zeit*. Spiegelman notes the reluctance of mainstream publications such as the *New Yorker*, the *New York Times*, and the *New York Review of Books* to publish these cartoons and points out that his only success in finding a willing publisher was with *Forward*, a descendant of an Yiddish broadsheet paper.

This difficulty in finding an American venue to publish his cartoons corresponds with Spiegelman's general disenchantment with American democracy expressed in the preface: "When the government began to move into full dystopian Big Brother mode and hurtle America into a colonialist adventure in Iraq—while doing very little to make America genuinely safer beyond confiscating nail clippers at airports—all the rage I'd suppressed after the 2000 election [. . .] returned with a vengeance." In this angry and emotional personal outburst, Spiegelman touches on the twin sources of political disenchantment that compromise the conception of the U.S. as an idyllic democracy. The first is the charge of imperialism, which taints the military action in Iraq. The second is the reference to the controversial election of George W. Bush to office in 2000, only with the aid of a Supreme Court ruling in a bitterly contested election against Al Gore. The drawings that follow in the broadsheets expand on these issues, which for Spiegelman have severely reduced the credentials of American democracy. In the panels on broadsheets, we find clear expression of Spiegelman's agreement with the idea of post-9/11 U.S. as a de facto state of exception, which Agamben using Schmitt had compared to the Nazi concentration camp. There is an attempt to represent the erosion of the values embedded in the U.S. Constitution. Spiegelman's drawings are engaged not only in the recording of the transformation of the U.S. into a state where democratic laws are suspended, but also in the creation of an alternative visual archive of 9/11 and its aftermath. In the same way that Donald Pease charts the creation of the fantasy of the homeland state, by transforming citizens into spectators of violence, which is eventually overturned by the arrival of alternative visual images, Spiegelman's drawings are an attempt to dismantle the fantasy of the Bush homeland state by the presentation of an alternative set of visual images and commentary that debunk the narratives of American innocence, victimhood, democracy, nationalism, and the ethics of the wars in Afghanistan and Iraq.

On the second broadsheet of the memoir, Spiegelman once again depicts himself as a mouse, in human attire, slouching over a table, with an Al Qaeda figure on one side, sporting a long beard, black Islamic priestly attire, and flashing a blood-drenched sword and a figure resembling George W. Bush in a grey suit, carrying an American flag on the other side of the table. This panel carries the caption "Equally terrorized by Al-Qaeda and by his own government." On pages 9 and 10 of the graphic memoir, Spiegelman depicts himself as a mouse, again. In these instances, it is not just to reinforce his connection with his family's experience of the Holocaust, but to underscore his sense of victimhood under the Bush administration and its policies on war with Afghanistan and Iraq, as responses to the national trauma of 9/11. The author depicts himself as ranting and mouthing expletives against the regime in power, feeling an overwhelming sense of frustration and helplessness. The final column before the memoir crosses over to the reproduction of old comics also depicts the author as a mouse against the backdrop of the Republican National Convention in New York City. The textual description of this scene dates the event as September 2004 and laments the fact "tragedy is transformed to travesty" (10).

Spiegelman also presents a scathing image of the 2000 election. On the seventh broadsheet, he presents a map of the U.S. predominantly shaded in red and two flags below it, the blue one containing stars and the red one donning only stripes with the captions "the united blue zone of America" and "the united red zone of America" appearing below the two flags. The text that runs as a heading to this drawing reads: "The stars and stripes are symbol of unity that many people see as a war banner. A detailed county by county map of the 2000 election—the one that put the loser in office—made it clear that we're actually a nation under two flags" (7). This division of the country along party lines and its devastating effects on the democratic system is underscored in the panel titled "Ostrich Party," where the text describes the Republicans as elephants and the Democrats as "dimwitted donkeys" (5). The rhetoric is fairly bombastic and calls for a new and revolutionary party. This party, however, is the Ostrich Party and its members are represented as burying their heads in the ground. This panel is clearly a satirical and parodic depiction of the state of American democracy. Not only is the country divided ideologically by party line, a large third group of Americans only subscribes to the political ideology of ignorance and apathy. The implicit question seems to be "Can the U.S. have a functional democracy when the majority of the people are not involved in political life?" In fact, in an opinion piece in the wake of the 2011 protests against collective bargaining rights of public employees, economist Paul Krugman has characterized the U.S. as an oligarchy.

In this section of the graphic memoir, Spiegelman is engaged in a lively polemic, expressing in several panels his strong opposition to the Bush administration. He clearly views Bush and his colleagues as oppressors of liberty. In the panel at the center of page 8, Bush is caricatured as a goblin-like figure with pointy ears and wearing a conjuror's hat with stars and stripes, wielding a hammer like a judge. To his stars and stripes hat, a rope is attached; the other end of the rope is tied around the Statue of Liberty's neck like a noose that is pulling her down from her pedestal. This is the most literal representation of the metaphorical attack on civil liberties under the Patriot Act of George W. Bush. Other panels that directly attack the Bush regime include one on page 4 in which Bush and Cheney are represented as recognizable cartoons riding on an albatross. Bush is saying "let's roll," while Cheney asks "Why do they hate us?" In another explicit attack on the Bush administration, Spiegelman represents Bush, Rumsfeld, and Ashcroft as the three cards in the Collector's pack titled "The Architects of Armageddon." This is followed by instructions in a red circle "Collect the Set . . . Available Wherever Finer Petroleum Products Are Sold" (9). In this panel, Spiegelman seems to be obliquely referencing the integral connection of state of exception with imperialist wars, which ultimately further the next stage of capitalism. Similar to what Naomi Klein has revealed in her study, Spiegelman's images also emphasize the seamy underside of the mission to spread democracy. It is more about finding cheap sources of oil and capturing the new markets that will be opened up as a result of the created need to rebuild Iraq.

The most powerful and recurring image of the broadsheets is the image of the burning twin towers. This is an image that has been imprinted in the public consciousness with innumerable replays on television networks and the internet. Spiegelman depicts this scene not as the brick and mortar buildings crashing, but as "the image of the looming north tower's bones just before it vaporized" (Preface). This is the image that is repeated many times in the early pages. In some early panels the towers are depicted as long structures in orange, with only the skeleton grid of the building visible. On page two, the glowing towers appear in a series of smaller panels at the bottom of the page. With each panel the tower shrinks and the sky appears to occupy more space, till in the final panel, where there is no vestige of the tower and the orange glow of the fire has merged into the blue sky.

Graphic Memoir and Artistic Autonomy

In my analysis of Spiegelman's graphic memoir, I have highlighted his personal relationship with a history of trauma and the manner in which he moves from the deeply personal to an intervention in the public discourse on 9/11 through his graphic memoir. He expresses strong political differences with the ideology of the Bush administration and voices a critique of its foreign and domestic policies. He uses a variety of literary and artistic strategies such as parody, satire, and photographic realism to undercut the official narratives of post-9/11 history, simultaneously debunking the fantasy of the homeland as virgin land under attack from foreign terrorists. The graphic memoir moves from this feisty tirade against the regime in power to a more self-reflexive moment, in which he traces a historical lineage of the genre of the newspaper cartoon and ends the memoir with a reproduction of seven plates of early twentieth-century comics. This sequence of older comics gives *In the Shadow of No Towers* an identity as an inheritor of the newspaper comic genre. It separates it from being just a political or journalistic tract. Even though it is a work passionately advocating against the Bush regime, its success and attempt at literary and artistic longevity is accomplished by self-consciously inserting itself into the history and canon of cartoon art. This section of the memoir helps to give this work an autonomous artistic space, which according to Frankfurt School writers such as Adorno, Marcuse, and Benjamin is essential to the success of a work of art. In my essay "Crossing Cultures/ Crossing Genres: The Reinvention of the Graphic Memoir in *Persepolis* and *Persepolis 2*," I argue that the form of the graphic memoir lends itself to artistic autonomy.

Among theorists of the autonomy of artistic forms, Herbert Marcuse defines aesthetic form as "the result of transformation of a given content (actual, historical, personal or social fact) into a self contained whole: a poem, play, novel, etc. The work is thus 'taken out' of the constant process of reality and assumes a significance and truth of its own" (8). Thus the work of art exists in a close relationship with reality but it does not exist on a coequal plane. Marcuse argues, "The criteria for the progressive character of art are given only in the work itself as a whole: in what it says and how it says it" (19). This idea is echoed in Walter Benjamin's famous statement in "The Author as Producer," where he writes, "I should like to show you that the tendency of a literary work can only be politically correct if it is also literarily correct. That is to say that the politically correct tendency includes a literary tendency" (256). Thus for Frankfurt School writers such as Adorno, Marcuse, and Benjamin the formal, aesthetic aspect of a work of art rather than its political content is what defines its progressive, political character. *In the Shadow of No Towers* is already a work defined by a political agenda. However, it is in its formal, self-conscious attention to its artistic form that it is able to establish a distance from the immediacy of its political context. This memoir has to preserve a fine balance between being a polemical text while preserving its artistic autonomy.

Spiegelman is able to preserve the artistic integrity of his graphic memoir not only by his careful and painstaking attention to the images, but by juxtaposing these recent images with older images from the cartoon archives of newspapers of the early twentieth century. The most striking of these is "The Glorious Fourth of July" plate, which is reproduced as Plate IV in the Appendix. In this plate, we see Foxy Grandpa's attempts to read "The Declaration of Independence" consistently foiled by the prankster kids. The kids succeed in dynamiting the speaker's podium, which leads one character to comment, "I detest the Fourth of July." The choice of this panel is significant since it echoes many of Spiegelman's own panels which question the foundational myths of American nationalism and most importantly reject the new fantasy of the homeland state that needs protection from terrorists with the help of security measures that compromise civil liberties. Spiegelman is not alone in his skepticism of triumphalist American nationalism and he draws on his predecessors in the comic art tradition, who had undercut the formalism and pomposity of nationalist rhetoric with parodic laughter and slapstick comedy. The disruption of the reading is on one hand a prank engineered by children, but it is symbolic of the unfulfilled promises of life, liberty, and pursuit of happiness, ideals that were envisioned in the foundational document of the American nation, but ideals which were unfulfilled in the early twentieth century, the time the cartoon was produced originally in the *New York American* comic supplement. In the context of 2004, Spiegelman's reproduction of this comment with its specific allusion to the Declaration of Independence seems to reinsert the question of the ideals of the Declaration and their erosion in the light of Patriot Act legislation, which limits civil liberties of a large number of Americans and foreigners who may be under suspicion of terrorism.

While the Fourth of July plate seems to resonate with Spiegelman's reflections on the state of American democracy, other plates seem to eerily prefigure the traumatic events of the destruction of the Twin Towers. The plate titled "Bringing up Father," published in the *New York American* on May 24, 1921, depicts a rustic character's discomfort with the Leaning Tower of Pisa. He is traumatized by dreams of the Leaning Tower exploding and falling and cannot accept the fact that it was built like that. He ends up arranging stilts around the tower to provide what he believes are necessary supports to prevent the tower from toppling. The image of a tall and famous building collapsing and the image of such destruction infiltrating the psychic life of the protagonist parallels the early pages of Spiegelman's memoir, where the image of the burning towers reduced to their skeletal frames recurs as the traumatic memory that the author cannot escape.

Finally, the plate titled "Little Nemo in Slumberland" is remarkable in its vivid drawings of Manhattan skyscrapers and the city's waterways. Nemo is lost in the city and disoriented. In the final panel of this plate, Nemo appears to be in bed, comforted by a parental figure. The entire sequence appearing before was Nemo's terrifying nightmare. Once again, this plate resonates with the early panels in *In the Shadow of No Towers*, where Spiegelman and his wife are disoriented in the immediate aftermath of the destruction of the Twin Towers and struggling to make their way to the schools of their children.

Lauren Berlant has described the transformation of the political public sphere into "an intimate public sphere" (4), where "acts which are not civic acts, like sex, are having to bear the burden of defining proper citizenship" (5). Berlant argues that citizenship in the U.S. is being increasingly stripped of its association with public movements initiated by adults and is being replaced by limiting notions of normative heterosexual intimacy. With the shrinking of the public sphere as a space for democratic protest, Spiegelman's graphic memoir oscillates between a direct critique against the political administration and a shift to reproducing an archive of early twentieth-century comics. Like the poetry readings referred to as therapeutic acts in the aftermath of 9/11, this is a self-reflexive act of recovering as a graphic memoirist by reconnecting with an older artistic tradition. Although Spiegelman's retreat into the archive of old comics may appear to be a shift into a notion of citizenship defined by intimate or personal practices, the acts of attending poetry readings and reading old comics are not devoid of their public interventionist dimensions. A poetry reading, while not as overtly political as a demonstration, is a gathering of people who may be inspired to act politically as a result of being exposed to moving testimonies in verse. Similarly, Spiegelman's turn to the older tradition of comics is not an evasion or escape from politics, but an attempt to seek artistic inspiration beyond the immediate moment. Thus, while the climate of the Patriot Act legislation places severe limits on political and artistic actions, Spiegelman is able to successfully transform an intimate space of reading comics in solitude to a space of powerful artistic and civic engagement.

Rereading old comics is also an act of harnessing the autonomous space of art to initiate resistance against the "state of exception" created in the U.S. after the events of September 11, 2001. Spiegelman's memoir successfully negotiates the role of art as polemic as well as art as autonomous from the political sphere. His reproduction of old comics debunks the idea of the artist as an alienated Romantic poet and posits instead the image of an artistic community, where ideas may be transferred across generations through the survival of comic masterpieces, and where art has the ability to inspire critical thinking and action, across temporal and geographic boundaries.

Works Cited

Agamben, Giorgio. *State of Exception.* Trans. Kevin Attell. Chicago: U of Chicago P, 2003. Print.

Basu, Lopamudra. "Crossing Cultures/ Crossing Genres: The Reinvention of the Graphic Memoir in *Persepolis* and *Persepolis 2.*" *Nebula* 4.3 (2007): 1–19. Web. 30 May 2012.

Begley, Adam. "Image of Twin Towers Ablaze Haunts Narcissistic Cartoonist." Review of *In the Shadow of No Towers* by Art Spiegelman. *New York Observer.* 13 Sep. 2004. Web. 15 May 2012.

Benjamin, Walter. "The Author as Producer." *The Essential Frankfurt School Reader.* Eds. Andrew Arato and Eike Gebhardt. New York: Continuum, 1997. 254–69. Print.

Berlant, Lauren. *The Queen of America Goes to Washington City: Essays on Sex and Citizenship.* Durham, NC: Duke UP, 1997. Print.

Berlatsky, Noah. "In the Shadow of No Talent." Review of *In the Shadow of No Towers* by Art Spiegelman. *Comics Journal* 264 (2004): 64–68. the *Hooded Utilitarian.* 10 Sep. 2008. Web. 24 May 2012.

Brenkman, John. *The Cultural Contradictions of Democracy: Political Thought Since 9/11.* Princeton, NJ: Princeton UP, 2007. Print.

Caruth, Cathy. *Unclaimed Experience: Trauma, Narrative, and History.* Baltimore: Johns Hopkins UP, 1996. Print.

Hajdu, David. "Homeland Insecurity." Review of *In the Shadow of No Towers* by Art Spiegelman. *New York Times.* 12 Sep. 2004. Web. 14 May 2012.

Kakutani, Michiko. "Books of the Times: Portraying 9/11 as a Katzenjammer Catastrophe." Review of *In the Shadow of No Towers* by Art Spiegelman. *New York Times.* 31 Aug. 2004. Web. 14 May 2012.

Klein, Naomi. *The Shock Doctrine: The Rise of Disaster Capitalism.* New York: Henry Holt, 2007. Print.

Krugman, Paul. "Wisconsin Power Play." *New York Times.* 20 Feb. 2011. Web. Mar. 15, 2012.

Marcuse, Herbert. *The Aesthetic Dimension: Toward a Critique of Marxist Aesthetics.* Boston: Beacon, 1972. Print.

Pease, Donald. *The New American Exceptionalism.* Minneapolis: U of Minnesota P, 2009. Print.

Spiegelman, Art. *In the Shadow of No Towers.* New York: Pantheon, 2004. Print.

———. *Maus 1: A Survivor's Tale.* New York: Pantheon, 1986. Print.

———. *Maus 2: A Survivor's Tale.* New York: Pantheon, 1992. Print.

Versluys, Kristiaan. "Art Spiegelman's *In the Shadow of No Towers*: 9/11 and the Representation of Trauma." *Modern Fiction Studies* 52.4 (2006): 980–1,003. *Project Muse.* Web. 15 Mar. 2012.

History, Memory, and Trauma

Confronting Dominant Interpretations of 9/11 in Alissa Torres's
American Widow and Art Spiegelman's *In the Shadow of No Towers*

—Davida Pines

Nearly three thousand people died in the September 11, 2001, terrorist attacks on the World Trade Center, with countless others directly and indirectly affected by the disaster. Yet despite a multiplicity of stories, experiences, and perspectives on the attacks, a limited series of images have come to stand in for 9/11. Among them are: a deep and cloudless blue sky, the Twin Towers ringed in flames and smoke, the uncanny approach of the second plane, bodies falling from unimaginable heights, the collapsing skyscrapers, embattled rescue workers, the wreckage at Ground Zero, "missing" posters and make-shift memorials, ubiquitous American flags, the altered Manhattan skyline.

Marianne Hirsch addresses the need to reduce atrocity to a few still images: "In the work of cultural memory, their multiplicity may be overwhelming, and thus the archive of atrocity photos is quickly limited to just a few emblematic images repeated over and over. In their iconicity and repetition, they may lose their power to wound" (1212). Yet, while constant exposure to a limited number of images can immunize viewers against trauma, it can also desensitize them to the images and encourage disconnection from the event. In addition, the replaying of key images contributes to the construction of a dominant or "official" version of the events and a consequent blotting out of individual memories, experiences, and interpretations, both verbal and visual.

Several 9/11 memory projects worked against the reduction of the event to a few representative images. The SoHo exhibit titled *Here is New York: A Democracy of Photographs*, for example, invited "anyone and everyone who has taken pictures relating to the tragedy" to submit their images (*Here is New York* 2001). The exhibit ultimately showcased more than 5,000 unframed anonymous photographs, intermingling shots by professional and amateur photographers. Refusing to elevate or otherwise distinguish one photograph, or way of seeing, from another, the exhibit underscored the sheer number of individual witnesses to the events of 9/11. *Portraits of Grief*, an *in memorium* series published daily in the *New York Times* from September 15–December 31 likewise gave equal space to each of its 1,910 subjects. With each profile no longer than a few paragraphs, none of the portraits overshadowed another; in fact, the brief pieces—more anecdote, Nancy K. Miller notes, than obituary—intended to conjure ordinary moments: "Like the snapshot, the anecdote, through the brevity of its narrative, catches life in its everyday dimensions" (Miller 115). And while one might question, as Miller does, the "codes of idealization" that characterized the portraits—"We can only guess by what is reported elsewhere about family feuds the details that have been suppressed or edited out" (121)—in the relentless coverage of the dead, the *Times* series underscored how many lives had been lost.

One forum that focused less on the sheer numbers of individual witnesses and victims of the disaster and more on the relationship between the actual experiences of individuals and the public narratives constructed in the wake of the attacks was the "The September 11, 2001, Oral History Narrative and Memory Project" at Columbia University's Oral History Research Office and Institute for Social and Economic Research. As Mary Marshall Clark notes in her "First Report" on the project, "Oral historians have often claimed that the lived experience of history is more complex than subsequent interpretations reveal" (569). In an effort to gain insight into the "lived experience" of 9/11 as compared to the dominant interpretations that arose quickly in the aftermath of the attacks, oral historians at Columbia's Research Office conducted interviews with 200 individuals both directly and indirectly affected by 9/11. According to the study, the "dominant account portrayed a nation unified in grief; it allowed government officials to claim that there is a public consensus that September 11 was a turning point in the nation's history that has clear implications for national and foreign policy" (569). In fact, the interviews revealed a gap between public and private interpretations of the attacks: "our interviewers gathered evidence of massive and overwhelming trauma from people who suffered from isolation and despair, responding to an environment in which there was little public understanding of their experiences" (Clark

574). Moreover, Clark observes, "While many of the genuinely heroic stories did indeed help promote unity in grief for the short term, they failed to account for long-range trauma and loss on both collective and individual levels. These stories included portraits of the September 11 rescuer as national hero/patriot, of New York City as 'wounded' but bouncing back, and by extension of the September 11 survivors as 'one in grief and mourning'" (574). James Berger's comments on "the transformation of overwhelming loss into a kind of victory" in the immediate aftermath of 9/11 underscore Clark's report. Berger observed, "The media soon spoke more about the heroes of September 11 than of the dead" (55).

In their respective representations of 9/11, Alissa Torres (*American Widow*), with art by Sungyoon Choi, and Art Spiegelman (*In the Shadow of No Towers*) use the comics medium to capture the specifics of their lived experiences of September 11th and the months following. Their works actively challenge the public narratives of unity, triumph, and heroism denoted in Clark's report, so much so, in fact, that Spiegelman's work, completed serially over the course of 2001–2002, was refused publication by mainstream American publishers until 2004. As Spiegelman himself notes in his introductory essay "The Sky Is Falling!," "Outside the left-leaning alternative press, mainstream publications that had actively solicited work from me (including the *New York Review of Books* and the *New York Times* as well as *The New Yorker*) fled when I offered these pages or excerpts from the series." The work's bitter critique of the Bush Administration's response to the attacks was deemed too dangerous for the mainstream American press to risk association with the work.

The early unenthusiastic reception of Spiegelman's work notwithstanding, comics, with its mingling of the verbal and the visual, offers a particularly apt medium for the representation of individual and collective trauma of 9/11. By offering a space for visual representation, the comics medium permits the introduction of 9/11 images that were neither captured nor continually replayed by the media. Moreover, comics enables the inclusion of deeply private perspectives, for example, the nightmarish or recurrent hallucinatory images so often connected with an individual's post-traumatic stress. In challenging the dominant verbal and visual narratives of 9/11 through their respective comics works, Torres and Spiegelman ask: to whom do the images and interpretations of 9/11 belong? What is the relationship between individual and collective cultural memory? How do we ensure that public interpretations of 9/11 reflect the complexity and specificity of lived experiences?

In its reliance on the active participation of the reader to make sense of juxtaposed words and images, the comics medium involves the reader in the construction and reconstruction of history, and specifically individual and collective memory. In Scott McCloud's language, comics depends on the reader to "commit closure" (63)—that is, to make connections and to fill in the gaps. McCloud elaborates: "Every act committed to paper by the comics artist is aided and abetted by a silent accomplice. An equal partner in crime known as the reader" (68). In requiring that readers take an active role in meaning (and memory) making, the medium of comics works against the passive consumption of prescribed verbal and visual narratives and encourages readers' participation in the construction of complex history.

In the introduction to their collection of essays *The Image and the Witness: Trauma, Memory, and Visual Culture*, Frances Guerin and Roger Hallas posit "an image-based process of bearing witness," in which the "intersubjective relations generated by the presence of the image opens up a space for a witness who did not directly observe or participate in the traumatic historical event'" (12). Rather than "'secondary' or 'retrospective' witnessing," Guerin and Hallas argue that the witnessing of representational images of trauma "is in fact primary to the collective cultural memory of traumatic historical events" (12). Accordingly, in their use of comics to represent the traumatic public and private history of 9/11, Torres and Spiegelman not only call on the reader to construct new meanings and interpretations of the history but also to bear witness to experiences not seen before and thus to strengthen and broaden the collective cultural memory of 9/11.

I. Witnessing Loss in *American Widow*

In her graphic memoir *American Widow*, with illustrations by Songyoon Choi, Alissa Torres uses the comics form to tell the story of losing her husband in the September 11th terrorist attacks on the World Trade Center. At 8:46 am on September 11th, Luis Eduardo Torres—Eddie—was at his second day of work at Cantor Fitzgerald, a brokerage firm whose offices took up the 101st–105th floors of the North Tower of the World Trade Center. He was one of the firm's 658 employees—and one of the 2,750 people in New York City—who perished in the September 11th attacks. At the time, Eddie's wife, Alissa, was seven and a half months pregnant with their son.

Prior to the events of September 11th, Alissa Torres had never created a graphic narrative. She was neither a visual artist nor a cartoonist. In the year following the event, she wrote a series of articles on her experiences as a so-called "9/11 Widow." She explains, "I wrote through my grief. I kept journals and published personal essays" (Alissa Torres). Yet in shaping her experiences into a memoir, Torres chose comics, a form that combines words and images. In a 2008 interview, Torres explained her choice in terms of the deeply visual nature of the events, both on a public and private level. Not only, she explains, did she, like so many others, contend with the flood of recurring media images ("that bombardment of the towers burning"), but also with a flood of personal images: "I was bombarding myself, looking at pictures of my husband" (*Newsarama*). And while Torres initially sought to avoid the public images, "listening to the radio instead for all the new developments" ("The Reluctant Icon"), she eventually felt the need to assert her own way of seeing and experiencing and making sense of the events. Her memoir ultimately challenges the dominant verbal and visual narratives of the events, using the medium of comics to help readers apprehend the specificity as well as the depth of her loss.

Given Torres's commitment to asserting her own vision and story, the question of the relationship between Torres' vision and artist Sungyoon Choi's drawings arises. Torres herself rejects a notion of the book as "a collaboration process" (*Newsarama*). Describing the evolution of the book, she explains that she created an early draft using Microsoft Word, "making boxes and then putting little text boxes inside, kind of like dialogue balloons" (*Newsarama*), and then later wrote a more formal comic book script in which she detailed the projected contents and layout of each page of the work. Ultimately, Torres gave the script to Choi who created the final version of the drawings. Commenting on Choi's work, Torres notes, "Sometimes she went right by the script"; sometimes, Torres admits, Choi followed her own inspiration. Torres calls the artist "intuitive," noting that "she got what I needed, I'm going to say 98% of the time" (*Newsarama*).

In his discussion of authorship in the work of Harvey Pekar, Thomas Bredehoft references Thierry Groenstein's argument "for the primacy of the spatial (images and their relationships) over the linguistic as the definitive formal criterion of comics" (98). Since Pekar wrote but did not draw his comic book series *American Splendor*, Bredehoft observes, "Pekar is the author if we continue to privilege the linguistic at all costs, but the degree to which he does and does not control the visual aspects of his comics—the images and their relationships—suggests the possibility of slippage or uncertainty in our ability to identify Pekar (as the subject of the comics) with the unique author of the images" (98). In addition to the "slippage or uncertainty" that might occur between Torres and Choi, an additional slippage might be said to occur when it comes to the representation of the collective history of the events of September 11th. As the works of both Torres and Spiegelman suggest, a key question when it comes to 9/11 is whose interpretation of the events will take priority? Which words and images will fairly represent what happened? Both texts are overtly critical of the "slippage" that occurs between private experiences of 9/11 and how those events were presented through politics and the media.

Moreover, when it comes to the representation of trauma, there is inevitably some "slippage or uncertainty" between the experience and the representation of that experience. As Michael Bernard-Donals asserts, referencing Blanchot, "The move from event to experience, from what happened to a recollection of what happened, is a forgetting that compels language" ("Conflations" 76). Writer and artist compensate for the loss, or "forgetting," of the primary experience by transposing the event into words and images. That Torres's readers might experience a double loss—first, the loss of her own firsthand experience, and second, the representation of that loss by another artist—does not call the authenticity or autobiographical nature of the work into question. In considering Pekar's texts, Bredhoft suggests that "stylistic heteroglossia"—that is, the use of different artists to represent Pekar's autobiographical narratives—"[threatens] to undermine the stylistic coherence of the whole" (100). By contrast, I propose that the stylistic heteroglossia apparent in *American Widow* enacts the complexity of capturing individual and collective memory: readers (who inevitably bring their own individual and collective memories of 9/11 to the text) witness the multi-tiered process of shaping memory and history. Given the challenge mounted by the text against the assertion of one official or dominant account of 9/11, the incorporation of more than one way of seeing within the text seems particularly apt. As Kristiaan Versluys notes in his discussion of Spiegelman's *No Towers*, the chaos of the event dictated against "an easy, unproblematic rendering of the historical facts" (989). Likewise, the writing of memory and history involves multiple voices and perspectives.

The active role played by the reader of comics likewise works against the passive acceptance of a single way of seeing. Given a series of static images, the reader of comics must find and enact the logical links between and among these images and ultimately "animate" them. It is the reader who makes sense of the gaps between panels (whether bordered or borderless) by reading back and forth across the "gutter" (or the empty space between panels) and assessing what has changed in time and space. Likewise, the reader toggles between words and images, assessing the sometimes clear, sometimes contradictory, relationship between text and drawings. In this way, the reader plays an integral role in the telling (or the recreating) of the story. It is this role that provides the answer to one of Scott McCloud's illustrative questions: "Why—Are—We—So—Involved?" (30). As readers, we fill in the gaps: we make sense.

The disruptions that are intrinsic to comics make it a particularly apt form for the representation of trauma. Referencing the gap between experience and understanding, Cathy Caruth asserts, "trauma victims become the symptom of a history that they cannot entirely possess" (4). Throughout her memoir, Torres references and enacts the experience of simultaneously possessing and disowning the reality of Eddie's death. Indeed, her use of the direct address (much of the narration is Alissa's one-sided conversation with Eddie) underscores her acceptance and rejection of the reality of Eddie's death: she fills him in on what happened after he died. When others in New York are posting images of their missing loved ones around the city, Torres confides, "I made a poster, too, even though I knew you were dead" (*American Widow* 117). And later, on a visit to Ground Zero intended to convince herself of the reality of the loss, she admits: "Yes I understood you died here, although this reality would continue to escape me. This visit did nothing to change that. It just made me remember" (118–19).

Just as Torres uses text to illustrate the experience of trauma and the symptoms of post-traumatic stress, she also utilizes images. Caruth denotes the signs of post-traumatic stress as "repeated, intrusive hallucinations, dreams, thoughts or behaviors stemming from the event" (4). As Alissa ventures into the treacherous waters of 9/11 victim assistance programs, ghost images of Eddie appear, unbidden. We first witness the phantom image of Eddie as Alissa embarks on her battle to secure visas for Eddie's family so they can attend his funeral (58). Alissa's moves are mapped out in clear, scene-to-scene progression: she arrives at the door of the Colombian Consulate; she takes her place at the end of a long line of people; she sits at a desk across from a Consulate employee who, it seems, cannot help her after all; she receives her next assignment: to find "Steven" at the Family Center. As Alissa travels from bordered panel to bordered panel, caught in a bureaucratic maze, Eddie floats in an unbordered circle of blue-green on the left side of the page (61). No direct mention is made of this image. Reading across the panels, the reader gains access to Alissa's internal and external realities.

At other times in the story, dream sequences break down the barriers separating Alissa and Eddie. In one such sequence, we witness Alissa's deeply personal and painfully fleeting dream of uniting with Eddie (124). The physical "electricity" Alissa experiences in her sleep finds its visual equivalent in swathes of swirls and bubbles. For once, Alissa joins Eddie in the unbordered circle of blue-green. When she wakes to the reality of being, again alone, no words are necessary to fill in the gap: the black silhouette of Alissa, sitting up silently in the bed, says it all (125).

In addition to their encounter with Alissa's inner life, readers of *American Widow* travel with her through the flat and silent world of trauma. On the first page of the book, the reader encounters a full-page square of seafoam blue. A hazy equivalent of the sharp and searing blue sky of that September 11th morning, the square of color evokes the 9/11 sky moments before it erupted into flames and smoke. Far from signaling our entrance into a world and a consciousness gone extravagantly mad, as in Spiegelman's *In the Shadow of No Towers*, the muted opening foreshadows the eerie and reverberating silence that follows a deafening explosion. On the next page, a tiny seagull shape appears to have been cut out of the paper. A silhouette of the seagull flies just above the cutout. The quiet fragility of this paper-thin world breaks on page three as the reader is bombarded by the verbal and visual cacophony of redundant calls by a center-stage TV to "Turn on Your TV" (5). Yet even as the words in the word balloons blare at the reader, only a barebones sketch of the smoking twin towers appears. By referencing, but not including, actual or detailed examples of the day's relentless and repetitive media coverage, Torres, with Choi, chooses not to reinforce the dominant, public images of the event. Instead, by permitting the reader to witness other, deeply private 9/11 images, Torres begins to reshape the collective cultural memory of the event.

Another way the text invites the reader to share Torres's trauma occurs on the first page of chapter five. Here, no panels divide the space into measurable increments of time. Instead, a black background encompasses the page. In the center, as though at the eye of a tornado cloud, Alissa, like Dorothy in the *Wizard of Oz*, lies on a floating, if not flying, bed. She lies on her side, her eyes tethered to an apparent photo that hangs in space in front of her. Circling the bed like well-meaning vultures, six close-up shots of the faces of Alissa's friends and family form a ring around the faraway center image. Though each person calls out to Alissa, seeking contact, Alissa herself is unreachable.

As we turn the page, the black background gives way to empty white space. Two bordered panels appear at the top of the page, like two eyes of a face. The left panel depicts a close-up of Alissa as she stares past the reader. The right panel brings the amorphous image she is staring at into focus: taped to the wall next to her is a photograph of Eddie, sleeping. This image appears several times throughout the book, with three references to it on these two pages alone (43–44), another a few pages later (51), and finally, at the end of the book, two color reproductions of the same image included in a collage of photos (198–99). Just as the repeating and uncanny image became part of Alissa's visual memory of 9/11, so too does it become part of the reader's collective memory.

Even as Alissa appears to float in a sea of grief (in the middle of this page she lies on a bed of emptiness), she begins to forge meaning through narration. At the bottom of the page, underneath what appears to be a mound of earth, a sentence referencing *The Book of Genesis* breaks the silence: "In the beginning there was a clear blue sky on a beautiful day" (44). In Joan Didion's language, Alissa here "imposes a narrative line" on the chaos of her 9/11 experience (Didion 1). Including what appears to be a child's jagged rendering of the approaching plane and burning buildings, Alissa weaves a mythical narrative over the catastrophic reality: "And there were two winged beasts of metal, no different than any other that flew . . . except that on this day they were piloted by insane men with sharp purpose and weapons. And then the metal beasts unleashed monsters of fire that consumed all they could" (45). If this is the story that Torres will eventually tell her young son, on the next page we find the story she will tell herself: "You jumped" (46). The caption presides over a rough approximation of "Richard Drew's 'Falling Man'" photograph. The panel appears in the top center of the page, against a black background. As though moving backwards in time, the panel placed directly underneath (forming a tower shape) depicts Eddie staring through a broken window: "You said, 'Fuck it, I'm out of here,'" the caption reads. The third panel—the would-be foundation of this emerging tower shape—is missing. Captions flank the top and bottom edges of the phantom panel, marking where the borders *would* be if the panel, and the foundation, were not engulfed in darkness. "And that was that," the ribbon of narration announces at the top edge of the phantom panel. "That was Day 1," the caption on the bottom counters,

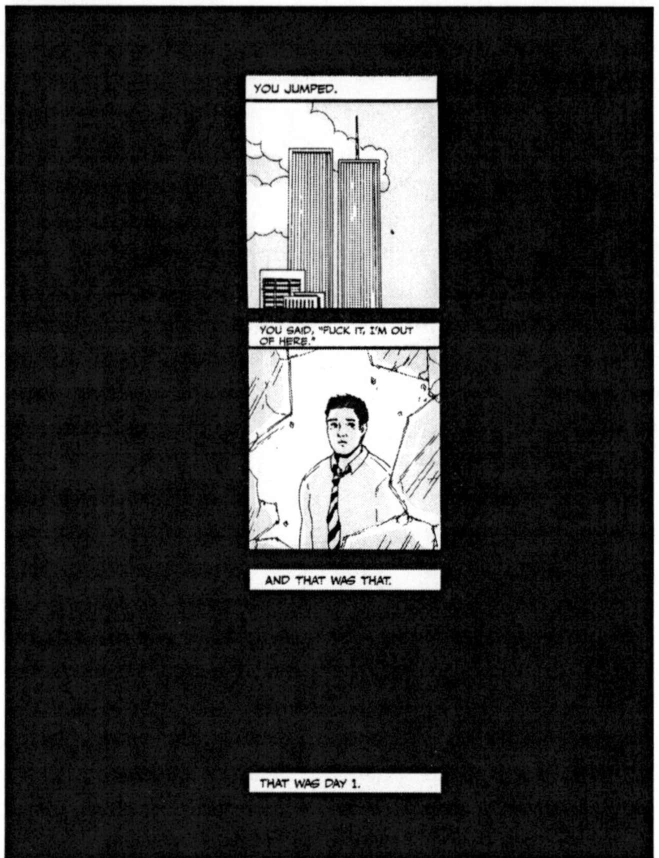

9.1. Alissa Torres. *American Widow*. p. 46.

confirming that Alissa's journey towards understanding and acceptance has only just begun.

As the reader travels with Alissa from the internal to the external world, we witness the disjunction between the public and private narratives. On Day 1, Alissa doesn't yet contend with the public elements of the catastrophe. As the chapter continues, she finds herself coming up against public narratives that fail to encompass or adequately define her private experience. On a city bus two weeks after September 11, Alissa's cell phone rings (65). It is her mother. From just a few contextualizing words, everyone on the bus seems to know Alissa's story: she's become a type rather than an individual. For the moment, she has a sympathetic audience who, having cast her as a "9/11 Widow," look on knowingly. Embarrassed, all too aware that her loss is anything but heroic—as she tells her mother, "I'm just try-ing to hold it together"—Alissa ducks her head (65).

The next scene depicts a similarly uncomfortable intersection between public and private experiences of September 11th, but in this case Alissa's representative status is received much less sympathetically. The scene is a maternity store, and Alissa has come with a friend to buy a black dress to wear to Eddie's funeral. The store manager, friendly at first, turns quickly away when she learns of Alissa's grim mission. The woman is visibly relieved when Alissa and her friend retreat from the store. Recalling James Berger's comments, it seems that in representing "overwhelming loss," Alissa not only undermines the excited optimism of a maternity store but perhaps also the media-driven preference for a collective narrative of vic-tory. Rather than feeling part of "a nation unified in grief" (Clark 569), Alissa finds herself alienated from fellow New Yorkers who were spared the kind of loss that she sustained. As Tim Gauthier asserts, "The belief that we all had an equal share in this tragedy . . . is an assumption that *American Widow* strongly contests" (376).

It is only at the end of the memoir that the public and private aspects of Alissa's experience collide in an explosive and ultimately important way. The scene is the Independent Women's Forum luncheon, an event orga-nized in honor of women who were pregnant when their husbands were killed on September 11th. Alissa was reluctant to accept the invitation, aware that it would only afford the press another opportunity to erase the specificity of her experience and to reinforce her identity as a "9/11 Widow." Nonetheless, she attends, and finds herself listening to the reading of a let-ter signed by First Lady Laura Bush who praises the assembled women for "the courage you demonstrate for your family and for the rest of us who may not know you personally but know you as one of the bravest heroes of September 11" (196). Just as the language of the letter elides individual identity ("[we] may not know you personally") in order to impose politi-cal identity ("but [we] know you as one of the bravest heroes of Septem-ber 11"), the comic literally asserts an individual and protesting voice (that is, the bolded sounds of a baby crying) over the political rhetoric of the letter. Specifically, parts of the First Lady's letter—reprinted on the page in full—are obscured by the all-caps "WAAAA! WAAAA!" of an infant. "Is that my baby?" Alissa wonders. With this breakthrough of sound and voice (as image) comes the introduction of color. Suddenly, there is dark red and deep blue, as the red, white, and blue centerpiece on Alissa's table comes to life, as though patriotism emerges in the rejection of a political

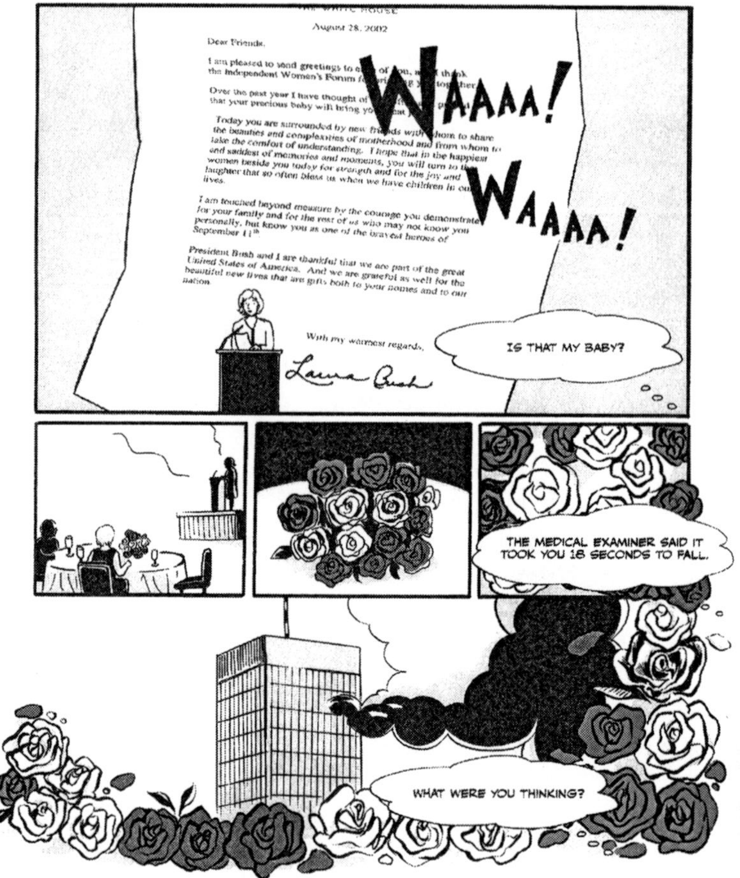

9.2. Alissa Torres. *American Widow*. p. 196.

narrative of 9/11. Mingling with the black smoke that rises from the image of the North Tower at the bottom of the page, the colors also suggest the painful return of life and blood to numbed limbs. It is as though Alissa is alive for the first time in the book, awakened, suddenly, by the need to resist her official, idealized status as an "American Widow" and to embrace her own and her child's lived experience. Not coincidentally, the next page confronts the reader with a full-page rendering of the famous "Falling Man" photograph. A simple drawing that depends in part on the reader's memory of the censored media shot, the image nonetheless takes the breath away. In the moment of silence and awe that it produces, we absorb the narrative that Alissa once again claims: he jumped.

In the terrible hush of that moment, the reader turns the page. There, facing us, taking up every possible bit of white space, is a two-page color collage of photographs of Eddie—a full-bodied, fully alive Eddie. After the flatness and quiet of Choi's pale comics world, Eddie's physicality jumps off the page: he is sexy, rugged, handsome; there are several shots of him without a shirt and several shots of him sleeping; in almost all of the shots, he appears relaxed and at ease in his body. He appears in a bathing suit; sitting among the dunes on a beach; standing in the fog. We witness him as a watchful child and as a serious young man in military dress. We come upon him as he's talking on the phone, waiting to blow out candles on a birthday cake, emerging from the sea after snorkeling. Mingled with the images are the contents of Eddie's wallet: the page is sprinkled with business cards, a driver's license, a video store card. Here is evidence of a life in full swing. And then we turn the page.

Eddie is gone. Alissa sits alone at her table, trapped once again in what now seems, by comparison, to be the stale and airless world of comics. In the split second between glimpsing Eddie in photographs and re-entering the comics world, Eddie came to life. Bernard-Donals defines "forgetful memory" as something like "a flash of seeing, in which the witness is not quite sure what he has seen, but understands its connections to his temporal and spatial present" ("Conflations" 76). For the reader of *American Widow*, the "flash of seeing"—our momentary access to a felt sense of Eddie's absence—occurs in-between pages. It is not the photographs themselves that provide access to the "forgetful memory" of Eddie but rather the space between the photographs and the comics world. We are most acutely aware of his having been present when we no longer see him. In effect, we see Eddie by looking away. In considering the writing of history, and specifically traumatic history, Bernard-Donals asserts, "the historian only has access to what resides behind the written memory . . . in the discontinuities in that narrative, its silences, and its idiosyncrasies" ("Conflations" 75). Just so, Eddie emerges neither through Choi's drawings nor the actual photographs but rather through the juxtaposition of these images and worlds; he emerges through the discontinuities created by comics.

Guerin and Hallas argue that "the act of bearing witness is not the communication of a truth that is already known, but its actual production through this performative act. In this process the listener becomes a witness to the witness, not only facilitating the very possibility of testimony, but also subsequently, sharing its burden" (11). In this view, then, not only does Torres become a firsthand witness to the verbal and visual narratives that make up *American Widow*, but the reader, too, becomes a primary witness to these narratives and as such incorporates them into his or her own collective memory of 9/11. In addition, given the active role that comics thrusts the reader into, I suggest that the reader not only witnesses Torres's trauma, but in re-enacting the moment of having, and losing, Eddie, the reader creates a memory of his or her own.

II. Constructing Memory in Spiegelman's *In the Shadow of No Towers*

Like *American Widow*, Spiegelman's *In the Shadow of No Towers* challenges the dominant verbal and visual narratives that were constructed in the immediate aftermath of 9/11. Instead of the recurring television images, Spiegelman shows images and captures moments that were not captured by the media but which nonetheless defined his experience and became part of his memories of the event. An eyewitness to the disaster (he and his wife Françoise were only blocks from the towers when the first plane struck), he finds himself questioning the reality of what he saw, as endlessly replaying media images crowd out his firsthand observations. As Katalin Orbán asserts, "the book is written precisely from the perspective of that on-site real-time witness whose privileged status is called into question and rendered supplementary by the global televisual witnessing of the event" (72).

Spiegelman's work speaks in particular to the problem that Mary Marshall Clark articulates in her discussion of "The September 11, 2001, Oral History Narrative and Memory Project." Clark observes: "One of the dilemmas in the debate over whether memory or history dominates the interpretation of major events is that few opportunities exist to study how people reconstruct the past before a dominant public narrative has been created by those who have a vested interest in defining the political meaning of events" (569). Spiegelman's *No Towers* enacts the difficulty of maintaining one's own way of seeing and remembering in the face of powerful media representations and political narratives of the events. While the work starts off as a verbal and visual diary of the moments and hours following the initial attacks, it gradually becomes a record of Spiegelman's increasing anger and frustration at the political use that he believes is being made of the events by the Bush administration. Critical of the work's intensive focus on Spiegelman's private experiences of and responses to

9/11, Orbán regrets its lack of "investment in causality and agency within the understanding of a historical process" (85). In other words, Orbán suggests that Spiegelman substitutes memory for history, and in doing so contributes a far less significant work on 9/11 than he might have otherwise. By contrast, I argue that in re-enacting the experience of overwhelming trauma, subjecting readers to an onslaught of alarming, distorted, and crowded images and what Orbán refers to as "micronarratives" (85), Spiegelman challenges the reader to assimilate the disparate parts of the work and to find the necessary distance, both from the text as well as from the events themselves, to make sense of history.

Whereas the reader of *American Widow* enters a world of pained silences and understated line drawings, the reader of *No Towers* grapples with a complicated, crowded, and literally towering verbal and visual text. Large and heavy, with thick cardboard pages approximating the "giant scale of the [early twentieth century] color newsprint pages," the book literally cannot be taken lightly ("The Sky is Falling!"). By presenting readers with an actual physical structure—a tower—Spiegelman confirms his commitment to comics pages as "architectural structures" ("The Comic Supplement"). Just as he claims that "the narrative rows of panels are like stories of a building," so too does he imply that the literal structure of the book (its actual physical presence) is like (or perhaps all he plans to offer with regard to) a narrative structure. In fact, the book is difficult to encapsulate: within its covers one encounters a reprint of the front page of a historical newspaper, two introductory (expository) essays, historical comics pages, and ten episodes of a new comics series (*In the Shadow of No Towers*) in which characters from historical comic strips figure prominently. Rather than a linear narrative, the book offers readers what appears to be a multifaceted, multidimensional scrapbook. Spiegelman explains: "I wanted to sort out the fragments of what I'd experienced from the media images that threatened to engulf what I actually saw, and the collagelike nature of a newspaper page encouraged my impulse to juxtapose fragmentary thoughts in different styles" ("The Sky Is Falling!").

The centerpiece of the work is the ten-episode *No Towers* series. Though stylistically similar and thematically linked, the episodes, initially published serially, are largely stand-alone pieces. While they generally follow Spiegelman forward in time, with each episode exploring (and exploiting) a particular theme relevant to key trends and/or (mostly local) incidents from the two-year period following the attacks, each episode also verbally and visually recalls the initial trauma. Thus, even as the episodes move forward in time [admittedly with a time lag: "I had anticipated that the shadows of the towers might fade while I was slowly sorting through my grief and putting it into boxes" ("The Sky Is Falling!")], they simultaneously remain fixed in one time and place.

The recurring, representative image that consistently brings Spiegelman and the reader back to the moment of private as well as public trauma is an image that Spiegelman witnessed but which did not become part of the battery of 9/11 media images. "The pivotal image from my 9/11 morning," Spiegelman explains "one that didn't get photographed or videotaped into public memory but still remains burned onto the inside of my eyelids several years later—was the image of the looming north tower's glowing bones just before it vaporized" ("The Sky Is Falling!"). In that frozen second, the tower, still visually intact, nonetheless appears broken up into swirling, particulate matter. As Spiegelman admits, it took repeated tries to approximate the image and it was only digitally, on his computer, that he was able to capture "the vision of disintegration" ("The Sky Is Falling"). The image is depicted variously throughout the ten episodes, appearing prominently in the early episodes and then receding in the later ones, until one has to look carefully to find evidence of the moment. In addition, a circular panel containing a glossy detail of the fiery image appears on the first page of the book, creating the illusion that the reader is looking through the lens of a telescope, straight through the reprinted front page of the September 11, 1901, newspaper to the literal and figurative heart of the book. In superimposing this keyhole image onto the historical newspaper, Spiegelman implies that an understanding of the present can only be achieved by boring deeply into the past.

The reader witnesses a large-scale version of Spiegelman's "pivotal" image in Episode 1. Running down the right side of the page and forming an imposing column are five rectangular panels (two and a half above the fold, two and a half below), each depicting a segment of the glowing, particulate tower set against a placid blue sky. With the exception of the first panel, which juts out at an angle, overlapping the corner of the second image and creating a cascading effect, the panels themselves line up perfectly, each one separated by a white gutter. By contrast, the sections of the tower that are displayed *within* each panel do not line up, but instead call to mind a series of puzzle pieces that have been placed in the wrong order. Thus, the narrow width of the tower segment shown in panel two does not align properly with the wider, close-up segment depicted in panel three; additionally, each of the segments appears to have been captured at a slightly different, or even opposing angle, from the one before, thereby creating a teetering effect. Overall, the misalignment of the separate, disintegrating images suggests that the tower, if not Spiegelman's memory of the image, is moments away from complete eradication. In creating a discontinuous line of images, Spiegelman challenges readers to transcend the gutters and imagine the "glowing tower" for themselves (Episode 1). In working to fathom both the image as portrayed on the page as well as the impossible reality to which it refers, readers begin to commit Spiegelman's vision to memory. And by offering variations of this image throughout each of the ten episodes, Spiegelman not only dramatizes the symptom of what he refers to as his post-traumatic stress disorder, but also works diligently to ensure that by the end of the work, this image enters the collective visual vocabulary of 9/11.

In Episode 4, Spiegelman launches a full-scale challenge to the official verbal and visual narratives that arose in the immediate aftermath of 9/11 (see fig. 9.3). While each episode confronts readers with large, colorful images and multiple, overlapping comic strips, all of which compete for our attention, this episode in particular withholds a clear path through the enormous page; readers need to chart their own course through this visual landscape. Rather than an underlying grid organizing oversized panels into vertical and horizontal strips, as we find in most of the other episodes, the bottom layer of this page reveals an enormous, close-up shot of a colorful comics page featuring what can be seen of Rudolph Dirks's early twentieth-century Katzenjammer Kids, recast as Spiegelman's naughty Tower Twins, those "rascals, icons of a more innocent age" (Epsiode 2). The surface of the comics page appears broken up into its constitutive dots, as though over-magnified, linking the image visually and thematically to Spiegelman's glowing, pixelated tower, a long shot of which runs from the top to the bottom of the left side of the page.

Presiding over the page is a tragicomic image of George Bush and Dick Cheney hijacking the enormous American bald eagle that served in Episode 2 as the literal albatross around Spiegelman's neck, compelling him to tell and retell the story of 9/11. Absconding with the lived experiences of 9/11 (the eagle's talons grip the underlying comics panels, literally flying away with the events as they happened), Cheney slits the eagle's throat while Bush happily holds on to Cheney's coattails, shouting "Let's Roll!" Spiegelman implies that the two effectively rolled the cameras again, creating a new narrative in order to justify war with Iraq.

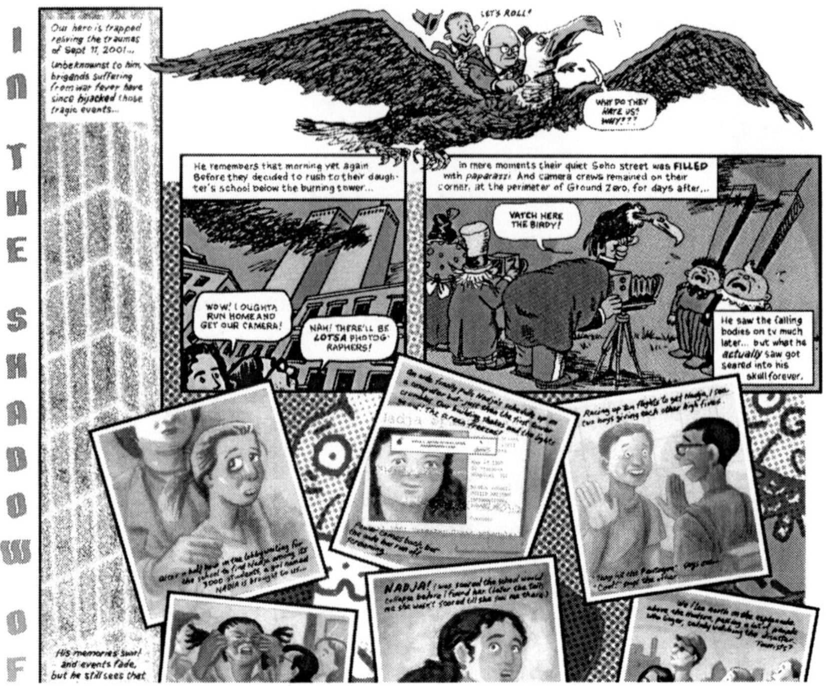

9.3. Art Spiegelman. *In the Shadow of No Towers*. p. 4. (detail)

The comics panels directly underneath the eagle capture the story of the moments shortly after the attack on the first tower: "He remembers that morning yet, again," the third-person narration reads, "Before they decided to rush to their daughter's school below the burning tower . . ." (Episode 4). Staring up at the towers, Art's wife exclaims, "Wow! I ought to run home and get our camera." "Nah!" Art replies. "There'll be LOTSA photographers!" The irony is that they are both right: there are indeed lots of photographers, but the public images won't necessarily translate into accurate or even recognizable representations of their private experiences. Remarking on the discrepancy between mediated and unmediated images, Spiegelman narrates: "He saw the falling bodies on tv much later . . . but what he actually saw got seared into his skull forever" (Episode 4).

To counteract the obscuring of personal memories by politics and the media, Spiegelman devotes the central section of the page to snapshots of his own memories of that morning. Here in the center, lying on top of the dotted image of the fleeing Tower Twins is a scatter of the photos that did not get taken, or assimilated into, the public discourse of the event. There

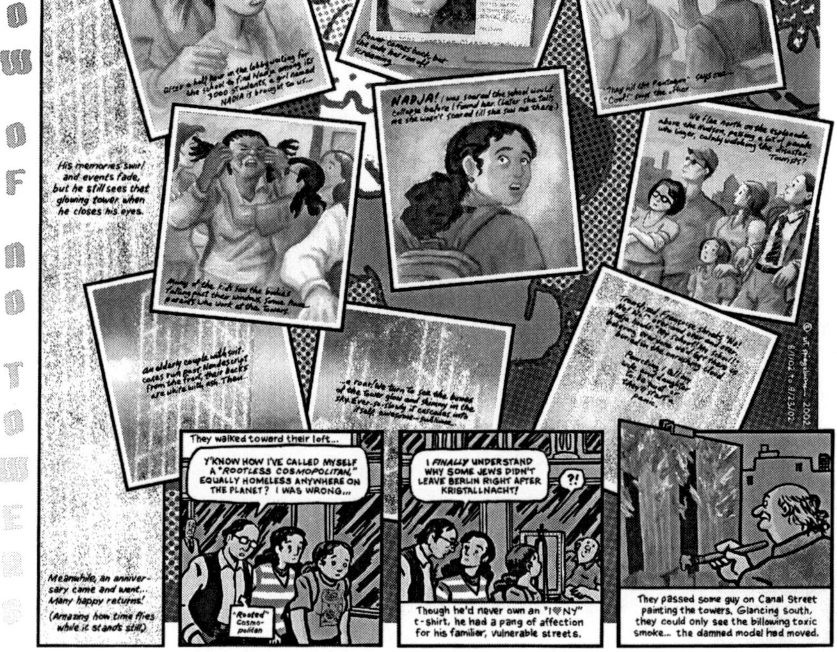

9.4. Art Spiegelman. *In the Shadow of No Towers*. p. 4. (detail)

is the moment when Art and his wife find their daughter Nadja, safe in her school, unaware of the scale of the chaos outside; there is, once again, the moment when "we turn to see the bones of the tower glow and shimmy in the sky" (Episode 4). While it is clear that he could have included countless images, he contributes these nine to the reader's collective memory of the day.

Bounding the images on the bottom of the page is another horizontal comic strip that picks up the above narrative at a later point (see fig. 9.4). It is after their panicked race through the streets of lower Manhattan to rescue their daughter, and now Art and his wife and daughter walk slowly and soberly home. The episode's gag emanates from the surprised expression on a street artist's face as he peers around his canvas. As smoke obscures the towers completely, Spiegelman comments wryly on the painter's behalf: "the damned model had moved" (Episode 4). The strip underscores the time advantage that digital photography has over the other visual arts.

While Spiegelman's comics representation of the events of 9/11, like the artist's painting of the burning towers, cannot keep up with the passage of time, digital photography captures history as it happens. As Orbán notes, "*No Towers* acknowledges the key role of the mediatized image—never denying its power, even while subjecting it to bitter sarcasm" (80). Even though it was digital technology that finally permitted Spiegelman to capture his own pivotal 9/11 image, it is also clear that the media's use of the same digital technology leads to the blotting out of individual ways of seeing. Orbán argues that a work focused as narrowly as Spiegelman's on the author's private experiences on and in the immediate aftermath of September 11th ultimately falls short of contributing to the historical discourse on 9/11. Recognizing the "double bind" that digital photography puts Spiegelman in, she observes: "So the author has two questionable options: to speak too soon or, virtually at the same moment [as the events are occurring], already too late" (86). The speed with which the media captures (and capitalizes on) historic events, Orbán suggests, "foreclose[s] a process of historicization" (86): the dominant public narrative defines the events before those who lived through them have an opportunity to make sense of their own experiences within a larger historical context. Interestingly, in standing back from the page and looking at the shape that the many disparate images in this episode create, it is possible to discern the form of an analog camera: the tip of the tall tower on the left forms the button that one depresses to take a picture; the scatter of photographs in the middle of the page suggests the aperture (see fig. 9.3). The reader is thus implicitly encouraged to take his or her own pictures, in his or her own time, to make and keep his or her own memories, and ultimately not to accept without questioning the public narratives of 9/11.

Faced with an increasingly electronic world in which history will continue to be recorded digitally, with less and less time in between the event and the visual representation of that event, it becomes increasingly important to capture multiple perspectives. While Spiegelman draws his own images, his work, like *American Widow*, demonstrates "stylistic heteroglossia," incorporating other voices, time periods, and ways of seeing. By impersonating comics characters from different times and places, specifically from his own *Maus* comic book, as well as from the strips that originated in the early twentieth century, Spiegelman puts his own experiences into different historical contexts and sees them, literally, from different angles. The incorporation of other ways of seeing offsets the apparent focus on his private trauma. Spiegelman uses comics to toggle between memory and history, encouraging the reader, too, to straddle the various gaps and to try to make sense.

Works Cited

Berger, James. "There is No Backhand to This." *Trauma at Home: After 9/11*. Ed. Judith Greenberg. Lincoln, Nebraska: University of Nebraska Press, 2003. 52–59. Print.

Bernard-Donals, Michael F. "Conflations of Memory: Or, What They Saw at the Holocaust Museum After 9/11." *CR: The New Centennial Review* 5.2 (2005): 73–106. Web. 13 June 2012. DOI: 10.1353/ncr.2005.0040.

———. "Forgetful Memory and Images of the Holocaust." *College English* 66.4 (2004): 380–402. Web. 13 June 2012. http://www.jstor.org/stable/4140708.

Bredehoft, Thomas. "Style, Voice, and Authorship in Harvey Pekar's (Auto)(Bio) Graphical Comics. *College Literature* 38.3 (2011): 97–110. *Project MUSE*. Web. 22 July 2012. http://muse.jhu.edu/.

Caruth, Cathy. *Trauma: Explorations in Memory*. Baltimore: Johns Hopkins University Press, 1995. Print.

Clark, Mary Marshall. "The September 11, 2001, Oral History Narrative and Memory Project: A First Report." *The Journal of American History* (2002): 569–79. Print.

Didion, Joan. "The White Album." *The White Album*. New York: Washington Square Press, 1979. 1–47. Print.

Gauthier, Tim. "9/11, Image Control, and the Graphic Narrative: Spiegelman, Rehr, Torres." *Journal of Postcolonial Writing* 46.3–4 (2010): 369–80. Web. 9 June 2011. DOI: 10.1080/17449855.2010.482420.

Hirsch, Marianne. "Editor's Column: Collateral Damage." *PMLA* 119.5 (2004): 1,209–215. Print.

Lorah, Michael C. "9/11's Legacy: Alissa Torres, *American Widow*." *Newsarama*. 11 Sept. 2008. Web. 12 June 2012. http://www.newsarama.com/comics/090811 -AmericanWidow.html.

McCloud, Scott. *Understanding Comics: The Invisible Art*. New York: Harper Collins, 1993. Print.

Miller, Nancy K. "'Portraits of Grief': Telling Details and the Testimony of Trauma." *Differences: A Journal of Feminist Cultural Studies* 14.3 (2005): 112–135. Web. 14 June 2012. http://muse.jhu.edu.

Orbán, Katalin. "Trauma and Visuality: Art Spiegelman's *Maus* and *In the Shadow of No Towers*." *Representations* 97 (2007): 57–89. Web. 14 Jan. 2011. http://www.jstor.org/ stable/10.1525/rep.2007.97.1.57..

Peress, Gilles, et al. *Here is New York: A Democracy of Photos*. 7 July 2011. Web. 6 June 2012. http://hereisnewyork.org.

Spiegelman, Art. *In the Shadow of No Towers*. New York: Pantheon, 2004. Print.

Torres, Alissa. *Alissa Torres*. Web. 6 June 2012. http://alissatorres.com.

———. *American Widow*. Illus. Sungyoon Choi. New York: Villard, 2008. Print.

———. "9/11 Widow: The Media Duped Us." *Salon*. 7 Sept. 2010. Web. 12 June 2012. http://www.salon.com/2010/09/08/we_are_not_experts_on_park_51.

———. "The Reluctant Icon." *Salon*. 25 Jan. 2002. Web. 8 June 2012. http://www.salon
.com/2002/01/25/widow_speaks.
Versluys, Kristiaan. "Art Spiegelman's *In the Shadow of No Towers*: and the
Representation of Trauma." *Modern Fiction Studies* 52.4 (2006): 980–1,003.
Web. 15 July 2012. DOI: 10.1353/mfs.2007.0011.

You Must Look at the Personal Clutter

Diaristic Indulgence, Female Adolescence, and Feminist Autobiography

—Alisia Chase

In 1975, pioneering feminist artist Carolee Schneemann performed what would eventually become one of art history's landmark works. Titled "Interior Scroll," the piece began when the fully clothed Schneemann entered the room, disrobed, and wrapped herself in a white sheet. She then divested herself of the sheet, climbed onto a table, and began to enact the poses of a traditional artist's model, her alternately draped and exposed female form arguably intimating that of silent muse rather than vocal maker. Then, taking mud-colored pigment in hand, Schneemann began to paint her flesh in a forceful, definitive manner, almost as if she were recreating herself, fashioning an art historical icon more reminiscent of a soil-covered primeval creator resurrected from the Paleolithic Period than a passive post-Renaissance odalisque.[1] The most critically significant moment of the work, however, occurred when Schneemann planted her feet firmly on the table, reached into her vaginal canal, and slowly extracted a long, crumpled scroll. As it unraveled, she began to read from the paper that seemed to originate in her womb, as Anna Chave suggests, "like so much contraband" (Chave 133). (fig. 10.1) Its text was a prose poem detailing Schneemann's conversation with a derisive male filmmaker, and I'll share a key part of it with you here:

> *there are certain films*
> *we cannot look at*
> *the personal clutter*
> (Schneemann, *Imaging* 159–60)

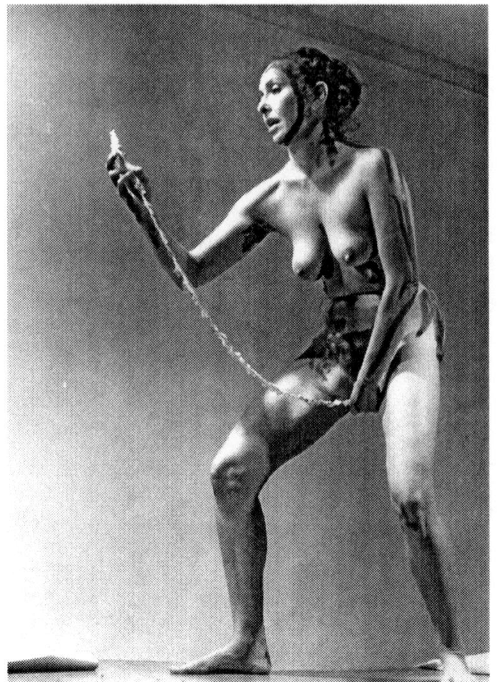

10.1. Carolee Schneemann. "Interior Scroll" 1975
(Performance)

The poem presents film criticism as being "in only one gender." The physical act of pulling something forth from one's vagina was routinely familiar to any woman in the audience who had witnessed or given birth, used a tampon, or douched. Yet, it was also visually shocking given the strictures of the then male-dominated art world, as well as revolutionary in its suggestion that poetry, and by extension, art, could issue forth from this region of the female body. But the work was rebellious beyond its obvious corporeal properties, primarily because it both exposed and challenged the sexist rhetoric that disparaged the "hand-touch sensibility and primitive techniques" of female creativity as being antithetical to the goals of modern art, which at that time were aesthetically exemplified by minimalist Donald Judd's factory-ordered pine boxes and puritanical Lucite cubes.[2] Most significantly, the reproving comments in the poem echoed the constant criticism aimed at feminist artwork of the early '70s: that by virtue of its focus on a female creator's life and subjectivity, it wasn't, nor could ever hope to be, up to artistic snuff.

It's no surprise, coming of age in the late 1980s during a renaissance of macho New York painters and their mammoth canvases, that I knew nothing about Schneemann's radical act, but when I finally did discover it as a young professor teaching a Women in Art class for the first time, I was struck by the visual force of the performance stills, as well as the ludicrous idea that "personal clutter, persistence of feelings, and diaristic indulgence" were considered condemnatory elements within a work of art. Certainly it was these very same qualities that had attracted me (and many others) to the artistic production of British multimedia artist Tracey Emin or the installation work of French photographer Sophie Calle, to name just two visual artists of the last decade whose focus on the autobiographical has won them widespread acclaim. But nowhere did I see these powerfully emotive qualities so pronounced as in the world of "alternative" or "independent" comics, a realm in which baring one's neuroses wasn't considered all that freakish or obscene, whether the artist was male or female. Additionally, the very hallmark of alternative comics is its emphasis on each artist's individual cartooning style and lettering, and thus, the field privileged, rather than degraded, a "hand-touch sensibility." It was in the graphic work of female cartoonists, however, where I most frequently encountered "personal clutter, persistence of feelings, and diaristic indulgence." Images such as this one, by Megan Kelso, in which the central character tears her broken, bloody heart out of her chest cavity, only to retrieve it because she knows that she cannot live without the ability to love (fig. 10.2), or Ariel Bordeaux's phenomenal third frame of her comic, *Tit Chat* (fig. 10.3), in which a woman recognizes that her breasts are significant not for their size but because they encircle the heart, were typical of such works that centered on the female protagonist's feelings. It was these women artists' ability to lay oneself emotionally bare—as visually symbolized by Schneemann, to pull from one's deepest recesses—that seemed to me, as a female viewer, the most compelling aspect of their work.

The art exhibition "Alternative Girlhood: Diaristic Indulgence and Contemporary Female Artists," which I curated with the guidance of Kelso in 2006, featured many of the now countless female comics creators whose work embraced such qualities, and it is really such an extensive topic that it could be the subject of a monograph. But I found the most powerful resonance of Schneemann's themes, particularly that of "diaristic indulgence," in three of these artists: Phoebe Gloeckner, Debbie Drechsler, and Julie Doucet. Additionally, given my field, I was drawn to their clear allusions to the canon of visual art, and how their work,

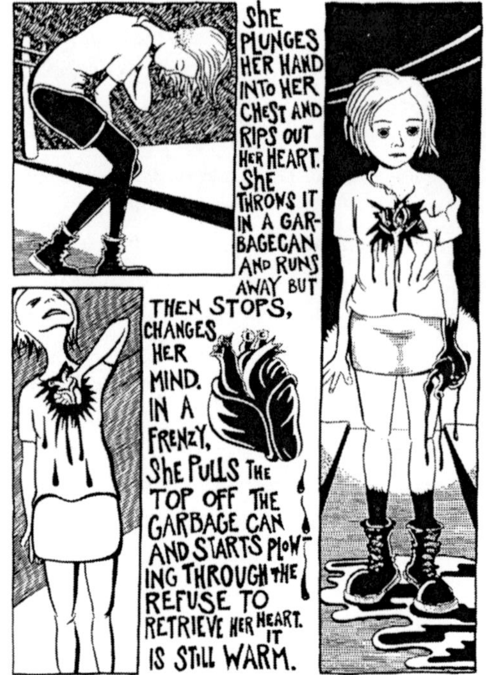

10.2. Megan Kelso.

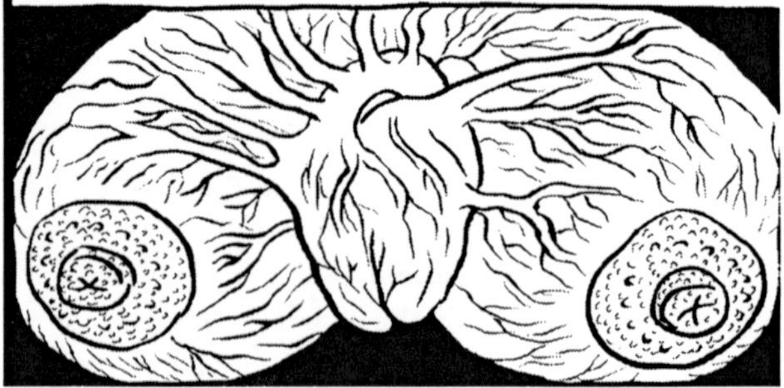

10.3. Ariel Bordeaux. *Tit Chat.*

like Scheemann's, could function as a feminist counterpoint. Gloeckner, Drechsler, and Doucet have all achieved public notoriety for their stories of young women's lives, and their resultant black and white "diaries," as well as individual comics, stand as an "alternative" vision of growing up female, one far more telling than the glittering pink and sparkling purple, highly sanitized fantasy proffered by most mainstream media. By laboring to make visible that which is normally obscured, to give voice to that which society would prefer remain unspoken about growing up as a girl in late twentieth-century North America, Gloeckner, Drechsler, and Doucet carry on the legacy of Schneemann and her second-wave feminist peers, who struggled to make the real life experiences of women legitimate subject matter for art.[3] I would argue, too, that as primitive in technique as comics might seem when compared to glossy media visuals of Hannah Montana on the Disney Channel or her real-world counterpart Miley Cyrus, whose Daddy's always got her back and a million in the bank to boot, these diaries present a world far more realistically in synch with many contemporary young women's authentic experiences. Throughout these potent works, the reader is confronted with a vision of female adolescence that is literally not pretty. On the contrary, it is often linguistically hyperbolic and hyper-grotesque in image; these are lives that have been irrevocably marred by incestuous father figures, mother figures in denial, promiscuous or non-consensual sex, and illicit drug use. The frames are quite often filled to the brim, so to speak, not only with junkie roommates, demanding phalluses, and menstrual blood, but packed with a visual "clutter" that can be read as symbolic shorthand for the emotional confusion that accompanied the lived experiences of the protagonists as well as their subsequent artistic narration by the creators. With *Interior Scroll*, Schneemann was not only asserting that the female body could be the site of artistic production, but also contending that female subjectivity was an essential component of her art. Like Schneemann, it is Gloeckner, Doucet, and Dreschler's *insistence* on "diaristic indulgence"—the persistent, emotional vacillations of a young woman, as well as the facts of female biology and one's subjective experience based on this biology—their very willingness to share moments that are both shocking in their intimacy and, to female viewers, far too familiar at once—that gives their work its aesthetic and cultural strength.

As such, I seek to illustrate not whether these autobiographies are historically truthful, but rather, to show how emotionally and socially *resonant* they are, by virtue of the artists' desire to share female intimacies that are customarily kept covert.[4] From its inception, the power of graphic art lies not in its ability to show things as they should be, nor as they really are, but in such a way that the horrible is heightened and the monstrous is magnified so that the viewer is moved to respond to the events being portrayed. Indeed, Gloeckner, Drechsler, and Doucet create powerful visual and textual metaphors for the visceral experiences of their early womanhood, and their liberal indulgence with the "truth" seems motivated by a desire to invoke both recognition and catharsis within the reader. To wit, both Gloeckner and Drechsler themselves have stated their overt desire to manipulate their lived "truths" in order to better narrate those stories. To quote Drechsler, "I realized that if I wrote straight autobiography the stories would suffer, so I began to take things that had happened and expand upon them, and mold them into stories that worked better than the 'honest truth' could" (Vertsappen). Gloeckner's words are similar: "It's not so important to me that a story is 'the truth' in a literal sense, even when I'm writing something that has a basis in my own experience. I'm not creating documentary; I'm after some sort of emotional truth, like any artist, I think" (Sullivan). Doucet is less reticent about acknowledging that these stories are based upon her own life experiences. She describes autobiography as "a disease" she just can't shake, but the more fantastical storylines within her work (a bikini-wearing kitty and masturbating with a cookie in a rocket ship as just two such examples) suggest that Doucet also "molds" her stories to make them more effective (Ladygunn).

It is important to underscore that I approach this work from the perspective of a feminist art historian. As such, I tend to utilize other works of art to both illuminate and aesthetically contextualize these comics within the continuum of art history; it is my opinion that the academic analysis of comics is too often housed in literature departments, where the overt emphasis on text and lack of emphasis on a cartoonist's art historical influences results in detrimentally biased readings. Additionally, in the majority of instances here, the stylistic and/or compositional precedents were created by a male artist. I believe that Gloeckner, Drechsler, and Doucet are most likely overtly or subliminally self-conscious of the ways in which their works are performative acts that negotiate, appropriate, and adapt these representations. These negotiations, in feminist art fashion, simultaneously "affirm and critique" those earlier works (Smith and Watson 15). I also concur with Hillary Chute and Marianne DeKoven, who suggest that "the lens of gender has been largely absent from recent academic considerations of comics" (Chute and DeKoven

776); as I have illustrated elsewhere, I believe that "old school feminist interventions" can provide comics scholars with constructive, and at this juncture, critically necessary methodologies (Chase). In no manner am I suggesting that this work is devoid of preceding or contemporary comic influences; on the contrary, the peerless Lynda Barry is clearly the major progenitor of adolescent female characters in comics, but Marlys's maker deserves her own monograph, not just a cursory shout-out in an article. The other obvious predecessor, at least as regards pioneering the autobiographical and the excessive, is Aline Kominsky-Crumb, whose work Chute has adroitly assayed in her text *Graphic Women*.[5] In asserting that Gloeckner, Drechsler, and Doucet's work carries on the difficult feminist art agenda of transforming women's circumstances into artistic subject matter—ultimately hoping that this subject matter will reveal the whole human condition, as art by men has been perceived to do for centuries— my impulse is to consider their work within the context of feminist art. In "Autography's Biography," Jared Gardner rightfully asserts that the gestation of the autobiographical form in comics was partly inspired by "the feminist movement and revolutionary politics that were very much in the air" in southern California in the early 1970s, but I would flesh out his proposition by suggesting that feminist artists' consciousness-raising sessions from the mid-1960s onward were another important influence on the rise of the confessional form (Gardner 14). At such sessions, women not only encouraged one another to share their "neuroses, body-issues, and sexuality" (as Gardner points out Kominsky-Crumb would later do in her *Twisted Sisters* comix and anthologies) but helped each other recognize that these psychological hang-ups were largely due to one's biological gender and the institutional sexism that prevented women from making equitable social progress in the art world and elsewhere. In sum, to recognize that the personal was indeed political. What Gardner describes as the greatest surprise of the first comics autobiographers: "that the most personal stories became the ones that forged the most meaningful connections with others, opening up a dialogue with audiences and a sense of communal experience and release," might just as easily describe how feminist artists felt when they discovered that art about the female experience liberated the psyches of makers and audiences alike (Gardner 13). The same year that Trina Robbins started the *Wimmen's Comix* collective in San Francisco, and Joyce Farmer and Lyn Chevley published their first edition of *Tits N' Clits*, Judy Chicago and Miriam Schapiro established the first feminist art program at California Institute of the Arts in Valencia,

California, and female audiences who visited their collaborative installation, *Womanhouse*, experienced similarly instinctive feelings of communion: crying, laughing, gasping in recognition, and nodding their heads in agreement at the revamped domestic scenes and tableaux vivants of women's daily lives.[6] Additionally, in the same manner that it was the bridal gowns, bed linens, tampons, pantyhose, and overflowing shoe closets that helped elicit a shock of recognition within *Womanhouse* attendees, I propose that it is these contemporary female comic artists' similar use of feminine iconography, or as Schneemann termed it, "personal clutter"—whether it be a Nick Cave album or earth shoes—that educes identification and empathy in the reader.

Gillian Whitlock, in her insightful article about the unique power of comics autobiography, what she has termed "autographics," posits that this art form in particular has the potential to speak across cultural divides, and I extrapolate her suggestion to presume that biological gender and its embodied experiences is simply one more cultural chasm that comics may be more easily able to bridge. Still, Whitlock warns that despite Scott McCloud's conviction that cartoon imagery possesses universality other visual forms lack, scholars should "be wary of claiming universality in mediations of comics and cartoon drawings" (Whitlock 970). By asserting that the themes within these comics universally speak to women, I certainly run the risk of what theorists have disparagingly referred to as "essentializing" these artists and their female readers. But here I follow the model of feminist art historians such as Anna Chave, who espouses feminist activism, artmaking, and scholarship that both acknowledges the unique traumas women experience as a result of their biological gender, and privileges, as Schneemann stated, "an ethic about knowledge—received from and in the body" (Chave 133). Similarly, despite many scholars' belief that to discuss art about women's experiences as if it expressed a depoliticized, monolithic point of view is both politically dangerous and woefully ignorant, I support Mary D. Garrard's bold assertion that it may not be as misdirected as it first seems: "[This] complaint that Woman is a fiction and myth, that real women are not unitary in class, race, and other aspects . . . is perhaps not particularly relevant to art made by women (or men), which must consolidate and idealize—in new terms of course, if it is to present an expressive model of imaginative emancipation both for artist and audiences. Unlike living women, images *may have to be* essentialist to work" (Garrard 142, emphasis is my own). In their influential anthology, *Interfaces: Women/Autobiography/Image/Performance*, Sidonie Smith and Julia Watson draw attention to the frequency with which women's visual art during the twentieth century has engaged the autobiographical, not only in order to illustrate the politics of self-representation, but to, as stated above, politicize the personal, and by doing so, to offer it up as mode of communication with the viewer. They also propose that feminist autobiography frequently occurs at what they call the "interface" of image and word, illustrating how this intentional, and frequently jarring, juncture of two separate discursive modes provides a way for female artists to rupture conventional and expected meanings, ultimately providing a site of artistic resistance to patriarchal culture. Chute and DeKoven make a similar point about comics when they suggest that because the comics medium is "cross-discursive," that is to say, "composed of verbal and visual narratives that . . . remain distinct," a female reader may be able to resist the passive spectatorship so problematic in film spectatorship (Chute and DeKoven 770). Merging these two assessments, one can posit that the comics form is capable of both liberating the female reader from a traditional, linear, and thus masculinist method of reading/interpretation, as well as providing a site of resistance and agency for female creators, who can capitalize on the multitude of ways in which image and text confirm, contradict, and/or complement one another. Additionally, by sharing the individual articulation of their subjective experience with a wider readership—which is really a consciousness-raising session in a reproducible and circulating form—comic artists clearly seek to make the personal public, and as such, must be optimistically viewed as attempting to engage with a more universal audience.

In 1977, Miriam Schapiro, one of the founders of that inaugural feminist art program at Cal Arts, declared that part of the feminist project was to redress the trivialization of women's experiences, and Phoebe Gloeckner certainly attempts to give both vision and voice to those whose intellectual, emotional, and biological concerns have historically been accorded scant consideration. In her collection of drawings and cartoons, *A Child's Life*, the viewer is confronted repeatedly with the "personal clutter" of female lives and experiences. Frames such as the title page to the comic, *An Object Lesson in Bitter Fruit*, despite being packed to the edges with idiosyncratic bric-a-brac, tend to be overlooked due to their relative lack of narrative action (fig. 10.4). But Gloeckner's girlhood iconography reveals reams of emotional information, and this relatively detailed image is exemplary of her agenda to illustrate her own life in order to speak to others, especially young women.[7] The composition owes more than a

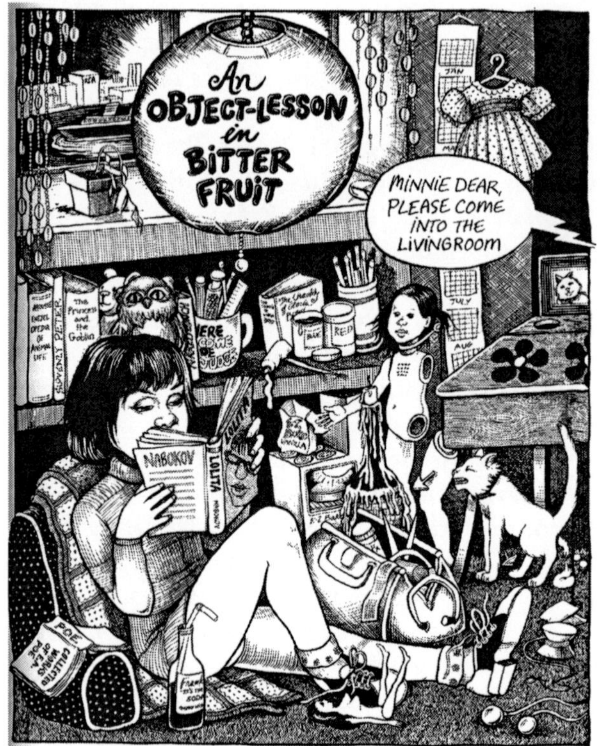

10.4. Phoebe Gloeckner. *An Object Lesson in Bitter Fruit* (title page).

passing debt to Albrecht Dürer's *Melancholia I* of 1514, an engraving that art historian Erwin Panofsky believed to be the artist's "spiritual self-portrait" (fig. 10.5). In the medieval period, melancholy was believed to be the humor most inclined to madness. As revised by Renaissance thought, however, it symbolized creative genius, and in Dürer's work the hulking female angel represents the artist who is both exhausted and paralyzed by the "terrible risks" that accompany her gift of keen perception. In Gloeckner's version, the ennui-laden goddess is a young girl of the mid-1970s, but she is no less symbolic of the universal artist's innate struggles as she comes to terms with life's hypocrisies. Specifically, the room is illustrative of the chasm between society's nostalgic fictions about young girls and the more sordid truths, as well as a landscape of conflicting female emotional stages and desires. Like Dürer's extremely hermeneutic image, Gloeckner's use of symbolism can be seen as her desire to convey "what it is to be human" (Groth 90). Here the young Minnie's bookcase is filled not

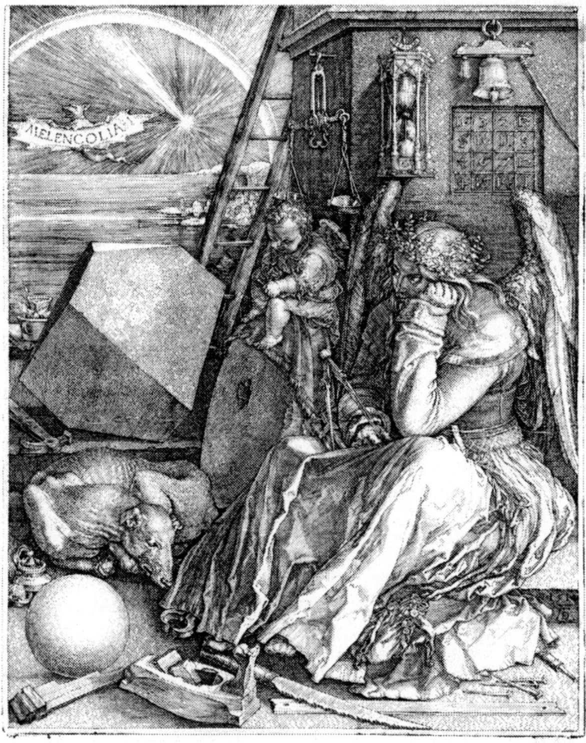

10.5. Albrecht Dürer. *Melancholia I.*

with the charming stories of the precocious children's heroines Madeline or Eloise, but, as we can see from the text in her hand, a more sinister femme-enfant, Vladimir Nabokov's Lolita, and the book is a self-evident harbinger for Minnie's first, albeit inappropriate, sexual relationship. Here, the intellectual curiosity of the adolescent girl is given primacy over the ruffled dress that hangs like a discarded emblem of toddlerdom in the upper right corner, and it is perhaps this visual binary that best foreshadows the following narrative, wherein which Minnie's mother and stepfather insult both her dignity and intelligence by asking her if she is aware that she will soon physically become a woman, with her stepfather enunciating "men-stru-a-tion" in a manner that is both patronizing and perverse. Even an eight-year-old girl has a clear sense of personal dignity; and as Gloeckner shows time and time again, it is adults who lose their moral footing. By showing Minnie reading *Lolita* in the first frame, and William Burrough's pederastic *Naked Lunch* in the third, Gloeckner suggests that

Minnie most likely does know all about these sensitive topics, and her cross-hatched cheeks are further visual affirmation of her knowledge as well as her embarrassment.[8]

That a young women's childhood stories, ergo their autobiographies, are darker and less sweet than most adults might otherwise envision them is additionally borne out by the fact that the title *The Princess and the Goblin*, a fairy tale, shares bookshelf space with *Slovenly Peter*, the grimmest of Germanic children's literature in which nail biters get their fingers cut off to bloody stumps. There also sits the aforementioned *Naked Lunch*, and more tellingly, *The Chastity of Gloria Boyd*, a cheesy mass-market paperback whose real life subtitle states, "The intimate story of a girl who became a woman the hard way." Another cultural lie is insinuated in the figure of the sadistically hung and de-limbed doll who pathetically points to the saccharine vanilla cake cooking in an EZ bake oven. The doll is obviously a minier Minnie in her hair color and features, but she's rendered far more poignant by the pitiful holes in her plastic breastbone, as if the recordings in the doll-body are all that society wants to hear. She is the equivalent of Dürer's despondent cherub: a figure that is normally drawn smiling and cheerful is here intentionally wrecked by the artist's hand. In this instance, a noose-type rope hangs around her neck, while an arrow pierces her detached thigh; like so many young women, she is first abused, then left abandoned. The Barbie at Minnie's feet can be viewed as the adult female body this doll will become, perpetually nude and on her back, her sexuality her only weapon, and as such, may be Gloeckner's version of the adamantine sword that lays at the feet of Dürer's angel.

The doll is a recurring motif within *A Child's Life*; the first comic within the anthology illustrates Minnie's nascent feminism as she endeavors to protect and find a good home for a motley assortment of "living dolls" who share their childhood stories of abandonment, abuse, and poverty (fig. 10.6). With their two-foot tall stature and diversity of costume and facial features, they can be interpreted as visual perversions of the extremely popular *American Girl* dolls, which are accompanied by autobiographical books that, while somewhat heroic and for the most part historically accurate, absolutely never address such taboo topics as divorce, starvation, or the more visceral ravages of war. Gloeckner herself sees them as representative of the more universal problems that plague humankind. When interviewed about their symbolic meaning, Gloeckner stated, "They also represent, in general, the problems in the world, and all the unfairness and sadness which I feel helpless to do much about but I wish I could. I do wish I could save those little girls" (Sullivan).

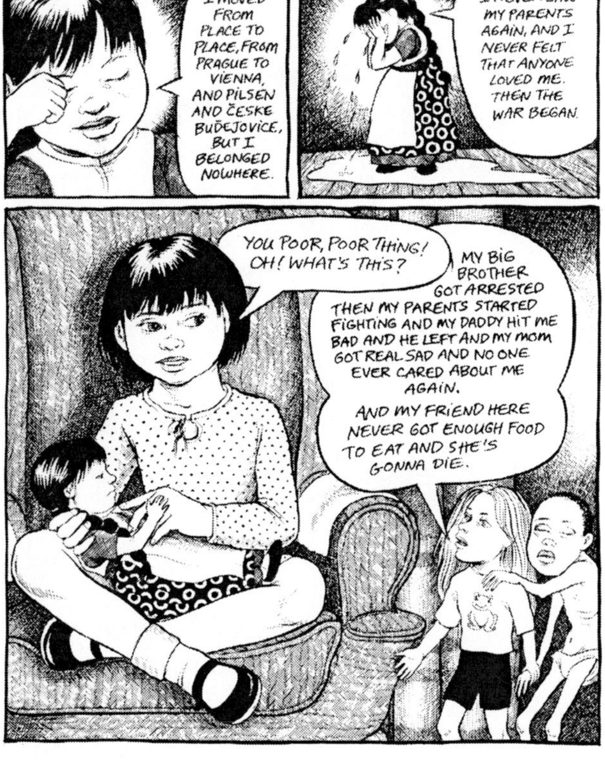

10.6. Phoebe Gloeckner. *A Child's Life.*

Such ostensibly trivial objects as baby dolls and Barbies, what Schnee-mann's fictional male speaker defined as the "personal clutter" of female lives, and these objects' ability to stand as potent iconography for a young woman's feelings, are also a significant element within Gloeckner's graphic novel, *Diary of a Teenage Girl,* the story of the same Minnie's teenage years in San Francisco and her troubled sexual coming of age at the hands of her mother's boyfriend. Reviewing the novel in the *Comics Journal* in 2004, Donald Phelps affirmed that Gloeckner's genius lay in her revision of the traditional Bildungsroman. Not only to illustrate the desires and frustrations of a young woman, as opposed to that of a young man, but to underscore that despite Minnie's moments of turpitude, her accumulated life experiences are what will eventually produce a great artist: "Minnie's progress . . . is not, like that of Hogarth's rake, a progress of dissolution; rather it is a voyage of assemblage, triply-motivated. Even as she lags and dawdles her way through school after school, to declining grades

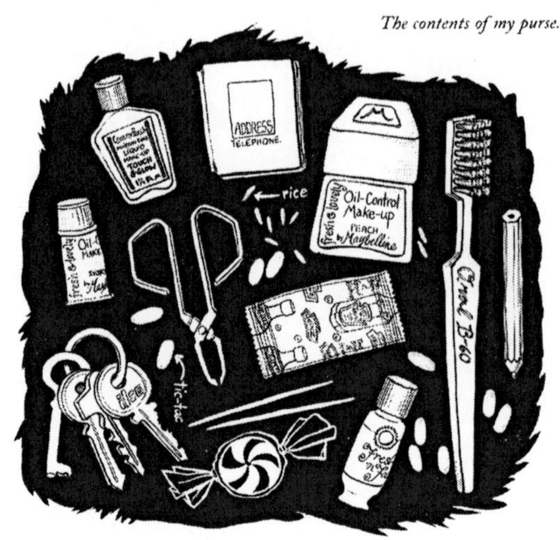

10.7. Phoebe Gloeckner. "The Contents of My Purse," *Diary of a Teenage Girl.*

and attendance records, Minnie is earnestly concerned with charting the new nation of her identity, in the piecemeal, picaresque way eternally familiar to young adolescence" (Phelps 76). Gloeckner's text is indeed, as Phelps states, "a form of ancient familiarity," but one that finally includes the embodied experiences of the other half of the population. Gloeckner's decision within the novel to include seemingly mundane objects as contemporary visual counterparts to Marcel Proust's madeleines suggests that they have an emotional resonance above and beyond what might normally be assumed. One such cartoon, the small drawing titled "The contents of my purse," at first glance might initially be read as nothing more than an accompanying illustration to the proximate text, and yet, nothing on the preceding or following pages has anything to do with Minnie's pocketbook (fig. 10.7). Nevertheless, I would argue that to a female viewer, the drawing is as emblematic of the aspirations of teenage girlhood and the construction of one's superficial identity as are such naïvely profound lines of the diary as "I want to somehow leave a mark that will eternally relate me to the animate world" that *are* found on the surrounding pages. The drawing shows us things we might expect to find in a handbag—tweezers, keys, address book, pencil, and various vials of makeup. Yet when one reads the four cosmetic bottles more closely, their labels are pathetic indications of a young woman's wish to be seen as "fresh and lovely" or "fresh and fair," and the youthfully erroneous belief that one product will magically transform the awkward teenage girl into the beautiful adult woman. The polarization of one's self-image in these years is emphasized by the contradictory "oil-free" and "moisturizing," both in the same glowing peach shade.

Likewise, Gloeckner's split image, titled "The left side of my room" and "The right side of my room" (fig. 10.8 and 10.9 respectively), reveals the mental and physical schisms endemic to teenage girls as they struggle to discover themselves, not only in its actual cleaving of the room by three full pages of text and one full page comic tellingly titled "Identity Crisis," but also by Gloeckner's overall composition and choice of iconographic elements. On the left side of Minnie's room, the bed is of central focus, but what sits upon it is not what we might expect given the heroine's testimonials of her voracious sensual desires. Rather, the typewriter and open journal on and in which the diary entries were written become a material substitute for her body, and insinuate that having sexual experiences is less important than having sexual experiences so that one can write about them—emphasizing the contrast between her actual physical self and the diaristically indulgent drama she narrates. Perhaps a truer portrait of the contradictions within the female protagonist is found in the room's conflicting visual details: a spilt bottle of wine on the left cancels out the bottle of Bonne Bell skin cleanser on the right, the girly platforms are balanced by the heavy boots, and the prim floral nightgown is at odds with the op-art mini-dress of this nymphet novelist who seemingly commands her own sexual destiny and finds her literary inspiration in the cult Surrealist poetry of Isidore Ducasse. As in the aforementioned frame from *A Child's Life*, Gloeckner's repeated insistence that images deceive us, that the world is an illusion, and that female selves are performances we try on, is evidenced by her choice to mirror her own hazy reflection in the looking glass with the dynamic poster of hippie chanteuse Janis Joplin on the wall above her bed. The young Minnie, try as she might to emulate the dissolute Haight Street lifestyle with its drug-addled denizens and free-love ethos, is but an apparition, unsure of herself and who she really is or can be. Every young woman's fragile understanding of her ever-evolving self-identity during these years is echoed in an interview with Gloeckner about adolescence: "There is still a certain innocence, this hope mixed with neediness and dreams . . . It's a very vulnerable time" (Groth 112).

The trials of coming of age in less than picture perfect circumstances, and a young woman's tenuous hold on "normalcy" as she struggles to define

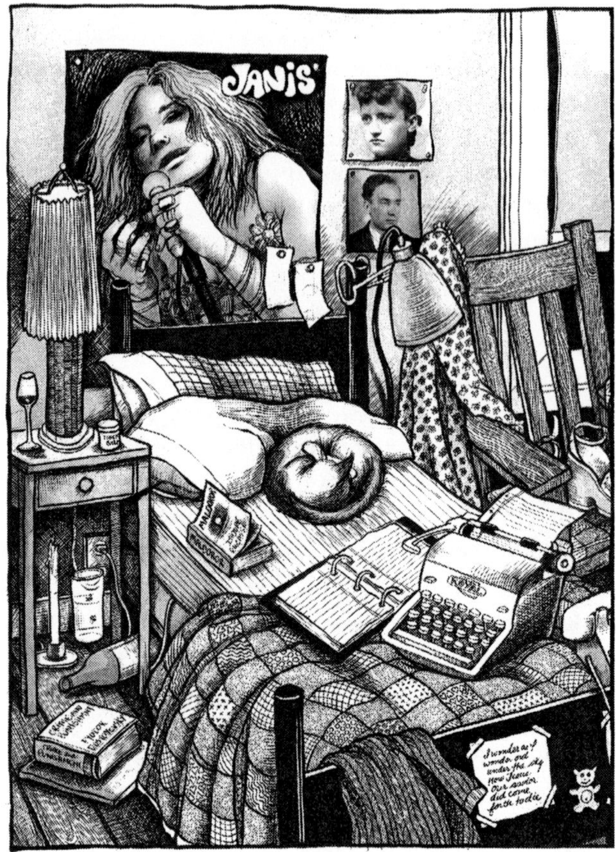

The left side of my room.

10.8. Phoebe Gloeckner. "The left side of my room," *Diary of a
Teenage Girl.*

herself in the wake of horrifically inappropriate sexual advances, are also
the topic of Debbie Dreschler's graphic novel *Daddy's Girl.*[9] As in Gloeckner's *Diary of a Teenage Girl*, there is an absurdly paradoxical schism
between reality and what is scribed within the diary, and it is Dreschler's
intentional sequencing that underscores her heroine's tortured emotional
flux in dealing with an incestuous father. In the one-page cartoon titled
"Dear Diary," Dreschler illustrates the quotidian teen girl's vacillating
emotions. In the first frame, Lily is thrilled with her mother for giving her
a journal in which she can record her "most deep dark secrets," in the next

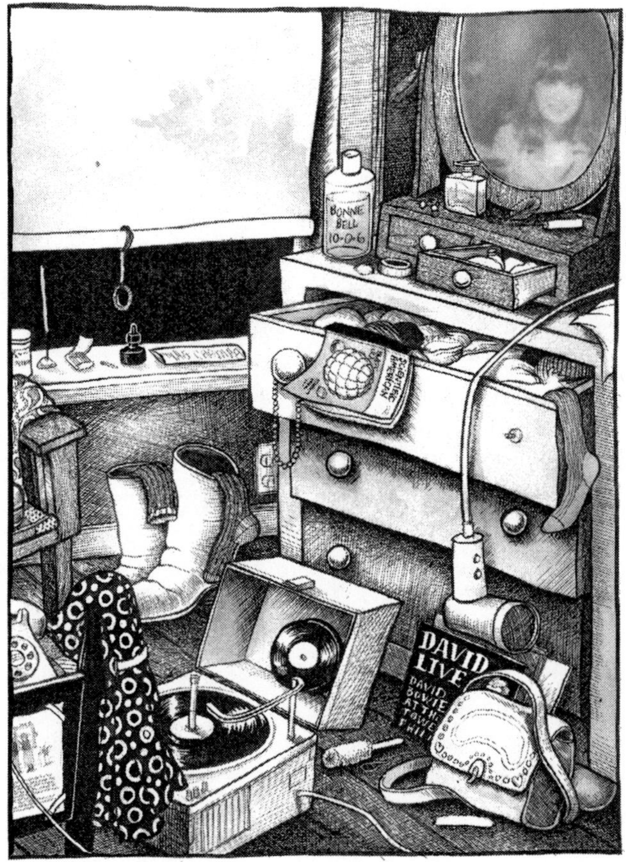

The right side of my room.

10.9. Phoebe Gloeckner. "The right side of my room," *Diary of a
Teenage Girl.*

she's calling her a bitch because she won't let her visit a friend's house: presumably commonplace stuff. And yet, the cartoons titled "Visitors in the
Night" and "Marvin," which bookend "Dear Diary," are grim renderings
of grotesque nighttime visits from a father hell-bent on sexually pleasur-
ing himself at the expense of his adolescent daughter. Although a diary is
stereotypically believed to be the place wherein which one's "most deep
dark" secrets are recorded, here Drechsler suggests that this event was so
traumatic that Lily could not bear to acknowledge it. Instead, the diary
becomes the place to erase the memory of her father's visits by pretending

that it never happened and perform the quotidian girlhood complaints of the sort a television heroine like Jan Brady might have had to endure. As Laura R. Micciche has written, "[One's reading of Daddy's Girl] is not simple, objective or total. It is directed by [Drechsler's] impulse to make us care about Lily and by extension, to care about the secrets that women's bodies and minds are too often forced to bear" (Miccichi 19).

Certainly, Drechsler's drawing style is reminiscent of Norwegian artist Edvard Munch's expressionistic line in his widely known work *The Scream*, a particular obvious formal point that has been noted by a number of other writers, including Micciche (fig. 10.10 and 10.11 respectively). The epigraph Munch composed to accompany the painting ends with Munch's understanding that his friends have abandoned him, and as such, his scream is elicited by the existential recognition that he is ultimately alone in the world. Lily, likewise, has been emotionally abandoned. Not only by her sister, whom the reader sees passively watching the horrific nocturnal events, but also, we must presume, by her mother. But I posit that a more accurate visual precedent to Drechsler's work is another, lesser-known painting by Munch, his 1895 *Puberty*, in which a wide-eyed, seemingly anguished young woman sits nude upon a bed while a ghostlike form hovers her left shoulder and head (fig. 10.12). Most critics assert the abstract specter symbolizes Munch's fear of female sexuality, and betrays this clearly adolescent female as an erotically dangerous figure, despite her modest pose. In Drechsler's telling revision, however, the surging, curvilinear forms are not shadowy phantoms symbolizing a young girl's fear of her own sexuality, nor a fledgling eroticism that threatens to disempower the potency of the male artist, but well-intended undulating angels who have come to give Lily the emotional reassurance her family cannot provide (fig. 10.13). As they float above her, they intone, "We'll come whenever you need us . . . we wish we could do more . . . but we can't. We love you Lily . . . now go to sleep." The desire to reclaim the representation of the female body and its gendered experiences was certainly part of the feminist art agenda, and here, in Dreschler's renderings, it's the girl's story, the girl's vision, the girl's voice, that is finally told, and the resulting artwork and all its persistence of feelings breaks the viewer's heart. By appropriating and adapting these forms to insinuate a young woman's desire for emotional reassurance in the aftermath of such egregious sexual exploitation, Drechsler not only gives the reader her individual revision of what it feels like to be simultaneously surrounded by people and alone as hell, but to be so as a physically vulnerable female child under the reign of patriarchical control.[10] Referring to the medium of comics, Micciche notes, "Drechsler critiques the culture of male violence and its traumatizing effects on women's bodies and minds while working within a male-dominated form," but the aforementioned comparison suggests that she is also doing so within the realm of fine art (Micciche 21). If one of the goals of early modernism was to create innovative forms that could visually articulate both subjective and universal emotions, then Drechsler's art is expressionism at its most skilled.

Schneemann also wanted to show that the female body could be a source of pride rather than the shame many male artists, such as Munch, imbued it with. "My culture," she declared, "denies females an honorable genital" (Schneeman, "Obscene" 28). To rectify Western culture's distortion and damnation of woman's inward and outward organs, Schneemann wanted to assert that the vaginal canal was the place where both biological, and by extension, cultural, creativity originate. She also proposed that society reconsider "the vagina—in many ways—physically, conceptually: as a sculptural form, an architectural referent, the source of sacred knowledge, ecstasy, birth, transformation" (Schneemann, "Interior Scroll"). This sentiment was exemplary of second-wave feminists' desire to be "cunt positive" despite the social complications of doing so, and these issues are thoroughly resonant in the work of Julie Doucet, whose original comic series called *Dirty Plotte* ("plotte" means cunt in Québecois slang) is filled with stories focusing on this socially degraded orifice. Arguably, Western society hasn't progressed far from Germaine Greer's claim that the shame surrounding "female genitalia stems from actual distaste. The worst name anyone can be called is *cunt*. The best thing a cunt can be is small and unobtrusive . . . No woman wants to find out that she has a twat like a horse-collar . . . [nor one that is] sloppy or smelly" (Greer 45), and Doucet's decision to put the adjective "dirty" in front of "plotte" is a way of underscoring and reaffirming the problematical nature of having pride in one's vagina, even in late twentieth-century Canada. Throughout the series, Doucet's insistence on sharing the intimacies of her cunt—its uncontrollable desires, most fulfilling pleasures, and fabulously unruly fluids—introduces subjects familiar to female readers but shocking given their rarity in visual art and mainstream media.

In one such comic, "Alone Again with Julie Doucet," the artist portrays herself lying on her bed in a position reminiscent of one of those mute reclining nudes of Art History, specifically that of Edoaurd Manet, whose 1863 painting *Olympia* shocked the bourgeoisie for daring to show

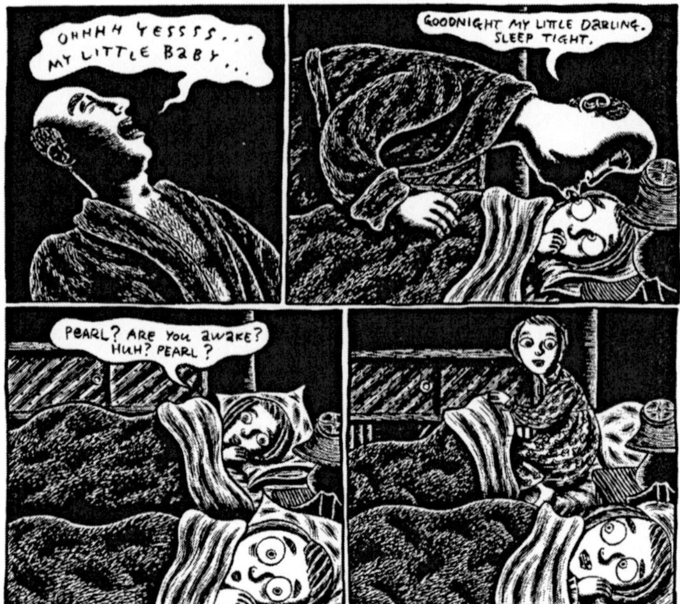

10.10. Debbie Dreschler, *Daddy's Girl*.

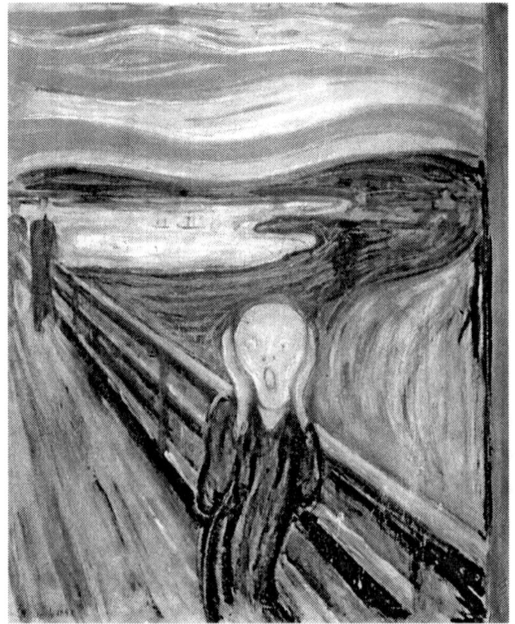

10.11. Edvard Munch. *The Scream* (1893).

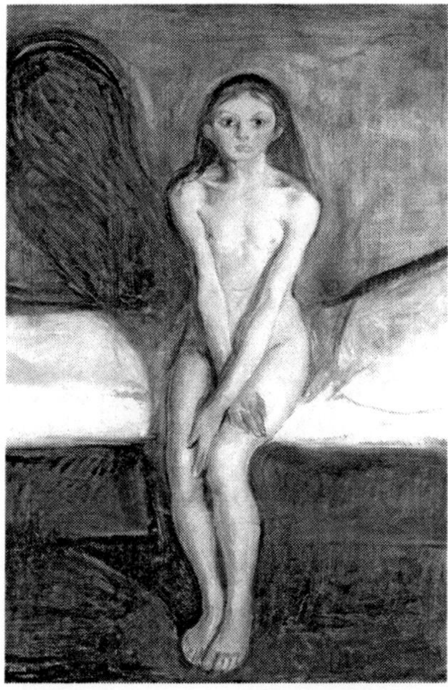

10.12. Edvard Munch. *Puberty* (1895).

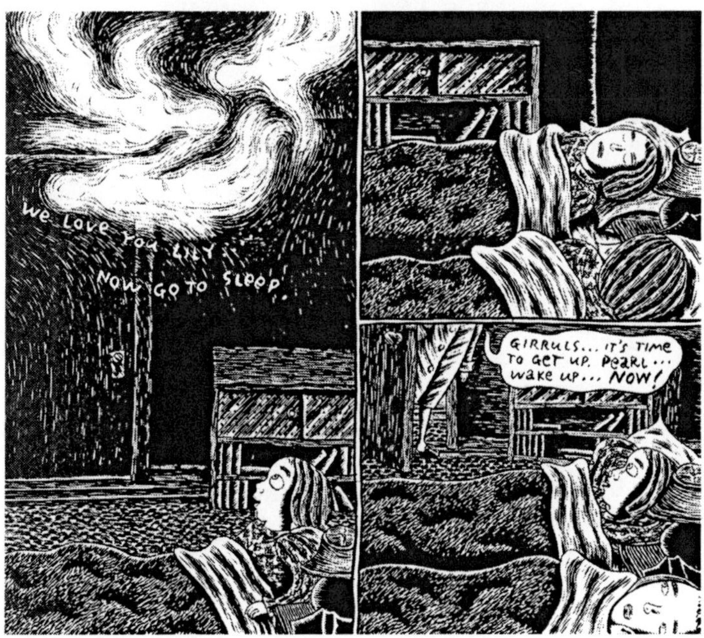

10.13. Debbie Dreschler. *Daddy's Girl.*

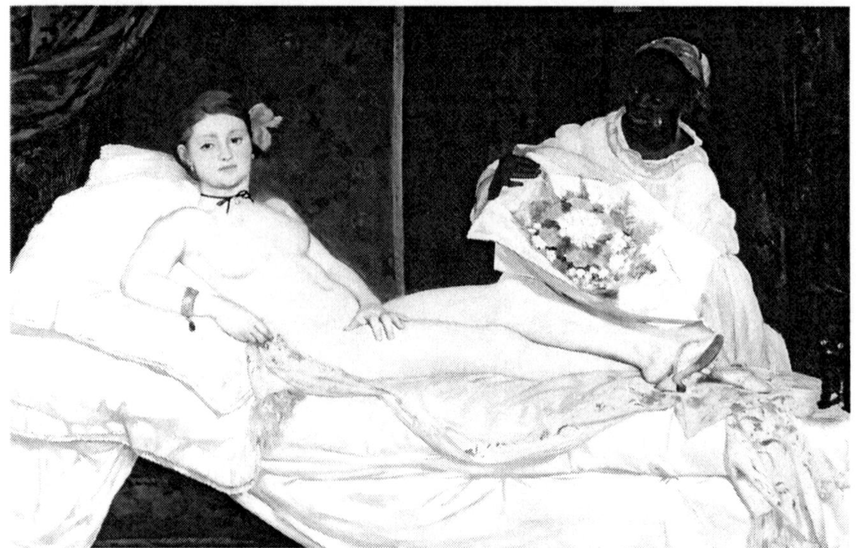

10.14. Edoaurd Manet. *Olympia* (1863).

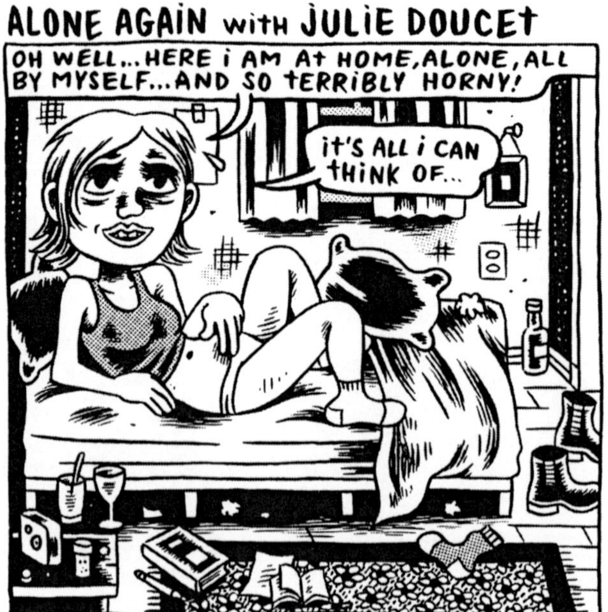

10.15. Julie Doucet. "Alone Again with Julie Doucet," *Dirty Plotte* #12 (1998).

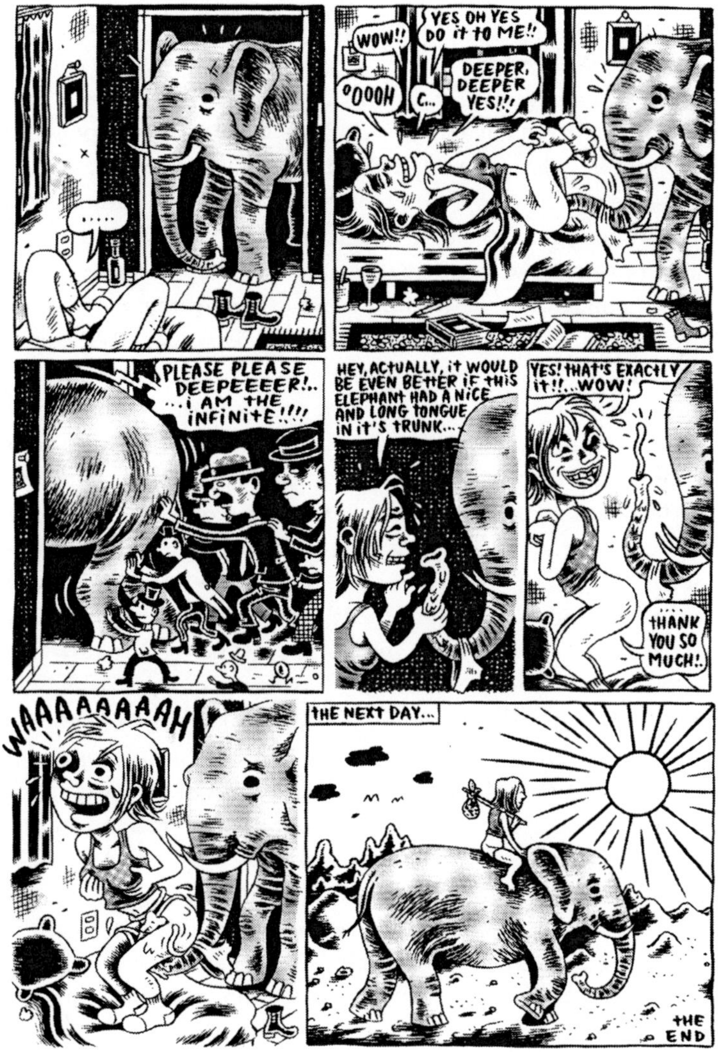

10.16. Julie Doucet. "Alone Again with Julie Doucet" *Dirty Plotte* #12 (1998).

a courtesan who looked directly at the viewer rather than demurely avert her eyes (fig. 10.14). But Doucet takes it further than Manet did, as the object of the ostensibly male viewer's gaze (and desire), revised and emancipated by the female artist, now addresses us with both eyes and words. With voice, the word balloon, she becomes the subject, the masturbator who controls her own fantasy, one in which she conjures up the ultimate phallus, one that will "[f]ill her up completely inside, totally!! Once and for good" (fig. 10.15). But as the frames progress, it is slowly revealed that no man's bodily appendages are large enough to satisfy her desire. It is only an elephant's trunk, magically equipped with a "nice and long tongue" that is the ideal counterpart for the artist (fig. 10.16). Like Schneemann unrolling her impressively long scroll, Doucet's boast, "I am the infinite" reclaims the power of the vaginal canal. It is no longer the negative and barren lack, but what Schneemann called "a vulvic space" so impressively vast that the male provides inadequate satisfaction. In the final frame, the heroine rides off, not on a prince's white horse, but on her own sexually gifted pachyderm—the fairy tale rewritten.

What comes from the cunt, and society's fear of its symbolic power, was also of concern to second-wave feminist artists. In 1971, hoping to rupture social taboos regarding female menstruation, Judy Chicago made a photolithograph, *Red Flag*, that showed a blood-drenched tampon emerging from her vagina as a visible marker of difference and a symbol of women's ability to not only bear life, but to choose when they want to do so, for the female body that bleeds is not one that will easily submit to patriarchal control. The following year, she created the now infamous *Menstruation Bathroom* installation of *Womanhouse*, in which a trash-can overflowing with bloody sanitary pads was set atop a white pedestal, and thus, exalted menstruation as by elevating it to the status of a high art object. Part of her agenda was to erase the cultural stigmas associated with such a normal and regular biological occurrence, and to make it visible was one way to persuade women to embrace what society has both shunned and visually erased. As Chicago stated, "However we feel about our own menstruation is how we feel about seeing its image in front of us" (Delaney et al. 276). Schneemann remarked, "For woman, blood is symbolic of life, but because a man has to be injured to bleed male culture often projects this fear into the female experience" (Schneemann, *Imaging* 245). In *A Child's Life*, Gloeckner illustrates this culturally indoctrinated shame that surrounds a woman's menses in her poignant comic "Developmental Developments." The first frame shows Minnie scrutinizing a woman's magazine Kotex advertisement featuring a bespectacled and somewhat disgruntled-looking teen girl with the words DEAR MOTHER NATURE: DROP DEAD emblazoned across her T-shirt, and this image works to establish Minnie's state of mind about menstruation. In short: that it's a bother but not insurmountable. Thus, when her neighbor Cheryl invites Minnie over to her house and proudly holds up a pair of bloodied underwear, proclaiming, "I got it even earlier than my sister," Minnie's seemingly casual inspection of the stained panties seems devoid of embarrassment. Cheryl then helpfully gives the dubious Minnie a sanitary pad in preparation for her own unavoidable advance into womanhood. "[It's] for your hope chest—," the ebullient Cheryl counsels. But the jubilant tone of the comic quickly turns dark when Cheryl's father comes up to punish her for leaving milk on the counter, and Minnie is forced to hide under her friend's bed. Gloeckner's consecutive frame—Minnie crouched below the wooden slats of Cheryl's twin bed, Kotex pad clutched in her hand, the words WHIP WHIP laid upon the image—encapsulates the private and public humiliation of being a "woman," and this visual perspective intentionally traps the reader with the anguished Minnie as she crouches in fear (fig. 10.17). The next frame, while more literal, is no less emotive, and likewise suggests the stigma women bear once they get their periods: an aerial point of view of Cheryl's exposed buttocks covered with fresh gashes from her father's lashing with a metal dog leash. Again, it's Gloeckner's use of a girl's "personal clutter"—the stuffed bunny tucked under Cheryl's arm and the pitiful toy mouse on the other side of the bed—that serve to poignantly underscore how vulnerable these girls are. No matter how much they may know about the clinical facts of life, they are still innocent about the atrocious violence enacted upon women's bodies. The last frame, which fills an entire page, shows Minnie on her own bed, tenderly holding the sanitary napkin to her cheek. On a superficial level, the pad could be viewed as an ice pack Minnie uses to dull the pain she feels for her friend (fig. 10.18). But Gloeckner's composition evinces Pablo Picasso's *Weeping Woman* motif, which evolved out of the howling pieta in *Guernica* (1937), his visual critique of the Spanish Civil War. The grief-stricken female form is widely believed to be representative of universal suffering. But the successive Weeping Woman paintings of his mistress Dora Maar holding a handkerchief to her Cubistically-fractured, visually distraught cheek were important, as Picasso himself infamously remarked, "because women are suffering machines" (Malraux 138) (fig. 10.19). In the same way that the mammoth handkerchief becomes a visual extension of Maar's tears—so massive that they fold and flow down the page, so Minnie's maxipad (what holds and contains one's menstrual flow) serves to magnify and reify her more than justifiable grief.

In her 1972 piece, *Blood Work Diary*, Schneemann stained various squares of tissue paper with her menstrual blood, and then laid them on a silver paper-backed grid. The serial miniature "canvases," encased in

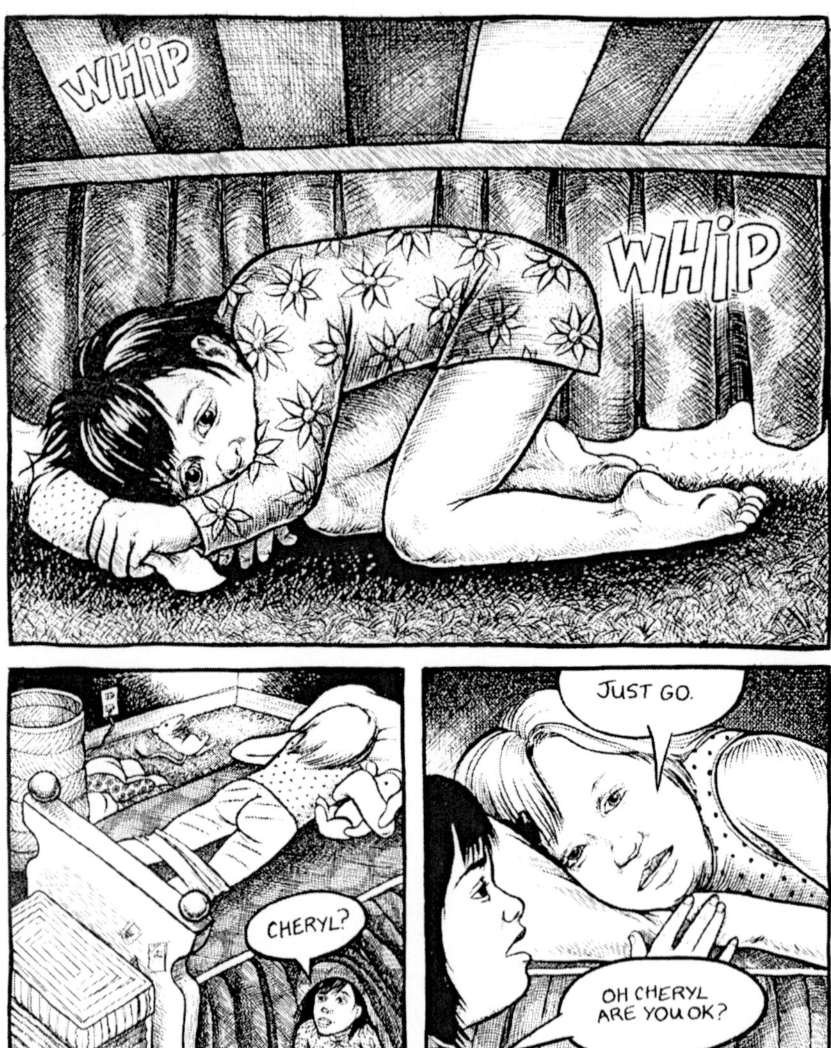

10.17. Phoebe Gloeckner. *A Child's Life.*

their orderly, individual frames, were Schneemann's attempt to expose the taboo aspect of a woman's period. From a distance, the central images appear to be the ambiguously fluid forms of Abstract Expressionism; only upon closer inspection of the title and the piece does the viewer realize how deeply engrained their repulsion towards this organic matter truly is.

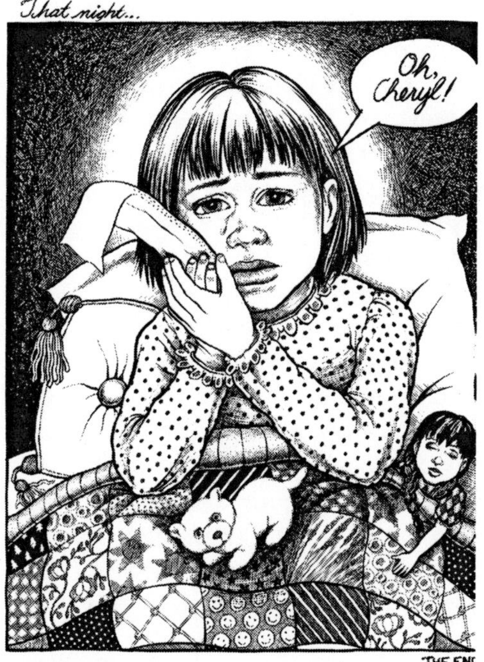

10.18. Phoebe Gloeckner. *A Child's Life*.

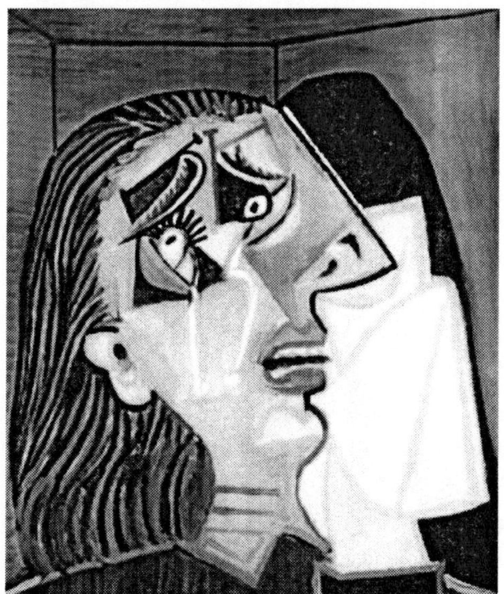

10.19. Pablo Picasso. *Weeping Woman* (1937).

In the same way that Schneemann's red stains are barely contained within organizational device of the grid, Doucet's revelation of her bodily secretions threatens to rupture the masculine rigidity of the comics frame. The hormonal fluctuations and conflicting, often overwhelming emotions a young woman undergoes as a result of her period are borne out in the different treatments of the subject as seen in "Heavy Flow" and an untitled comic from "Dirty Plotte No. One" and Doucet seems determined to normalize the myriad ways in which women experience their menses, given the frequency with which she makes it the main subject of her comics. In both works, the protagonist's menstrual flow is heavy, but her ability to cope with it varies dramatically, and this is appropriately borne out in the look of the protagonist in each comic. In "Heavy Flow," the central character becomes, in a Hulk-like instance of transformation, the monstrous female body, overwhelmed by its inability to control the fluid gushing from between her legs. Ripping male bodies from nearby buildings like a cartoon version of the fifty-foot woman, the blood begins to flood the town, sweeping everything along in its path (fig. 10.20). Her mammoth scale, obviously, is artistic shorthand for the hormonal irrationality engulfing all in her wake. But Doucet's decision to smear her self-portrait with the painterly mess of the fertile, but not pregnant, female body makes her form visually analogous to Schneemann's pigment-covered goddess evocation of *Interior Scroll*, and one can draw parallels between the two artists' pointed refusal to deny the facts of the biological female body. It is a clear visual allusion to Francisco Goya's horrific *Saturn Devouring One of His Sons* (1820), and Doucet's cooption of this image and her employment of hieratic scale are also meant to affirm a woman's ability to both create life and destroy it (fig. 10.21). Doucet's drawing brings to mind Barbara Creed's belief that "the monstrous is produced at the border which separates those who take up their proper gender roles and those who do not" (Creed 11). In the untitled comic, Doucet's mood is more serene, and her sublimated wish to reach the bathroom without releasing any of her menstrual blood is attributed to the right side of her brain, the intuitive hemisphere often associated with women and abstract creativity. The last frame of the untitled comic is overt in its proclamation of the power of woman's biological specificity; it reads in all capitals: LIVE BETTER EACH DAY THANKS TO THE POWER OF THE RIGHT SIDE YOUR BRAIN (fig. 10.22). The latter cartoon also shares an agenda with Schneemann's 1983 piece *Fresh Blood: A Dream Morphology*, a visual and sound collage based on a menstrual dream in which the artist reclaimed her

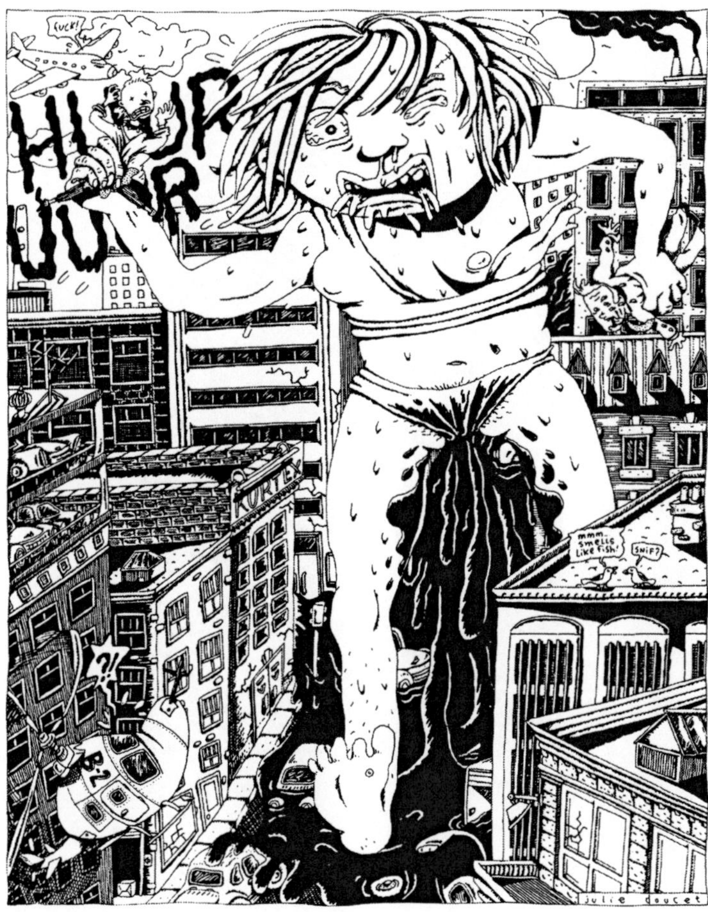

10.20. Julie Doucet. *Heavy Flow*.

body's functions as normative and the human basis of continuing life, not as something other, something transgressive, something "not male."

It's probably considered unfashionable in a post-feminist age to situate this work in such a context, or as I stated at the outset, naïve to claim that individual, obviously subjective autobiographical material can be representative of universal experiences, but it is inarguable that the production of these artists carries on the difficult agenda begun by Schneemann and her peers of legitimizing female lives and experiences as a valuable subject matter for art. The art historian Griselda Pollock, whom I revere for so many reasons, admonishes such "interpretations" when she writes:

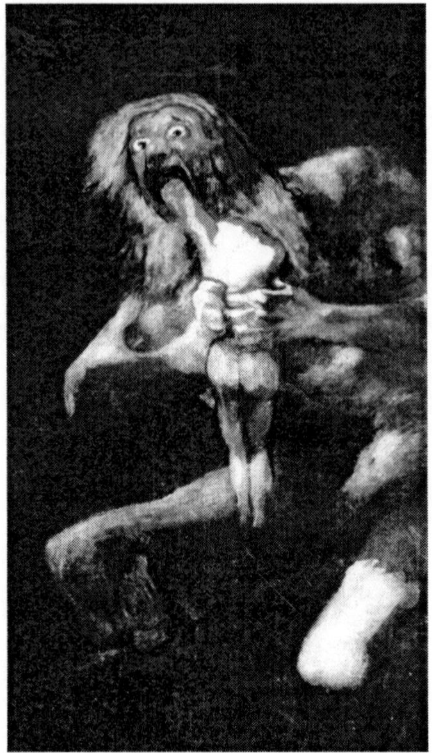

10.21. Francisco Goya. *Saturn Devouring One of His Sons* (1820).

"At present, women's culture suffers unbearably from too 'much reading in.' Critics appear confident in their interpretations of artwork by women: it means this; she is saying that; it is feminist because she shows this. . . . Apparently, we already know what women are, feel, experience as women. The work remains tied in a loop of current ideological constructions of femininities" (Pollock 75). True as that may be, and as important as it is for feminist scholars to remember, I return to Garrard's point about images needing to be "essentialist in order to work." In order for artists to convey coherent and comprehensible meaning to their audiences, they must on some level use symbolic content that both reveals their personal subjectivity and resonates beyond it. That these comics speak to young women, that they reveal an alternative story that isn't told nearly as often as it is lived, that it presents a graphic reality far more like many girls' contemporary lives, is evidenced by such

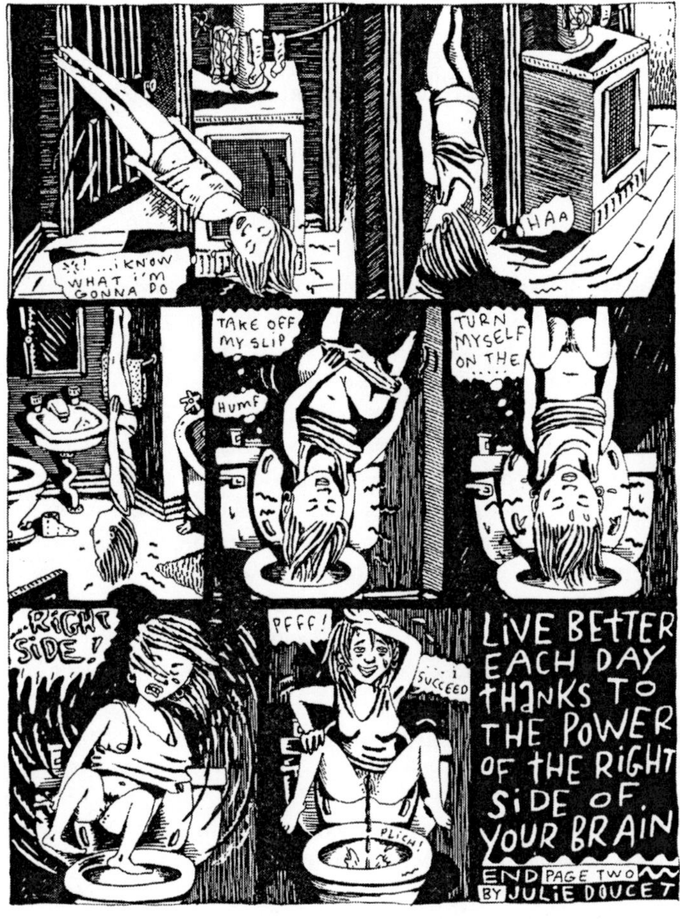

10.22. Julie Doucet Untitled comic from Dirty Plotte No. One. (1990).

apocryphal stories as the one told about the Contemporary Women's Lit class held at McGill, when after reading Doucet's *My NY Diary*, a female student stood up and shouted, "This is my life!"[11] Or, perhaps the more verifiable claim by Gloeckner that she's had many teenage girls write to her and say, "That character is *me*. How did you know how I felt?" (Groth 107). As Gloeckner herself states, "The basic question of art, of any art is, "What is it to be alive?" (Groth 90). And these artists' greatest feat is to show us what it means not only to be alive in our time, but to be alive as a young woman. To make the personal political, and make it universally understood.

Notes

1. The basic description of the performance follows Schneemann's in *Imaging Her Erotics*; the art historical comparisons and interpretations are my own, based on her extensive writings.

2. Although Schneemann later revealed that the poem was provoked by a conversation with a female film critic, making her critic male allowed her to, as Anna Chave has written, "Perform the role of the embodied gender to pointedly excessive effect" and thus illustrate the "opposing . . . obsessions of the corporeal female with the cerebral male" (Chave 33). Despite the similarity between Chave's introduction and my own, it is important to note that my paper was first presented in 2005 at the International Comics Art Festival in Washington, D.C., and as such, this similarity is simply coincidental (the bodies and theses of the papers are not similar).

3. I realize that in calling this work feminist, I may indeed be challenging the artists themselves. Here I concur with the assessment of Helena Reckitt, who writes, "[Woman artists] have at times denied being feminists. This should not mean, however, that their work is not necessarily "not-feminist," that it has not influenced feminist artists, or cannot be interpreted within a feminist perspective. Sometimes the work's implicit feminism contradicts the artist's words" (Reckitt 12–13).

4. In this regard, I follow Timothy Dow Adams, who has elucidated the potency of the autobiographical form as: ". . . the story of an attempt to reconcile one's life with one's self . . . [it] is not, therefore, meant to be taken as historically accurate but as *metaphorically* authentic" (Adams, ix).

5. This nod to Chute's text is cursory; the final draft of this essay was submitted before the release of Chute's text, and the original version presented, as noted above, in 2005.

6. Recalling their emotional responses, Schapiro believes their emotional outpouring was due to that fact that they *recognized* what they saw: "At Womanhouse, women, particularly, walked into what was essentially their home ground, knowing instinctively how to react." In short, they saw their "lives" (Shapiro 270).

7. Gloeckner told Michael Martin that while she was writing *Diary of a Teenage Girl*, she "kept holding in [her] heart a vision of a teenage girl who would read it [and relate to it]."

8. Likewise, if *A Child's Life* is read in sequence, the preceding comic, "Developmental Developments," narrates the story of Minnie's friend Cheryl and her first period, and thus the reader is aware Minnie knows all about "men-stru-a-tion."

9. Most of these comics were originally printed in a series of comics titled *Nowhere*, which to me insinuates that the events could happen anywhere, and most likely have happened everywhere.

10. About her readers' responses, Drechsler stated, "I found that a lot of adults were very moved by the stories. People who had experienced incest felt that I'd described

what they'd experienced in a way that they couldn't and people who hadn't had that experience found a deeper understanding of it."

11. As shared with me by Peggy Burns, vice-president of Drawn & Quarterly, the publishers of Doucet's work.

Works Cited

Adams, Timothy Dow. *Telling Lies in American Autobiography*. Chapel Hill, NC: University of North Carolina Press, 1990: ix, Print.

Chase, Alisia Grace. "Draws Like a Girl: The Necessity of Old School Feminist Interventions in the World of Comics and Graphic Novels." *Feminism Reframed*. Ed. Alexandra Kokoli. Cambridge: Cambridge Scholars Publishing, 2008: 61–85. Print.

Chave, Anna. "'Normal Ills': On Embodiment, Victimization, and the Origins of Feminist Art." *Trauma and Visuality in Modernity*. Eds. Lisa Saltzman and Eric Rosenberg. Hanover: Dartmouth College Press, 2006: 132–57. Print.

Chute, Hillary. *Graphic Women: Life Narrative & Contemporary Comics*. New York: Columbia UP, 2010. Print.

Chute, Hillary L., and Marianne DeKoven. "Introduction: Graphic Narrative." *Modern Fiction Studies* 52:4 (2006): 767–82. Print.

Creed, Barbara. *The Monstrous Feminine: Film, Feminism, and Psychoanalysis*. London: Routledge, 1993. Print.

Delaney, Janice, et al. *The Curse: A Cultural History of Menstruation*. Chicago: U of Illinois P, 1988. Print.

Gardner, Jared. "Autography's Biography, 1972–2007." *Biography* 31.1 (2008): 1–26. Print.

Garrard, Mary D. *Artemisia Gentileschi Around 1622: The Shaping and Reshaping of an Artistic Identity*. Berkeley: U of California P, 2001. Print.

Greer, Germaine. *The Female Eunuch*. New York: Harper Collins, 2008. Print.

Groth, Gary. "Interview with Phoebe Gloeckner." *Comics Journal* 261 (2004): 79–123. Print.

Ladygunn. "Interview with Julie Doucet." *Ladygunn*. 8 Aug. 2010. Web. 9 Sept. 2010.

Martin, Michael. "Phoebe Gloeckner: Inside Her Explicit Diary of a Teenage Girl." *Nerve*. 6 Mar. 2003. Web. 12 Aug. 2005.

Micciche, Laura R. "Seeing and Reading Incest: A Study of Debbie Drechsler's 'Daddy's Girl.'" *Rhetoric Review* 23:1 (2004): 5–20. Print.

Phelps, Donald. "Review: The Diary of a Teenage Girl." *Comics Journal* 261 (2004): 74–77. Print.

Pollock, Griselda. "Inscriptions in the Feminine." *Inside the Visible: An Elliptical Traverse of 20th Century Art in, of, and From the Feminine*. Ed. M. Catherine de Zegher. Cambridge, MA and London: The MIT Press, 1995. Print.

Schneemann, Carolee. "Interior Scroll." *Carolee Schneemann*. No date given on site. Web. 22 July 2010.

Schneemann, Carolee. *Imaging Her Erotics*. Cambridge: MIT Press, 2001. Print.

Schneemann, Carolee. "Obscene Body Politic." *Art Journal* 50:4 (1991): 2835. Print.

Schapiro, Miriam. "The Education of Women as Artists: Project Womanhouse." *Art Journal* (1972): Vol. 31, no. 3. 26870. Print.

Smith, Sidonie, and Watson, Julia, eds. "Introduction: Mapping Women's Self-Representation at Visual/Textual Interfaces." *Interfaces: Women/Autobiography/Image/Performance*. Ann Arbor: U of Michigan P, 2002. Print.

Sullivan, Gary. "Interview with Phoebe Gloeckner." *READERME: An Online Magazine of Poetics*. No date of interview on website. Web. 22 June 2010.

Verstappen, Nicolas. "Interview with Debbie Drechsler." Du9: L'autre bande desinée, July 2008. Web. Oct. 2, 2009.

Whitlock, Gillian "Autographics: The Seeing "I" of the Comics." *Modern Fiction Studies* 52:4 (2006): 96579.

A Female Prophet?

Authority and Inheritance in Marjane Satrapi

—Rachel Trousdale

Marjane Satrapi's *Persepolis* is a book about rebellions, both the large-scale rebellion of the uprising against the Shah and the personal rebellions of teenagers listening to rock music. But the formal rebellions of the book—whether performed by the Islamic Revolution, punk children, or Viennese anarchists—are constrained, regimented, and reactive: the protesters and police alike are drawn as interchangeable figures in a Persian frieze, and the punk kids wear uniforms just as prescribed as soldiers or fundamentalist women.[1]

Throughout the memoir, however, Satrapi proposes her family as a parallel lineage of authority, one that does not strictly prescribe individual actions and thus against which it is not necessary to rebel. The whole family participates in creating a cumulative moral authority, which is traced back to Marji's great-grandfather, the last emperor of Persia. Within the memoir as a whole, the family's moral system has a primary spokesperson: Satrapi's grandmother. Despite Marjane Satrapi's deliberately schematic drawings, Grandma Satrapi is one of the book's most consistently recognizable individual figures: her unusual hair color shows even beneath a veil, and the lines on her face mark both her age and her uniqueness. The grandmother provides Marji (the protagonist of the memoir) and Satrapi (its author) with an authority worth obeying: not an external set of rules, but a personal sense of integrity shaped by the actions and affections of past generations.

Satrapi's treatment of "the fundamentalist woman" and "the modern woman" initially suggests that women's self-representations, whether conformist or anti-conformist, are dictated by prefabricated ideological positions. Such claims, however, inevitably turn out to be reductive. Satrapi's self-representations in her memoir are equivocal and ever-changing: she both claims and rejects the status of exemplary Iranian woman just as both she claims and rejects the notion that she could be the next prophet. Through her depictions of her grandmother in *Persepolis* and in *Embroideries*, Satrapi suggests how we can read one woman as both individual and emblematic, traditional and liberated—and thus how to read the memoir itself as a document simultaneously about an individual's life in retrospect and about the history of a country. For Satrapi, the tensions between official and personal narratives can be partially resolved by recourse to her lineage of female storytellers, who teach her—and us—to see the nuances in the black and white of history.

Persepolis appears to stage a conflict between West and East, modernity and fundamentalism, individualism and collectivity. But while Satrapi's drawings are starkly black and white, the thematic dichotomies in her memoir systematically break down, suggesting a carefully negotiated reconciliation of the apparently incommensurable private and public personae the memoir represents. Satrapi's memoir constructs an alternative to the polarizing ideologies she encounters, a moral system grounded not in abstractions or absolutism but in personal affection and individual autonomy. She roots this moral system in a female lineage, in which the individual is both free to make her own decisions and supported by a family history of independent women and exacting maternal love.

The complexities of *Persepolis*'s ambivalent relationship to authority and autonomy are easy to miss, in part because the second volume of the memoir contains a strong nihilist streak. Early reviewers treated *Persepolis* as a "liberal and humanist" text—and thus as a text that validates Western readers' preexisting ideas (Naghibi and O'Malley 226). These readers understand Satrapi's memoir as a "universal" story with which they are free to identify. They base their readings of the memoir on the premise that childhood is a common, cross-cultural experience; they suggest that, since we too have experienced childhood, Marji's naïve lens renders the complexities of Iranian life comprehensible to outsiders because her reactions and ours are analogous. But as Nima Naghibi and Andrew O'Malley point out, "*Persepolis* subverts at every turn the very assumptions of universality and simplicity reviewers have widely ascribed to it and which the book itself encourages" (243). Instead, Satrapi's ethical claims are rooted in a highly specific cultural context: not just that of Iran during the Islamic Revolution, and Iranians' suffering during the Iran-Iraq war,[2] but her own family's history, which is both interwoven with and apart from the history of the Iranian Republic. At the same time, however, Satrapi's memoir instructs us to look for and transcend the barriers to individuality within any homogenous society—whether Iran or Austria, where, as Jennifer Worth notes, Marji still must "hide [. . .] herself under a succession of various symbolic 'veils'" (155).

Theresa M. Tensuan writes that Satrapi shows how "the transition from childhood to adulthood" is "overdetermined by narratives of development that set gendered roles, define class distinctions, articulate racial demarcations, inscribe religious differences, and establish parameters around sexual exploration" (952). Satrapi's memoir examines just how much we can avoid such predetermined narratives. At the same time, however, Satrapi, as a storyteller and a memoirist, seeks to reclaim narrative as an empowering rather than a confining framework for understanding her own life, making storytelling a retroactive analysis rather than a preemptive limitation on the events she describes, and drawing what Georges Gusdorf describes as the "diagram of a destiny" (40). In *Persepolis*, just as her cartoony drawing style balances between the reductive and the expressive, Satrapi is constantly attempting to replace prescriptive with descriptive storytelling, and traditional authority figures with family-sanctioned self-determination.

God and Grandma

Satrapi introduces the primary conflicts in the memoir (tradition/modernity, east/west, rebellion/conformity) through the rivalry for her allegiance between Marx and God. Despite her secular upbringing, young Marji is deeply religious. Her God—drawn as a ghostlike white pyramid, whose flowing beard blends into his flowing robes—is both a parental figure and her imaginary friend, visiting her every night and holding her in a comforting embrace. God completely surrounds and supports Marji, cradling her like a baby, with only her head showing (see fig. 11.1).

However devout she may be, however, Marji's religious beliefs are unorthodox. She is the center of her own moral universe—and intends not simply to remain central for herself, but to become central for others. "At the age of six," the narrative voice tells us, "I was already sure I was the last prophet" (see fig. 11.2). Marji's self-image as prophet separates her from those around her, both spiritually and physically. She imagines awed,

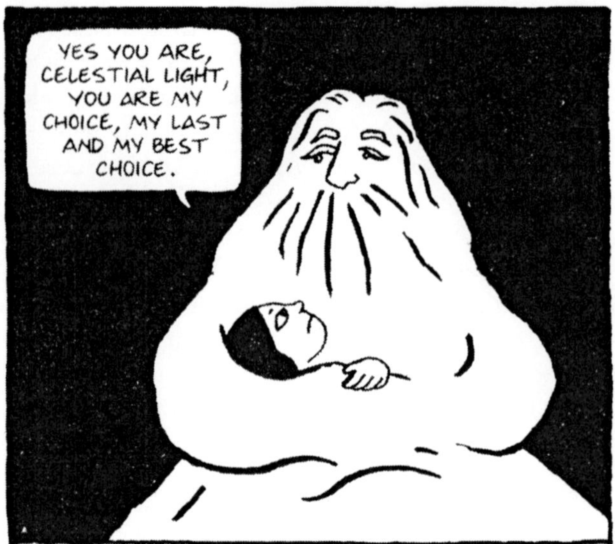

11.1. Marjane Satrapi. *Persepolis.* p. 8.

rejoicing worshippers kneeling to her, while her hair is replaced by rays of light like those of a child's drawing of the sun. Her halo both marks her as a supernatural figure and removes her from the gendered realm of veiling: rather than having hair she must cover (already an issue, as the very first page of the book discusses the veil), her head is surrounded by "celestial light." She believes that she has superior knowledge of her grandmother's body, thinking, "Don't worry. Soon you won't have any more pain. You'll see." Marji, picturing herself as a prophet, imagines not only that she is unconstrained by ordinary human concerns, but that she has the power to liberate others from them.

The six-year-old Marji's religion, however, is influenced by real-world pressures and problems. She recognizes her difference from the "others," the line of iconic prophetic figures in the upper right-hand panel, who are depicted with beards and, as far as the small drawing can show us, vague facial expressions as they stare in various directions, presumably contemplating the infinite. When Marji enters the line of prophets in the next panel, with her halo emphasizing her holiness and her short stature and cute smile emphasizing her youth, the earlier prophets shift their positions, standing in a tighter row, their expressions suddenly uniform as they scowl at her. The thought—unattributed by a thought balloon, and thus equally attributed to all of them—"A woman?" floats over their heads.

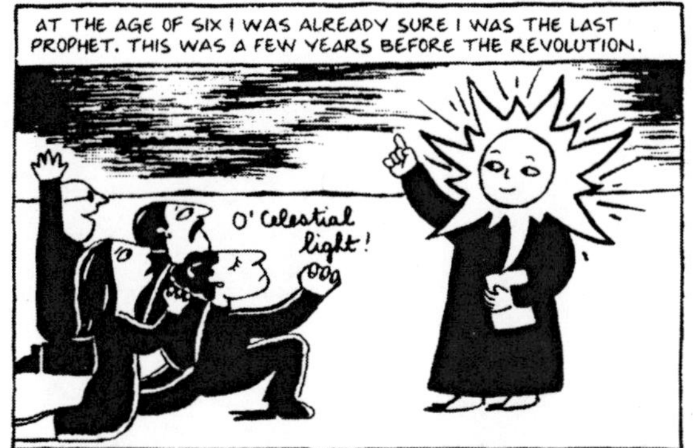

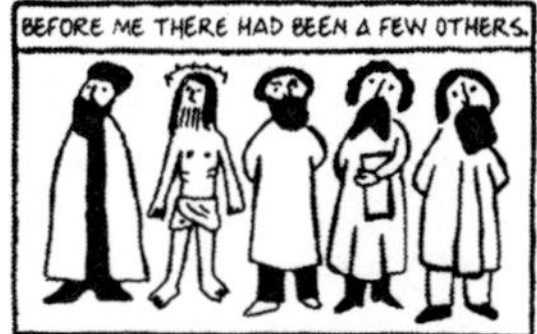

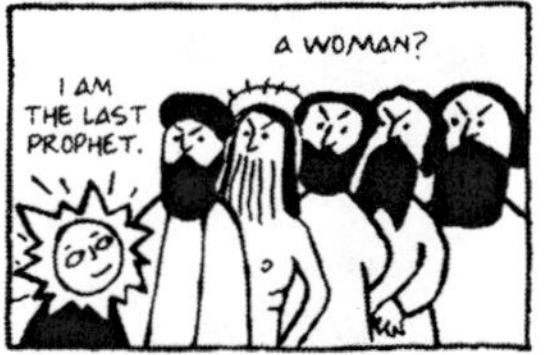

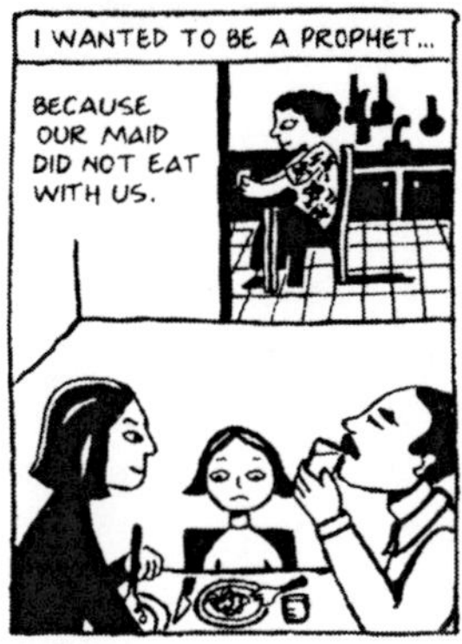

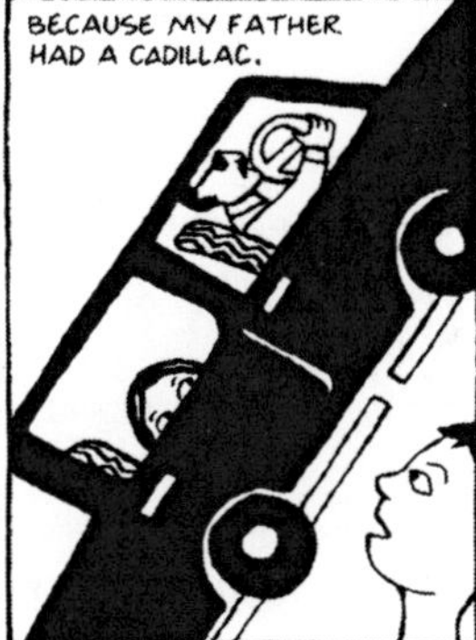

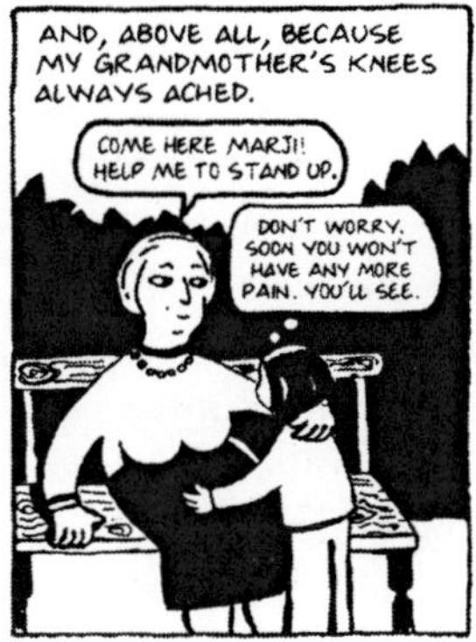

11.2. Marjane Satrapi. *Persepolis.* p. 6.

For all her certainty of her own prophetic status, even at the age of six Marji is aware her gender sets her apart from earlier prophets. Her desire to situate herself within the prophetic tradition, then, turns out to be highly un-traditional. Marji's very first religious stance is both conformist, in its desire to emulate traditional models, and transgressive, because she is choosing models that, as a woman, she is not supposed to emulate.

Marji's prophetic impulse, as it turns out, comes from the combination of her religious faith and her awareness of real-world injustice and suffering: she wants to be a prophet "because our maid did not eat with us. Because my father had a Cadillac." She is set apart both by her privilege and by her awareness of privilege. In the panel depicting the Satrapi family's class-segregated meals, Marji is the only person, including the maid, not smiling; in the panel depicting the Cadillac, her shamed eyes peek out the window of the car. This sequence cartoons class inequity, in Scott McCloud's sense of cartooning as "amplification through simplification," in

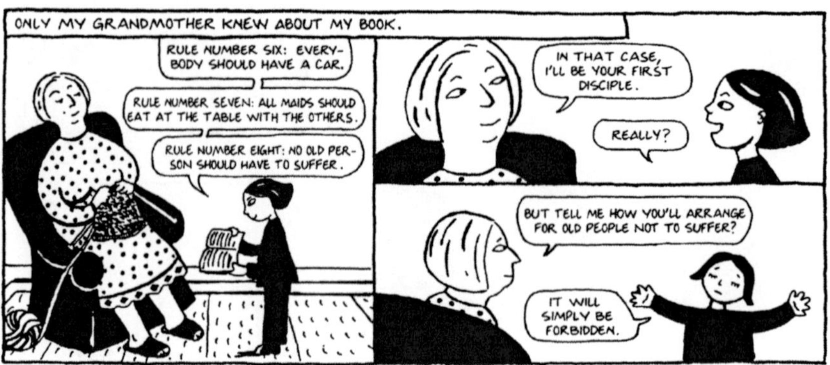

11.3. Marjane Satrapi. *Persepolis.* p. 7.

which simple drawings render complex truths more legible (30); the impossibly steep angle up which the car appears to be driving and the awed look on the face of the watching pedestrian suggest how extreme the difference is between the lives of rich and poor. Satrapi's treatment of Marji's early religious ambition does not distinguish between categories that will come into conflict later in the memoir: Marji's first beliefs are both supernatural and materialist, just as they are both traditionalist and transgressive.

The final panel of the sequence explaining Marji's desire to be a prophet is not about social injustice, however: instead, it comes from her sympathy with her grandmother's aging. Her grandmother is the only person who listens to Marji's plans (see fig. 11.3). The panels here are drawn without gutters, suggesting the intimacy of the conversation, and the smile on the grandmother's face echoes that on the face of Marji's imagined prophetic self. This conversation, however, emphasizes just how impossible Marji's desires are. While her awareness of class inequity suggests that Marji is paying attention to the real world, and the earlier prophets' objection "A woman?" suggests that she is aware of the struggle she is likely to face, Marji's plan that the suffering of the old "will simply be forbidden" does not seem very effective. The grandmother's physical suffering presents a challenge to any moral system from which it is viewed: neither the traditional religion Marji wants to participate in nor the economic struggle she intuits will directly solve the grandmother's problems. This first interaction between Marji and Grandma Satrapi establishes the grandmother's role throughout the memoir: Grandma Satrapi is Marji's greatest challenge, a loving and beloved individual who will not accept the pat answers provided by any of the ideological systems Marji explores.

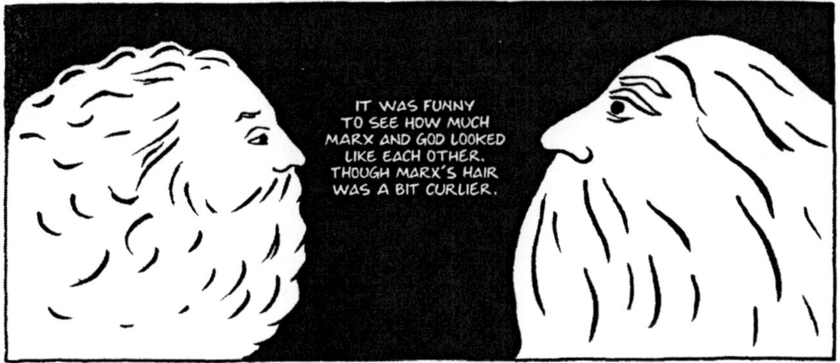

11.4. Marjane Satrapi. *Persepolis.* p. 13.

God and Marx

Marji's faith in God soon comes into overt conflict with her observations of social injustice. God's authority is challenged by another bearded authority figure who replaces the collection of prophets in Marji's personal pantheon: Karl Marx. Marji is aware of differences between the two. While God is comforting and affectionate, Marx is a troublemaker. In Marji's comic book *Dialectical Materialism*, he cackles and flings a stone at Descartes's head to emphasize the reality of the material world. Nonetheless, Marx and God are strikingly similar (see fig. 11.4). This juxtaposition of God and Marx suggests several apparently contradictory ideas. To begin with, it implies that young Marji's understanding of God and Marx is superficial, since the ideologies the two figures represent are at least in principle opposed to each other, and the two figureheads have very different natures. God is an incorporeal, immortal, omnipotent being, who stands at the head of a moral system based on the supernatural; Marx is a human being who stands at the head of a moral system based on the primacy of the material world. Moreover, the two ideologies are explicitly opposed: Marx rejects religion entirely. The fact that the figurehead of each ideology has a beard is a small similarity in light of such differences.

While God and Marx are profoundly different, however, their visual similarity in the panel also points toward deeper commonalities. By treating God as a concrete and knowable figure, who has a particular kind of beard or nose, Satrapi represents him as an individual analogous to the mortal, individual Marx. This representation, while perhaps reductive, is to some extent accurate: Western readers will be familiar with this portrait of a robed, bearded, paternal God regardless of their personal beliefs. Given this image's familiarity, it is fair to say that God and Marx look alike. The similarity revealed by the cartooned double portrait ironically undercuts Marx's claims to liberate us from the chains of religion; from Marji's point of view, Marx is very much a part of the same patriarchal system that the God-as-bearded-man image represents, in which a bearded male figure provides authoritative moral instruction to his followers. While neither figure precisely resembles the memoir's recurring image of the bearded fundamentalist man—Satrapi generally draws the fundamentalists' beards as black and carefully trimmed—her choice of the beard as the sign of authority suggests that God and Marx are implicitly linked to the Guardians of the Revolution. The bearded figure, for Satrapi, conflates religious with political power and has been hopelessly compromised by the Iranian regime.

Just as God and Marx are compromised by their similarities, so are the ideologies each figure represents. To Marji's eyes, there are essential structural parallels between theism and Marxism. Both systems demand faith from their followers; both require the subordination of individual needs and desires to the larger movement; both inspire Marji to emulate their leaders, whether prophets or Che Guevara; and both initially provide comfort in the face of adversity (God's embrace, Uncle Anoosh's certainty that "Everything will be alright" [*sic*, 65]) by reassuring their adherents that one individual's suffering is a necessary part of a larger movement. Most importantly, however, each system turns out to require the sacrifice of individual human lives for the greater good—a sacrifice Marji finds unacceptable.

The weakness of each moral system is exposed by the death of Marji's beloved Uncle Anoosh. Anoosh is one of Marx's main proponents in the memoir. He treats Marx as a kind of sacred figure, turning to his ideology for comfort as well as for guidance. At the news of the Shah's overthrow, he is confident, fist raised like the triumphant protesters: "The religious leaders don't know how to govern. They will return to their mosques. The proletariat shall rule! It's inevitable!!! That's just what Lenin explained in 'The State and the Revolution'" (62). The multiple exclamation points indicate his enthusiasm and certainty; at the same time, his Marxist jargon and his claim that "it's inevitable!!!" suggest, to readers who know the revolution's outcome, his naïveté.

Anoosh's confidence is somewhat shaken after the murder of his friend Mohsen. He reacts to the news of Mohsen's death optimistically, saying

"Everything will be alright!" (65). His fist is lowered, however, his eyes downcast, and his eyebrows tilt to show distress. Nonetheless, he retains some of his hope: he still faces directly out of the frame, and retains one of his exclamation points. The last panel in this sequence, however, suggests that while Anoosh repeats "Everything will be alright . . ." one more time (66), he does not believe it: in the final panel, after more bad news, his head is lowered, his eyes hardly visible, and the confident exclamation point is replaced with an ellipsis.

If Anoosh's faith is shaken by the regime's violence, Marji's is ultimately destroyed when God and Marx fail equally at saving Anoosh from execution. His death is a double blow to Marji, depriving her of both of her competing, comforting ideological systems at once. As she grieves for Anoosh—whose death is announced by an anti-Communist newspaper headline: "Russian Spy Executed"—God comes to visit her, and she yells at him: "I never want to see you again! Get out!" (70). God obeys, leaving her, as a full-page panel shows us, adrift in a dark universe at the start of the Iran-Iraq War. Only seventy pages into a book more than three hundred pages long, the narrative abandons both of its proposed moral centers.

The Fundamentalist Woman

After Marji's loss of faith and the success of the Islamic Revolution, the benevolent robed figure of God is replaced by the black silhouette of the veiled fundamentalist woman. Like God, the fundamentalist robed figure also embraces people, but her embrace is tragic and confining rather than comforting, enfolding not the hopeful young Marji but the figure of a dead martyr (see fig. 11.5). The comforting image of God is replaced by an image that is disturbing on several levels. The Fundamentalist Woman lacks autonomy, instead allowing her shape and appearance to be determined by the mullahs. Her association with martyrdom makes her complicit with violence, and her image is used to promote participation in the war. At the same time, this figure becomes a focal point of duplicity: the image is taken from Marji's entrance examination for art school, in which Marji models her drawing not just on the fundamentalist visual rhetoric surrounding her on walls and posters, but on Michaelangelo's *Pietà*.[3] Unlike the similarly shaped figure of God, then, the Fundamentalist Woman's robes hide something: not only her body, but also her motives and her origins. Satrapi's *pietà* is a peculiar form of rebellion: it is hard to say whether,

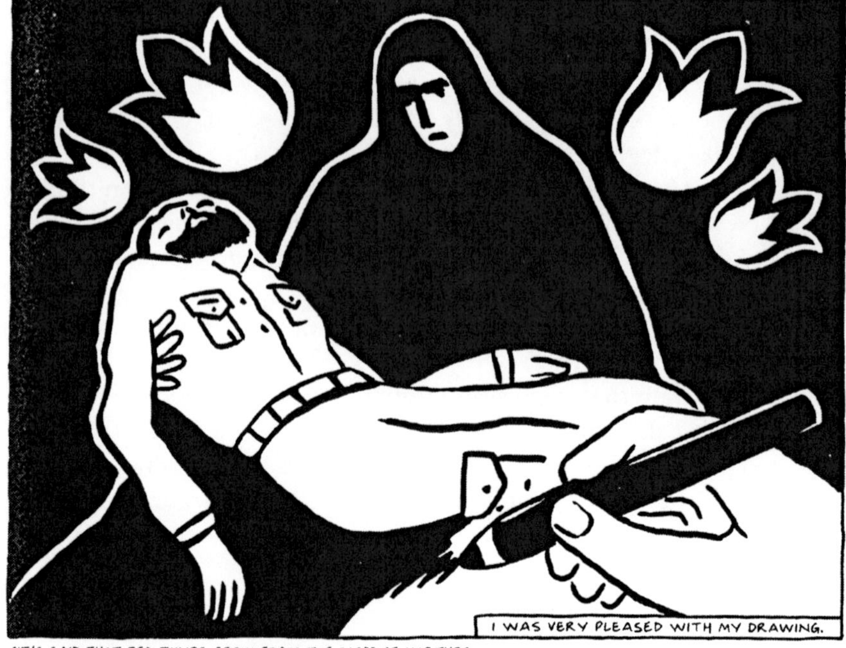

11.5. Marjane Satrapi. *Persepolis* 2. p. 127.

by veiling her Western source under a chador, she is more subversive of or complicit with the regime.

In art school, too, the robed figure hides something Marji values. The model in life drawing class is entirely veiled, her downcast eyes echoing those of the earlier martyr/*pietà*, no other part of her body visible (see fig. 11.6). The veiled artists retain their individuality: Marji is identifiable by her mole, her friend Niyoosha by her light eyes and hair. The model, however, has no distinguishing characteristics: her eyes are closed, her hair fully covered, her body entirely shrouded. The pyramidal form that was associated with God's comforting embrace at the beginning of the memoir is entirely replaced with the identity-effacing veil. Marji's God has been rendered doubly problematic by the regime's visual rhetoric: he has the beard of the fundamentalist man and the robes of the fundamentalist woman. The regime's gendering of God's visual attributes—beards

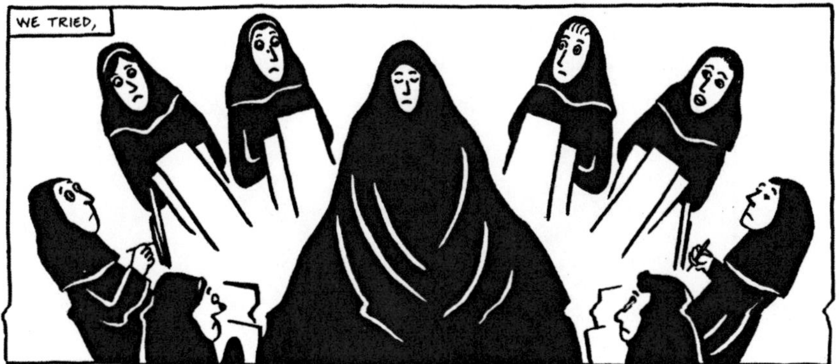

11.6. Marjane Satrapi. *Persepolis 2.* p. 145.

are male, robes female—suggest how limited and obsessive the Guardians' notions of gender are. Satrapi, thoroughly disillusioned with theism, makes no attempt to reclaim this iconography once it has been appropriated by the fundamentalists.

Scripted Rebellions

The Fundamentalist Woman has a counterpart: the Modern Woman. While one figure supports the regime and the other opposes it, both women's appearances are equally determined by the rules of the Revolution (see fig. 11.7). The Iranian regime allows exactly two forms of self-representation: the obedient and the rebellious, each of which is defined in very narrow terms. The result is not simply that women's appearances are dictated for them. Their thoughts are also circumscribed by the regime's rules: "The regime had understood that one person leaving her house while asking herself: 'Are my trousers long enough? Is my veil in place? Can my makeup be seen? Are they going to whip me?' no longer asks herself: 'Where is my freedom of thought? Where is my freedom of speech? My life, is it livable? What's going on in the political prisons?" (*P2*, 148). Resistance to authority, in this account, is just as scripted as obedience.

Marji's time in Vienna does not present her with useful alternatives to the regime's narratives. The robed, pyramidal authority figure follows her in the form of the nuns—more veiled religious women—and even her rejection of patriarchal authority figures begins by drawing on yet another bearded man: the anarchist philosopher Bakunin, recommended to her

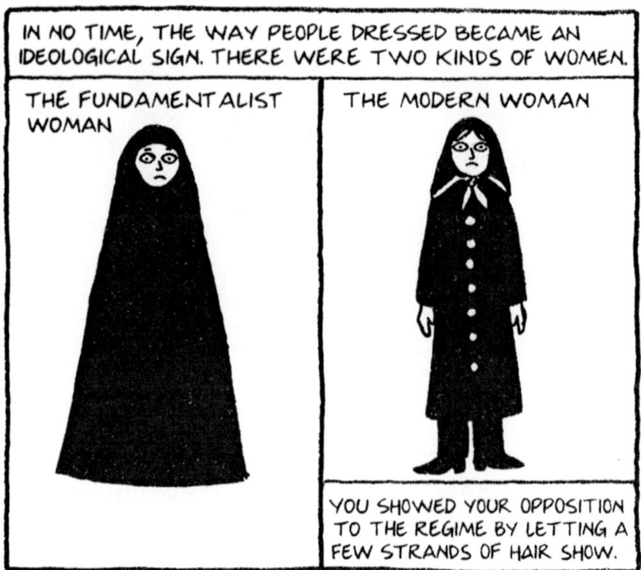

11.7. Marjane Satrapi. *Persepolis.* p. 75.

by her punk friend Momo. The rebellion against authority Momo offers her is entirely unsatisfactory: his fascination with Marji because she has "known war" (*P2*, 12) reveals him as both callous and ignorant, and the anarchist party Marji attends seems more like a preschool outing than a serious alternative to God, Marx, or the regime's moral systems. Satrapi's Viennese anarchists invent nothing new; they merely react against the authorities they encounter, without constructing any viable alternatives. More disturbingly, as Marji herself is slowly removed from her familiar economy of obedience and rebellion in Vienna, she lacks a clear moral authority to either follow or resist and is cast adrift emotionally and physically, dealing in drugs and eventually becoming homeless.

Persepolis initially suggests that Marji is stuck choosing between patriarchal systems: she can be either a fundamentalist or a Marxist, either follow tradition or have her rebellions dictated by it. In Iran, she has two choices: she can be the "fundamentalist woman" or the "modern woman," each of whom must wear a uniform. If Satrapi is really to escape from the Iranian regime psychologically as well as physically, she must construct an alternative system of authority, one which allows her not simply to rebel, but to move in an entirely different direction—the moral equivalent of her emigration to France.

Individuals, Families, and Grounded Autonomy

While God and Marx are both discredited, the memoir retains a moral center: Satrapi's grandmother, who embraces Marji in a different way than the patriarchal figure of God or the patriarchy-shrouded figure of the fundamentalist woman. While the pain in the grandmother's knees helps discredit Marji's initial prophetic idealism, her words and her body also provide Satrapi with a link to an alternative moral system. The grandmother, in both *Persepolis* and Satrapi's short book *Embroideries*, rejects Manichean binaries, resisting easy categorization as traditional or modern, Eastern or Western; aside from the moment of the embrace, the grandmother resembles no other character in the memoir, retaining her individuality and thus her moral integrity. For Satrapi, the grandmother provides a personal, feminine alternative to the authoritarian, masculine, "schizophrenic" options presented both by the regime and by the West (*P2*, 151). Grandma Satrapi provides these narratives directly through storytelling: just as her detailed accounts of her own life provide a model for Satrapi's memoir, her oral history provides a counter-narrative to the official historical narratives of the regime.

In *Embroideries*, the grandmother is bawdy, fond of innuendo, and unrepentant about her sexuality and her several divorces. She playfully suggests that her granddaughter give her the present of "a full embroidery," a surgical reconstruction of the hymen to create the illusion of virginity (88). Grandma Satrapi parodies Iranian sexual mores, emphasizing the "embroidered"—decorative, insubstantial, superficial—understanding of female virtue that traditional Iranian sexual codes promote. Her request at once embraces and mocks the equation of virginity with sexual desirability and morality; by pretending to want to deny her sexual history, she reminds us both of her past fertility and of her continuing sexuality. At the same time, she reconfigures six-year-old Marji's impossible ban on the suffering of the old into a playful claim that her body can return to youth through a simple (and biologically trivial) surgical procedure. The version of Grandma Satrapi in *Embroideries* is presented through the eyes of an adult granddaughter, one capable of recognizing the complexity of the older woman's experiences—and of appreciating her charisma. The benign, smiling grandmother who promises to be six-year-old Marji's "first disciple" turns out to be the leader of a large group of women, who turn to her not just for advice but for the stories—the gossip—which provide the test cases and reference points of their own moral codes.

If *Embroideries* makes Grandma Satrapi the spokesperson for an Iranian approach to liberated sexuality, *Persepolis* makes her the embodiment of a familial, rather than patriarchal, approach to morality. This familial morality is tied to both a heritage of political power and a history of anti-authoritarian activism. Grandma Satrapi's husband, Marji's grandfather, was a son of the last emperor of Persia. He and some of his sons spent years in prison under the Shah for their Communist ideals. The fact that Marjane Satrapi shares her grandmother's surname makes the younger woman's place in this politically active lineage affiliative as well as a filiative: Grandma Satrapi is Marji's maternal grandmother, so their shared surname must be the result of a conscious decision (whether Marjane Satrapi's or her parents' we are never told).

Grandma Satrapi sees the basis of good behavior in individual rather than group identity. According to her, each individual is responsible only to herself. At the same time, this responsibility is understood within the context of family affection and a shared dedication to individual self-determination, in which an individual person's identity and value come both from her own choices and from her allegiance to the people who love her.

The grandmother articulates her moral code when she visits Marji the night before Marji's departure for Vienna (see fig. 11.8). Like God, Marji's grandmother embraces her. Unlike God, however, the grandmother does not hold her in the pyramidal *pietà* shape. Instead, grandmother and granddaughter lie together in bed, in a less stratified embrace. This image has far fewer implications of sacrifice than the vertical cradling of the *pietà*; instead, it is a moment of comfort and intimacy. The grandmother's advice to Marji, "always keep your dignity and be true to yourself," is both an assertion of individualism—"*your* dignity," "true to *your*self"—and a reminder of the individual's connection to her family: this advice on independence is valuable because it comes from someone the child loves, who is holding her in her own bed. Like Marji after her rejection of God, the figures in this panel are surrounded by darkness. But on the eve of her departure for Vienna, Marji is no longer alone.

The grandmother is not the first person to give Marji advice on how to live. Anoosh, telling Marji about his own life and that of his brothers, instructs her to remember her history: "Our family memory must not be lost. Even if it's not easy for you, even if you don't understand it all . . ." and Marji replies, "Don't worry, I'll never forget" (*P1*, 60). But while Anoosh emphasizes Marji's relationality—her duty is retaining "our family

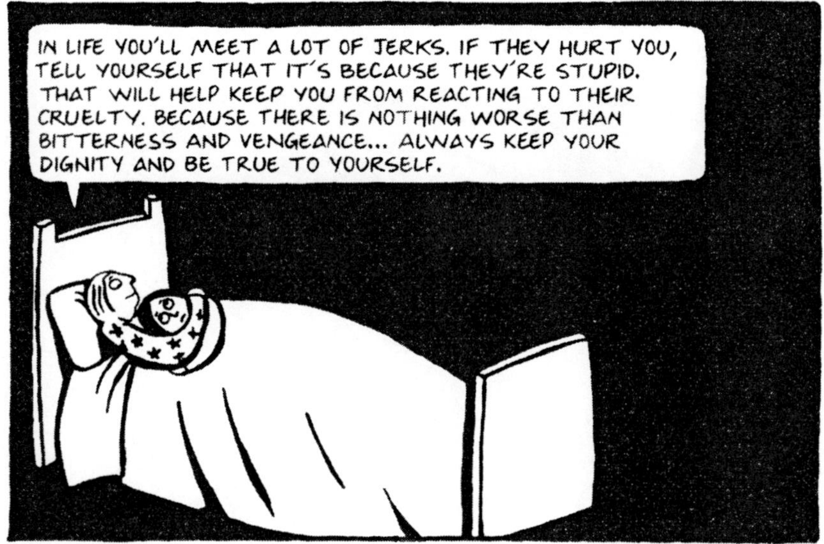

11.8. Marjane Satrapi. *Persepolis*. p. 150.

memory"—the grandmother leaves relations implicit: it is enough that this advice comes during an embrace in Marji's bedroom. The moment of deepest familial intimacy is also the moment in which the grandmother most clearly articulates the necessity for individual autonomy.

The grandmother's emphasis on self-sufficiency is presented not as an end in itself, but as an alternative to "reacting." "In life you'll meet a lot of jerks," she says. "If they hurt you, tell yourself that it's because they're stupid. That will help keep you from reacting to their cruelty. Because there is nothing worse than bitterness and vengeance." The grandmother's advice, in other words, is a clear alternative to Momo's anarchist rejection of authority. To react to cruelty or the abuse of power is still to participate in the abusive system. Self-sufficiency, as articulated by Grandma Satrapi, removes the individual from the oppressive system entirely.

While the regime alienates Marji from her childhood religion, this scene also helps reclaim the ethical underpinnings of her first moral beliefs. The grandmother's embrace of Marji in bed is visually linked to Marji's earliest prophetic impulses. Not only is the grandmother the same old woman whose knees Marji was concerned about, but the woman and the girl lying in bed together echo an embrace that happens because of Marji's childhood concern for the family maid. Little Marji helps the maid carry on a correspondence with the boy next door; eventually, Marji's father

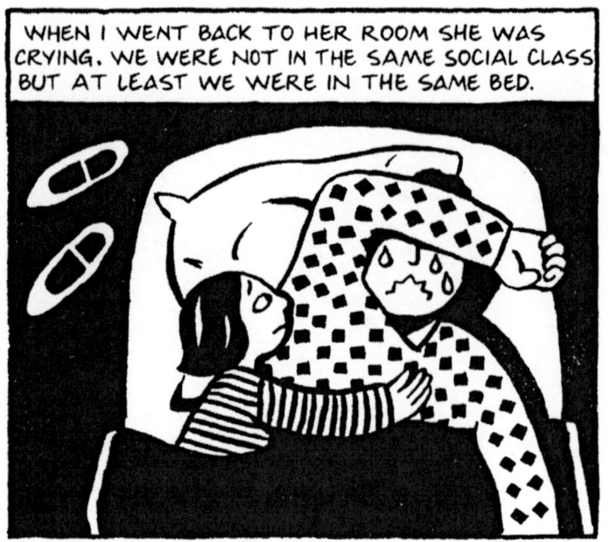

11.9. Marjane Satrapi. *Persepolis.* p. 37.

discovers and puts a stop to it, explaining, "in this country you must stay within your own social class" (37). Marji is appalled by this injustice and by her Marxist father's inconsistency: "Dad," she asks, "are you for or against social classes?" We do not see his response; instead, the next panel shows Marji embracing the maid (see fig. 11.9). Here Marji is the one doing the comforting, but the moment prefigures the scene with the grandmother: both panels contain Marji and an older woman side by side, in bed, with Marji's head at breast level. In both cases, too, the question under consideration is whether an individual—and particularly a woman—can act independently from social constraints, being true to herself and her own desires rather than being constrained to either follow or rebel against repressive social norms. Unlike the unfortunate maid, Marji, the child of well-to-do free-thinkers, is in a position to forge her own path.

Responsibility

The grandmother's authority—and the nature of the responsibility she sees in individualism—are most clearly established after Marji's greatest moral failure. In the second volume of the memoir, after her return from Vienna, Marji goes out wearing heavy makeup and encounters a group of Guardians of the Revolution. Frightened that her makeup will get her arrested, she preempts the Guardians by claiming that a nearby man has made an obscene remark to her. The Guardians arrest him; we last see him begging Marji to tell them that he has done nothing wrong, but the heavily made up Marji only scowls at him.

In this incident, Marji believes that she has no choice but to react to the "jerks." By going out in public wearing more makeup than usual—which she does to please her boyfriend, who habitually criticizes her for being "not made-up enough" (131)—she reacts against the Guardians; when she encounters them, she panics, and reacts in the other direction, setting them against a hapless bystander as a way of directing their violence away from her. The incident demonstrates how thoroughly the rebellion of the Iranian "modern woman" is dictated by and part of the system of the regime: the makeup she wears does not reflect her own tastes, but her boyfriend's desires and the Guardians' regulations. By following the script of rebellion, Marji abandons her own choices—and thus makes herself vulnerable to other scripted behaviors, which she follows in order to escape punishment. She is never so complicit with the Guardians as when she pushes too hard against them.

After escaping, she meets her boyfriend, who thinks the whole incident is hilarious. When she comes home, however, she tells her grandmother, who is disgusted (see fig. 11.10). Like God and Marx, Marji and her grandmother face each other in profile. Unlike the two bearded men, or the book's many uniformly veiled women, however, these two faces cannot possibly be mistaken for each other. Marji is still in her heavy makeup, with bold lips and a plucked, arched eyebrow; her grandmother, on the other hand, has white hair, wrinkles, a hooked nose, and a sagging chin. The most striking difference is in their facial expressions: Marji is shocked at her grandmother's reaction, her eye round with surprise, whereas the grandmother is furious. The power of the grandmother's reaction is emphasized by her placement in the panel; while the two women are nose to nose, the grandmother's head is drawn slightly larger and slightly higher than Marji's, giving her a dominant position in the otherwise symmetrically composed panel.

Just as when the prophets ask "a woman?" a word balloon is missing in this panel. While we know the grandmother is speaking, the lack of a balloon suggests that her words fill the air, coming not only from the grandmother's lips but from a larger moral judgment, one which may be assigned to Marji's conscience as well as to her grandmother. The

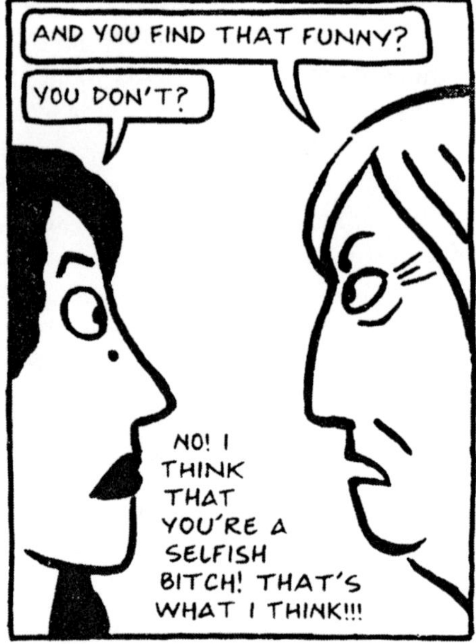

11.10. Marjane Satrapi. *Persepolis 2*. p. 137.

grandmother's use of the word "bitch" emphasizes the gendered nature of Marji's crime: her accusation against the stranger makes her complicit with the regime not only in her dishonesty and ruthlessness but in her use of the regime's sexual mores to protect herself.

The grandmother invokes Marji's male relatives, still without a word balloon surrounding the words: "Have you forgotten who your grandfather was? He spent a third of his life in prison for having defended some innocents. And your uncle Anoosh? Have you forgotten him too???! He gave his life for his ideas! What have I taught you? Hunh??? "Integrity"!!! Does this word mean anything to you?" (137). Marji's individual actions are her own responsibility, but they are to be judged in the context of her family's history. She is not only obliged to bear witness, as Anoosh implies; instead, the memory of her family should teach her to pattern her own actions not on a script but on "integrity." The face-off panel's composition is repeated in the panel immediately below it, as Marji looks ruefully at her own image in the mirror; Marji must learn to hold herself to this standard, not depend on her grandmother to correct her.

The grandmother's speech emphasizes the need to be loyal not to a distant figurehead (Marx, God) but to known individuals (the grandfather,

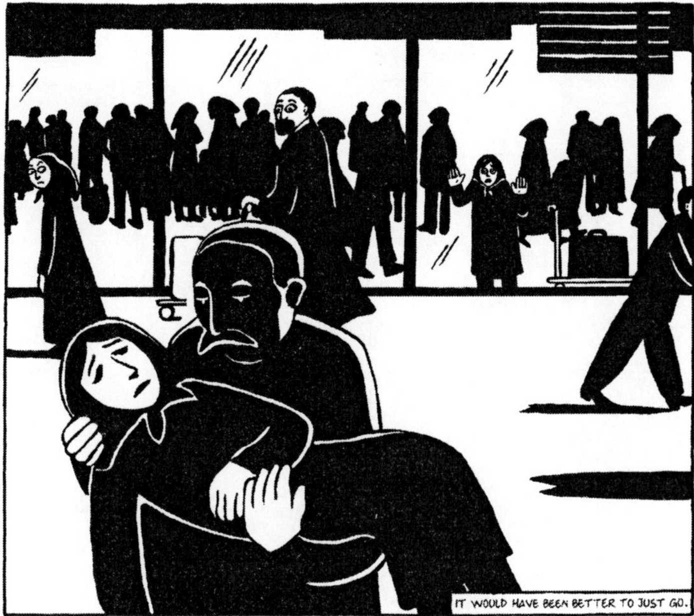

11.11. Marjane Satrapi. *Persepolis*. p. 153.

Anoosh) and to internal truths ("his ideas"). In this formulation, Anoosh's death does not come from following Marx as one would follow a prophet, but from remaining true to himself.

The Price of Freedom

Satrapi stages her own liberation—and the way that liberation depends on her family history—in the two final panels of the two volumes of *Persepolis*. The ending of the first volume is distressing (see fig. 11.11). In the foreground, Marji's mother has fainted and is supported by her father in another echo of the *pietà* pose; a horrified Marji, ignored and alone, looks on from behind a pane of glass. The panel emphasizes the mother's suffering—her martyrdom by the regime, her sacrifice for Marji—but it does so without suggesting that this suffering is redemptive or that the sacrifice is worthwhile; instead, the volume closes on the family's pain and shock.

The final panel of the second volume repeats the scene, but with important variations (see fig. 11.12). Whereas in the first airport panel, all the sightlines converge on Marji's mother's white face, thrown into relief by

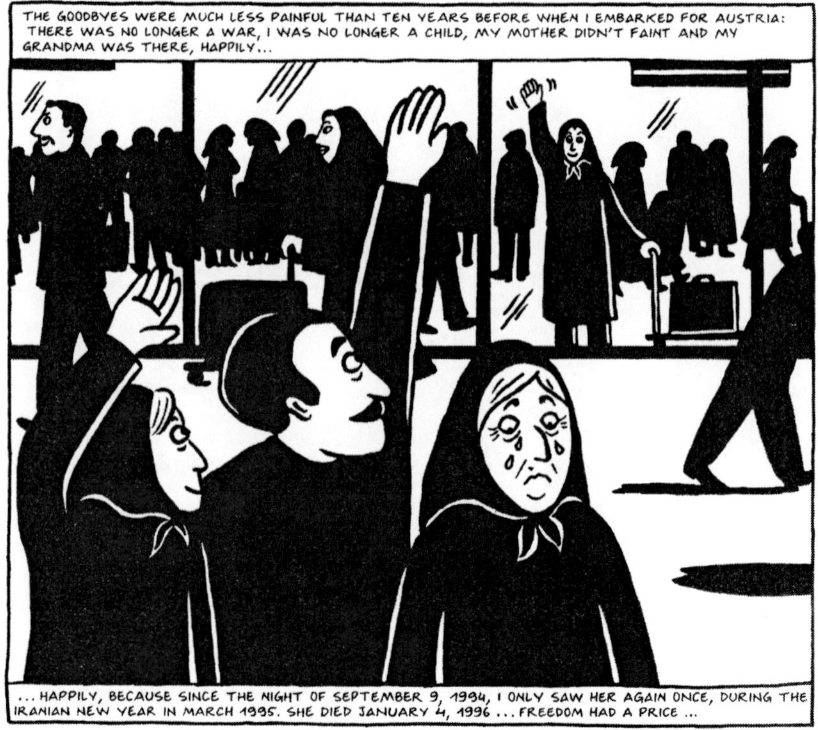

11.12. Marjane Satrapi. *Persepolis 2.* p. 187.

the black body and face of the father, in the second panel, there is no single focal point in the image. Marji, no longer a child, looks happy and composed, and her parents—though sad to see her go, as the lines under their eyes suggest—are able to keep smiling. The one sad face is the grandmother's: she looks away from Marji, toward us, crying. The final caption of the memoir emphasizes the grandmother's exceptionality in the panel: "since the night of September 9, 1994, I only saw her again once, during the Iranian New Year in March 1995. She died January 4, 1996 . . . Freedom had a price . . ."

This ending, while sad, is oddly equivocal. The farewell to the grandmother here is both final and not. On the one hand, Grandma Satrapi is looking away from Marji, crying, and we learn that she will die soon; but we also learn Marji will see her one more time. The separation at the airport is momentous, and Satrapi treats it as symbolic of her final parting from Iran, but the narrative voice also diminishes the finality of the occasion by admitting there will be one more meeting. Even in Satrapi's own memoir, the grandmother resists orderly narratives.

The final panel gives us a rare image of the grandmother veiled. In this panel, she is both visibly herself and briefly acceding to the rules; the result is an acknowledgement that her moral code does not exempt her from at least appearing to obey social strictures. In this panel, the whole family has succeeded in negotiating with the regime, gaining Marji's freedom and absolving her of guilt at leaving her loved ones. At the same time, the grandmother's impending death marks the difference between her localized moral system and the all-encompassing systems of God and Marx. But despite appearances, the price of freedom is not the total loss of the grandmother. Marji *does* see her again, as she acknowledges, and after Grandma Satrapi's death, Marji consciously embraces the tradition her grandmother stood for. Satrapi does not pretend that staying true to her grandmother's spirit negates the loss of the real person. But if the price of freedom is mortality, it is not much different from the price of living.

Satrapi's refusal to call herself a feminist reflects her understanding of this balance between public and private identity. Nancy Miller shows how *Persepolis* places itself and its narrator in a feminist lineage via her mother's activism and reading of Simone de Beauvoir, and the memoir's proposition of female authority as a corrective and alternative to hegemonic national identity is clearly linked to feminist discourse (19). But a central aspect of that alternative, for Satrapi, is its separation from named ideologies and movements, motivated by the tendency of such movements to eclipse individuals' autonomy and complexity.[4] Feminists may recognize their values in Satrapi's work, but however convincing readers may find their claims, Satrapi's rejection of the label is consistent with her memoir's rejection of ideological affiliations.

Critics who read the memoir as "universal" may downplay Satrapi's commitment to bearing witness to the suffering of the Iran-Iraq war, the Iranian intellectuals' resistance to the regime, and her own family's history of principled action. But her memoir makes the case for an individualism that is both rooted in family relationships and released from scripted ideologies—and thus, if not "universal" in its origins, at least detachable from the context in which she approaches it. Six-year-old Marji dreamed of becoming a prophet and of teaching her disciples a moral code; the adult Satrapi, instead, shows how individuals must carry their own moral authority within themselves.

Notes

1. Theresa M. Tensuan argues that the way critics discuss Satrapi's use of Persian miniatures is a useful metonym for how Satrapi herself is treated as emblematic of her culture (956). Hillary Chute notes that Persian miniatures particularly influence the "frequent scenes in which public skirmishes appear as stylized and even symmetrical formations of bodies" (98). The repeated use of miniature style in depicting demonstrations regardless of the ideology of the demonstrators suggests that identifications with national history and ideologies make people more uniform—as opposed, for example, to the chaos in the opening playground scene where Marji's schoolmates play with their veils. Pauline Uchmanowicz also discusses the appearances of miniatures in the memoir, arguing that miniature style is part of the "cultural parameters associated with allegiance to Islam," although it is noteworthy that some of the groups depicted in that style are "modern" anti-fundamentalists (371).

2. Unlike reviewers who treat the memoir as a "universal" story, Kimberly Wedeven Segall emphasizes that much of its subject is Iranians' trauma during the war: "The *Persepolis* books document collective melancholy and thus formulate an intimate witnessing to intergenerational loss, in contrast to media versions of Middle East violence" (38).

3. Gillian Whitlock comments on Satrapi's use of Michelangelo (975–76). Nancy K. Miller also traces the recurring *pietà* image through *Persepolis*.

4. Lopamudra Basu discusses how the ambivalent relationship between Western feminism and "third world women" plays out in *Persepolis* (8–9).

Works Cited

Basu, Lopamudra. "Crossing Cultures/Crossing Genres: The Re- invention of the Graphic Memoir in *Persepolis and Persepolis 2*." *Nebula* 4.3 (2007): 1–19. Web. 18 May 2012.

Chute, Hillary. "The Texture of Retracing in Marjane Satrapi's *Persepolis*." *Women's Studies Quarterly* 36: 1–2 (2008): 92–110. Web. 3 Oct. 2010.

Gusdorf, Georges. "Conditions and Limits of Autobiography." Trans. James Olney. *Autobiography: Essays Theoretical and Critical*. Ed. James Olney. Princeton: Princeton UP, 1980. 28–48. Print.

McCloud, Scott. *Understanding Comics: The Invisible Art*. New York: HarperPerennial, 1994. Print.

Miller, Nancy K. "Out of the Family: Generations of Women in Marjane Satrapi's *Persepolis*." *Life Writing* 4 (2007): 13–29. Print.

Naghibi, Nima, and Andrew O'Malley. "Estranging the Familiar: "East" and "West" in Satrapi's *Persepolis*." *English Studies in Canada* 31: 2–3 (2005): 223–47. Web. 3 Oct. 2010.

Satrapi, Marjane. *Embroideries*. Trans. Anjali Singh. New York: Pantheon, 2005. Print.

———. *Persepolis: The Story of a Childhood*. Trans. Mattias Ripa and Blake Ferris. New York: Pantheon, 2003. Print.

———. *Persepolis 2: The Story of a Return*. Trans. Anjali Singh. New York: Pantheon, 2004. Print.

Segall, Kimberly Wedeven. "Melancholy Ties: Intergenerational Loss and Exile in *Persepolis*." *Comparative Studies of South Asia, Africa and the Middle East* 28 (2008): 38–49. Web. 3 Oct. 2010.

Tensuan, Theresa M. "Comic Visions and Revisions in the Work of Lynda Barry and Marjane Satrapi." *Modern Fiction Studies* 52 (2006): 947–64. Web. 3 Oct. 2010.

Uchmanowicz, Pauline. "Graphic Novel Decoded: Towards a Poetics of Comics." *International Journal of Comic Art* 11:1 (2009): 363–85. Print.

Whitlock, Gillian. "Autographics: The Seeing "I" of the Comics." *Modern Fiction Studies* 52 (2006): 965–79. Web. 3 Oct. 2010.

Worth, Jennifer. "Unveiling: *Persepolis* as Embodied Performance." *Theatre Research International* 32 (2007): 143–60. Web. 3 Oct. 2010.

Showing the Voice of the Body

Brian Fies's *Mom's Cancer*, the Graphic Illness Memoir,
and the Narrative of Hope

—Sharon O'Brien

> *Why do we read? We read to know that we are not alone.*
> —C. S. LEWIS

The cover illustration of Brian Fies's graphic memoir *Mom's Cancer* shows a person with a bald head.[1] Only a few stray lines suggest wisps of hair. The person, who is wearing pink and white striped pajamas, is leaning forward, more out of weariness than anticipation: she, or he, cannot hold the body up straight. There is a graying bandage attached to the neck with two crossed pieces of tape. The cheeks are sunken, the mouth drooping. The person is alone, isolated. The frame of a window marks a vertical down the left side of the frame, and outside we see an expanse of night sky. But the person is not looking at the larger view we can see: she or he is looking straight ahead, unaware or uncaring that the universe expands outward outside the window. We are not even sure that the person is seeing anything. She or he inhabits a space of numbness and depression. I use the pronouns "he or she" here because without the title words "Mom's Cancer," in large san serif font in the lower right, we would not know if this person was male or female. Only the title tells us she is a woman, and, we assume, the mother of the author. The image here tells a story that the words cannot: that this illness, this cancer, this chemotherapy, has turned a woman into a genderless sufferer and into someone who can no longer "mother" her children.

The cover belies the optimistic American narrative that illness will lead to recovery, cancer to cure. Cancer and its brutal treatment have

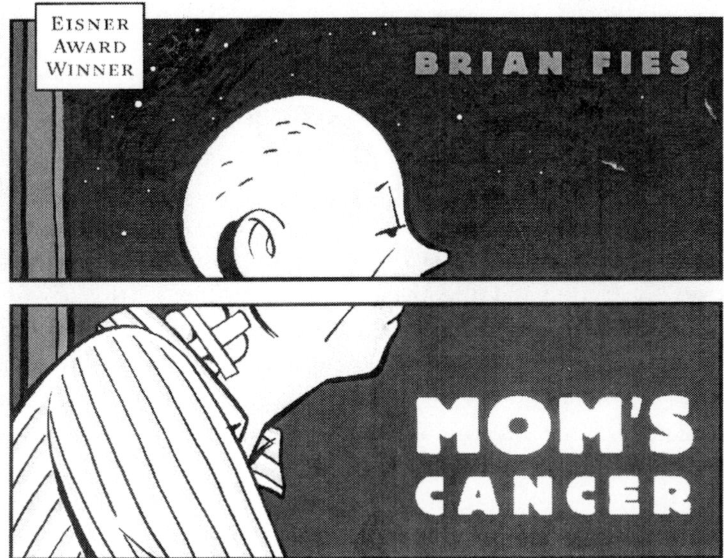

12.1. Brian Fies. *Mom's Cancer*. Cover Art.

interrupted the life of this woman and of her family; Fies conveys the "before and after" disruption of time through the visual representation of space. A line cuts through the middle of the frame, severing the mother's body, passing over her head, creating the illusion that she is behind bars, incarcerated by her illness. Upon closer inspection, we see that the night sky with its specks of stars figures only in the top half of the illustration. Below the line the dark night sky gradually shifts to blue, and the stars disappear. Mom has entered what Sontag termed the "kingdom of the ill," having left the "kingdom of the well," perhaps not to return. The darkening sky recalls Sontag's description of illness as the "night-side of life," a night that does not, inevitably, lead into day.[2]

No one wants to hear the words "Mom" and "cancer" in the same sentence. As Charles Kochman writes in his "Introduction" to the memoir, "Mom. Cancer. How could the juxtaposition of those words *not* make us stop and take notice?" No one's mom should ever get cancer, ever cause us to put those two words together. Mom is supposed to take care of you and to live forever. Cancer changes these illusions; the mother's cancer transforms the midlife son or daughter back into a child who must perform an adult's role—taking Mom to the hospital, reassuring Mom, caring for Mom physically and emotionally. At the same time, the adult child may not want to hear her story; her fear and pain are too frightening. And so she may be silenced. What would Mom say if she could speak, and if her children could hear? The use of the word "Mom" in the title suggests that Fies both saw and heard his mother's story. If he had chosen "Mother's Cancer" as his title we would have felt distanced; not many of us call our moms "mother." So when we read the title, that simple, scary phrase and see that the bald person behind bars is *Mom*, we *do* stop and take notice.

The threads of the story Fies will tell in *Mom's Cancer* are woven into this cover illustration and title: the impact of a mother's struggle with cancer on her children; the ways in which cancer creates a dark world that replaces the brighter world we once knew; how American platitudes about the "positive" gifts of illness are belied by experience; how the language of medicine needs to be interrupted in order to tell the ill person's story; how a story of hope can be marked by loss and a story of loss marked by hope.

What this cover illustration also represents is the unique ability of a graphic memoir to convey the experience of illness.[3] As Arthur Frank observes in his groundbreaking theoretical work on illness narratives, *The Wounded Storyteller*, illness challenges the representational power of words because pain and fear can never be fully translated into language. "Bodies need voices," he writes, but how can they speak, and who will hear them?[4] Through his skill as a graphic artist who can interweave illustration with language, Fies can give a voice to the inarticulate but powerful speech of his mother's body and soul. In this essay, I want to tease out these threads and so to explore not just the artistic power of *Mom's Cancer* but also the particular gift of graphic memoir to show and tell the voice of the ill body.

Graphic Memoir

Before we explore Fies's narrative, we need to be clear about the two genres to which it belongs. Most obviously, it is a graphic narrative, or what most critics and readers would call a "graphic novel." Many critics use the latter term loosely, including memoirs. (Charles Kochman terms *Mom's Cancer* a "graphic novel" in his introduction.) I am not going to use this term, however, preferring "graphic memoir" instead since *Mom's Cancer* also belongs to the genre of memoir. Even though fiction and memoir have much in common, the genres are not the same; scholars make distinctions between "novel" and "memoir" for non-graphic narratives, and the same distinctions, in my view, should apply to graphic ones.

How are novel and memoir similar? These genres share many literary techniques and effects. Both tell stories, and memoir draws on the methods of fiction—the creation of scenes, the use of dialogue, the preference for "showing" more than "telling," the creation of character. The memoirist must also face the novelist's decision about structure: will he or she move around in time, or tell the story chronologically?

Like the novelist, the memoirist must make a choice about point of view. Who is telling the story? Whose stories will be represented by the narrator, whose will be passed over or silenced? Since all memoirs involve both self and other, both autobiography and biography, a memoir writer may decide to tell a portion of the story from another's point of view. This leap into another consciousness might derive solely from the writer's imagination and memory, or it might be also based on interviews, documents, archives, or photographs. In *Mom's Cancer* Fies often represents the world he imagines his mother experiencing, as in the series of panels showing her as a tightrope walker negotiating cancer treatment's frightening "balancing act," receiving enough chemotherapy to kill the "bad" cells but not too much to irreparably damage the "good" ones (60–61).

Then what *does* distinguish memoir from fiction? As the writer Judith Barrington observes in *Writing the Memoir*, we expect the memoirist— who will need to invent dialogue, who may collapse two scenes from "real" life into one for the sake of the reader—to ground the story in lived experience and to tell what she terms "emotional truth."[5] The memoirist may invent, as in creating dialogue, but she does not lie or intentionally fabricate: she tells a "true story" because of the "obligation" she feels toward the reader to be honest:

> I sometimes reorder events to make the narrative work. I approximate dialogue that I can't recall word for word. I frequently leave out whatever makes the story too complicated for a stranger to grasp. At the same time, while taking these liberties, I feel honor bound to capture the essence of the interaction in the events as I order them and in the dialogue as I recreate it. Memoir is, after all, supposed to be a true story (one that represents as closely as possible the experience); you have an obligation to the reader to make it that. (Barrington, 65)

In his "Preface," Fies acknowledges this doubleness of memoir: that it is a story, but a true story derived from his own experience. "Members of my family remember some of these events very differently," he writes. Looking back at Mom's experience with cancer and even more with its treatment and resulting torment—radiation, chemotherapy, weakness, nausea, fatigue—his two sisters and Mom herself would see a different story and create a different memoir. Even though he knows his memory is not objective, however, as a memoir writer Fies has followed Barrington's directive to tell emotional truth and create what he calls an "honest, earnest" story.

By contrast, we do not expect the first-person narrator in a novel to share the same race, sex, sexuality, or any form of identity with the author; the novelist is free to invent the storyteller and to describe events not directly experienced in his or her life. We may feel betrayed if we discover that the author of a memoir has fabricated most, or all, of the events described, while we may expect that the novelist will do so.

The other major difference between memoir and fiction has to do with plot. In most novels, we expect something to *happen*, and that at least some happenings will be presented sequentially. The drama in memoir is much quieter: it is the drama of the narrator's search for meaning, her search to understand the past. It is this quest that underlies all memoir. The "search for patterns and connections is the real point [of memoir] observes writer Sven Birkits.[6] Whereas in a graphic novel (or a comic) featuring, let's say, a superhero, the search (perhaps for an evildoer) will involve character, event, journey, complication, resolution—in a graphic memoir such as *Mom's Cancer*, the narrator, who does not possess super powers, has the quest to understand his mother's story and to find a way to represent that understanding in art. This quest may well be invisible to most readers, since the writer's journey toward understanding took place in the time between the events experienced and the act of writing. The text that we read is the end point of the journey.

Hence, as Birkits points out, the passage of time in the writer's life is key to the creation of memoir. These works of writing "are about circumstance become meaningful when seen from a certain remove," he comments. "They all, to greater or lesser degree, use the vantage point of the present to gain access to what might be called the hidden narrative of the past. Each is in its own way an account of detection, a realized effort to assemble the puzzle of what happened in the light of the subsequent realization" (8). The poignant cover Fies created for *Mom's Cancer* showing how his mother's life was broken in two by her illness reflects a process of understanding that could only have taken place over time.

That time, however, in Fies's case was quite short. He began what would become *Mom's Cancer* as a blog he kept during his mother's illness. He was writing and drawing the present very close to events as they happened, not knowing the "plot," not knowing how his mother's battle with cancer would play out. "I began serializing *Mom's Cancer* on the Internet in early 2004 as . . . dispatches from the front lines of a battle into which my family stumbled unprepared," he writes in his preface. When he was writing his internet serial, Fies did not know if his mother would live or die, just as the war correspondent does not know if the nation from which she comes will win a war. And so, unlike the memoir writer who looks back in time after many years have passed, Fies in his internet serial may have had only days or even less to reflect on events. We do not know how he reimagined or rewrote his serial when he shaped his memoir; his publisher required that he remove *Mom's Cancer* from its online life. So we do not know how, or if, Fies reordered events, cut or added sections. But we do know that his structure (mostly chronological) is true to his experience of Mom's cancer: the memoir moves from diagnosis to treatment to an unlikely remission. The final step in the sequence is Mom's death, not from cancer but from complications associated with steroids taken to control inflammation. We do not find this out until the last, untitled page of the book, when Fies tells us that she died "just as *Mom's Cancer* was going to press." So we know, then, that Fies did not write or rewrite his memoir knowing that his mother's story was headed so quickly toward death after cancer's remission. Were he to write his memoir now, it might have a different structure.

Even though the time between Fies's real-life experience and representing his mother's story in art was brief, he nevertheless demonstrates what I call "retrospective narration," the memoir writer's telling of a story from a later vantage point. As a graphic memoir, *Mom's Cancer* is a shaped narrative, no less artful than a novel. No matter how close he was to the events described and shown, Fies transforms aesthetically the raw emotional material he represents. So there is a difference between the writer/artist and the self he portrays in the memoir. As I explore *Mom's Cancer* I will thus be using "Fies" or "Brian Fies" to refer to the writer, and "Brian" to refer to the writer's represented self in the memoir. When I refer to the "narrator," I am speaking of the voice the writer adopts in the explanatory narratives interwoven throughout the memoir. Some of these are juxtaposed to panels, while others are placed in boxes within panels. The words in the bubbles spoken by "Brian" constitute the dialogue Fies has given to earlier self. These aesthetic distinctions will help us understand how Fies is working with the art of memoir in graphic form.

12.2. Brian Fies. *Mom's Cancer*. p 39.

Medical Talk

In his important theoretical work on illness narratives, *The Wounded Storyteller*, sociologist Arthur Frank observes that the "body sets in motion the need for new stories when its disease disrupts the old stories" (5). The "old" stories are ones that a person who is not ill may not even recognize: the story that one will make dinner and enjoy eating it; the story that one will take a vacation; the story that there will be a future with yourself in it. Once a grave, life-threatening disease like cancer claims the body these stories no longer hold true. The poet Jane Kenyon beautifully captures the "before" story of health with the later story of illness and death only imagined in her frequently quoted poem "Otherwise":

I got out of bed
on two strong legs.
It might have been
otherwise..[7]

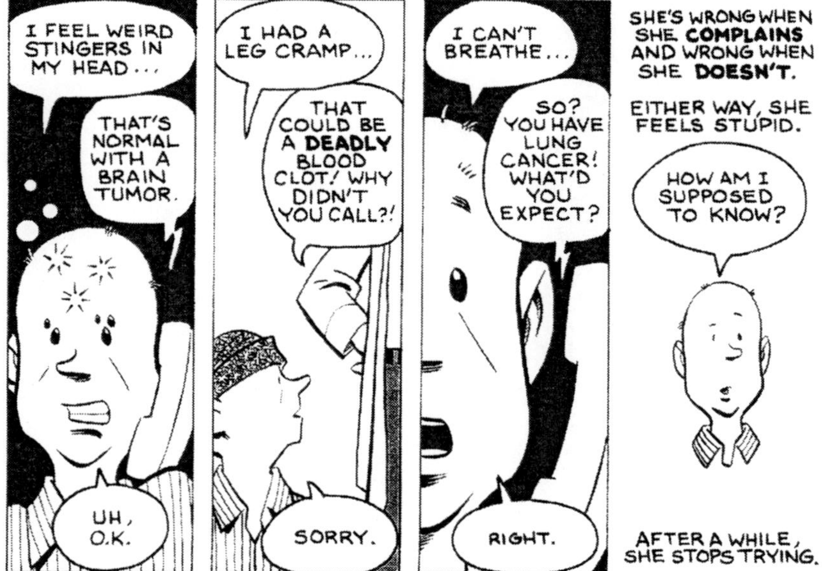

12.3. Brian Fies. *Mom's Cancer.* p 40.

The poem acknowledges that some day, it will be otherwise. When one enters the country of "otherwise," leaving behind the enjoyments of strong body, ripe peach, one confronts not just the difficulty of finding the words to express experience. As Frank observes, a major challenge the ill person faces in trying to tell a "new" story is the powerful defining force of medical discourse. "The story of illness that trumps all others in the modern period is the medical narrative," he writes. "The story told by the physician becomes the one against which all others are ultimately judged true or false, useful or not" (5).

Fies shows the power of the physician's words to undermine the patient's authority in "The Usual Unusual." "Call immediately if you notice anything unusual," four physicians say in unison in the first panel, sharing the same word balloon (they are all speaking medical talk). (39) In the next panel Mom tells a doctor "I have a headache. . ." "Yeah, don't worry about it," is the answer. In the next panel she tells a doctor "I had a deep cough. . . ." "**What?!** You should have called at once!" exclaims an annoyed doctor. As Fies's use of ellipses here demonstrates, the doctor has the power to interrupt the patient who is always speaking tentatively. (In this sequence doctors get bold face and exclamation points in their word balloons, Mom gets

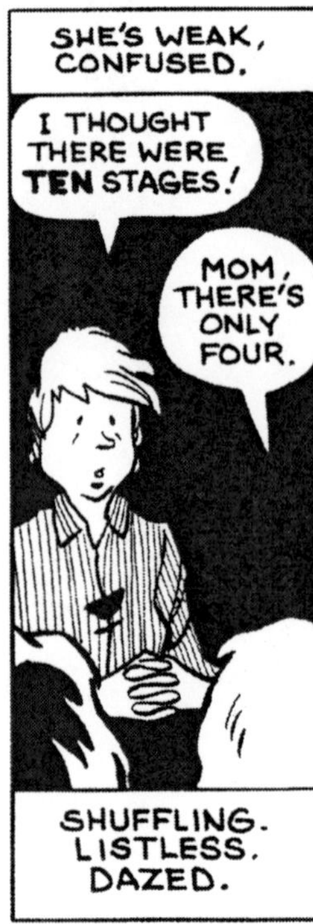

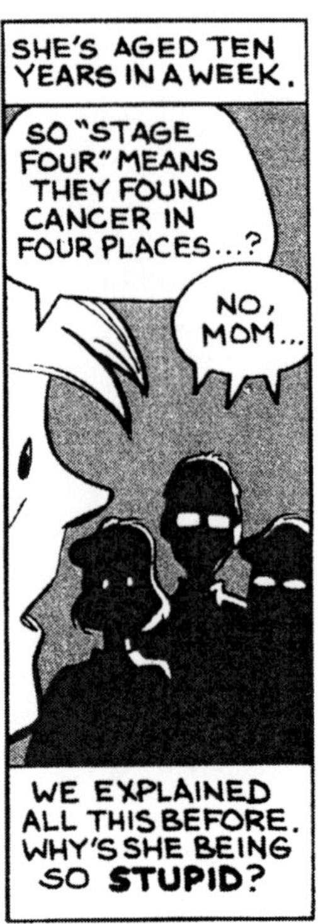

12.4. Brian Fies. *Mom's Cancer*. p 10.

question marks and ellipses. Punctuation reflects power.) The physicians get to define what is "unusual," and the patient is left helpless and unsure.

The patient's bafflement and dependence on the doctor is reinforced by what Frank calls "medical talk"—the technical, specialized language doctors use to refer to symptoms, diagnoses, illnesses, treatments, and bodies (6). Fies shows Brian's annoyance with Mom's unfamiliarity with the medical language of cancer "stages" in "A Family Meeting." By this point it is clear that Mom's brain tumor has its origin in her lung cancer. Mom is concentrating on the upcoming operation to remove the tumor ("they'll take it out!") and an annoyed Brian says, "But the **real** problem is lung cancer." "At least it's just a **stage four!**" replies Mom. "You know stage four is **bad,** right?" asks Brian. "I thought there were **ten** stages," Mom answers, confused (9–10). She seems "stupid" to her son—after all, we all know there are four stages to demarcate the progress of cancer, right?

But in fact her confusion reveals how arbitrary "medical talk" is. Oncologists decided on four stages, but perhaps there could have been three, or

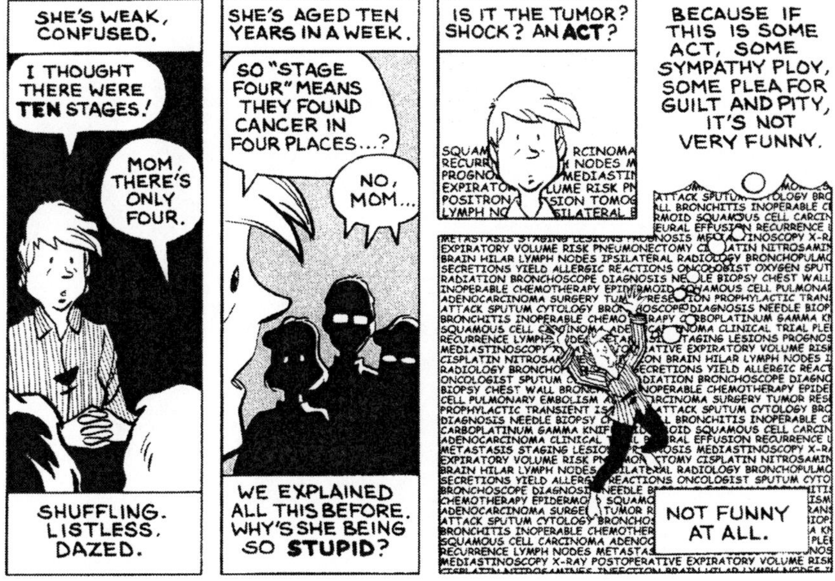

12.5. Brian Fies. *Mom's Cancer*. p 10.

five? The use of the number suggests an objectivity and a scientific fact that the body, in all its variety and variability, may in fact belie. And cancer is still a mysterious disease: its origins unclear, its treatments guesswork, its outcomes uncertain. Oncologists do the best they can, but often they are just working from educated guesses, not sure themselves if their medicines will work. Brian realizes their imperfect knowledge after Mom has been through radiation and is starting chemotherapy. "It takes a while to figure out that oncology is an **improvisational** art," he writes. "They make it up as they go. Today's results determine tomorrow's treatment" (71). Doctors have the power of medical talk, but as "improvisational" artists they cannot construct sequential narratives that lead from illness to cure. Like the patient, they have to wait and see what happens, see how the body responds.

In three panels grouped on one page Fies juxtaposes Brian's annoyance with Mom for not "getting" the medical talk with the writer/artist's deeper understanding of her fear, bewilderment, and isolation (10).

In the first panel, where Mom tells her children she assumed there were ten stages, Fies shows Mom confronted by Brian and one of his sisters (we can see only the backs of their heads). In the second panel Mom's ignorance extends—maybe "stage four" means they "found cancer in four

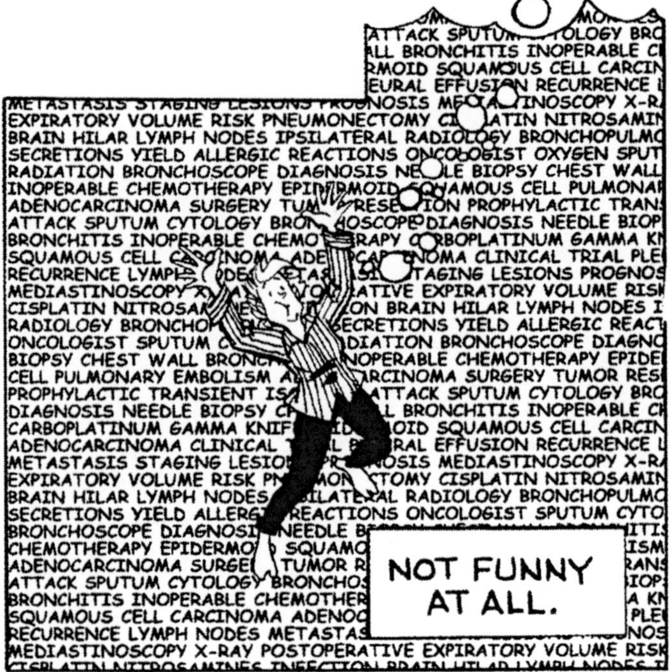

12.6. Brian Fies. *Mom's Cancer.* p 10.

places?" In this panel Fies shows how, to Mom, her three children can seem like a united and unsympathetic crowd by silhouetting them in black and giving them the same word balloon ("No, Mom. . . .") In the last panel, twice as big, Fies shows how Mom may feel she is drowning in a sea of technical words, unable to speak herself. Here the balloons that we often see in comics do not signify thoughts or unspoken words—but Mom's gasping breaths as she drowns. Her tiny figure represents her powerlessness. Fies makes the technical "medical talk" words so small that readers will have a hard time reading them, a way of making us feel some of Mom's helplessness. Fies repeats his horizontal list of medical words in this ocean of terms, a way of showing how there is no progress for the patient: we can never master them, just as we cannot master the illness. The same words will just come streaming by just as long as we are ill, without break, without punctuation, words like: *needle biopsy lesions prognosis expiratory bronchoscope chemotherapy cisplatin radiation oncologist sputum lymph nodes pulmonary embolism adenocarcinoma squamous cell yield allergic reaction clinical trial prophylactic inoperable needle biopsy lesions*

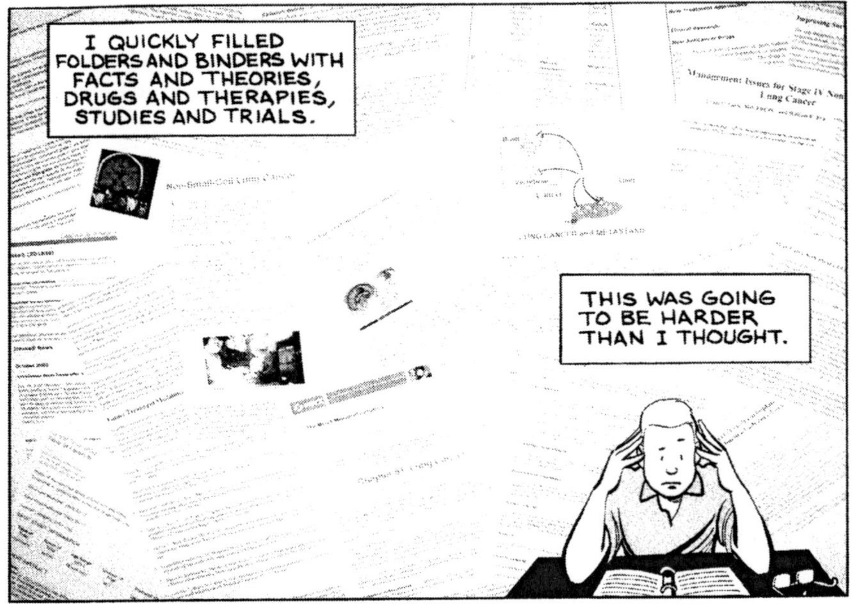

12.7. Brian Fies. *Mom's Cancer*. p 24.

*prognosis. . . . (*10) Fies cuts off the page in the middle of the last row of words, letting us know that this ocean has no bottom, the stream of words no end.

In the later sequence "A Terrible Thing to Waste," Fies takes on medical numbers and shows them to be part of the same discourse as medical talk: the physicians' way of defining reality that seems objective, and yet is incomprehensible. "Your brain tumor is 24 millimeters," the doctor tells Mom. "How big is that?" she asks. A good question: not only are we Americans not on the metric system, we patients don't know if 24 millimeters is "big" or "small" for a brain tumor, or something in-between. Brian hears this question—we don't see an answer—and decides he needs to switch on his "scary-smart" brain and "figure things out" by reading. He will become a comic-book hero, draw on his superpowers (his "scary-smart" brain), study books and articles and **"cure cancer"** (23). For information, Brian turns, as many Americans now do, to the internet.

To show the results of his heroic research, Fies gives us a full-page panel showing cartoon Brian surrounded by real (and tiny) copies of all the information he's collected, binders filled with "facts and theories, drugs and therapies, studies and trials" (24). Brian's bewildered expression now links him with Mom. He's not drowning, but he's surrounded by studies and reports he cannot master. "This was going to be harder than I thought," he realizes; the know-it-all kid now his comeuppance. Near the end of the memoir when experience has made him wiser, Fies knows not to use "cure" and "cancer" in the same sentence. Mom's lung and brain cancer has vanished from the scans, but she's "not out of the woods yet," he writes. "She'll **never** be out of the woods" (102).

In his memoir, Fies interrupts "medical talk" with the narrative of Mom's experience, using her story to provide a counternarrative to medical discourse. By showing us what Arthur Frank calls "a specialized knowledge that is unfamiliar and overwhelming," Fies shows us the human reality hidden by the "official story of an illness" told by doctors, charts, scans, and MRI's.[8]

Showing the Voice of the Body

Interrupting the official story is just a beginning. In order to provide a fuller narrative of illness, the writer needs to do something difficult: give a voice to the body. The ill and changed body needs its new story, but as Frank observes, "the body eludes language" (2). The ill body "is not mute," he reminds us, for "it speaks eloquently in pain and symptoms—but it is inarticulate." When a writer tries to narrate illness she must "speak for the body," but "such speech is quickly frustrated: speech presents itself as being about the body rather than of it. The body is often alienated, literally 'made strange,' as it is told in stories that are instigated by the need to make it familiar" (2).

What Frank suggests here is that even the memoirist who is writing about his or her own illness—let alone that of another—is translating the body, speaking "about" the body, representing it in a language external to the body's experience. Even when those of us who are ill speak about our body's experience to sympathetic listeners, we are faced with this challenge of translation and know that language can never fully capture our pains and symptoms. Stories of illness, whether written or spoken, are *about* the body; how, Frank asks, can we describe stories told *"through"* the body?

Although all forms of representation are social constructions—not objective windows into experience—the graphic memoir of illness has the additional resource of visual imagery to supplement (and even

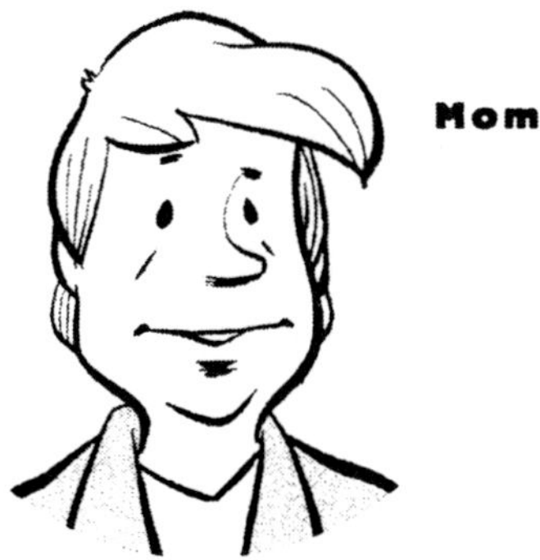

In her early sixties and diagnosed
with lung cancer that metastasized
to her brain after a lifetime of
cigarette smoking, she is determined
to overcome grave odds.

12.8. Brian Fies. *Mom's Cancer*. Opening. Non paginated.

overshadow) language. Because of his skill as an illustrator and his training in graphic fiction, Fies makes full use of visual imagery in order to show the story of Mom's cancer. He represents her experience more strongly in pictures than in words, drawing on a variety of artistic resources in order to do so. There are dozens of images of Mom in the memoir; I will be discussing those that best show Fies's ability to *hear* the stories Mom's body is telling and, in turn, to show them to us—so that we can become listeners as well as viewers.

Fies gives us the first visual image of Mom in "The Characters." She's shown with a cowlick, black button eyes, and a half smile; she looks like a goofy cartoon character.

When healthy Mom becomes ill and we see the ravages of cancer and chemotherapy, her appearance takes on dignity and bravery as Fies shows her suffering and fragile endurance. Even before we've seen healthy Mom if we've looked at the frontispiece, we've seen ill Mom's bowed figure.

In "Arrangement in Gray and Black," we see a full-page representation of Mom in a hospital chair undergoing chemotherapy, two IV bags hanging above her head. There is no speech in this panel (Mom is sleeping, or in a chemo doze), but Fies makes use of verbal labels ("misc. syringe," "I.V. pump," "strawberry shake") (33). It's the visual image that speaks most

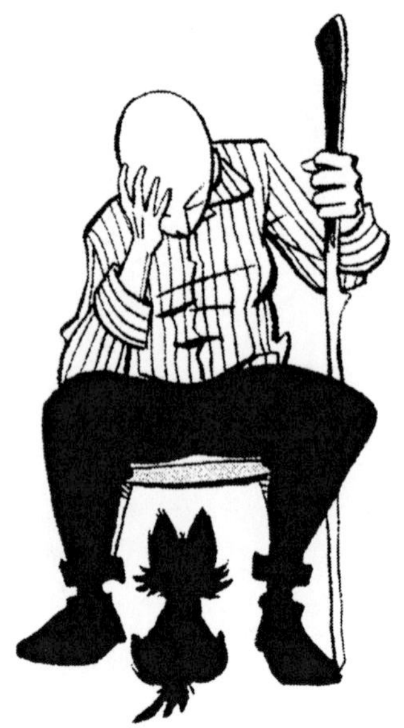

12.9. Brian Fies. *Mom's Cancer*. Title page. Non paginated.

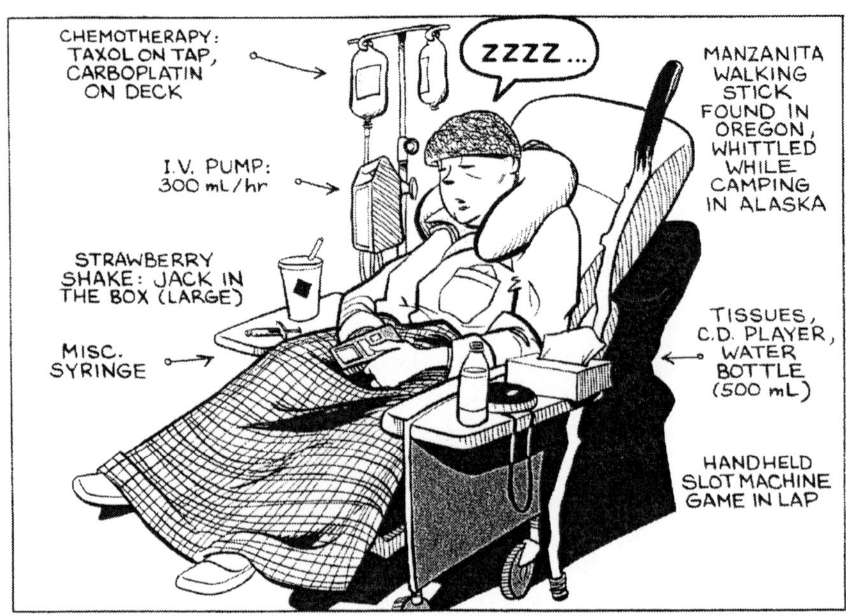

12.10. Brian Fies. *Mom's Cancer*. p 33.

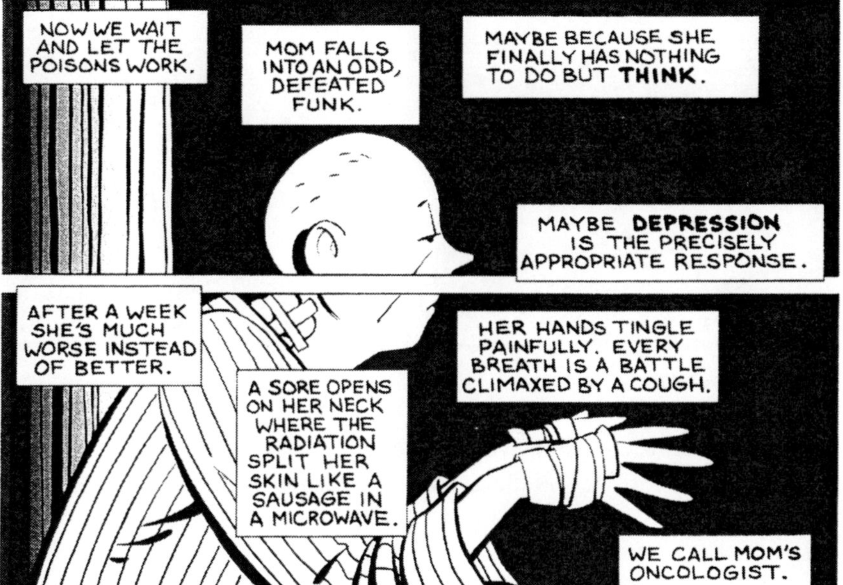

12.11. Brian Fies. *Mom's Cancer.* p 47.

strongly, however, showing us the voice that Mom does not have. We see her human figure surrounded by hospital equipment and implements; she's a captive. Her feet are slightly splayed, their position determined by the footrest positions the standard-issue chair provides. The hand we can see is limply holding a slot machine game (perhaps given her by one of her children?), showing us that her weak body, fatigued by chemotherapy, has no power for play. Her head tilts to one side, and though she is cradled by a neck pillow we see that her body is not comforted. The walking stick leaning against the chair reminds us of hiking and camping, but now its presence has a different meaning: Mom needs it because she is too weak to walk unassisted.

The next full-page representation of Mom occurs a few pages later, showing her after six weeks of chemotherapy and radiation. This is a black and white version of the book cover image, here splattered with narrative boxes in which the narrator represents both her body and her weakened spirit. We see more of Mom in this image than on the cover—now visible are her hands, splinted and wrapped in bandages ("Her hands tingle painfully.") The patch on her neck is explained: "A sore opens on her neck where the radiation split her skin like a sausage in a microwave." "And now

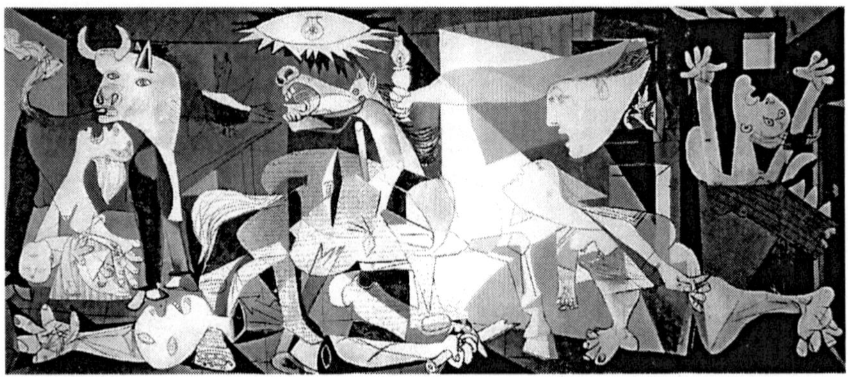

12.12. *Guernica* by Pablo Picasso (1937).

we wait and let the poisons work," Fies writes, using "poison" rather than the more euphemistic "medicine" or "chemical." In this version of his ill mother we see his fullest challenge to the heroic narrative of the "fight" against cancer. The truth? Mom is in a "defeated funk." She is depressed, not relieved; her "battle" is not against cancer, but a struggle to breathe.[9] Fies loses some of the visual power of the cover by using so many words in this panel, but he relies on language as well as image to tell Mom's story because she has fallen silent.

Weeks later, Mom has recovered enough from chemo to—have more chemo. "This'll be rough," the oncologist tells her. "Because you were getting radiation before, we didn't give you a full dose of chemo." "Let's go for it!" Mom says, her bald head juxtaposed to the doctor's blond hair. She raises her fist. She's ready to fight.

We turn the page and see the impact of these new rounds of chemo, each one being a "breath-taking punch to the gut." Mom's not the powerful fighter here, she's the battered victim; Fies takes a risk and draws on imagery from Picasso's *Guernica* (1937) to show Mom's suffering.

Some might find his visual linkage of one woman's suffering from chemotherapy to the mass slaughter of innocent civilians during the Spanish Civil War problematic, but Fies has a good reason for his choice of reference: he wants to make Mom's suffering more universal, knowing that many others have shared this struggle. Mom's body is presented in such a stylized, two-dimensional fashion and her upside-down face so distorted that she could be *anyone*, and so this image seems to honor all those who suffer from illness and the treatments for illness. Like many others, mom is engaged in a "grinding battle of endurance," knowing that if she walks

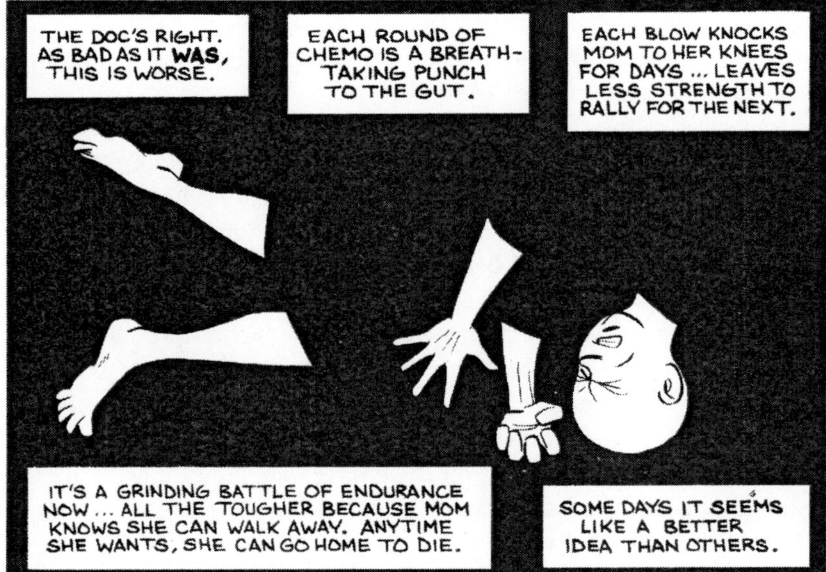

12.13. Brian Fies. *Mom's Cancer.* p 72.

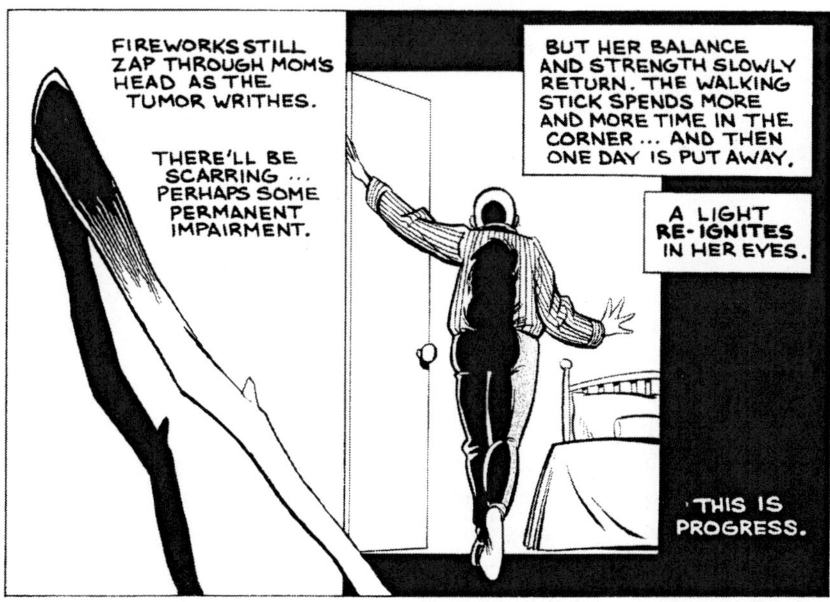

12.14. Brian Fies. *Mom's Cancer.* p. 80.

away from this devastating treatment she'll be walking into her own death. "Some days it seems like a better idea than others," Fies writes (72). Some days, death doesn't seem like a bad idea.

Mom survives the chemotherapy and begins to walk without the hiking stick. Fies devotes another full-page panel to his image of Mom's "progress." This is not a sentimental image of a return to health. The walking stick, although leaning against the wall, is still larger than Mom's bowed figure. Her left hand touches the wall for balance and her right hand, fingers extended, stretches out—waiting for another surface to provide stability (80).

Although we can see the progress and believe the narrator, he reminds us that improvement is not "recovery." There will be scarring, perhaps "permanent impairment." A hopeful sign is the light that reignites in her eyes, but Fies purposely shows her figure from the back so that we cannot see this spark and assume that all is well. Her small figure, with another smaller figure inscribed on her back in shadow, tells us that her body's narrative of health is tentative.

Cancer is not portrayed as conquered, but at bay.

The Counternarrative of Hope

We are now almost at the end of the memoir. Like the family, we are overjoyed to learn that Mom's cancer has disappeared; she is one of the "five per cent" who has made it across the ocean of illness and words to the other shore. This ending was unexpected, and may be due to chance. "We know how lucky we are" (102). Since the memoir had its origins in the blog Fies kept during his mother's illness, he did not know what the outcome would be. "When I started [the blog] I thought my story was about **death**," he writes. "It turned out to be about **hope**" (104).

Fies illustrates the unexpected outcome of hope in "An Epilogue," all in color. Mom and her two daughters decide to move to Hollywood, the land of dreams. "Mom always wanted to live in southern California. I guess she figured it was now or never," Fies concludes. The final two panels of "An Epilogue" echo the blue, star-covered background of the cover illustration. Here the lines are different. There are no figures in the first panel, but the center line leads to the vanishing point of the horizon, above which we see the expanse of stars (real stars, not the celebrity stars of Hollywood).

Each word summary tells us what is happening to another "character" as Fies reflects the ending of (Hollywood) films that tell us what the major

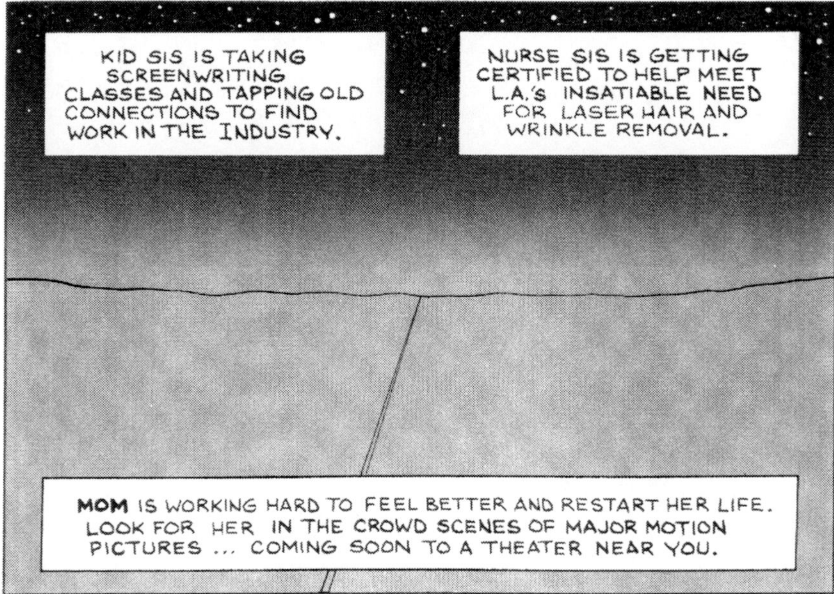

12.15. Brian Fies. *Mom's Cancer*. p 111.

characters are up to. "Kid Sis" is looking for work in the movie business, "Nurse Sis" is getting certified "to meet L.A.s insatiable need for laser hair and wrinkle removal." And Mom? She is "working hard to feel better and restart her life." She once had a non-speaking role in a movie, and Fies humorously imagines her future for us: "Look for her in the crowd scenes of major motion pictures . . . coming soon to a theater near you" (111).

The final panel of the memoir is simply visual and echoes both the "Hollywood" panel and the cover illustration. The blue rectangle now has been divided in two, the white space of the gutter suggesting both Mom's move from cancer to remission and the possibility that the "interruption" illness brought to her life may return (112).

The sky in the top rectangle is darker than the blue of the bottom, almost black, and we can see only one star distinctly. Perhaps that star is Mom? Perhaps that star suggests the fragility of hope? However we read this final, empty panel, we are placed in the role of the family members—looking ahead and up toward the sky, not knowing what will come next, but hoping for the best. This is not, then, a "Hollywood ending."

In shaping the narrative of hope he did not expect when he began the blog, Fies does not give us the simple plot of what I call the recovery

12.16. Brian Fies. *Mom's Cancer*. p 112.

narrative. On the contrary: he provides a counter-narrative to the recovery narrative.

This narrative, which always tells the story "once I was sick, but now I am well," echoes the American ideology of upward mobility incarnated in Horatio Alger stories ("I was poor, but now, through hard work, I am rich") as well as the spiritual tale of conversion ("I was blind, but now I see"). Such a story may be comforting to some, but it can be oppressive to the many people with chronic illnesses or illnesses that cannot be "cured." Fies will not give us, or himself, this easy consolation that masks troubling reality. This story of willed optimism does not offer the speech of the body; in fact, it can silence the body as well the soul. If I am dying from cancer or suffering from a chronic illness like depression, I may not be able to speak: it would upset people! We want the recovery narrative because then we do not have to listen to an ill person's disturbing voice.

The recovery narrative reflects what Barbara Ehrenreich terms the "ideology of optimism," which is different from the narrative of hope. The first is a belief system, the second an emotion. In her recent book *Bright-Sided: How the Relentless Promotion of Positive Thinking Has Undermined America*, Ehrenreich argues that "positivity" and optimism are not a mood or a feeling, but "part of our ideology—the way we explain the world and think we ought to function within it."[10] As she observes, optimism differs from hope. Hope is a "yearning," while optimism is a "cognitive stance." Optimism is also a "conscious expectation" that Americans hold for themselves and others. And the underside of this willed optimism is anxiety. "If the universe tends toward happiness and abundance, then why bother with the mental effort of positive thinking?" Ehrenreich asks. "Obviously, because we do not fully believe things will get better on their own."[11]

The intellectual framing Ehrenreich provides can help us understand why *Mom's Cancer* has been important to the many readers who thanked Fies for creating the memoir.[12] His readers want honesty, not ideology; they want hope, not optimism. Hope can counter despair and depression, but it does not promise the formulaic "happy ending" proffered by Hollywood movies.

The final page of the memoir—untitled—tells us that Mom's hope, while real, did not guarantee many years of life after her cancer went into remission. She did have a happy, but brief, time in Los Angeles. "I don't think I ever saw her happier living anywhere than she was in Hollywood," Fies writes on this last, un-numbered page. "She loved her new neighborhood. . . . It was where she needed to be." Her time there was short, because even though she had "beaten" cancer, her body had been broken down, Fies tells us, by the steroids she had to take to control brain inflammation. They had to be reduced, the brain inflammation returned, and then "the end came quickly." So Mom "died free of cancer," perhaps ironically, but the medicines the physicians needed to use could not stop the side effects of the brain tumor for very long.

Fies's last words are positive but not "positive thinking." "Hope is never in vain," he writes. His mother had found purpose in life because her story had given other people hope. "Her name was Barbara, and she lived and died well. I will miss making new memories with her."

By writing and publishing *Mom's Cancer*, Fies extends comfort to readers who can identify with Mom's sufferings, take courage from her perseverance, and find hope in the honesty of her story. Illness narratives are powerful and important because they allow readers to feel that they are not alone. These are the first words Fies writes in his "Preface":

You are not alone.

Because there are so few honest illness narratives in our culture, readers find those that exist powerful and important because they give voice to their own silenced or submerged stories. "I was astonished by how many readers saw their own stories in ours," Fies writes in the preface. He had felt the lack of such stories when he began his blog: "I created *Mom's Cancer* because I wish someone had created it for me." Drawing on the resources of visual art and verbal honesty, Fies creates a narrative that creates companionship for readers. "My family shared many of the experiences of the author's family during my mother's cancer," a reader, Joe Smith (pseudonym?), writes on Amazon.com about *Mom's Cancer*. "It's compelling, touching, and hopeful."[13]

By telling and showing the voice of the body—and that of the heart, soul, and spirit—Fies creates the kind of narrative that Arthur Frank called for in *The Wounded Storyteller*: a story that interrupts medical talk with human expression, a story told by an individual voice that achieves "collective force" (12). The collective force of *Mom's Cancer* now lies in the community of readers it has created and will continue to create.

A year ago I taught a course titled "Health, Illness, and Narrative in American Culture." I included *Mom's Cancer*, feeling a little unsure because I did not know if some of my students might have parents or grandparents who had experienced cancer, perhaps died from cancer. Would they find it upsetting? My students did not seem to, but several were silent during our discussion. One student, whom I'll call Brian, was silent through most of the course. Did he dislike the course? Dislike me? Find *Mom's Cancer* boring, frightening? Was he even listening? Even doing the reading? Last summer I got an email from Brian. "Thank you for teaching that course," he wrote. "You must continue to teach it, and include *Mom's Cancer*. I just found out that my mom has breast cancer, and I re-read it. People in my family aren't talking about the cancer much. So this is the one book that's helping me make sense of things."

I'm going to continue to teach it.

Notes

1. Brian Fies, *Mom's Cancer* (New York: Abrams Comicarts, 2006). All page references in the text will be to this edition. The "Introduction" and "Preface" are not paginated.

2. Susan Sontag, *Illness as Metaphor and AIDS and Its Metaphors* (New York: Doubleday, 1988), 3.

3. For a thoughtful discussion of the resources graphic narratives can offer illness narratives, see Susan Squier, "Literature and Medicine, Future Tense: Making It Graphic," *Literature and Medicine* (Fall 2008), 124–52.

4. Arthur Frank, "When bodies need voices" in *The Wounded Storyteller: Body, Illness, and Ethics* (Chicago: U of Chicago Press, 1995).

5. Judith Barrington, *Writing the Memoir* (Portland, OR: The Eighth Mountain Press, 2002), 65.

6. Sven Birkits, *The Art of Time in Memoir: Then, Again.* (Saint Paul, MN: Graywolf Press, 2008), 6.

7. Jane Kenyon, "Otherwise," in Jane Kenyon, *Otherwise: New & Selected Poems* (Saint Paul, MN: Graywolf Press, 1996), 214.

8. Frank, p. 6.

9. In *Illness as Metaphor*, Sontag critiques the use of the "language of warfare"—words such as "invasive," "colonize," "defenses," "kill," "magic bullet"—to describe cancer, its treatment, and the patient's experience (Sontag, 64–65). She calls for a language to describe illness that is "resistant to, metaphoric thinking" (Sontag, 3). Fies, however, finds the language of battle and struggle useful to convey his mother's experience.

10. Barbara Ehrenreich, *Bright-sided: How the Relentless Promotion of Positive Thinking Has Undermined America* (New York: Metropolitan Books, 2009), 4.

11. Ehrenreich, 5.

12. http://tinyurl.com/3ezagow.

13. http://tinyurl.com/3ezagow.

Works Cited

Barrington, Judith. *Writing the Memoir*. Portland, OR: The Eighth Mountain Press, 2002. Print.

Birkits, Sven. *The Art of Time in Memoir: Then, Again.* Saint Paul, MN: Graywolf Press, 2008. Print.

Ehrenreich, Barbara. *Bright-sided: How the Relentless Promotion of Positive Thinking Has Undermined America.* New York: Metropolitan Books, 2009. Print.

Fies, Brian. *Mom's Cancer*. New York: Abrams Comicarts, 2006. Print.

Frank, Arthur. *The Wounded Storyteller: Body, Illness, and Ethics.* Chicago: University of Chicago Press, 1995. Print.

Kenyon, Jane. "Otherwise." *Othewise: New & Selected Poems.* Saint Paul, MN: Graywolf Press, 1996. 214. Print.

Smith, Joe. "Reader Review." Amazon.com. 4 May 2006. Web. 1 Aug. 2012.

Sontag, Susan. *Illness as Metaphor and AIDS and Its Metaphors.* New York: Doubleday, 1988. Print.

Squier, Susan. "Literature and Medicine, Future Tense: Making It Graphic." *Literature and Medicine.* (Fall 2008): 124–52. Print.

Contributors

Jan Baetens is professor of literary and cultural studies at the University of Leuven (Belgium). His research on literature and medium innovation is supported by BELSPO, in the framework of an IAP (Interuniversity Attraction Pole, Phase VII) program. He has published widely on word and image studies as well as on poetry and photography, in journals such as *Critical Inquiry, History of Photgraphy, Substance, Poetics Today, English Language Notes,* and *PMLA.* In his work as a published poet, he often collaborates with graphic novelist Olivier Deprez, most recently in *Autres nuages* (Brussels: Les Impressions Nouvelles, 2012). His faculty page is: https://www.kuleuven.be/wieiswie/en/person/00004749.

David M. Ball is an associate professor of English at Dickinson College and currently visiting associate professor of English at Princeton University. His coedited collection of essays, *The Comics of Chris Ware: Drawing Is a Way of Thinking,* was published by the University Press of Mississippi in 2010, and his monograph, *False Starts: The Rhetoric of Failure and the Making of American Modernism,* is forthcoming from Northwestern University Press. He serves as editor to the Critical Approaches to Comics Artists series published by the University Press of Mississippi

Lopamudra Basu is an associate professor of English and director of Honors College, University of Wisconsin-Stout. Her current research interests include contemporary world literature, transnational feminist theory, U.S. ethnic literatures, graphic fiction and autobiography and globalization studies. She is the coeditor of *Passage to Manhattan: Critical Essays on Meena Alexander,* Cambridge Scholars Publishing, UK, 2009. Her articles, interviews, and reviews have been published in *South Asian Review, Nebula, Social Text, Journal of Commonwealth and Postcolonial Studies, Remarkings,* and in the anthology *Rites of Passage in*

Postcolonial Women's Writing (Rodopi, 2010). Her faculty page is: http://www .uwstout.edu/faculty/basul/.

Christopher Bush is associate professor of French and comparative literary studies at Northwestern University. His research and teaching focus on comparative and interdisciplinary approaches to literary modernisms, especially the interactions between Euro-American and East Asian aesthetic theory, avant-gardes, and media. His current book project, *The Floating World: Japoniste Aesthetics and Global Modernity*, challenges conventional notions of "japonisme" as a nostalgic reverie of a vanishing Old Japan. He is the author of *Ideographic Modernism: China, Writing, Media* (Oxford, 2010) and the coeditor and cotranslator of Victor Segalen's *Stèles* (Wesleyan, 2007). His faculty page is: http://www.frenchand italian.northwestern.edu/people/faculty/bush.html.

Isaac Cates is a comics artist, poet, and lecturer in the Department of English at the University of Vermont. He is the author of *The Graphic Novel: How Comics Grew Up* (forthcoming) and the coeditor, with Ken Parille, of *Daniel Clowes: Conversations* (University Press of Mississippi). His faculty page is: http://www.uvm.edu/~english/?Page=IsaacCates.php.

Michael A. Chaney is associate professor of English at Dartmouth College. He is the author of *Fugitive Vision: Slave Image and Black Identity in Antebellum Narrative* (Indiana, 2008) and editor of *Graphic Subjects: Critical Essays on Autobiography and Graphic Novels* (Wisconsin, 2011). His essays on the interrelation of verbal and visual art have appeared in such journals as *American Literature, College Literature, MELUS,* and *International Journal of Comic Art.* His forthcoming book explores graphic novels as forms of pedagogy and examines them for their embedded lessons in reading and seeing. His faculty webpage is: http://www .dartmouth.edu/~english/faculty/chaney.html.

Alisia Chase is associate professor of art history and visual culture in the Art Department of SUNY Brockport. Her research focuses on American extra-cinematic culture, contemporary art, and graphic novels and comics by female artists. She has published articles in *The Great American Makeover: Television, History and Nation*; *Virgin Territory: Representing Sexual Inexperience on Film*; *Difference Reframed: Considering the Legacy of Feminist Art History*; and *Habits of Being*, Vol. II, among others.

Additionally, she has written the introductory essays for two graphic novels, *Moomin: The Complete Tove Jansson Comic Strip* and *AYA*, as well as regular exhibition reviews for *AFTERIMAGE: The Journal of Media Arts and Cultural Criticism* and *Film Quarterly*. In addition to her research, Dr. Chase presently serves as reviews editor for the journal *Fashion, Film, and Consumption*. Her faculty page is: http://www.brockport.edu/art/faculty/achase.html.

Sharon O'Brien is James Hope Caldwell Professor of American Cultures at Dickinson College where she teaches in the American Studies and English Departments. She is the author of two biographies of Willa Cather and of a memoir, *The Family Silver: A Memoir of Depression and Inheritance*. Her teaching interests include courses in health, illness, and narrative; in multiple identities; and in politics and the novel. She teaches memoir in the creative writing program. Her faculty page is: http://users.dickinson.edu/~obrien/.

Davida Pines is associate professor of rhetoric at Boston University in the College of General Studies. Her book *The Marriage Paradox: Modernist Novels and the Cultural Imperative to Marry* was published by the University Press of Florida in 2005. She teaches courses in writing and research, as well as graphic narrative. She is currently working on a monograph on the representation of traumatic history in long-form comics. Her faculty page is: http//www.bu.edu/cgs/faculty/rhetoric-faculty-profiles/davida-pines/.

Yaël Schlick is professor of English at Queen's University (Canada) where she teaches courses on travel writing, autobiography, and modern literature. She has published articles on travel writing, colonial literature, and modern fiction. Her translation of Victor Segalen's *Essay on Exoticism* appeared in 2002. More recently she has coedited a volume of essays on the figure of the coquette with Shelley King and published the book *Feminism and the Politics of Travel after the Enlightenment*. Her faculty page is: http://www.queensu.ca/english/faculty/schlick.php.

Jane Tolmie is an associate professor of gender studies and cultural studies, cross-appointed to English, at Queen's University (Canada). Selected publications appear in *Topia, French Studies, lectio difficilior, Journal of Gender Studies, Journal of Historical Pragmatics, Early Theatre, Mediaevalia,*

Arthuriana, and *Wit's End*. With Jane Toswell, she edited and contributed to an international collection of sixteen essays on medieval mourning and cultural production, *Laments for the Lost in Medieval Literature* (Brepols, 2010). Her current research is on memory, trauma, and women's art activism in comics and theatre. She is working on a monograph on women's comic art, focusing on eight writers/artists and tentatively titled *Portraits of the Art-Activist*. She is a poet, feminist activist, and blogger. Her faculty page is: http://www.queensu.ca/gnds/tolmie.php.

Rachel Trousdale is an associate professor of English at Agnes Scott College in Decatur, Georgia. Her book *Nabokov, Rushdie, and the Transnational Imagination: Novels of Exile and Alternate Worlds* was published by Palgrave Macmillan in 2010. She has published articles on James Merrill, Marianne Moore, Virginia Woolf, Michael Chabon, and Isak Dinesen. Her current project is a book on humor in twentieth-century American poetry; she also writes poetry. More information is available at: www.racheltrousdale.com.

Benjamin Widiss is visiting assistant professor at Hamilton College. He is the author of *Obscure Invitations: The Persistence of the Author in Twentieth-Century American Literature* (Stanford University Press, 2011). He is working on a second book, *Flirting with Embodiment: Textual Metaphors and Textual Presences in Contemporary Narrative*, which explores a constellation of relationships between mass production and individual bodily presence, conceptions of temporality and loss, and constructions of adolescence and maturity as a means to articulate the aesthetic postures of an emergent post-postmodernism in novels, comics and films. His faculty page is: http://www.hamilton.edu/academics/departments/faculty?dept=english.

Index

CPSIA information can be obtained at www.ICGtesting.com
Printed in the USA
BVOW01s1535201214

379734BV00002B/6/P